Metamorphoses of the Body

José Gil

Translated by Stephen Muecke

Theory out of Bounds *Volume 12*

University of Minnesota Press

Minneapolis • London

The University of Minnesota Press gratefully acknowledges
financial assistance provided by
the French Ministry of Culture for the translation of this book.

Originally published as *Métamorphoses du corps*, copyright 1985 Éditions de la Différence.

Published by the University of Minnesota Press
111 Third Avenue South, Suite 290
Minneapolis, MN 55401-2520
http://www.upress.umn.edu

Printed in the United States of America on acid-free paper

LIBRARY OF CONGRESS CATALOGING-IN-PUBLICATION DATA
Gil, José.
[Métamorphoses du corps. English]
Metamorphoses of the body / José Gil ; translated by Stephen
Muecke.
p.   cm. — (Theory out of bounds ; v. 12)
Includes bibliographical references and index.
ISBN 0-8166-2682-0 (hardcover : alk. paper). — ISBN 0-8166-2683-9
(pbk. : alk. paper)
1. Political anthropology.   2. Power (Social sciences)   3. Body,
Human—Social aspects.   I. Title.   II. Series.
GN492.2.G5513   1998
306.4—dc21   97-37835

The University of Minnesota
is an equal-opportunity educator and employer.

10   09   08   07   06   05   04   03   02   01   00   99   98   10   9   8   7   6   5   4   3   2   1

Metamorphoses of the Body

Edited by

Sandra Buckley

Michael Hardt

Brian Massumi

THEORY OUT OF BOUNDS

Contents

Translator's Preface

TWO OF the strongest paradigms in the human sciences of the twentieth century have been those of society and language. In this work José Gil works within and beyond the boundaries circumscribed by these domains. A newer vocabulary inevitably emerges as he engages with questions of the body and the transformations it enacts in social domains characterized by certain sorts of power. His explanations for "what happens" to the body do not revert to the social categories of "system," "structure," or "function"; nor do they engage a language-based hermeneutics to find a "meaning" for what is happening to the body as it is transformed by rituals like curing (of the ill) or enthronement (in the case of kings).

The operative concepts of those engaged in ritual (from traditional through modern societies) are not likely to seek higher authority in structuralist or functionalist theory, or to strive for meaning through exegesis; rather the concepts deployed will be primarily related to the aim of making the ritual effective, to make it *work*. This is the level at which Gil's analysis engages. Accordingly, "power" and "force" are concepts significantly elaborated in this work. The rendering of these terms, especially that of power, is noted as the translation proceeds. Working on power using the philosophical technique of the antinomy, Gil develops an approach, almost a new discipline, that he has called the "anthropology of forces."

"Exfoliation" is one of his new terms, which describes the way in which the body is always already unfolding into the spaces it occupies, and the examples given in the text develop the potential of this fruitful concept. "Infralanguage" is another of his terms, which is introduced to explain the transformative capacities of bodies in relation to objects. "Preverbal meaning matrix" goes some way toward defining it, but in addition it depends on understanding abstract forms and rhythms creating a space of the body that is defined neither by subjective experience nor by objective perception, which is why Gil's examples come also from dance, mime, and the "body-image pathology" of some psychiatry. The concept of infralanguage allows us to describe the multiplicities and discontinuities of the body in the singularity of lived experience. The analysis can thus transcend the representationalism of received ideas of "body-image" as well as the more romantic ideals of the sexually liberated body. The book culminates in an analysis of the investments of all sorts of bodily energies and forces in State apparatuses, defining in this way the operation of power in today's societies. However regularized these power mechanisms seem to be, they are never free of the magical-symbolic forces more prevalent, perhaps, in societies we like to call Other.

I would like to thank those who have helped me work through the difficulties of the translation, or who have made specific contributions: Prudence Black, Paul Gillen, Noel King, Brian Massumi, Frances Muecke, and Julian Pefanis.

Stephen Muecke

Introduction

THIS BOOK is about tribal societies,[1] and this could mean that it is as much about us as it is about exotic peoples. I haven't gone looking for the ideal image of a "good savage" in these societies, or for the equally reductive image of an "other" who is always at the horizon of our perception. All this would bring about the risk of methodological error; and if I were to make these bold isomorphisms, or comparisons, or give in to fascination or repulsion, this might only encourage feelings of moral superiority while remaining politically safe.

I was thinking about something quite different. Even accepting from the start that our relations with traditional societies are ones of both filiation and rupture, I wanted, for once, to create an alliance, a clandestine one since this effort to understand tribal people demanded a "becoming-primitive." This is a strange undertaking, especially if it has theoretical ambitions as well — but *A Thousand Plateaus* by Gilles Deleuze and Félix Guattari already provided examples of it.[2] Let's look again at their terms. To become primitive is not to "do the primitive," to mimic or borrow their cultural expressions (in the Picasso drawn to African art there is a certain mixture of an authentic becoming-primitive and an imitation of their artistic forms). Becoming-primitive is to understand oneself experiencing — and grasping in *theoretical images* — the circuits of intensity that emerge as one leaves, via a kind of methodological breakout, the domain mapped out by our signs. Although this is more a question of technique than of method, it leads us to begin to connect with *forces*, that is, to make contact with that which constitutes, in their own words, the substance of tribal peoples' universes.

So in the course of this study on power and the body I have been drawn by an interest in the effects of forces, and especially those which, in spilling out of the domain of social exchange, continually escape it. These are floating energies that are not yet fixed or invested in techniques and signs. In order to sketch out another sphere where this equilibrium is upset, next to the stable domain where powers are divided up, I shall be asking questions about how forces are captured, and how they are overcome so that apparatuses of power can be made out of them, and how these apparatuses engage in relations of tension with social power as it is already constituted. I shall be talking about spheres of power, a stable one where powers are evenly distributed and another where this balance is upset, where energies escape and forces are worked upon by particular mechanisms — especially magical and political — in short, a domain of "underpower" and one of "overpower."

The usual perspective of the ethnologist will thus be displaced. It will no longer be a question of studying the relations of power and the sacred, or the sacrificial role in sacrifice, but in either case, the nature of the forces at play, the way in which they are manipulated, and how they escape peoples' control, through which techniques they are modulated, intensified, "wasted," or transformed; and, in general (in the contexts of therapy, rites, juridical and political processes), what channels tribal peoples construct in order to make these forces come and go from the field of overpower and make them appear in that of established powers.

Such an approach does not carry with it a set image of tribal societies, nor does it derive functional models for our own societies. Nevertheless, on at least one point the temptation emerges to use them as a model (for heuristic rather than ideological or political ends), because it seems to be the case that we have here societies that are in permanent confrontation with forces, living with their powerful dynamism on an everyday basis, yet that are strangely frozen. Whatever position one takes up in the debate on the presence or absence of history (or of "historicity") in tribal societies, one thing is certain: tribal peoples only conceive their institutions according to a single pattern, finding any way they can to assimilate all innovations into the traditional frameworks of their inherited practices. This contrasts starkly with our modern societies, which, oriented toward the future, always stalked by change, construct project after project to resolve new problems that are always cropping up. And these "problems" result from the effects of free forces, that is, unmastered ones, that haven't been through the mill of technique and habitualization. Thus, in a certain way, the answer that tribal peoples bring to the sudden appearance of novelty could perhaps be exemplary for the study of our own societies, even if the nature of this innovation is not the same in both cases. But neither is it entirely different. Whatever the field of power, where tribal peoples only have a single model of thought, we are always looking for answers by multiplying the alternatives. This applies to the fields of economy, law, politics, education, psychiatry, and culture.

All these domains make up spheres of power. The comparison between modern mobile and innovative societies and tribal societies thus takes the form of an interrogation: why do the former admit several possible types of power, while the latter only function with a single model?

This book will, as a whole, attempt to answer this question.

The first part brings together the alternatives appearing in the discourse on power (in all domains) in the form of several "antinomies," because it can be shown that these alternatives are antinomical. In the case of each antinomy, an answer found by a traditional society is presented—a solution that becomes clear, I think, thanks to the notion of the "field of overpower." All of these answers are implied by and are founded in a certain way of thinking and of mastering time in its articulation with space. In particular this is achieved through the agency of magico-symbolic thought and practice; thus traditional or tribal peoples accord themselves the supreme power of holding back time by working on free forces in very subtle ways.

The second part proposes a new approach to the study of the body. It flows from the first because it developed in response to a question that emerged in relation to the solutions to the antinomies of power: What is the operating factor in this spatialization of time in symbolism that prevents "historicity" from appearing in the social temporality of tribal peoples? The analysis of one of these practices brings out the central role of the body. It is one of those rituals that constitute "machines for eliminating time," as Edmund Leach says, paraphrasing Claude Lévi-Strauss.[3] How does the body function in the ritual of possession in such a manner as to "bring back" a prior global time? The set of developments one could place under the heading of "metamorphoses of the body" will try to provide an answer. For the most part we will leave the domain of the anthropological and move toward "modern" countries where phenomena appear that are similar to those which take place in the body during magical ceremonies. In particular these include phenomena linked to what I have called "the space of the body." These are found in psychiatry, literature, and art.

Finally, in the third part, I set about examining a particular relation between political power and the body. What are the reasons for the first forms of transcendent political power (in particular, magical royalties) being represented by the image of the body of the king? This interrogation led to the examination of the mechanisms that allow the emergence of state organizations in societies that did not previously have them and, at the same time, to the study of the upheavals caused by the emergence of the state in the regime of signs, in social exchanges, in legal processes, and in the "space of the body."

This work is about the relations between power and the body. This does not mean those which result from the effects of the former on the latter (which includes a gamut of things from the "techniques of the body" first studied by Marcel Mauss to psychiatric, educational, and carceral practices studied more recently). Nor does it include those which come from the action of the body on power, which covers a domain occupied by all sorts of ideologies and "liberatory" doctrines of the body. It is about the effects of the circulation of bodily powers that nourish formations of power in all fields. In other words, and we must stress this notion, it is not a question of studying *forces* (magical, religious, prestigious, or whatever) according to their representational contents, but to grasp them in the way they function in their own right, that is, in the way they may differ from the signs and symbols that are attached to them.

This has led back, in one way or another, to taking indigenous languages seriously. This is because in tribal or traditional societies there are always "forces," "potencies," and "powers" that traditional peoples quite regularly distinguish from signs, beings, or symbols. Force has its own reality, which manifests itself in a specific way. It is not only "lived" in the strong sense, individually or collectively, it is "operational," manipulable. What are the specific manifestations through which force is translated? How can it be treated conceptually, without falling back on the signs that represent it? One path seemed a good one to take: to stop giving prime attention to the *meaning* of signs, to their representational contents, and to focus instead on their *practical effects;* to give up trying to decode the significance hidden behind symbols, and instead to ask what forces they draw on or shore up, and through which mechanisms they are likely to trigger certain effects; to cease interrogating the semantic charge of forces, but rather to interrogate the energetic power of signs. From this point the study of forces becomes possible, and the point of view is reversed; a given system of signs implies a given circulation of forces, such that one can speak about "regimes of signs." Now, a given ritual practice engages signs and forces, implying a given articulation between circuits of forces and regimes of signs. It is this principle that has governed my exploration of curing mechanisms in therapeutic rituals and my analysis of traditional legal processes.

This reflection on tribal societies runs the risk of annoying anthropologists who would say, "What gives you the right to draw general conclusions from tribal societies without having made a thorough comparative study in the first place?" Coincidentally, they are not talking to their colleagues, wary that there is a danger of losing the prerogatives of their "field," and, particularly possessive about their own fieldwork, they take on the intruder: "What right has he, or any philosopher for that matter, to come hunting on our lands?"

Still, this is not really about encroaching on other peoples' territory. The aim of the philosopher thinking about tribal societies is not the same as that of the anthropologist. The former is trying to establish general relations among facts, relations that can be verified across all tribal societies; the latter has no determined object; his or her thought can take sacrifice as its object, for instance, in order to work out a certain type of relation to the sacred, and, while it is always a good idea to have gathered the most possible facts, there is no absolute need to have done so. Sometimes even a single example can do. This has an obvious relation to the very nature of philosophical method. The questions raised there are quite different from the ones put forward by anthropology as a field of empirical research, or as a science. If it is a matter of creating models, then the philosopher starts at a level of abstraction that is not anthropological. Taking an empirical object, for example, one that might already be a scientific object, the philosopher uses categories belonging to the discipline of philosophy in order to choose certain privileged relations. While the anthropologist, proceeding by comparison and generalization, observes a strict respect for experience, the philosopher permits himself or herself to work from an infraempirical level, a more radical or pristine experiential level, to a level that is supraempirical and where abstraction attains a maximum degree. The greater heuristic scope of these models runs greater risks, and this is the price one has to pay. On the one hand, the heuristic procedures of science (whatever extrascientific material the scientist may make use of in his or her personal research) are situated within definite limits set out in advance, which can eventually be displaced or transformed, but they remain to be worked on from the inside. On the other hand, philosophical procedures are located outside the scientific sphere, which nonetheless is visited from time to time with an apparent lack of respect, which comes from the innocence that its freedom brings.

This is why scientists often throw up their hands in horror at the "speculations" of philosophers, but why they are also fascinated sometimes by the feeling that a line of thought might be opening up new fields to scientific inquiry.

PART I

The Antinomies of Power

WHAT EXACTLY are we referring to when we speak of power? A thing? An idea? A being? Can we say that the object of power is accessible to our senses? After all, there is nothing more concrete than the effects of political power on society. But as soon as you want to understand power, it becomes impenetrable; when you try to pin it down, it is suddenly everywhere; when you try to approach it, it disappears.

Is power, then, political power? If we turn toward political organizations to try to get a fix on the object of power, we find that even the most cursory examination immediately shows up the ramifications, dependencies, and fragilities of political power. Other formations of power appear before us—social, religious, magical, therapeutic. They are also systems of power. They are dependent on each other and on political power, such that "power" is both everywhere and nowhere. Nowhere, in fact, since this proteiform object is radically unthinkable; and yet it is always there, its most ostensible effects proclaiming the fact of its existence. It is like Lévi-Strauss describing the "antinomical" properties of *mana* as "force and action, quality and state; substantive, adjective and verb all at once, abstract and concrete, omnipresent and localized."[1]

So what is the material out of which power seems to be made? Doesn't it constitute the very essence of all potentiality? In every case it is a question of strategies. We have to try to grasp what seems to be the basic material of power, and then build apparatuses that can tame it, fix it, and maintain it. In this way "sites" and "machines" of power are created. But before the construction of these sites and appropriate apparatuses to manipulate power, there is no power; and yet, without this material, the apparatuses cannot function.

The question arises as to whether this difficulty in knowing the object of power is related to the nature of the object itself or to the methods used to approach it. As usual, in these cases, the answer is linked to both. But here, perhaps, it is in a slightly special way.

First, if one looks for different ways of defining power based on its appearances—or its effects—one quickly comes up against the fact that whatever definition one pauses on, there is likely to be an opposite statement, which is equally plausible and equally unverifiable: the discourse on power is an antinomical discourse.

Suddenly this fact takes on a dramatic resonance—doesn't every society want to look after itself, to build up its defenses? Isn't it initially the job of political power to take on this task? But if every discourse on power only represents one side of the two faces of an antinomy, if it allows that there is always an antinomical discourse with the same claims to the truth (which are translated into real social struggles), then isn't there necessarily a *democratic illusion* or a *monarchical illusion*, an illusion of liberal economic discourse, and one of socialist economic discourse, and so on? These illusions do not bear comparison with those which Kant spoke of in relation to the transcendental appearance that makes us believe that we can know God, the soul, and the world. Democracy exists and we know how it works. The illusion in question here is the one that believes that democracy or monarchy produces the best, the strongest, or the most stable form of power, that they embody the very essence of political power.

In this case the illusion relates neither to the object nor to the tools used to find out about it, but mostly to the one that comes to the fore when it is *produced* by a certain knowledge that one thinks one has about it. Let me explain. Democracy is what we might call an "ideological reality." It is not a tree or a feeling. It is also a product of the way people think about themselves and about reality. But this thinking has effects on its object, it fashions them and orients them. And it is only a way of thinking that is full of beliefs, illusions, and particular points of view. This, nevertheless, is going to condition the very nature of the object that one is constructing; and democracy, through the struggles and relations of forces, comes about, socially and historically, as the product of all these ideological discourses — legal, political, moral, and philosophical — that people inhabit. If, then, there is an illusion about the power of democracy, then it has its roots already in the very reality of its object. So it is not surprising that the knowledge of this object, as an effect of power, would be illusory.

In fact the illusion relates to a precise point. It emerges when one tries to define the object of power in an exclusive fashion, in whatever domain. For instance, this happens when one tries to make democracy the essence of power, when one asserts that modern technology has a claim on true, efficient, or absolute power (to the exclusion of magic). So the illusion is born because one pretends to be able to embrace the totality of power in a single definition that applies to an exclusive object. Here the comparison with Kant becomes necessary. Kant showed that the illusion that leads us to believe that we can know God, the soul, or the world came from the fact that the understanding exceeded the limits of perceptibility, making too great a claim in relation to the available facts. We do not have perceptible facts that allow us to say, as some do, that the world has a beginning in time. The case of power is a little different. When we assert that democracy is the most powerful political system, we do not exceed the limits of empirical experience, we *reduce* the facts that it offers us. What facts? Those which pertain back to power itself; power has effects *in all domains*. There is no knowledge that doesn't rub up against it. But the definition of a political system (or for that matter a legal system or a therapeutic method) that claims to encompass all power in its formulation of it falls necessarily into the trap of illusion, because it didn't take into account this first fact, which is that one of the features of power (one of its effects) is precisely to *escape* from a real or logical order. Therefore there is always more power in the real world than one can know about. Wherever there are leaks, overflows, or disorder, power appears there, too. But any definition of an object as being a source and an effect of power leads inexorably to the desire to enclose *all* power in that object, to present it as *the* source and the seat of power. Equally, discourses on this object will be reductive, partial, and falsely totalizing. And at the very spot where one thinks one finally has the truth all tied up, the breach opens and all the power runs away. From this point another discourse that is antinomical to the first starts to take shape. This still has the same logic as the one at work in the Kantian antinomies.

A further question is whether we are dealing with antinomies of power or with discourses on power. Given the "ideological" nature of the reality of objects of power, the two become confused. There are corresponding discourses that reply to the real, social effects of antinomies like democracy/monarchy or psychiatry/antipsychiatry. And as the former constitute, in turn, effects of power, they too can be considered like concrete objects, as forces in action. I will designate the oppositions that traverse this discourse-reality complex with the simplified expression of "antinomies of power."

Antinomies exist because of reductions of the whole of power to a single object or perspective. But why cannot power be seen to be enclosed in a sole object? Because of history. And this is why we have societies without "historicity"—traditional societies—resisting innovation, always assimilating it into traditional models, which have created particular apparatuses precisely in order to give themselves the maximum of power. They have built up networks for the capture of floating potency, leaving it floating, the better to integrate it. In these societies there is only one perspective on objects of power, the one that has been "handed down by the ancestors"—applying equally to the form of political institutions, to magical rites, to therapy, to kinship organizations, to the way of educating children, to cooking and the techniques of hunting and fishing. Here, there are no antinomies because there are no innovations that condition the passing of time, as in our modern societies. Here, time is recurrent, "repetitive" to a certain extent. There are no antinomies because the way in which traditional peoples think their time (as social and cosmic) has allowed them effectively to maneuver—in particular instances like therapeutic rituals or the overall organization of their societies—all the power that is at their disposal. It is not that these people are in possession of the transparent control of their social mechanisms, but that in a sense this control exists in the very form of their social system.

On the other hand, as soon as "historicity" gains entry to traditional societies, antinomical discourses and rival factions emerge that want to promote one or another object of power. It is with history that we see a certain balance beginning to sway, then power ignites, and forces that people no longer have control of begin to act. This is why they are obsessed with wanting to link up the totality of power with a single one of its effects.

The antinomies that I will present here retrace the trajectory that I have just sketched out. First the antinomies will be set out in four categories, then I will research the reason for this in their conceptual formation, and finally attempt to show what answers ancient societies have given to them.

If four antinomies have been chosen, it is clearly for ease of presentation, and I have not wished to shirk the fact that the reference to Kant would lend an air of affectation to the argument. But this is also justified by the content of the problematic that is put forward.

Why four antinomies and not five or six, why these four and not others? I could have presented different ones, in a greater number — the effects of power are multiple and diverse, and it would not be difficult to gather them under categories other than the ones chosen (sign/force, one/multiple, life/death, finite/infinite). But, as always happens in such cases, we would have found, under these new categories, those which we had left aside. So in a way the choice is arbitrary. But it is arbitrary because an imperative internal to the categories that make the effects of power conceivable means that they closely imply them, such that they can all be found in the small number that have been chosen.

Besides, my approach is not aiming to define power, but to establish the conditions that have made possible its antinomical thought — this covers all the fields of power. It was therefore not necessary to worry too much about the mode of entry in order to reach the heart of the problem. So I have chosen, for convenience, the most economical and direct way.

O   N   E

First Antinomy
(on the Means of Power)

THESIS: POWER lies in signs and their relations, and not in force.

Antithesis: Power is force, and signs could never create power of their own accord.

Proof of the Thesis: If power lay in force alone, one would have to concede that it would be measured by its capacity to overcome resistance. This capacity would not be controlled, oriented, or determined in either space or time; otherwise it would have to be subordinated to the organization of signs. The power of force would be completely haphazard, blind, fortuitous, and at the whim of circumstance (as Rousseau says, there is always one force greater than another). It would thus depend on factors on which force would have no power. So power exists only by virtue of signs and their relations, which are capable of establishing norms and laws.

Proof of the Antithesis: If power lay in signs alone, it would become assimilated to the capacity of signs to quash the impetus of a force. But only a force can oppose another one; if signs were to have that capacity, it would mean that they are forces, or that they conceal or produce forces. Only force can create power.

1.1.

This antinomy is about the means of power, means that the Thesis locates in signs, and the Antithesis in forces. Nothing could be more misleading than to attempt to resolve the antinomy by way of a "synthesis." It is indeed the case that there are two possible ways of thinking about power, which will continue to go in opposite directions as long as one upholds a certain conception of forces and signs that the Thesis shares with the Antithesis. They both think of force as a gross fact, without intelligence or meaning, made up of raw energy and, in the final analysis, without direction. The sign is thought of as having the power to signify by itself, such that force would not be graspable, and would probably not exist, were it not for this signifying capacity of the sign. In a word, the blind force and the sterile sign.

The antinomy covers a broad range of domains where thinking about power is exercised: legal philosophy, where legalist theories on the foundation of the law are opposed to doctrines that see its origin in forces; political philosophy, where the essence of power is on the one hand situated in a relation of more or less direct domination and submission, and on the other in decision and control systems benefiting from the significant informational contents available to them; the therapeutic practice that stresses the "economic" or energetic aspect, where the cure is seen above all in terms of the distribution of forces, or its "guiding principles" are set according to the organization of representations, signs, or signifiers; different conceptions of magical powers that are discovered in the course of different ethnological approaches, some seeing them as coming from outside the social domain of institutions and language (these would be irrational forces), others assigning them particular functions in the overall functioning of a society, reducing them to variants of the same type of phenomena (witchcraft would thus be explicable in terms of kinship structure, or whatever); and, in general, in every field where the force-sign dichotomy is found.

1.2. Forces, operators, and signs.

Forces and signs can be conceived of in another way. It is true that force is not just a raw fact, meaningless and made up of unencodable energy, because it would be impossible to talk about such a thing; it is equally certain that a sign would not be able to signify by itself, since it does not even exist in itself, but only in relation to a receiver, which entails a message, a communication, decoding. In a word, there are forces that make the sign mean something for someone. One can also say (as the Proof of the Antithesis has done) that a force would only be able to recognize resistance in another force. According to this view, a force is only what it is for another force if it is signified as such. Whether it is a political, social, logical, or warlike force, it can only exercise its "force," produce its effects, if it is "translated" as it does so. This translation is not a simple encoding through a system of signs, because in a way it consists of an irreducible, untranslatable, and quite specific encoding. Let us say that it is an encoding where signs also remain forces. In the arena of economic struggles, the forces that confront each other are certainly economic; as such they are only "understandable" or "readable" for other forces of the same type. What creates the specificity of force is this particular decoding apparatus, which makes a sign a force for another force in the same code, and which doesn't reduce the sign to a pure arbitrary signifier, "cut loose" from the signified. When two forces clash, they signify their opposition, and their combat unfolds because of, and through, this way of being in opposition to each other. This is why each individual encounter has its own individual rules—which, in each case, have the effect of purifying the forces of the foreign bodies that they have brought with them, so that the fight can be just, loyal, balanced, and without exterior support, making it purely economic, intellectual, or political. The apparatus that encodes forces in this particular way (to reiterate: it makes them significant for other forces of the same type, and not for other forces of different types, which makes it an operation similar to that for the encoding of information) can be called the operator of force. This is a technical apparatus that transforms a force and stores it. It has a role that is simultaneously expressive, communicative, and active. It is expressive because it signifies the force in advance, communicative because it places it in communication (and keeps it there), and active because it produces effects on the other force (tools are technical agents, the body can and is used as an agent, as are weapons, and so on).

This leads us to assume that (1) it is necessary to distinguish among several similar notions, such as "energy," "force," "potency" (*puissance*), and "power" (*pouvoir*)[1] and (2) there is a certain affinity between forces and signs such that the former can transform themselves and move, in part or in whole, into the latter.

Since the Thesis and the Antithesis represent in effect two attempts to define power, I shall limit myself for the time being to the distinction between "energy" and "force." Energy is force that is not determined or coded; it is the intensive feature of force and its specificity as the motor of a mechanism or a process. In the generally accepted definition, energy is both the most concrete and the most abstract thing, the most particular and the most universal; the most determined (since it produces particular discoverable effects) and the most indeterminate (since it appears in a way to be undifferentiated, permeating everything). On the other hand, force seems to be an oriented energy, implying a "resistance." While energy is related to the pure positivity of a flux, force implies fault lines produced in this flux and in particular points at which energy is coded by some agent. Energy becomes force inside a "field," acquiring a vectorial aspect, undergoing cracks and fragmentations that are part and parcel of the individualization of force. Since there is force only for another force, it has to be admitted that in the process of the individualization of energy the tension between forces is already in play, or, in other words, opposing vectors are in conflict.

As we have just seen, the Thesis and the Antithesis are in place because of the radical separation of forces and signs. But if any force is the result of a coding of energy and if force exists in more than one mode (those which cannot enter into direct relationships: of opposition, reciprocal stimulation, repulsion, or attraction), these latter are the work of the operator that transforms signs into forces. In fact, every sign carries a force within it, and is already a force: there is a force of representation, a force of speech, a force of the symptom, and so on. By the same token, there is no force that does not contain some aspects of the sign (and in particular that of signifying for another force, that is, to have a value as something else — apart from pure energy — for another thing). Thus it is the same operator who starts with energy, individualizes it into force and encodes it in such a way that it can act as such in a field of forces. The operator's role seems to be a double one. First determining what the force is, then transforming it. In other words, the process of identification tends to make it something other than what it is. It is in this sense that one can say that force doesn't exist: when it is the movement from one sign to another. But as movement, with its characteristic feature of energy, its existence is final and irreducible.

Problems arise with the particular transformation of forces into signs (and signs into forces, when the former "dissolve"). There are different regimes of forces: one could be a play among signs creating a tension or a symbolic confrontation. Nonetheless it is still a question of forces in action. And the relations between signs and forces are always multiple and complex. There are signs, and relations of signs, which absorb force (or its energy) in such a way that they reveal it only as reduced, diminished, and evaporating. Because of certain properties of the sign, and in specific contexts (such as that of representation), it soaks up the impetus of the force that it comes from and tends to make it disappear. So here there is a sort of entropy that is an integral part of sign systems and that reduces their signifying capacity.

If two forces are set up in opposition to each other, then the force that has the upper hand in the struggle gives rise to and leaves behind a remainder. This remainder, which is the measure of the relation between the forces and the gap between them, also measures the power of the one over the other. Now the remainder is no longer a force with a meaning related to the other force since the action of the operator has stopped; some of the remainder may form a precipitate constituting a *sign*, in residual form. Thus the sign emerges because of the absence of the operator, as a distant repercussion of force. It is both a memory of the actions of the operator and the result of their ceasing. As long as forces act, signs do not emerge. There is only the pure activity of operators producing things, which may become, in due course, signs for quite different forces. So these considerations on the meaning of the sign lead us to think that it relates to this original differential gap coming from the relations of forces.

Now, what "work" does the operator do? It acts on a force and on its internal features and places it in communication with other forces. The first aspect refers to another characteristic of forces: their intensity has the property of being able to grow or diminish without changing in nature. This means it has the capacity to work with internal differentiations or rhythmic heterogeneities without losing its wholeness or even creating a division in its heart. The intensity of a force is not enough to give birth to meaning (force would not have this privilege of being able to produce meaning all by itself). For that to come about, some other limitation would have to apply to the intensity of forces. This limitation would be the result of its opposition to an external force, and the "remainder" would add to the internal gap a double determination. It gives the force an orientation and, coming from the outside with an absolute limit, recalibrates the system of internal gaps around (while opening it up to) another system of references.

As a precipitate of the remainder, the sign thus refers both to another system of signs and a relation of forces. It refers to a relation of forces because it is the result of whatever flies off from the struggle between two specific forces. It refers, by itself, to a body of signs because it is the result of a transformation of determinations that are internal to force. In starting up this transformation in this way the operator paradoxically makes a force meaningful for a force of the same type, and at the same time makes it susceptible to the actions of other external operators. This is where the translatability of the sign comes from, why it is treated "fetishistically," giving it the power to mean all by itself (Thesis) and making it dependent on forces (Antithesis).

In any case we can see how power is intimately related to meaning. At the same time as the sign and its meaning are cast in relations of force, the very foundations of power are laid—this remainder, this original gap between the two forces, which is transformed into a sign destined, however, to carry its meaning indefinitely to the horizon beyond all possible meaning.

1.3. Prestige.

Here I will be investigating phenomena closely tied to the formation of power, which have the advantage of being at the cutting edge of the creation of forces and signs in power.

If one defines power in a quite general fashion as the capacity to produce the desired effect on people or things, then it becomes identified with the exercise of a competence. This is such a broad definition that it says nothing about the specificity of power or about its internal mechanisms. However it is useful to keep it in mind in approaching the idea of prestige. Prestige arises when one attributes a certain competence to someone, and this competence exceeds the usual performances expected of it. Prestige is therefore the consequence of a judgment and an evaluation of a domain of competence as it is carried out by other subjects. Since this evaluation enlarges the field of competence, it necessarily ends in the attribution of a surplus of force compared with that which was calculated as corresponding to the first competence. This would be the force of a larger, or even unlimited, competence, since there is no available criterion to circumscribe this new domain. And thus prestige begins to spread, by way of its authority (that is, its recognized power) over other quite precise domains of competence. Since evaluation is involved, then there is a relation of forces. The surplus that emerges is only a figure of the "remainder" that is the precipitate of a struggle. The act of attributing prestige must therefore produce signs, on the one hand, and on the other reassign them to other competencies. It does little good to know if "truth" is involved or not; in any case the evaluation that gave birth to prestige implies an inequality and an illusion, even if it is later confirmed that the subject did indeed possess the competencies attributed to him or her. Persons who take advantage of the situation and "up the ante" on the evaluations others make of their competencies, elevating their own prestige, will make haste to produce the necessary signs. The deliberate and reckless gesture of manifesting these signs will build up the impression that one has hidden knowledge and power. But it is not sufficient to make people believe in power in order to obtain it; forces have to be worked, the remainder attributed; forces have to be called upon, communicated, and made active and efficient. Unless this happens, there will be no power (since, as Machiavelli noted, power is only what it is if it is held, so that the way in which power is maintained will structure its internal organization). This task devolves to the technical operator of the power of prestige, who must turn this remainder into a force which relates to other forces.

Since it is a question of producing power, then what has to be done is to turn the surplus of attributed force into a meaningful force. One has to make sense of the gap between the competencies of the prestigious person and those of the people who are making judgments. And this extra force that has been attributed has to be inscribed in the general network of other forces that are circulating in the social arena and that signify them and make them significant. To sum up: out of the relationship of forces arising between the performance capacities of a person and those who judge them arises a remainder, a surplus that favors the former. People will say, for instance, that a person has exceptional "gifts." Certain competencies go beyond normal performance. The remainder is a force that is yet to be understood. It is not coded, it is not located in the usual network of criteria — it is prestige. As a surplus that is not yet meaningful, it exceeds the normal field of meaning. The transformation of prestige into power comes through the work of the operator who translates the remainder into particular signs at the same time as keeping the force as it is — that is, as a "surplus of force."

If we assume power to be based essentially on prestige, then in this case the operator is simply directing a scenario that has the aim of producing signs that make people believe there are forces there (signs of wealth, nobility, competence, beauty, and so on) that are always greater than normal. Lévi-Strauss tells us in *Tristes Tropiques* that Chief Nambikwara scribbled illegible letters in order to imitate the writing of the ethnographer, and that he understood just how much he could get out of this in order to build up his prestige among his people. Pen, paper, and the act of writing constituted the operator of force that he used in order to conjure up an incomprehensible (from the point of view of the Nambikwara) surplus of prestige, which was nevertheless seen as a sign of superior competence that only the White Man possessed. What he did was to stage an operator connecting the signs produced to obscure forces.

However, if power is continually obliged to produce a surplus of incomprehensible force, it is equally obliged to turn it into something that can be understood. In this way there is a continual disjunction and rematching going on between forces and signs; power has to act both as a pure surplus of meaning (nonsense) and as the normal change of meaning. This is why prestige, which is the basic material on which power works, is always there keeping it company, offering itself as the inexhaustible source of power.

This example shows that force has to be considered not as a lack of meaning, but as something with too much meaning. And the sign, not as something that meaning depends on—and never quite matches up to—but as something that is always trying to attach itself to a surplus of meaning in order to signify.

1.3.1.

If prestige is born in the attribution of a surplus of force corresponding to a know-how that, while beginning locally, quickly becomes a gift that exceeds its initial boundaries, then one can say that the surplus that is accorded a prestigious person is also accompanied by the subtraction of an equal quantity of force from those who have declared themselves less competent. So there is a social transfer of force in operation. Prestigious persons base their power on giving themselves social goals and on guaranteeing that the power they have control of has extraordinary and general functions. In this manner prestigious persons socialize forces and introduce mechanisms of domination: grants of prestige are accompanied by rites, prohibitions, avoidance behavior, and a whole series of representations and beliefs that imply subjection to the force that is feared. Thus the allegiance shown to the person of power is a first gesture in the establishment of power.

Moreover, it can be seen that the socialization of forces always maintains a point of contact with that aspect of the force that cannot be assigned or encoded. In ceremonies like potlatch, prestige is accrued in proportion to the destruction of the signs of power. Beyond powers—understandable, institutional, and coded—lies power.[2] In many African kingdoms—those magical kingdoms studied by Luc de Heusch[3]—power is installed through heroic exploits. The next in line, the son of the king, must perform some feat (often in war, as in the kingdoms of Uganda) that demonstrates his vital force, which will then come to replace and replenish the declining forces of the aging king. And as the king is required to revitalize the world through magic (good harvests, births, and so on), the heroic-magical feat that installs the new power harks back, in fact, to the same genesis of royal power. That is, a struggle gives rise to a surplus of forces, magical forces, and this rite symbolizes this birth, celebrating that which is beyond all forms of power and which creates and nurtures them. In this sense prestige is closely related to charisma. We could talk here of "graces" (*charis*), overendowments that, while accompanying exchanges, lubricate them and make them work.[4]

We must note that whatever signs are produced to accompany prestige, the power that eventually emerges is marked by a particular sign that is different from the others in its nature. It is not the sign of greater age, greater wealth, greater courage, larger family, or greater cleverness. It is the sign of the force that is the force from/in the sign, since it is a thing endowed with magical virtues: a royal scepter, the statuette of an ancestor (among the Shilluk of the Upper Nile), a sacred drum, or a throne.

1.4. Witchcraft.

Surplus of force, surplus of meaning. This last notion seems obscure, if not absurdly redundant, as if one said that one square is more square than another one. Yet, if it is admitted that power corresponds to an excess of force; that it is defined by the capacity to distribute this surplus along the lines of signs and social channels, and in doing this it directs signs and forces according to meaningful relations; and that in any case it has as its aim not only to exercise itself, but also to maintain its existence—in always reproducing its origin and genesis, which obliges it to ceaselessly recreate forces without meaning—one comes up against the idea of an "excess" of meaning, corresponding to the excess of force. An example will help us understand this difficult point.

The originality of Jeanne Favret-Saada's book on witchcraft in the Norman Bocage[5] lies no doubt in her reversal of the usual terms of analysis of witchcraft in classical ethnology. She is no longer trying to find relations—of causality, of structural or functional complementarity, or of genealogical descendance—between the discourse and the representations of witchcraft and social and practical structures; for example, to link this discourse to the social status of the witch or the bewitched, and more generally to a socioeconomic structure or function; or, again, to try to establish general relationships—as Edmund Leach does between marriage and the "mystical influences" of witchcraft[6]—between kinship and witchcraft relations; or finally, to make a meticulous catalog of activities, medicines, and therapeutic practices of magicians and "unwitchers"[7] to fit them into a particular symbolic network. While all this is not to be dismissed out of hand, the approach is now somewhat different. The words of the bewitched are now taken seriously, and the following questions are asked: Why do they adopt such a special language to talk of their misfortune? Why do they tie the symptoms of their repeated misfortune—sickness, pain, and death—to "forces" (and not to "the usual symbolic mediations" or to known social "rational" causes)? Why can't the conflicts that this discourse speaks of be seen as resolvable by way of justice in the courts of law?

Favret-Saada's rejection of the traditional way of approaching witchcraft and her new approach presuppose a heterogeneity, in a radical sense, between the discourse of witchcraft and other types of practices and discourses. If the latter were to account for the former, they would make it say things it doesn't say and doesn't signify. If one lines up the effects of fate next to the symbolic forms of personhood, then relates them to social, economic, or political groupings, then one is introducing into the discourse of witchcraft precisely what it can't and doesn't want to say. On the other hand, if one begins by taking as given the gap between social discourse (which is also that of classical ethnology) and the discourse of the bewitched, then the representations belonging to the latter can begin to take shape (in the form of concepts, or "diagrams") without reference to the former. What at first glance seems impossible (and Favret-Saada succeeded in doing it) is a translation of a dynamic of forces by direct conceptualization. The writer speaks of forces by way of concepts, but does not introduce foreign matter (at the end of the book the difference between "magic force" and "vital force" is abandoned) into the discourses of the bewitched or of the exorcists. One then has to ask what the basis is for the conceptual framework if there is no primordial reference to other codes, and if the desire to hold strictly to the discourse of witchcraft is thoroughly respected.

The reference to codes is certainly there, but not in such a way that one code is privileged, such as the economic, the kinship, or the therapeutic. What Favret-Saada calls the "domain" of an individual (who is in some relationship involving sorcery) includes these references, but they are amalgamated in a totality that a "force" is opposed to and acts upon. The domain of the bewitched, so defined by the name (which marks its possessions), encompasses all that normally pertains to quite precise categorizations and social mediations. If the discourse of witchcraft puts all that in the same basket (under the same name), it is to distance itself from it: the discourse about forces speaks of that which it is normally impossible to talk. So what does one normally speak about? About things that make sense. And what does witchcraft speak about? Things that have no meaning, like incomprehensible ills, adversity, and death, which strike haphazardly and inexplicably return. Now this gap between sense and nonsense, between ordinary discourse and the discourse of witchcraft, makes sense for everybody, even those who would deny it. And yet it remains out of reach, unsayable, and in a certain way incomprehensible. It is the same gap that separates Favret-Saada's ethnological discourse on sorcery and that of ordinary ethnological discourse. It places the meaning produced by the first in excess over that of the second—the same way that witchcraft is in excess over other discourses. They add extra meaning because they speak of a surplus, which while it lacks sense in itself, nevertheless constitutes an inexhaustible source of meaning for life and the world. This reinforces the feeling generated by reading *Deadly Words*. It is one of inexplicable obviousness. She doesn't build up a "grammar" of forces, or even a "syntax." Rather there is an elementary logic of meaning; it is about the most fundamental events of life.

Ethnology has always endeavored to get a grip on sorcery by starting with its conditions and effects. What sorcery spoke most clearly about—"forces"—was simply heard as a vulgar way of expressing that which ethnology had the job of rendering intelligible, by referring their manifestations to signs, representations, beliefs, and social practices that would be useful, integrated or integratable, and understandable. Now this order seems to be reversed: forces don't have to be signified; they signify. They don't depend, in the first place, on other languages, symbols or meanings.

1.4.1.

The powers one always associates with sorcery and magic are those that hold sway over life and death.[8] These powers would not be nearly so terrifying if they could be easily understood and translated according to known partially common significations. If this can't be done it is not only because they store the most possible meaning, but also because this maximum meaning is beyond meaning: it is in the very forces that these powers carry along with them. Their meaning has its beginnings in this spilling out: the meaning of life *is* the effective power of life as a force, and that of death collapses and opens up to infinity in the real power of inflicting death. The surplus of meaning is only comprehensible because its intelligibility comes to a halt in the register of a sign-based translation, only to be extended in a dynamic of forces. One could put forward the hypothesis that the discourses of the magician and the bewitched draw their powers and their effectiveness from the region where the surplus of meaning becomes mingled with the surplus of force.

It is perhaps in this perspective that it would also be useful to consider the placement of various social powers, and the relations—or lack of relations—that exist in certain societies between the powers of sorcery and political power. What E. E. Evans-Pritchard suggested in *Witchcraft, Oracles, and Magic among the Azandie*[9]—namely a classification of the power of the sorcerer, of the magician, and of the prince, going from the margin to the center, from the "imaginary" to the "symbolic,"[10] the magician being the person who transforms the nonmediatized forces of the sorcerer into social behavior—does not depend on "functions" or on "different positions in the structure." But since all power—and especially political power—tends to rationally organize forces according to an order, it is not surprising that the instance that should produce the most sensible order (the political establishment) finds itself to be the furthest removed from the forces that rub shoulders with incomprehensibility and nonsense. This, however is a mere appearance. According to particular cases they could be widely separated, but they could also be in close proximity, and sometimes in a relation of forces. The political apparatus for the production of meaning and power tolerates, feeds off, or represses the powers of sorcery. Because politics, also, would like to become the meaning center for all social meanings.

1.5. The politics of repression.

There is an aspect of the antinomy of forces and signs that concerns the relative proportion of the one and the other, such that the most stable government is obtained. This is the classical problem of political thought. In this way, Plato opposed (in his *Politics*) the roughness of gymnastics to the gentleness of music, which the royal weaver would have to bring together. And Machiavelli also opposes the force of the lion and the cunning of the fox, two attributes that the prince should possess, and there is also, in a reversed perspective, the way that Estienne de La Boétie questions "voluntary servitude," taken up again by Wilhelm Reich in *The Mass Psychology of Fascism* and by Gilles Deleuze and Félix Guattari in *Anti-Oedipus*.[11]

It remains to be seen how despotic and authoritarian regimes of all sorts manage, surprisingly, to become stable. We need to ask how voluntary servitudes are forged: why would anyone want to be repressed? The power that is least likely to be contested or revolted against is that which knows how to impose voluntary obedience rather than forced submission.

The question can be approached from this angle: Why would anyone want to be repressed if they are under the illusion that this is a liberating process? The discussion can begin with belief: How is belief produced such that it is placed in the service of objectives that include the enslavement of the believer? The belief cannot be summed up by adherence to a banal type of illusion, because it impinges on an "object" in which the subject itself is included. In the final analysis, "voluntary servitude" contains belief that only brings about subjection because a pseudosubjection brings about belief. It is not an "appearance" that is offered up as reality, an "illusion of freedom" that comes from the outside to entrap an individual or a group. But the conditions of production of the appearance that invite allegiance should be such that they oblige the subject to become him or herself producer of the appearance, only to be all the better subjected, rather than be reduced to vulnerable passivity. This has a necessary relation to the energy provided, to the active forces at play in the production of the appearance. This is borne out in extreme cases, such as political regimes of fascism or in the diverse "personality cults" that accompany certain socialist regimes, but also in a revealing way in the esoteric religious sects that are widespread in the West these days. The relation of force, sign, and operator takes a particular form. In every domain of social activity, the operation takes the form of an apparatus that makes each individual force (each operator) into a sign that only gathers its force when it contributes to the functioning of the operator (itself a despotic sign and force). The more one works toward the liberation and the production of forces, and the more they are imprisoned in the sign (because this work, the movement of forces, is already the creation of signs), then the more force, operator, and sign tend to be confused in the belief resulting from and because of this imprisonment. Here we find ourselves in the presence of a fundamental mechanism in the formation of power. Given its generality, it can be more easily approached from the perspective of therapeutic power.[12] So from this point on I will be guided by the following points:

1   A theory of repression cannot remain wedded to a simplistic conception of brute force, or to the exclusively signifying sign.

2   It has to develop a theory of belief and, in particular, come to terms with the construction of a "scenic" apparatus in which, and thanks to which, the space of signs and the circulation of forces is put in place.

3   These can only be understood by way of reference to notions of the surplus of meaning and surplus of forces, because it is obvious that in all the cases in question (like fascism or sects), an exceptional deployment of forces and meanings occurs (especially the latter in the case of belief).

4   Finally, a theory of repression has to ask whether there is a general criterion deciding what is liberation or repression. This is a crucial question because it puts at issue the "subject of theory," and whether this subject ever has the "right" to speak on behalf of others. This question is always oversimplified by ideological discourses that adopt one clear criterion or another, or by simple legal reality, which assumes criteria whether one wants it to or not. In the end it is a necessary question because it throws doubt on the very manner of posing it: it is not a question of "values," but of a special circulation of energy and of life in the heart of the group.

There is a minor point. It could seem tempting to begin the analysis with the choice of a Freudian model, to compare the desire for obedience to all the evidence of the "death instinct" described in *Beyond the Pleasure Principle* and elsewhere: the repetition compulsion, the resistance to therapy, masochism, the need for punishment and melancholy. The existence of the desire for obedience would reveal problems of the same order: how can obedience produce pleasure, since that implies submission, inequality, injustice, and deprivation? These are all things that in other instances create such universal grief that the desire for obedience can only be explained by the activation of some death drive. The Freudian model would indicate a division of pleasure and displeasure according to different psychic apparatuses: pleasure for one (for the ego, for example) would be pain for the other (for the id, for example). The compulsion to repeat traumatic events, painful for the sick person and stopping him or her from getting better, would have primary and secondary benefits. Nevertheless, in cases where obedience to the group is cited, there is a total involvement in submission, without anything to dampen the delight of the voluntary slave. Here it is not a question of pleasure or pain, but of force and desire. Rather than hindrances, there is a guiltless liberation of energy in the social domain.

T W O

Second Antinomy
(on the Forms of Power)

THESIS: ONLY social power exists, and individuals get their power only from the totality of the social relations in which they are integrated.

Antithesis: Only individual power exists, and social power only comes about as the sum of all individual powers.

Proof of the Thesis: If individuals drew their power from other individuals, or from themselves, then each individual, in a given society, would be the exclusive origin and destination of social power. Society would be reduced to a totality of individuals, and outside of individual power it would have no power. The very idea of society would be canceled out. And it is hard to see how individuals could get their power from a relationship to other individuals, since the very idea of relationship implies the idea of a group. Alternatively, one would have to consider power as exclusively concentrated in one individual, and the result would be that all the others would find themselves stripped of it. Power would be absolute, but empty, without any social bearing. Therefore, power can only be social, and the individual manipulates only social power.

Proof of the Antithesis: If there were only social power, it would be divided among individuals who would draw their own power from society, and this "individual" power could never be used for egotistical ends. This distribution of power would be so smooth and harmonious that any relation of forces between individuals or between groups and individuals would be impossible, just as conflicts and separations would be unthinkable. But then, in turn, it would become unthinkable to entertain notions of power, society, and institution, which have the aim of regulating conflicts of power. Power is therefore uniquely individual and draws its origins only from individuals; in fact, all "social" power comes about only as the sum of all individual powers.

2.1.

This antinomy can be considered through the perspective of the divisibility of power. It could be formulated as follows: Thesis: power is multiple, and there is no privileged site where power is retained. Antithesis: power is necessarily defined by its indivisibility, by its unity, and even by its absoluteness. The classical aporias of political power emerge at this point. Is it divisible or indivisible? Can it be chopped up, or is there no sharing by definition, and so on? In the way that this antinomy has been phrased, we can find an advantage as well as a drawback. The first relates to the fact that the problem is put in concrete terms; the drawback lies in the notion of the "individual," which has a particular historically determined connotation. It can't be forgotten that the "individual" is associated with a recent construction that has accompanied the development of capitalism, that is, with a precise form of social power. For example, the clear expression of the antinomy can be seen in the problems arising from the division of power at the moment when the modern state was born in the West. Or alternatively, all the ideas and dead ends of the doctrinaires of the social contract are in the proofs of the Thesis and the Antithesis. What I mean by "individual" here is not just the idea of the individual that was sketched out in seventeenth-century Europe, but a notion that covers renderings as different as the "person" of traditional societies, the "subject" of psychoanalysis, or a shareholder in an oil company. "Individual" refers, therefore, to the singularity of a body. It is not by chance that the real social and political conundrums, expressed in this antinomy, are often striving toward solutions that take "the body" as (metaphorical) model. When power is too divided, it is weak. When it is too concentrated, it is too strong; in both cases it ends up impotent, that is, as the negation of power. So we are looking for compromise solutions that take the human organism, the individual body, as a model for social power, or, alternatively, solutions in which the power of an individual, of a king, for example, provides the cipher for the distribution or a sharing of powers according to functions, in the way in which the sections and organs of a body are divided.

2.1.1.

As far as the division and organization of powers in society are concerned, the antinomy interrogates the relations between social powers and political powers, between judicial power and society, or between the same power and instances of political government; between the individual and the group, for whom the former may have a representative task, within certain bounds; and so on. In short, it is about social dynamics, the role of the individual in society, and about history, to the extent that the future of a society depends on the factors that weigh most heavily in internal dynamics. Should one hand over to the economic aspect or to the demographic or the political the privilege of being the driving force in social life? Should one, on the contrary, see social life as being the result of the action of individuals? These are just so many questions arising in the clash between the Thesis and the Antithesis.

The importance of the problem is clear when one takes up the question of a general theory about powers or a theory of history. Has it not been said that Marx failed to construct a theory of political power, and that this lapse in Marxism allowed Stalinism to come about? The question, never solved, of the role of "superstructures" in historical and social dynamics and the periodic rearrangements that they are subject to are witness to the vigor of the stakes implicitly at work in the Thesis and the Antithesis of this antinomy of power. A general theory of power and powers, a theory of social and historical dynamics, a theory of crisis and revolution—all these depend on the way in which the sharing and unity of powers is thought through, the relative importance of this sharing and unity, and the ways in which they act respectively on the ensemble of the social body.

2.1.2.

In seeking its solution, this antinomy assumes a balance between social and political power. The latter is, in effect, the remainder of the dysfunction between social organizations and individuals or particular social units (like the family). The balanced distribution of power between society and these units would necessarily have as its political translation a type of power whose government would correspond to the needs brought up by the particular dysfunction. But what does "correspond" mean exactly? I will take it for granted that there is no balance between the two types of power, that political power fulfills its function without taking over any social power for its own advantage; or that the instances of government are so light compared with the weight of the power circulating in the social domain that there is no longer any incoherence among the diverse social forces; or even that there would be a general principle that politics doesn't increase the dysfunction between society and particular social units, but endlessly dissolves it.

This is a precarious balance. The example of democracy is enlightening. Government for the people by the people presupposes the principle of an equitable share of these two types of power. This is why the principle of justice must give a direction to democratic politics. As a "counterpolitics" it constitutes the most adequate arrangement to impede the accumulation of power on the political side, its role being to redistribute into the social domain forces that threaten to crystallize as power when conflicts arise.[1] But democracy does not escape the contradictions expressed by the second antinomy.

On the one hand, politics is an example of the totalization and unification of social forces; it hinders their dispersal and oppositional possibilities. On the other hand, it creates the hinge of social powers, at the points where individuals and groups meet: in "free zones," at points of constraint, regulation, or law that extend throughout society and change its workings because of the effects they have on the inside of these groups. A whole political *system* is built up, composed of institutions, agents, and functionaries for whom the fundamental activity is political: magistrates, administrators, members of parliament, and police. The need for a political leadership exudes another society, a body of institutions that is intimately involved with social life at the same time as maintaining a tendency to create another one, more or less autonomous to the first. The "free zones" are thus partially covered by the "civic body" (Aristotle), which is the State. However, this is not enough to unify social forces. The creation of a "political association" should not be seen as the simple filling of gaps or the mending of broken or torn social tissue. In any case it is hard to see how this would be sufficient to make the cloth whole. This will only come about through the specific effects of political work; not that any laws handed down are likely to assure the systematic coherence of the totality of behavior (in principle guaranteed by the axiomatics of fundamental constitutional laws), because this coherence always remains relative and aleatory; it doesn't impede — it even makes possible — free zones (in the negative form of normative constraints).[2] Real political coherence, which produces the stability of the totality of social life, is given by authority, by the principles of political obedience, and practically, through the fact that all members of society obey the same call to do so.[3] It is obedience that allows the unification of conduct inside a zone of liberty, by instigating a kind of *custom* (a constraint having the obligatory force of a normal behavior). This is the thing that homogenizes individual behavior in a certain way, bringing about the foundation of the unification of common life: peace. The "unification" of social goals does not mean anything else. The well-being of society and striving for a "quality of life," says Aristotle in *Politics*, are the aims of political associations. In order to achieve these, one has to first guarantee civil peace, or provide it at the same time in fact, because it is conflict that puts obstacles in the way of the unification of different social forces; and peace comes about through obedience, which is the permanent foundation for the behavior that is induced by the laws proscribing conflict. Any other coherence remains partial or purely theoretical.

Under these conditions, the democratic principle can be formulated with a first difficulty in mind. How can the social coherence necessary for everyone's well-being be obtained without resorting to political methods based on restraint? The solution lies initially in how one understands the political game. Democracy, since it assumes a constitution, cannot help but allow for political constraints. However, these constraints will be made to serve the interests of freedom. It will be determined that everyone is free, and that there are no civic duties beyond that of impeding individual freedom. This is a false solution. The fragmentation of social power that it brings about is amplified into a weakening of society, and demagogues can fall upon the power made available, and democracy devolves very quickly into the tyranny that represents its opposite: the maximization of politics unified by restraint.[4] What does this degradation of politics mean? That an "infiltration" of political liberty has come about and has penetrated into the very tissue of social exchanges: "freedom spread(s) to everything.... [It] filter(s) down to the private houses.... anarchy [is] planted in the very beasts.... a father...habituates himself to be like his child and fear his sons.... the teacher...is frightened of the pupils and fawns on them, so the students make light of the teachers," and the horses and asses, having caught this fever, "have gotten the habit of making their way quite freely and solemnly, bumping into whomever they happen to meet on the roads, if he doesn't stand aside," and the citizens "pay...no attention to the laws, written or unwritten."[5] The weakening of these bonds completely disrupts social life.

Democratic balance should therefore, above all, bring about a happy relationship between the overarching constraints of political power and the obligations attached to reciprocity. But it would seem that this is quite difficult if not impossible to put into practice, as soon as freedom is not flowing naturally from social relations but tends to be imposed on them from the outside. And how can political freedom flow naturally from social relations?

This issue displaces and broadens the problem. One would have to imagine a society where the political organization is so closely aligned to the cleavages of the social organization that politics can emerge "spontaneously" from the latter. Then political tasks would be confused with social relations. Acts of exchanging or giving would already be equivalent to governing or administering. And at the same time such harmony would, in the final analysis, obviate the need for a political system at all. The dynamics of social forces, would, by themselves, and without recourse to any instances of management or unification, accomplish in an immanent way tasks that are of a strictly political nature. There would therefore be a homogenization of forces, since they are driven exclusively, and from within, by the same aim; the idea of heterogeneous forces, or different groupings, tensions, and diversities, would lose all meaning (as the argument in the Antithesis showed).

The question of the organization of democracy will be held in abeyance while the problem of the balance between social and political power is put in classical juridical terms. Here, the relation of norms to singular forces will have to be taken into account. If democracy is always unstable, under threat, and incapable of resolving the question of the link between constraint and freedom, this is because one either envisages the norm according to its repressive side—signs overcome forces, singular forces being stripped of their power, leading to an authoritarian regime—or according to its libertarian side—forces breaking the yoke of signs only to establish their capacity for violent action, leading to anarchy. It is always this conception of forces and signs, present in the first antinomy, that is at stake. But if we conceive of the law first as that which allows forces to circulate, then as that which allows this circulation to slip out of control, a loss of control that is positively inscribed, as a right, in laws (this is also what the law has always been, both in state societies and societies without states), then it will be possible to conceive of systems of laws in which constraint acts automatically where there is an excess of constraint, and violence against the overabundance of violence. Democracy thus becomes, above all, a matter of the legal recognition of singular forces. Democratic order will be understood as that which recognizes in conflicts the possibility of guaranteeing peace; and it will only last if malfunctions and failures are sufficiently tolerated and institutionalized to assure the functioning of the group, if the preservation of singular forces and laws becomes the condition for the legitimacy of laws in common, if social constraints are conceived in the play of singular forces and political constraints are established for the service of the circulation of forces and not to paralyze or appropriate them; and finally, if equality and justice are founded on difference and the radical singularity of forces. Under these conditions the very idea of freedom changes. In the demographically small group of societies without a state, freedom is deployed in the space that covers and exceeds (covers because it exceeds) the agent who sets down the customary juridical norms. In state societies, freedom is circumscribed in the negative space of the law, or it exceeds it, exceeds it because it is entirely contained in the space of the law. But in these same large modern demographic groupings, a new conception of the law would locate liberty in the exclusive space of social dysfunction in relation to the global functioning of society. And since there would be recognition of singular forces and laws, the very creation of limited groups with their own norms would be inscribed in the law.

2.1.3.

This problematic implies a distinction between political power and social power, which has not been clearly made. The first is a "power over," linked to a surplus of force; the second is essentially a "power to" linked to a balance between forces and signs. The question of knowing how to operate a distribution of forces between individuals or particular social units, or between the social and the political, without an unjust accumulation of power—that is, an "overpower"—forming, requires an even finer distinction between the two types of power, because all "power to" seems also to double as a "power over"; and, vice versa, all political power is, in the first instance, social power.

Let us nevertheless provisionally pose the question in the following way. In relations between individuals (and between individuals and groups), whenever there is a surplus of force produced, what destiny can be assigned to it so that it would not be possible for it to be definitively appropriated for the benefit of the few? This question presupposes another. Where does this surplus of force, which is so regularly attached to political relations, come from?

2.2. The (political) power contract.

Certain tribal societies seem to have come up with a satisfying solution to the question of the relation between political power and social power. In state societies the numerous functions that devolve to the political establishment are carried out here by the regulation of diverse social systems: the kinship system, the magico-religious system, systems of age classes, and so on. In lineage-based societies of the segmentary type, for instance the Nuer, studied by Evans-Pritchard,[6] the imbrication of these systems allows the regulation of litigation to take place without a higher political power. The emergence of conflict depends a great deal on the fusion-fission dynamic; the units of the segmentation depend themselves on the system of descent and kinship; and the mediator controlling certain litigations, the man with the leopard skin, has magico-religious functions in relation to the supernatural significance of the acts motivating the litigation. Elsewhere the system disconnects authority from power, and the leopard skin chieftain does not retain any special prerogatives in the domain of political power. The juridical-political function is thus achieved in a way that is quasi-immanent to social organization, belonging to it without overshadowing it. Nevertheless, this immanence does not imply a harmony that would exclude all conflict. On the contrary, with the Nuer it is the system of conflicts that prevents the accumulation of political power, to the detriment of the social power of singular unities.

Now, if one looks in turn at the political organization of state societies, the transcendence of the political becomes immediately obvious. The leader always holds a part of the authority. This is the product of a consensus: there is no authority that is neither recognized nor allowed. The legitimate exercise of power emanates from authority. It presupposes the transfer of forces whereby prestige comes to acquire a surplus over initial competence. Authority is born of this surplus, here not only as a power that goes beyond the boundaries of initial competences, but as something that is autonomous and recognized, as a surplus in the self, as a "power of power." This is what the etymology of *auctoritas* gives us, as Emile Benveniste notes.[7] Its meaning is the capacity to confer power (the power of being or doing). Power, *potestas*, is the legal and real capacity to act. But this capacity does not derive from power itself (even though power tends, in certain cases—imperial political regimes—to claim it as its own). Whoever has authority is the *author* of power. *Augere*, related to *auctoritas*, contains the idea of engendering and of growth, of development, but also the idea of consent. Authority is the acquisition of a surplus of power by consent. It is not an attribute of prestige, it is one of power.

Individuals who recognize the authority of a chieftain (or an institution) accept that they *command*. We find social reciprocity relations have changed, because what is a given by one of the parties is not equivalent to that which is returned by the other. Consider the general idea of the political "contract," the way it appears in the tradition of the philosophy of natural (rationalist) law. The pact, which makes man pass from a natural to a social state, implies the delegation of individual powers to the superior political level. Civil peace is obtained at this price, the political level alone having the capacity to exercise power.

The general idea held by all its proponents is that the political contract is accompanied by a relation of reciprocity between the political establishment and the members of the community. What the latter gain from their political association is at least equivalent to what they have given up. The circuit of this exchange can be described as follows. On the one hand, individuals decide to shed their individual powers (in particular that of exercising violence); on the other hand, they receive in exchange the guarantee of civil peace, the benefits of collective life, and the protection of the state. The countergift of the state is paid off by the survival of the community and by its well-being, that is, by the maintenance or the improvement of the general conditions of social life. There are thus two relations of individuals to the political level: one direct, without mediation—it is the relation of obedience; the other, extremely mediatized, traverses all society and goes from the state to individuals, while diffusing itself in global society—it is the circuit through which the countergift of the state passes. So there is an exchange between obedience and the general benefits that should come about for the collective:

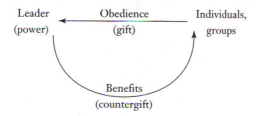

This model obliterates a fundamental nonequivalence at the same time as it establishes it. It tends to make the relation of command coincide with the state's acts of protection of society. Paradoxically, obedience to the state will become disconnected from the commandments delivered by it. With limit cases (as in Rousseau, where the state becomes, thanks to the notion of "common will," the authentic expression of individual powers), there would not even be any transcendent relation to the command; commands would be carried out by the sole function of protection and safeguarding of the community, accomplished by the political establishment.

Nevertheless, the relationship of obedience contained in the political pact presupposes an inexchangeable element. Consider, for instance, the rituals of "inversion" of power studied by ethnologists in numerous tribal societies, especially in African kingdoms. The fact that on certain occasions the subject-chieftain relation is inversed, that the latter is sacrificed, symbolically put to death, rendered destitute, defied, or insulted, is evidence of a tendency to reestablish the balance that the power contract cannot bring about. In fact, everything is reversed. Now it is the relation of domination that is being expressed in a mediatized (ritualized) way, as if symbolic violence came to recompense two vectors that were absent in the preceding model: one, which should accompany obedience (refusal of violence) in order to transform it into a symbolic relation (which would imply an internal reciprocity, making the unilateral obedience stop); the other, which really accompanies the countergift of the benefits of power, but which cannot be seen because it is too mediated (too symbolic). The king's symbolic aggression in the inversion rituals in African kingdoms reveals the nonequivalence of the power contract. It brings with it on the one side too much of the symbolic, too many overloaded circuits through which power is exercised (and is lost, dissolving as a violent relation of command)[8]— to such an extent that (bearing in mind the implicit obedience that shows up on the side of power, and the fact that it is a question of *rituals*, that is, of institutions belonging to global society) it can be modeled as shown in the accompanying diagram.

Obedience is a sham, it is not real. Aggression is real, but it is translated by a symbolic ritual. The inversion ritual tends to reestablish the balance, allowing the community to plunder the leader of the things he or she had taken inexchangeably in the power relation. In other words, political power actually hides something that cannot and has not been exchanged, something that cannot be mediatized, or symbolized, and is therefore nonsymbolic. This is no doubt the primary paradox of this power: being organized in an obedience contract, which is made up of rules of exchange and of reciprocity, it necessarily brings about a surplus of power without any possible return. This surplus is of the order of force, first of all; later it will dress itself in signs. It is embedded in the direct relation of body to body, force to force, which speaks immediately of obedience.

We therefore have to conclude that it is in politics and nowhere else that the surplus-value of power takes shape, *inasmuch as it is constituted in an autonomous fashion*, and inasmuch as it is going to function institutionally in social life. It is not that forces and the surpluses of forces do not exist everywhere, and in a way immanent to this life (we have seen how witchcraft speaks about it and lives off it; and we will see that there are "sites" that are like reservoirs for these surpluses of forces and powers). But it is not just social powers that, being attached to a certain belief, a certain practice, or a certain type of representation, participate entirely in their movement and position in the social dynamic—they appear and disappear with them and do not tend toward autonomy as surpluses of pure power. The shaman holds a surplus of power, which he uses to accomplish precise tasks and which is used up in each performance of this function. It is not the same in the case of the king.

So this is why political power is paradoxically the most powerful of all the (social and singular) powers. It offers itself as the generic of power because it is pure power, capable of unifying all powers as it harmonizes them, orienting them toward the same aim—in short, bringing them under its will. Unlike all the others it is a power that is not fixed on any aim or particular function. Making all powers dependent on it, and by right escaping the network of conditions that limit the other powers, it presents itself as the realization of the very essence of power.

2.2.1.

Two consequences flow from the obedience contract. (1) Certain attributes of power find their source in the constitution of this autonomous excess, which defines the power of power. Since it emerges while masking its origin (which is violence without symbolic equivalence), it seems to have existed forever and to have come from nowhere. The fetishism of power and its institutions, which makes them seem to be independent of the people who have produced them, as if they possess a value in themselves, an undisputed legitimacy that emanates from their very nature; the transcendence of power; its character of immortality, while those who embody it pass on—all this is covered by the idea of the excess of power created in the obedience contract. (2) The "surplus-value" of power is also based on this contract.[9] Since the excess of power cannot be exchanged, it accompanies political status and function in a permanent way. It is produced and reproduced each time this status and function are reiterated (on the occasion of rituals celebrating inaugurations of power); and elsewhere, obedience being translated by concrete behavior such as offerings of goods and services, the gestures necessary for the maintenance of the excess (and consequently for effective power) are constantly carried out. It is therefore always held in this position and never exchanged. There is no clear criterion to quantify the excess given as a pure quality. The leader and his or her subjects certainly know that beyond a certain threshold there are abuses of power, that the global balance of the "exchanges" of the contract is upset, to the extent that everything in the community is subject to strict surveillance by everybody. But there is a reason that always makes the illegitimate accumulation of power possible (and in a sense inexorable)—the illegitimate accumulation of power. Since there is no measure of exchange in the obedience contract (the only criterion being the result, the general situation society is in after the contract), since what is obtained rightfully by power is *absolute*, the translation into facts and practical applications can—actually—be indefinitely extended to domains unforeseen by the contract. Power hides an absolute principle of command that can often be, and in most cases is, tempered by apparatuses that limit its application. Nevertheless, these apparatuses of counterpower, since they are there in order to thwart, trap, or limit the practical exercise of power, are witness to its potential for indefinite growth.

The surplus value of power thus seems to be self-generating. Taking as a starting point this excess that emerges from the obedience contract, the growth of power does not imply a corresponding increase in countergifts or returns that would balance the exchange. This would no longer make sense, since the contract established the minimum conditions for the exercise of power so that the collective good could be guaranteed; it was only on this condition that a collective consensus was realized. If such increased well-being were to come about, the conditions of power would also have to change—in short, the power contract tends to establish, on all sides, a balance of exchanges, a balance in the imbalance. The growth of power can only be born where reciprocity fails (in relation to well-being, the payoff for obedience): once the balance is tipped, a possibility inscribed in the very nature of "the power of power," the leaders will try to give themselves real means for a social transformation that legitimizes their new power and that empirically confirms the new disequilibrium, as a generator for even more power. A new power contract is then put in place, by will or by force, with or without consensus, in real constitutional language or as a simulation of the law. Thus, this first surplus-value of power can engender others, and other systems that lead to worse effects, like tyrannies or despotisms.

2.2.2.

When Lévi-Strauss, in *Tristes tropiques*, analyses the political system of the Nambikwara Indians, a system he regards as one of the most impoverished in existence, as a way of laying bare the fundamental mechanisms of power, he arrives at the conclusion that it is *consent* that is at the basis of the political contract. Even though he attempts a reformulation of the "social contract" (as Rousseau "and his contemporaries" had conceived it), he does not seem to make the distinction—which the theoreticians of natural law had never clearly set out—between a "social pact" and a "political pact."

Lévi-Strauss finds himself to be in the presence of a "society reduced to its simplest expression"; it is "moribund," in all likelihood "degenerate,"[10] which does not solve his problem, because the social fabric seems to be so full of holes that it has to rely almost entirely on the political roles that the chief takes on. The very constitution and the survival of these Nambikwara bands depend on and result from these qualities of the chief: "Political power does not appear to result from the needs of the community; it is the group, rather, that owes its form, size, and even origin to the potential chief who was there before it came into being" (308). (An analogous situation appears among the African Bochiman of the south-west, even though among the Kung the role of the "chieftain," if it "preexists" the band, being inherited from father to oldest son, is nevertheless required by the "needs of the collectivity.")[11] Under these conditions, it was difficult to separate the politi-cal contract from the social contract. It is in this way that Lévi-Strauss seems to consider them identical, basing them on egalitarian exchanges: consent against gen-erosity, giving up of women for safety, and so on. Asking himself, nevertheless, what in this case—the case of the reciprocity between what the chief receives and what he gives and what the community receives and gives—leads certain men to want power (which, by the way, brings with it disagreeable burdens and risks), Lévi-Strauss deliberately sets aside the real benefits they get out of it, like polygamy or all the other social and sentimental advantages:

> There must be some further reason. When I try to recall the moral and psy-chological characteristics of the various Nambikwara chiefs and to grasp the elusive aspects of their personalities..., I am driven to the following con-clusion: chiefs exist because in every human group, there are men who dif-fer from their fellow beings in that they like prestige for its own sake and are attracted by responsibility, and for whom the burden of public affairs brings its own reward.[12]

This is an explanation that relates the ultimate cause for such things back to "basic psychological material from which all societies are constructed" (316), prohibiting it, at the same time, from seeing in this love of prestige for its own sake one of the effects of the nature of power. Nevertheless, Lévi-Strauss had just recognized that in the domain of political power, there are distinctly different motives from those which drive people to establish social relations among themselves. It is in the relation between reasons of a psychological order and whatever it is in the nature of power that seems likely to satisfy them that one has to look for the cause of the desire to be a chieftain.

2.2.3.

In a desire to establish a typology of sacred power, Luc de Heusch shows that the most ancient forms of political organization do not draw on magical attributes to create the character of chiefly authority.[13] The magician-king does not appear before the priest-king, and political-religious power does not seem to emerge from the evolution of magical royalty. Many African societies of linear descent, with segmentary political organization, manifest powers of a religious type, based on ancestor worship, the chieftain drawing his authority from his intermediate position between gods and mortals. Here, the sacralization of the chief is much less accentuated than in magical royalties; the latter do not embrace a clan system. Characteristic rituals (as in Rwanda, where the pretender breaks the bow of his father-king when he takes over from him) and norms structuring power (such as royal incest between mother and son-king) are there in order to signal that the political sphere is vastly separated from that of the social relations of kinship or the clan-based relations of filiation. The coexistence of simple political forms (segmentation) with more complex (religious) forms of the sacred, or of more complex political forms (based on kinship) with simpler versions of the sacred (magic), tends to prove that the political sphere is in reality autonomous and that, if it borrows modalities of power from other domains (notably the magical and religious), it is because the former have the privilege, among the different sectors of the social domain, of "containing" highly important surpluses of power.[14]

2.3.

If we go back to the question that was raised in 2.1.3 about dividing up powers, then we find that in order to answer it several points have to be made explicit before a satisfactory solution can be found for the second antinomy. Thus, now that we know one of the sources of political power, it is necessary to know those concerned with social power. We have seen that the solution to the antinomy should be looked for in the distribution of social power among singular unities, in such a way that the latter reinforce each other by reinforcing the former, and without any of them monopolizing power (the relation between social and political power). Since we have found an excess of power in politics, its distribution among singular unities also concerns social power and its division. So one can even ask oneself if there isn't some excess of power that is circulating in the social domain. This brings us therefore to the idea that social power has an inbuilt instability, which would show up by way of faults and excesses. And this in turn would lead us to interrogate more closely the destiny of forces in the repression that a stable order exercises. Thus we would bring into focus a kind of social organization that works with a fault in power rather than political power producing a surplus of power. So we would not be asking ourselves why various constitutions are unstable and necessarily precarious, but why a repression can bring about a political regime that is more or less stable. We will try to discover what, in the real world, can take the place of the possible and what, in this displacement, appears in the world of the possible as having the best chance of being real. We will thus have the mirror image, as it were, of the solution of the second antinomy, the model of an unjust distribution of power that gives birth to a lasting regime because both specific social units and political government establishments are entirely accounted for.

T H R E E

Third Antinomy
(on the Ends of Power)

THESIS: POWER is measured by its capacity to produce life, and all power is power of life. In this sense, the greatest power is that which can overcome death.

Antithesis: All power is power of death. Death is the strongest power because it produces the most powerful effect, the absolute effect, which has no equivalent among the things that life can produce.

Proof of the Thesis: If the power of death were the strongest, and in fact the essence of power, then all the other manifestations of power would only be the effects of the power of death. Whatever this power worked on would not be power, and the power of death would be reduced to a force without resistance, which contradicts the very notions of force and power. There is therefore no power of death, this being neither a power nor one of its effects. The first condition of power is to be and to persevere in its being. To be able to create being and life is therefore the measure of all powers. And the greatest power, that which maintains this measure at its highest degree, is the power to always create power: active immortality.

Proof of the Antithesis: If the power of life were the more powerful, nothing would be able to destroy it, since only a stronger power would be able to abolish the life that exists in all power of life. Now, every power of life is always outstripped by the death that destroys it. Destruction, the abolition of life, and the creation of nothingness are the measure of all life. It is therefore death that possesses the strongest, most absolute power, to which nothing is equivalent.

3.1.

The range of this antinomy only seems to cover thinking about power in a general way. But wherever there is an effect of power this antinomy comes into play. For example, at one time or another political activity will be faced with the problem of carrying out force to the point of death; the difference between the Indian doctrine of nonviolence (ahimsa: "absence of the desire to kill") and certain Western presuppositions concerning the necessity of violence in social conflicts and debates on capital punishment are founded on the same antinomical opposition. So the question of capital punishment turns on this axis: if the state has the right to kill, it becomes the holder of an absolute and unequaled privilege. So in a real and symbolic way it would have a power without any possible counterpart, which comes down to giving it the exclusive right to violence, thus introducing into the legal system the possibility, in principle, of granting itself absolute power in all areas.

A glance at the practices and institutions that are concerned with life and death, or at the ways in which societies have treated their dead through their representations and their legal and religious norms, by creating categories to think about them and apparatuses to dispose of them, shows that what is at stake in the third antinomy is quite real and links up with precise forms of social behavior. According to what they believe about life and death, people arrange things so that their beliefs become the effective means of their power; isn't this because it is life or death that translates its potentiality to these beliefs? If it were only a matter of analyzing the systems of representation that correspond to the Thesis and the Antithesis, one would certainly pass over the forces that are hidden between the lines, as Nietzsche noted in relation to the discourse on morality. The great Nietzschean split between "active" and "reactive" forces, forces of life and death, implies longstanding alternatives. Perhaps in researching tribal societies one might chance upon a way of grasping how these alternatives were able to come about and develop.

3.2.

When, in a given society, a person dies, it is a major event that has repercussions on all levels of social life: who inherits the goods of the deceased? In the case of a man leaving a wife or wives, over whom he had rights, whom can they remarry or go to live with? If the person had contracted debts, who will repay them? If it is a violent death, who will avenge it? After death, the presence of the deceased among the living would become intolerable without a set of strategies in place to respond practically to these problems. It is not just that there are questions associated with material goods or with pain and grief. There is also the death, which is both the most meaningful and the most meaningless event. What is it about the presence of someone who is definitively absent?

Jack Goody, speaking about "the contradiction involved in the very idea of an afterlife," asserts that "the minimum definition of survival implies that an entity or essence associated with a human body persists after death. The inevitable link between the personality of the individual in its living and dead states means that the ghost or spirit tends to be treated as if it still possessed the desires and wishes of the living."[1] We would thus be able to explain funeral rites in any society, rites of passage from one world to another; beliefs about the hereafter; "testamentary" legal procedures; and so on. "The major contradiction here lies in dismissing the dead with honor and yet retaining their property without loss,"[2] because one cannot accord the dead person "the full quantum of rights he held in life; for unless an irreducible minimum of these are separated from him and transferred to the survivors, the social system cannot perpetuate itself."[3] In other words, in generalizing the problem, the "status" of the dead can neither be their total disappearance, without which nothing would be understandable and society would break down (that is, if the dead did not make their presence felt at all after death), nor their unchanging presence, without any modification, as if the dead had only gone away temporarily. The status assigned to the dead must resolve this "contradiction," so signs of wealth are offered to the dead, emblems appropriate to their sex, as with the LoDagaba[4] (an African people whom the author is studying); one would form "the concept of a joint corporation, such as a lineage, consisting of both the living and the dead. . . . But neither of these ideas altogether solves the central difficulty that is reflected in the fear which the living have that the dead will attempt to perpetuate their network of social ties in ways dangerous to the survivors."[5] In fact, Goody asks himself why the beliefs attached to the dead make them appear terrifying to the living. The idea of descent is not an answer; it does not remove from the dead the danger they are supposed to represent and from which they draw their real power. Let's sketch out a scenario: the ancestors are not inherently good, they are always ready to thwart the living, and they always have to be softened up with offerings and sacrifices. And what if frightening us were their main role?

3.2.1.

Comparing the system of transmitting heritage among the Lo-Dagaba with sacrificial obligations (who sacrifices what to whom), Jack Goody comes to several conclusions: (1) One sacrifices only to those ancestors who are found in a direct line of inheritance, that is, those from whom one has received goods. (2) One sacrifices when (or because) one has gained a profit from these goods: "The underlying reason for the sacrifices was that the donor had accumulated wealth with the help of his agnatic ancestors [the case of the LoWiili, subgroup of the LoDagaba] and now had to make a return prestation."[6] (3) In general one sacrifices goods (cows, sheep, goats, poultry) chosen from among those one has inherited from the dead. (4) The ancestors are "agents of social control," because they "distribute authority among the living."[7] Among the LoWiili, for example, the authority of the father is reinforced through his position as the guardian of the sacred objects of his own dead father. In this way a whole hierarchy of different authorities is established, which is a relation of the place of the heir and the greater or lesser proximity of the dead. This has a considerable effect on the social relations between members of the same clan.

Thus, when the LoWiili say "the ancestors are angry" (*a kpime ziora*), they are speaking of their own agnatic forebears, and when the LoDagaba use a similar phrase (*a kpime zebra*), they may be referring either to a shrine of their mother's brother or to the shrines of duplicate clansmen. Both communities explain this situation in terms of the differences in the manner of inheritance, an explanation that our analysis fully supports. But the difference is not simply a matter of the projection of the roles of authority of the living onto the dead. It is the type of authority that is important, the control of money and livestock. The heirs gain control of these goods only at the death of the holder, an event that is therefore hoped for as well as feared; when it comes, the death arouses joy as well as sadness, the inheritance brings guilt as well as pleasure. For all concerned accept hostile thoughts as a sign of complicity. The idea that the bereaved had a hand in the death that is being mourned pervades a number of rites at the LoDagaba funeral. And it is the differences in the expectations of close kin that are reflected in the worship of the ancestors. In the main, it is those from whose death one benefits that one fears as ancestors.[8]

Jack Goody's subtle analysis nevertheless leaves us in the dark about a primordial aspect of the ancestor cult: the nature of the "exchange" between living and dead. On the one hand the goods, on the other the "moods," the pure forces. What is the role of this exchange in the general economy of a society, especially on the level of power?

Sacrifice is only conceived of as a ritualized activity: it implies a certain regulated relation between the sacrificer and the ancestor, and this has consequences for the relations between the sacrificer and the living. So the exchange between the living and the dead assumes a whole set of roles and statuses that would be inconceivable without sacrifice. In other words, sacrifice introduces separations, distances: a hierarchy among the members of the same clan. If there were no ancestor cult, expressed by sacrifice that marks the permanence of the rights of property of the dead over the goods of the living, if everything that belonged to a person ceased to belong to him or her at the moment of death, then all of that would have to come back equally to everyone and no one, to all the *living* without discrimination: death would become the criterion of possession for those whom it logically distinguished—on the one hand all the nonpossessing dead, and on the other all the living, undifferentiated possessors, gathered up in a single category. This could not come about. It would disrupt the whole system of classifications that marks the distances and the relations among the living. Because the dead continue to have rights after their death, and in this way a distance is opened up inside the clan, differences are established among the members. That the dead are no longer in a position to produce goods directly, and that death is an occasion for transmission (donation)—all this puts the deceased in a particular situation. On the one hand he gives and distributes his goods without any reciprocity being required, he shares as one does inside a family; on the other hand he is not quite inside the family, so his donation takes on the character of an exchange: he has to receive some return. But it is obvious that the return gift (carried by sacrifices and offerings) is not in response to a true reciprocity of exchanged goods, otherwise the exchange would have to stop. In order for it not to stop, it will have to open up onto another form of exchange, which totally changes its characteristics: (1) Goods will be traded with forces; (2) the exchange will deal with surpluses of goods (and surpluses of forces); and (3) the prestations involved actually constitute prestations of power.

By suddenly breaking the circle of gifts among the living, death prohibits the prolongation of this modality for the circulation of goods; at the same time it opens up the relations between the dead and the living onto a much broader domain, where one doesn't just share, one is already "exchanging." With Jack Goody we can say that sacrifice is but the continuation of this practice of sharing among members of a family or a clan, a practice that obliges them to keep giving, even after death; but if we were to stop at this point, we would not understand that this "sharing" brings about payments in return, "return gifts," obligations of reciprocity on the part of the dead—which locate it in the realm of exchanges.

3.3. The Gift of the Spirit.

We can go further. It seems that the exchange between the living and the dead has a direct impact on ordinary exchanges among the living. In his analysis of a classical text from a Maori informant, made famous by Marcel Mauss, Marshall Sahlins explains the presence and the necessity of a third term in the formal description of exchange, because of the need to "bring into evidence" the production of a surplus value.[9] In his desire to account for the two mysteries that had so intrigued Mauss[10]— the obligation to give back, and the presence, in the Maori text, of a third term to explain the exchange—Sahlins asserts that the text becomes clear if one takes into account the notion of "surplus," the profit that goods can bring to the people who receive them. The Maori informant says that three things are necessary for there to be an exchange, and Mauss asks himself, Why not two? Why can't we think of exchange as between only two people?

Sahlin's superb analysis, which puts the text back into its ritual context, shows, in summary, that the exchange in question brings with it in fact a first term, the fact of the initial gift, which is different from the others. This is the "forest," the "gods," which guarantee the production of all goods, including the ones that can be given away. The Maori text says: If someone gives me something and I give it to another, then this other person must give me something in return, on pain of falling sick or dying. Sahlins shows that the exchange cycle is even broader: I have to give back the equivalent of what someone has given me, in the form of sacrifices to the forest and its supernatural forces. The threat that comes from any possible withholding of goods is explained by the presence of the "forest gods" at the very heart of the exchange between people. What people exchange comes from supernatural presences and must be given back to them in one form or another. The cycle among the living thus makes up only part of a bigger ensemble that takes in the dead as well.

The informant stresses the fact that along with the thing being given comes the *hau* or the "spirit of the thing," but when it is my turn to give a thing, I also add my personal *hau*, the *hau* that Mauss makes the pivot of his explanation of the obligation to reciprocate (because one is not supposed to appropriate a spirit). Sahlins shows that the *hau* in the object has to be understood as the "surplus," which produces the goods that I give, in the hands of another: what comes back to me, when this person reciprocates the gift, is what I have given plus a "surplus" (if the payment is delayed, the Maoris increase it by a certain amount on top of the initial gift); and because this profit has been created thanks to the thing that was given, it has to be given back: the obligation to return the gift can be explained by the necessity to make the surplus circulate and disappear, in a society that does not allow the private accumulation of surplus value. The presence of the third term brings out the existence of the profit, because if there were only two terms, it would not be easy to see how a surplus value could emerge out of a simple reciprocity; the fact that what I give to someone is passed on to someone else makes this item into a specific item, with its own properties: it is not only my *hau* that I hand over with the item, it is something that it possesses in itself, the capacity to produce a profit coming from the powers of the forest.

But Sahlin's explanation ends on one obscure point. There is the *hau* of the forest (its fertility power), the *hau* of the thing, the *hau* of the person, the *hau* as the "profit" attached to the object: why is there a single term for all these meanings? Sahlins certainly knows there is a problem here:

> The *hau* of valuables in circulation means the yield thereby accrued, a concrete product of a concrete good; still there is the *hau* of the forest, and of man, and these do have spiritual quality...[this] suggest(s) that the *hau*-as-spirit is not unrelated to the *hau*-as-material-returns. Taking the two concepts together, one is able to reach a larger understanding of that mysterious *hau*.[11]

And at the end of a brief analysis, Sahlins concludes:

> So, as we had in fact already suspected, the *hau* of the forest is its fecundity, as the *hau* of the gift is its material yield. Just as in the mundane context of exchange *hau* is the return on a good, so as a spiritual quality *hau* is the principle of fertility. In the one equally as in the other, the benefits taken by man ought to be returned to their source, that it may be maintained as a source.[12]

Fine, but why, if there is a difference between the "profane" and the "spiritual," would the Maoris employ the same word *hau*?

Speaking of valuables, the Maori could conceive *hau* as the concrete product of exchange. Speaking of the forest, *hau* was what made the game birds abound, a force unseen but clearly appreciated by the Maori. But would the Maori in any case need to so distinguish the "spiritual" and the "material"?[13]

Sahlin's answer comes via Mauss: *hau* is a "total social fact," as Lévi-Strauss noted: "Does not the apparent "imprecision" of the term *hau* perfectly coincide with a society in which "economic," "social," "political" and "religious" are indiscriminately organized by the same relations and intermixed in the same activities?"[14] This quick definition of the total social fact is unclear on at least one point. It is not easy to see what the "linking" would be in the case of these "same relations" without the basic ideas of the "economy" and the "social" losing all meaning as distinct ideas. Because if the relation that is making them operate together here is the *hau*, then the relation must be of such a kind as to be able *both* to link the two terms and to maintain their distance from each other; and in order to do this, the *hau*, as an operator of the relation of distantiation and identification ("intermixed in the same activities"), must *harbor its own meaning within itself*. This linguistic[15] operator must *also* represent a foundation for meaning, acting as a translator of the common sense that would allow the "political" to relate to the "religious," and so on. Otherwise, it is hard to see how a "total social fact" would carry out its role of participating in or containing in itself all the instances of social life. If the *hau* did not possess its own meaning—unrelated to any of these individual instances— it wouldn't be able to "link" or "mix" politics with religion or the economy except by confusing them, that is in making them lose all signifying autonomy. But this is not what happens. They are mixed up, but they retain their specificity, because a Maori knows how to distinguish the monetary value of a thing from its ritual value. This is what is amazing. And this is because the *hau* that translates them identifies them by delineating its own domain of meaning, which is also the domain where these instances are intermingling.

That is what is missing from the description of the "antinomies" attached to the notion of *mana* (or of *hau*) that Lévi-Strauss sets out in the *Introduction to the Work of Marcel Mauss* ("Force and action; quality and state; substantive, adjective and verb all at once; abstract and concrete; omnipresent and localised"):[16] this empty or "floating" signifier, "able to take on any symbolic content," also has the property of not having to be translated in order to be "clearly understood by everyone" (Sahlins). So shouldn't we make some allowance for the "indigenous theories" of which Mauss would have been the victim, according to Lévi-Strauss?

How is it that *hau* (or *mana*) also contains an untranslatable meaning? It comes from what they call primordial or vital forces; *hau* is a principle of fertility and fecundity. But this principle has a direct relation to death and the dead. It is in this relation, which attaches the dead to the living, that one has to look for the origin of the property that *hau* has of relating only to itself: that it is power.

3.3.1.

Three types of facts can be derived from Sahlin's commentary on the Maori text: *hau* designates an excess (a profit drawn from the exchange, the "free" gift the forest endows); *hau* is associated with the idea of *mauri*, "breath of life"; the idea of *hau* seems to be disassociated from that of *wairua*, the "spirit that quits the body at death and proceeds to the spirit world, or hovers about its former home here on earth."[17] Of course I will not be able to bring all these ideas together; however, it strikes me that it is significant that the problematic of the *hau* as "excess" relates mostly to the last two of these in Sahlin's analysis. First, everything leads us to believe that the *hau* of exchanges is not only the same as the *hau* of the forest, but that the second constitutes, shall we say, the "original" source of the *hau* that can be extracted from goods. This is the whole thrust of the meaning of the three-term transaction that the Maori text is talking about: if the forest must have returned to it what the second term receives as a surplus, it is because, as Sahlins stresses, the forest makes an initial free gift ("without a price" [in Mauss]; "without any agreement about payment" [in Briggs]). So why must it be given back? Why does the return gift have to be made? Sahlins says this is because "we have to deal with a society in which freedom to gain at others' expense is not envisioned by the relations and forms of exchange" (162). Why is this? Why is this situation so typical of tribal societies? If one looks closer, the Maori text says the following: someone gives me an object for free, which I give to a third person; time goes by and this last person gives another object back to me in return: "this object is the *hau* of the other object"; I must return it otherwise I will fall sick or die. What is it that I must give back to the initial donor? Is it the "net profit" understood by Sahlins, who wants to strip the transaction of any "mystical" connotations — or rather, as the text puts it, *the object that is the* hau *of the first?* If the *hau* is the profit and if I must return an object because it has produced a profit, the obligation to give back is in no way explained. Because one would then have to accept that there would be no obligation to give back if there were no production of surplus value. But the text says: the object that someone gives me in exchange for the one I have given is the *hau* of the first. These are mysterious utterances; the *hau* would then be incorporated into the object I am being given, and the profit would be all the new object itself. From the other point of view, if I understand the *hau* as a pure "net profit" of the exchange, I am preventing myself from understanding the Maori words. By removing the benefit from the initial object, I can't see why I should give back another object, the one I obtained with the help of the first (given that the first was a free gift). It seems that for the Maoris surplus value is not simply an accountable matter. Let us imagine that the text sets out this equation:

$$\text{Object}_1 + X = \text{object}_2 \ (\text{object}_1 + \text{profit})$$

The meaning of the transaction seems to be getting clearer: X is what is being given with the first object and what is necessary to introduce into the equation to understand reciprocity in the obligation to give back. What does it designate? According to the equation, it corresponds to the surplus that appeared with the second transaction; one could say that it is that which permits an object to "be fruitful." The work of time could simply be seen there, the time during which the original donor no longer possesses the object, preventing himself from realizing the benefits of it; time that would have the equivalent value to the profit that the exchange has created. Time would measure this value, but not produce it: what produces it results from the use one can make of the object—it is therefore something that belongs to the object and the person who owns it. Let us call it the capacity that the object has to be able to produce a surplus, other objects. So we are in a position to see that along with object$_1$ the initial donor is also offering a power (to produce other objects), a power that comes about in the capacity of the donor to use it, translating himself therefore in his relation to object$_1$. He has relinquished this power as he handed over this object, and gotten it back when it was returned to him. This power is his *hau*, the principle of "growth" of objects, analogous to the principle of fertility or productivity of the forest. In all this there is nothing "mystical," except that in the desire to measure everything by the standards one believes to be those of reason, one prevents oneself from understanding the "mystical" itself.

The *hau* certainly "explains" the obligation for the return gift. Now we can see the reason why this notion is applied both to the "material" domain and to the "spiritual," and one can understand why Mauss and the other commentators could not stop themselves from seeing there a sort of spiritual principle of personhood attached to the gift.

Now why is it that with the gift there is also the power to produce a profit? Because the *hau* is also the *mauri*, the life force of each person, and because the *mauri* is that which is first of all placed (sacrificed) in the forest by the *tohunga* priests in order that it produce the birds that men will eventually kill.[18] The exchange that the Maori informant is speaking about is inserted in a ritual and sacrificial context. In that way one can see that the *mauri* corresponds exactly to that which is given in sacrifice by the priests to the forest in order that it be abundant in birds. Here we enter into a type of exchange that is similar (formally identical) to the one, between the living and the dead discussed by Jack Goody in relation to LoDagaba sacrifices.

Note also the affinity between *hau* and *wairua*, the spirit of the dead, the double. In numerous cultures, sacrifices are made to the dead so that they do not come back to haunt the living. It certainly seems that the world of the dead and that of the gods (or spirits—of the earth, the forest, and so on) enjoy the power of giving to or withholding from the living the surplus of goods for which they are the beneficiaries. And how do the dead and the gods manage to do this? Certainly not by directly giving or withholding goods, but by their capacity to produce a surplus. How? By exercising their power over life and death, by becoming angry or extending their goodwill toward humans. For such an exchange between the living and the dead (or the gods) to be effective, it must be "adequately" symbolized: there has to be symbolic effectiveness. A whole system of mediations will be established between the dead and the living to guarantee this effectiveness, including representational systems and beliefs pertaining to doubles,[19] the figurations of the person and the body, the organs, the blood, and so on. So, in and through these mechanisms, what the dead give will not be subject to mere faith.

3.3.2.

The dead give and deploy their forces; people offer goods (and sometimes also power and living things) that are in surplus to them. The exchange focuses on surpluses of power and things, not simply on the things themselves. The dead and the gods are like massive stores of energy, energy from which power is derived. Humans receive benefits from them, or become victims of their jealous dispositions. The world of the gods and the dead seems to play two roles (I am including in this "world" all the nonhuman figures whose actions impinge on the world of the living): (1) Exchanges between the living can take place by extending over a broader terrain. We have seen that the obligation to give back comes from the fact that the goods exchanged between the living incorporate the surplus that comes from elsewhere and must be returned there. This elsewhere is the world of gods and the dead, who are the primary donors in any exchange, and because they initially give a power, a surplus (the *hau* of the object), they create a sort of inextinguishable debt made up of endless obligations on the part of the living.[20] This explains why in tribal societies and in many traditional ones economic goods are often of a ritual or sacred value: they carry the powers (or superpowers [*sur-puissances*]) that come from the original donors. (2) In order for the dead and the gods to manifest their power or to bestow it by way of their dispositions, feelings, and forces, there is necessarily a reorganization of forces and things in the human world. If one of the effects of their presence is to bring about the destruction of the excess of goods that is born in the course of exchanges among the living, their action is not limited to a single economic effect; one only has to consider their role in witchcraft and its role in regulating all sorts of conflicts to be aware of this. One could say that exchanges with the dead impose a certain regulation of the relations between forces and things, and forces and signs. The power of the gods and the dead is frightening: the fear that they inspire in people is not only an instrument of "social control" through the obedience that it induces, but also a way of liquidating the excess of force among the living, which would otherwise generate conflicts. The human hubris disappears in the face of the gods' anger and the threat of their punishment. Wherever there is excess of goods or forces, we find gods and the dead, acting as regulators of the one or the other, distributing the right forces to goods or signs, holding back when too much is produced, giving when there isn't enough. But we should not think that this regulation acts purely mechanically, that it is limited to giving and withholding. In every society the magical-religious system has its own complexity, and intervenes in the "profane" world through apparatuses and mediations that are often highly subtle. The fact that this has real effects — thanks to the effectiveness of the symbolic — on people's forces (in appropriate instances limiting or multiplying them) is sufficient to convince us of the necessary presence of gods.

Their world is one of the most important sources of social power, including magical power, hunting skill, fortune in war, social rank, wealth, and health. All this depends on the power of the gods and the dead. All of these (which also deal with individual force) receive their life force from supernatural powers. Human power coming from the power of the gods. What is the anger of a god? It is an inexorable force that has no explanation but itself. It exists in its own right, and is not subordinated to any other will or law. It has the right to deploy itself. It has the right to be fair or unjust, wicked or good, destructive or creative. It carries its own self-justification and self-legitimation: it has no external source of authority. Why? Because the gods are omnipotent, they have the power. And having power is having the meaning of meaning.

3.3.3.

If the gods and the dead are the major reserves of social power,[21] then it is natural for political power to try to draw from them.[22] The relations between the two are sometimes constrained by a given demarcation (the religious authority of priests, the political power of kings), sometimes by accumulation, sometimes also by tensions and oppositions. If it is true that all political power finds itself sitting on the fence between offering itself as generic and legitimate, presenting itself as the most necessary *social* power, it tends naturally to resolve this contradiction (between its transcendence and its immanence) by having recourse to magical and religious authority.[23] The latter remains the "manager" of this source of social power, which is nevertheless above or beyond society. The history of the State in the West has been a long process of disengagement of political power from its religious roots, while at the same time seeking out a new sacred foundation for its authority. This would be an interminable task. Where is the transcendence of the secular State to be sited, if it is away from religious or divine sources? It seems that no modern State has satisfactorily resolved this question. But history is revealing; in the absence of being able to give itself a religious foundation, the State will transfer aspects of its sovereignty and authority toward the "nation," and the latter will be founded on the power of the dead.[24] It will try to take up where the church leaves off in the management of the dead, the church having done everything it could, during the Christianization of Europe, to become the mistress of funeral wealth, by controlling funerals and the relation of the living to the dead (thus appropriating "what accrues to the dead," the surplus that offerings were supposed to remove from the circuit of exchanges among the living; as Georges Duby shows,[25] the movement of this funeral treasure-hoarding toward Christian sanctuaries would supply, after A.D. 1000, the "renascence of the monetary economy"). The modern State will now manage the "patriotic dead" in appropriating the power of capital that they represent. To manage the dead to better suppress the living: this is the last avatar of the history of the techniques of control of the dead and the gods, the original donors of social power, nexes of "overpower" that it is appropriate for them to gain possession of.[26]

3.4.

The Thesis and the Antithesis of the third antinomy saw life and death as effects of power. Parallel to the preceding antinomies, these effects (starting here with the aims of power) were constituted as the essential attributes of an unambivalent definition of power that the Thesis as much as the Antithesis were aiming at. The analysis of the sources of social power, by means of examples taken from traditional societies, shows that we have to reverse the points of view expressed in the antinomy. For these societies there is no antinomical oscillation. Life powers are mixed with powers of death, life and death being neither powers nor effects of powers, but two different regimes of accumulation and circulation of forces. In this sense the abiding feature of traditional societies was to conceive death in the service of life. First, death is dead people; then, the dead maintain relations with the living in such a way as to guarantee that the latter have an equitable distribution of social power.[27]

Death and life should not be seen as two powers that are removed from the living and act unilaterally on them. But, since death and life appear as beings, the living have a certain control over them. Thus the solution to the antinomy, at least for tribal societies, can be formulated in the following way: the greatest power is not to take life away or to produce it, but to arrange things so that death can guarantee life. In order to reach this point, these societies constructed broad systems of thought and practice concerning the dead and their relation with the living. The primary condition for the edification of these systems is the idea of a manipulable death, that is to say death as a mode of being. From here, all thinking about time (and the organization of social time according to this thinking) is found to be subordinated to a tissue of relations among beings. Far from subordinating the construction of this tissue to a time that is impossible to control or to think about—a time that would open onto nothingness—traditional thought conditions thinking about time to a series of relations between things in space. The social organization of traditional peoples presupposes the idea of a "nonannihilating" time. It is in this sense that one can say that traditional societies "have no history." They have no historicity, they do not build themselves up by introducing nothingness, as we do, into the very heart of the social project. While historicity may well construct social temporality by thinking of itself as deployed against nothingness, historicity is the result of a construction where the thread of past time traverses the present in order to be able to point a vector toward the future. The present is thus knotted around this vector. Traditional societies, on the other hand, because their vector of the future is turned toward the past—toward the dead, toward ancestors—have history ("stories") without historicity.

We can now begin to understand the reason for these antinomies, at least the third antinomy: its Thesis and Antithesis presuppose a conception of death as nothingness and of life as all-exclusive of death, which implies, in turn, a certain conception of time. Time in death is irremediably nothing and non-life-producing, and is opposite to the ideas of tribal thought. In short, the antinomies of power seem to be born of historicity, that is, from a thought that can only think about power in (and because of) time that does not historically recur. In contrast, if tribal peoples manage to insert time in a recurrent flux—which prohibits them from having antinomical ideas of power—it is because they retain the tool that is both necessary and adequate to this task: symbolic thought.

F   O   U   R

Fourth Antinomy

(On the Limits of Power)

THESIS: ALL power has a beginning and an ending in time and has a limited spatial territory.

Antithesis: Power has neither a beginning nor an ending in time, nor does it have spatial limits.

Proof of the Thesis: If power had neither a beginning nor an ending in time, each power, at any given moment, could only constitute a part of or be a link in a vaster power that would have preceded it and would follow it. If this is the case, then each power would carry some element of impotence or weakness, which would be contrary to its definition. The Thesis can be proved in another way. If each power at any given moment were only a link in an endless chain in time, one would not know where it draws its strength from, nor what aim it had in sight. This would be an incomprehensible power, with no justification for its authority—and this is contradictory. As far as space is concerned, if power were to exceed all territorial limits, then it would either be obliged to share its power with other equally unlimited powers, or it would be at the mercy of all exterior powers—in each case its authority would be limited to its own territory; or rather, more precisely, it would be the only one in existence, and so would not have any particular site of activity, or "territory," so to speak, this factor ceasing to be one of the features of power.

Proof of the Antithesis: If power had an absolute beginning and end in time, there would be time preceding this beginning, and time after the end, when there would be no power (and nothing to relate to this power). We could not see from what source each power would get its foundation and origin, which are essential elements for a force to become a power. Nor could we see the outcome of any power, given that, inevitably having to end, it contains its negation in itself, as an internal feature (of its will, or of its potency). This contradicts its definition. And if its territory had limits, and if it only worked inside these limits, then each power would be without any relation to any other power that worked outside of its boundaries. And in the territory defined by these boundaries, there would be no way to know how to share or divide any power. The very idea of relations of forces or powers would thus find itself eliminated. Therefore, any power that has territorial frontiers must always cross them to better assure its power.

4.1.

When political power is set up, it is faced with the two sides of this antinomy. On one side it feels the imperial need to present itself as new, inaugural, creating a radical break with the past and the powers that preceded it. And on the other, it is led by a logical force that is greater than its individual agents to claim a (glorious) past for itself, to want to inscribe itself into a certain political tradition of the people it is now governing. The effect of the antinomy is felt everywhere, from the herald's cry of, "The king is dead, long live the king," to the revolutionary ideas of breaking with the "old world" and the advent of a communist society that is the necessary outcome of history—or, in an attenuated yet visible form, in the liberal discourse that promises both "change" and "continuity," or even in the fascist discourse that also wants to reinterpret the past and inscribe itself in the "true" tradition by announcing a radiant future after the destruction of "bourgeois and Marxist society."

But the antinomy is also about the discourse *on* power. This is clearly shown through the example of the controversy on the origin of the state. Was there any political power before the appearance of the state? Can a broad distinction be made between societies without a state and state societies, as do certain anthropologists (especially since the appearance of Evans-Pritchard and Fortes's *African Political Systems*[1]) and philosophers, to see in the former a kind of social organization that has succeeded in warding off political evil and in the latter the very essence of power? Or is everything already contained in potentialities of societies without states, at their multiple decision-making centers? The question remains as to whether state power has a beginning in time. The fact that the antinomy is found both in the discourse of power and in the discourse on power proves its generality and shows how high the stakes are.

As far as space is concerned, we have already noted fundamental questions on the definition of power, in the proofs of the Thesis and the Antithesis, that are put in quite concrete ways, that is, in legal, political, and military domains. It is enough to give as an example the problem of assuring the borders of states through the creation of an international body (a tribunal, executive, or parliament) entitled to settle conflicts between countries. The question becomes one of asking under what conditions this international body's decisions are viable, and how far its powers and authority can reach. And this question presupposes the solving of many other problems; for example, to what extent does the exterior power of a state condition its internal power? Are not internal and external power two absolutely indispensable sides to the definition of power? What territory is "appropriate" to a power? How can the exterior factor be taken into account in the definition of this appropriateness?

4.2.

A close reading of the proofs of the Thesis and the Antithesis is enough to see that the antinomy results from the fact that they both understand power as existing *in* time and doing its work *on* space.

Let us consider this last aspect: because power is understood as power over a territory, any definition beyond its limits will always be precarious. One could say that a power that is exercised over a limited surface is a limited power — therefore impotent from one point of view — and a power that dominates an unlimited territory is a false power because it is impossible to imagine. Therefore the problem for this antinomy comes from the existence, for any given power, of another space of power. But if all powers allow other powers to enter another space, is it not limited? And if it does not allow entry to the other power, if it occupies all the space, if it is unlimited, is it still a power? Doesn't the idea of power necessarily imply the idea of resistance or opposition of another power?

Thesis and Antithesis come about because space is conceived of as a surface that is offered up to the exercise of power. In other words, the definition of power via its limits is always a slippery one: a territory can be cut up or divided, and assumes another one beyond its borders. And if the totality of the territory is occupied, then power ceases to have any territory, because there is no *other* territory beyond its own. In short, it is because the space of power is mobile, indeterminate, and always in the process of being fixed that the antinomy exists, in other words because there is history and a history of spaces to conquer and occupy: the history of the State. The fourth antinomy is the product of the history of the State. It appears in a discourse that only allows one type of relation between power and space: occupation.

This is why the historical solution for the antinomy (which is always aborted) is imperialist war. With territorial expansion having become the prime aim of the State and the ultimate reason for power, this then means the actual limits of power are, at any given moment, overtaken by the demands of war. So power in time and power over space (which the Antithesis claims are weaknesses) can give themselves time and space as power (which are unlimited because they are unique, and therefore they are completed in space and time—required by the Thesis—because they fill up space and run out of time).

Another solution that is often put forward is the idea of a universal State deploying its power over the territory of the planet. But it certainly seems that this issue would only be made possible by allowing for a different relation between power and territory than that of occupation or exercise of power over space (because these latter imply war between States, therefore a minimum of two different States).

4.3.

As far as time is concerned, the idea of power as situated *in* time presupposed a conception of time as irreversible and opening onto nothingness. This is obvious in the case of the Antithesis, and does not require further elaboration. In the case of the Thesis—which seems to contest the notion of irreversible time—the end and beginning that it tries to assign to each power can still only be understood in time, situated on a temporal line that stretches before and beyond the birth and death of a given power organization. After this power, another would have to begin—this is the rejoinder from the Antithesis.

It is certain that if there is an antinomy, then this is due to the coexistence and opposition of two ideas on the nature of time in the Thesis and the Antithesis. They both posit a time that is substantial, that is like a self-sufficient being, and at the same time a nothingness-time that destroys all beings and all things (thus having the substantial insubstantiality of nothingness). So, the Thesis, in order to disallow the partial time of beings having substantiality—which unavoidably leads to the idea of a substance in no particular mode, or a plenitude of homogeneous and undifferentiated power—insists on the limits of power; and because power allows for the idea of nothingness-time, which contradicts the very notion of power, the Antithesis finds itself confusing power with time and attributing to the latter the substantiality of a being. In short, there is an opposition between power and time, which takes the fourth antinomy back to the third: is time more powerful than any power? Isn't the very essence of power the domination of time? (That is, not only nothingness-time, but also the antinomies of time, therefore also substance-time. But doesn't this antinomy of time result from the fact that we are in the time of the antinomy, that is to say of the impotence of the discourse on power?)

The antinomial oscillation is based on the irreversibility given to time. If the antinomy were no longer to exist, we would have to accept that power be both limited and untranscendable; that it be finite and unique; that it is born, dies, and yet remains. Now, this becomes possible if time is considered to be recurrent: every power can always be the same and nevertheless another, always self-identical since the beginning of time (according to the myth) and constantly changing with each generation or each cycle.

In this perspective time comes back because things come back, because power comes back. The latter is not "placed" on the time line open to infinity, but on the contrary, weaves it, puts a rhythm into it, and imprisons it through cyclical temporalization. Time, according to this view, is neither a substance, nor a being, nor nothingness. But being and nothingness rise up and succeed each other according to the way in which life (social behavior) allows time to be filtered, scanned, temporalized. We can see how the solution to the fourth antinomy links up with that of the third, and remains intimately tied to it: it is in the same way that death ceases to be taken as a power when power is given over to the dead, the same way that time ceases to be lived as nothingness when one brings out in it the particular temporal organization of beings.

In fact, all this presupposes a determinate relation to space. In order that time be perceived both as full and as empty at the same time, so that living beings and things are engaged in immutable and eternal cycles, so that cyclical time reiterates identity in difference — then between these beings and these things in space there have to be woven relationships and correspondences that never allow time to escape beyond their networks. So how would recurrent social time be found? Tribal societies have answered this question with symbolic thought.

The space of power is no longer subject to the antinomy. Space is limited, but in an absolute sense — there is no space outside the space of power, because power comes from space, it draws its efficacy from the earth.[2] And yet, it is always in relation to a (territorial, spatial) exteriority that each power in a space can think of itself as absolute and absolutely closed in on itself. This is possible because the other — the other territory, the other power, enemy, stranger, outside — comes to inhabit the very heart of space — the country, the ally, the countryman, the inside — as witnessed by the tribal beliefs associated with these figures.

Tribal societies thus present themselves as exemplary cases in the solution to the antinomy. Without wanting to make a universal model out of them, they can serve as a guiding light in the exploration of mechanisms that allow the correspondence of time and of space as a generator of recurrent time.

The way I have chosen is to examine a tribal therapeutic ritual. It constitutes one of the apparatuses that these societies make use of to bring about cyclical time.

4.4.

Victor Turner, in analyzing the ways in which Ndembu society, in Central Africa, sets about curing one of its members of an "afflicting" sickness, notes that they want to "redress breaches in the social structure, through exposure of hidden animosities, the renewal of social bonds in the course of a protracted ritual full of symbolism."[3] The cure involves members of the group who carry out their diverse tasks as doctors, assistant doctors, and so on. This is how the social context of the ritual is presented:

> Crises in the affairs of a social group often provoke ritual measures of redress. In most cases it is assumed that an unlucky or sick individual is afflicted by a shade; the whole matter speedily moves to a social plane and involves more or less everybody in the patient's local matrilineal descent group, the nuclear membership of a village.
>
> Trouble, which may be man-made or a result of what we would call a "natural disaster," may lead to a state of social relations in which feelings of anxiety, fear, and aggression become pervasive. Sentiments of mutual dependence are sooner or later mobilized by responsible persons; since the scale of action is public, this mobilization takes institutional forms, including recourse to divination to seek a ritual remedy. The ritual remedy thus invoked itself possesses a form similar to the whole process of crisis and redress. It originates in trouble, proceeds through the symbolization and mimesis of tribal causes of trouble and feelings associated with it, and concludes in an atmosphere of re-achieved amity and co-operativeness, with the hope of restored health, prosperity, and fertility.[4]

Let us summarize a sequence from the *Nkula* rite, which is used to cure women who are suffering menstrual problems (menorrhagia, amenorrhea, dysmenorrhea). *Nkula* has three sequences, the first establishing the space of the ritual: behind the patient's dwelling a little hut is built that is supposed to shelter the "shade"; a second phase called *Ku-lembeka*, which is sufficient to obtain a therapeutic effect and which consists in collecting the roots of plants needed to make the medicines the patient will be made to drink, and including other ritual gestures; and a third phase, *Ku-Tumbuka*, much more complicated than the preceding one, which proves necessary when *Ku-lembeka* has failed.

The sick person who has problems like menorrhagia (excess of menstrual flow), which stops her from having children, has previously consulted a soothsayer who has identified the cause of her sickness. She has been "seized" by the shade of a deceased relative (Turner shows the relation that exists between attacks from shades and matrilineal descent). The aim of the *Nkula* ritual and its sequences is therefore to reestablish fecundity.

Ku-lembeka is made up of several ritual episodes. First they collect the medicines in the bush (roots and leaves of various plants and bushes). The collectors are "doctors," men and women (the patient remains in the village), doctors who are nothing more than former victims of the "affliction" who have been cured, and who have thus acquired the power to cure. They leave an hour before sunset and first head toward a (*mukula*) tree, which is of great symbolic importance. (Among other things, the red gum that it secretes coagulates rapidly and has the generic meaning of "blood," in tune with Ndembu theories of fertility, which is supposed to come about when menstrual blood coagulates around the semen introduced by the husband. When menorrhagia occurs it is said to flow "uselessly.")

After collection, the medicines are prepared in the hut of the patient. The women crush the roots and leaves while singing. Later, the main doctor gives the patient a little of the prepared medicine to drink. He tips a little of it on the top of her head, "so that she can receive her shade," then he washes her shoulders and chest. And this is how he carries out the main part of the treatment:

> After washing her, the doctor catches the patient by the little finger [because she is taboo or sacred] and says, "Will you please go by the fire to warm yourself?" He gives her a *muswayi* rattle, then takes her again and lifts her high up with it in his right hand, still holding her little finger in his left hand. She must stand by the means of the doctor's power, not her own. . . .
>
> He leads her like this to the fire. . . . All the adepts follow them there. First the patient must wash herself, then the doctor gives her a little pot containing root medicine taken from the big *izawu* pot. She is given this mixed with warm medicine from the clay cooking pot. Then drums are beaten at the doctor's instructions. . . .

After a while the patient begins to tremble.... This is the first time she must shake during Nkula. The second is while the people are dancing. The third time is while the doctor gives the woman her shade by putting the red *ilembi* bead on her head. At that third time she must dance upright. Now she is sitting on a mat with her legs together in front of her. She is trembling because the shade has caught her. She moves her neck round and round. A woman adept can teach her friend to move her neck round, but not a male adept.[5]

A helper, who may be the husband, crouches behind her and drags her as far as the hut (the helper can also be a boy so long as he is circumcised). He places his hands on the shoulder of the patient and they retreat as far as the shade's little hut. There she drinks more of the medicine, and carries out some ritual gestures. Finally, they take her back to her hut so that she can rest: "She must go through the doorway backwards, like a girl novice (*kankang'a*) at the puberty ritual."[6] She continues to wash herself and to drink the medicine until there is none left. The ritual is over at midday of the day following the day it was begun (at sunset).

Turner analyzes each gesture and every important element of the sequence, trying to work out their symbolic significance. In this way color (chromatic code: especially red and white), temperature (thermal code: heat and cold), the plants whose names refer to other codes, the sex of the participants, their age, the time and the completion of certain activities, the position of the bodies of the patient and the person officiating, the path from one hut to another, the choice of medicine, the space of the ritual in contrast to the space of everyday life in the village, the consistency of certain medicines, the songs and drum playing, and so on—everything is charged with symbolic meaning and is tied up in the ritual. Let us remember that this therapeutic rite—and according to Turner all the Ndembu rituals to do with sickness—follow a course that represents a passage: they are rites of passage as Van Gennep understood them, and Turner explicitly refers to him.[7] Rites of passage incorporate three stages (separation, transition, incorporation) that obey the general form of passage, from death to rebirth. There is no doubt that the *Kulembeka* ritual follows this "rule," since the patient is supposed to pass, in one way or another, from the side of the dead. (She receives the ancestor's shade when she drinks the medicines, when the *ilembi* pearl is put on her head, and so on. On this point the *Ku-Tumbuka* sequence is unambiguous, the identification with the shade being obvious.)

Now, if one examines the ritual in the context of each of these two stages that come before and after it, one notices that it could in itself be considered a passage, an intermediate stage between two periods. One where the problem emerges, the problem, as Turner says, that requires institutional methods to be fought against; and the other, after the ritual, where the social tissue is reconstituted and order reestablished. These three stages must be seen as being inside an ensemble, because they are effectively linked. Here we are looking at the ritual not just in magical-religious terms, nor just as therapy, but as an apparatus that links up with many levels of social life and, in a sense, to its essential mechanism: in reorganizing the totality of this life, disturbed by the corporeal symptom, the therapeutic ritual appears as a lever supporting the global system of thought and practice of a culture. How is it possible, in fact, for the kinds of manipulations that anthropologists call "symbolic" (of certain signs, gestures, and words) to lead to what could be the total restructuring of a social ensemble? So the ritual seems to be like the control panel of a machine that manipulates activities by remote control (and it is hard to see clearly the links back to the center).

The levels on which the problem impacts (first stage) spread out through the whole of social life: individual (psychic, biological, or psychological), collective (throwing into question kinship relations; psychosocial); religious (since the cause of the sickness is the neglect of a matrilineal shade, and the ritual is equivalent to an "ancestor cult"); sociopolitical (since the cultural organizations of the doctors are the major repositories of social power among the Ndembu); and so on. So the ritual can be viewed from the point of view of one or the other of these different levels, either as a therapeutic process, or as a way of reestablishing kinship links that are under threat, or as an occasion for the celebration of the ancestor cult. Each perspective taken up would no doubt be relevant. Its analysis would necessarily lead the ethnologist to the examination of other symbolic or cultural fields that are implicated in the rite. And the rite itself is no doubt something else above and beyond each of these aspects.[8]

The three stages that I have noted for this ensemble, which could be called the ritual context, follow a cutting up of space and time (corresponding to three moments of the transformation of forces: impotence (sickness), action of potencies (process of cure), power (healing). This is how the three stages of *Ku-lem-beka* could be characterized:

1   In terms of space: first there is a space in which the problem is manifested (the first stage), due to the presence of the "shade" where she is not supposed to be found—the space of the daily life of the village, or the "profane" space (Turner is the one using the profane/sacred

terminology). In a certain way, therapy is about reestablishing normal boundaries between the dead and the living, reallocating them both in their respective worlds. But we must not forget that the dispute is also caused by the woman's too great proximity to her husband's family (marriage is virilocal), a dispute that has to be resolved by means of the ritual. The first stage allows a confused space to emerge, a space in which categories get mixed up.

The supposedly "sacred" space where the ritual takes place (the second stage) is not a prolongation of the first, but is cut off from it. It is a symbolic space, arranged in the space of the village, but a space where behavior from this point on must follow the rules of the rite. Here, subdivisions are marked out, a "shade hut" is built behind the sick person's one, and so on. The everyday space obeys the need to articulate symbolism with technique and economic structures; in other words, the symbolic meaning of places should correspond more or less with technical and utilitarian imperatives (without deciding whether the one is determining the other). This is equally the case, for instance, for the placement and orientation of family huts in the village. In return, the territory of the ritual process is mapped according to the requirements aiming to produce an exceptional event, via exceptional behavior and gestures. It is an extraordinary setting for an extraordinary event. And this event—as we shall later observe—consists of an upheaval, a total transformation of the space upset in the first stage. So what we can say about the ritual space is that it is a space of transformation or a site of metamorphosis.

The third stage sees the rebirth of profane space from which the problem has been eliminated: it is a restored profane space. The shade is no longer the cause of the sickness, and the limits between the two worlds and between the families of the wife and the husband are reestablished. The everyday space, which was thrown into confusion by the sickness, has found its original order again with its internal distances clearly defined.

2   In terms of time: the first stage (corresponding to the first stage under space) is daily time threatened with "escape," that is, irreversibility. The sick person's problems unleash conflicts and incoherent processes that don't connect up with each other and that cannot be controlled

by normal means. Because neither the patient nor the relatives nor the social fabric that guarantees the course of events in normal life is up to the task of understanding or combating the pathological behavior caused by the sickness, they run the risk of irrevocably rending the fabric itself. The therapeutic ritual wards off this danger: it battles against incomprehensible irreversibility.

The second stage unfolds in a particular time (corresponding to the second moment in space). The ritual process has the aim of taking the patient to a unique moment where she "receives" (or identifies herself with) the shade. Here the time of the living coincides with that of the dead. It is therefore a time that prepares the sick person for the event in which the ritual will take place. It is a symbolic time turned toward mythic time, a human symbolic time where gestures, behavior, and attitudes are different from those of everyday time. This stage is also a stage of transformation. The troubled time of the first stage is shed and evolves into a "mythic" time to the point where, the treatment having been carried out, the patient emerges from this temporality "in suspension."[9]

The third stage corresponds to a restored, ordered social space. Irreversibility has been defeated, and cyclical time once more punctuates human activity.

4.4.1.

In order for time to be "cyclical" or recurrent, its flow must not be seen as autonomous or independent of things and of beings. So it is essential that irreversibility not appear as an inherent attribute of time that would come along to upset the organization of space. Irreversibility tends to create irremediable gaps between things, gaps that are difficult if not impossible to structure into a totality, because the constant reproduction of the new impedes the perception of isomorphic forms, analogies, and the formation of structures. In fact, because the gaps in a structure are differential, these differences create the beginnings of a set of relations that can only be established on the basis of identity (complementarity, isomorphism, symmetry, inversion, and so on). Absolutely irreversible diachrony prohibits, by definition, a regular arrangement of differences, since the gap between one point in (past) time and another (past or present) cannot find another basis of comparison with the gap between two other points differently situated in time — time being irreversible — so the formation of a structure is impossible. And what could be the diachronic structure of a time that never repeated itself? And how can the unique be integrated in a structure with elements that are totally unique? The gaps cease to be relative and become absolute.

Cyclical time cannot allow irreversibility to triumph. On the contrary, irreversibility is subordinated to the constraints that stop it from "letting itself go" (especially thanks to the fact that space, thought symbolically, captures time in its links). One of these constraints is belief in the afterlife. If death were the absolute end of life, if there were nothing to attenuate this brutal severance with the world of the living, then time would be perceived as irreversible. If, on the other hand, the belief in the afterlife (with the whole set of beliefs and magical-religious practices that come along with it) guarantees a certain immortality to some part of the life of the defunct, then the world of the dead no longer appears as a *past* (a temporal dimension that incorporates two others, present and future), but precisely as a (present) *world* or a totality where time no longer flows. This world of the dead thus constitutes the barrier essential to the irreversible loss of time. That there might be a world where the dead go to live after life is over implies that there is another temporality, stronger than irreversible time, that stops the flow of this time and becomes like a period or a "place" between "prebirth" and "postdeath." Irreversibility is contained between two limits; temporal infinity no longer has any meaning inasmuch as it is the destroyer of meaning. Our temporal infinity (as a postulate of historic time) has no basis in reality for tribal societies.[10] Whereas in our history it is irreversibility that increasingly takes priority, such that it is in an irreversible continuum (a calendar for which the points of reference always change and are never repeated: "historic events") that the events of a life are inscribed, in tribal societies the duration of the individual life is only understood within genealogical cycles. Irreversibility is no doubt accompanied by singularity, but it is not a basis for making the world intelligible (or for organizing space).

Turner, quoting Max Gluckman's famous classification distinguishing "recurrent social systems" and "changing social systems," applies it to his own understanding of the Ndembu ritual.[11] For Gluckman, a "recurrent social system is a system for which the model allows a total resolution of conflicts and total cooperation." And Turner adds:

> In such a system we may find rivalry between individuals and interest groups for authority, prestige, wealth and other sources of power, but we do not find reformers or revolutionaries. There is the unquestioned adherence to certain axiomatic values, which gives the social structure itself almost the value of a creed.[12]

In these systems, according to Gluckman, "there is no possible change in the character of the parts of the system or in the model of their interdependence." On the other hand, in the "changing social systems," "new types of groups and social personalities constantly arise having among them endlessly changing relations." Now, the function that Turner assigns to the Ndembu sickness rituals is effectively one that stops change from happening, that creates recurrence. A ritual is a "drama" that has the object of regulating social conflicts:

> For the drama implies consensus as to the values and principles of the social structure. Indeed, it is these very values and principles that dictate the form and course that quarrels and disputes will follow in repetitive systems. In such systems social disputes tend, when prolonged, to become "social dramas," in which men establish identity, not as solitary individuals, but through their roles in tribal groups and sub-groups. In changing systems, however, disputes do not become dramas. They may well remain in what I call the phase of "crisis."[13]

Isn't this tantamount to saying that the ritual stops irreversibility and restores the threatened cycle? Turner adds, even more explicitly:

> A repetitive social system is constituted by customs that make for recurrent series of social events, like the rebellion cycle in the Zulu kingship, described by Gluckman, or the developmental cycle of the Yao village, discussed by Mitchell. But a cycle of social events does not complete its course smoothly. We are dealing with the periodic, not with the unvarying. And the periodic has phases of conflict.... Conflict and change were both *combined* within the repetitive cycle. A drama, social or ritual, exhibits a similar development, expressed in terms of a mounting conflict between its protagonists, which is at the same time a reduplication. A drama has a kind of circularity of form and intention. There is an intention of restoring an antecedent condition, in this case a condition of dynamic equilibrium between the parts of society.[14]

At the center of this cyclical structure of the rite, which reproduces the cyclicity of social time, there is the movement of the patient to the world of the dead, to the belief in the afterlife. But it is not enough to believe in the afterlife in order to have cycles; this belief must be integrated in the totality of practices such that the punctuation of the diachrony by certain events becomes a structure or can be organized as a structure. This is what shows the logic of time, such as it appears in the therapeutic ritual: the third stage brings about this "symbolic capture" of time necessary to the functioning of the cycle. The rite can thus be envisaged as a way (which has a paradigmatic value) of opening itself up to irreversibility, then closing again afterward.[15] For the "recurrent" society the threat comes from irreversibility, a history that dislocates meaning and is impossible to control.

4.4.2.

The decisive moment in the ritual, which clinches the cure, effects a kind of "inversion" in the play of signs in the rite. Everything that previously signified pathological disorder gives way to a healthy order. This "crucial" event does not come about by chance, but is the end result of the careful accomplishment of all the previous ritual stages. First of all the patient is prepared to put herself in a receptive state for the shade; that is, to move through the world of the dead (or to have contact with it, or to identify with one of its members). In order to do this she is symbolically brought closer to this world through particular rites—washing, for example: "Muchona told me that the pieces of leaves adhering to the patient's body are the symbol of the *Nkula* shade. The *ilembi* bead, too, symbolizes the Nkula shade, for when the patient is given this red bead she is said to have been 'given Nkula.'"[16] Or the drinking of medicines prepared from leaves and roots: the root of the *mukula* tree, which counts as the principle ingredient (the "principle medicine," *ishikenu*) of the brew the patient drinks, "stood for the shade."[17] So they are moving toward a genuine physiological assimilation of the shade. Other ritual sequences, such as the fact of being led into the shade's hut, witness this passage into the world of the ancestors. The patient is therefore transformed into an otherworldly being, but the process of this passage to another world is made up of two essential parts:

1. First the symptom, and in a sense the causal relation to the origin of the illness, is exaggerated. This aspect does not emerge in a highly evident way from the description of the *Ku-lembeka* rite, even though it is there: the songs the doctors chant while they are gathering medicines in the bush are composed of verses for which the meaning, according to Turner's informant, is clear:

> The song means that the woman patient "is a bad woman, useless [*wa-mukunkulwagyi*], she is powerless [*hawahetang'ovuku*]—you are destroying yourself, woman; you ought to have babies, by refusing men you will have no babies, you are an unworthy [*hawatelelaku*] woman, a guilty woman. You are a frigid woman [*wafwa mwitala*]. The genet cat has stripes; this woman, although she has been given her private part for men, has kept it useless, doing nothing with it."[18]

This relates to the Ndembu beliefs that attributes feminine menstrual problems to their refusal of fertility and, quite often, to their frigidity.

The "negative" side of the illness, accentuated during the ritual, is again shown in the use of hot medicines, in a way for homoeopathic effects, like those usually used in witchcraft: pain is used to cure pain:

> There are two sorts of medicine, "cold" and "hot." According to Muchona, cold medicine is used in order that the patient may feel "peaceful." He went on to explain that the greeting, "*Kwahola?*" (literally "Is there cold?") means, "Are you free from the action of witchcraft?" If someone answers, "*nehi, kwahola wanyi,*" "No, it isn't cold," it means that he is feeling "hot in the liver" [*yiyena mumuchima*], i.e., that witchcraft is being used against him.
>
> If cold medicine means benefiting the condition of the patient, hot medicine is used aggressively against witches, sorcerers and their familiars.[19]

In this example of ambivalence in the use of hot medicine we have another example of the process of exaggeration, during the cure, of the pathological side of the illness. One more sign:

> Other songs speak of *Nkula* (the shade-manifestation) "doing the dance with an axe in hand" (*ku-tomboka*) performed by Lunda war-leaders after victory, or by executioners after beheading their victims; and of "walking on the verandah behind (the patient's) hut" — "*Nkula wenda hekeki.*" In the first place the reference is to menstruation, for the Nkula manifestation, according to Muchona, "sheds the patient's blood." In the second place, the reference is to the shade-hut, placed just behind the patient's hut of residence.[20]

There is no doubt that Turner's remark establishes a relation between war and menstruation (or menorrhagia), which both spill blood; and the analogy between the Lunda warrior and *Nkula*, who is standing behind the patient's hut on the veranda (or hut) prepared for the ritual, makes one think that the latter also "stages" the attack that the patient suffers on the part of the shade, who is the cause of her sickness.[21] The very meaning of the term *Nkula* is ambivalent, or rather overdetermined. In the foundation myth,[22] it means "long menstruation"; elsewhere it designates the spirit or the shade who has brought about menstrual problems and who should now cure them.

2. The second part of the transformation of the patient, to the point where she becomes herself a shade, is directly opposed to the first. Far from exaggerating the symptom, every effort is made to suppress it by "pulling" the sick person toward the side of the forces of health, procreation, and fecundity. Most of the roots and leaves going into the composition of the medicines have virtues relat-

ing to these forces. The songs are made up of prayers and exhortations asking the shades and spirits to give the sick person back her health, full fertility, and so on.

Certain things show that the ritual process goes through an oscillation between the two poles of sickness and health; the alternating use of hot and cold medicines, certain actions, and movements, like shifting between the shade's hut and the fire and back again. This oscillation certainly brings with it a distortion of signs and ritual contexts; one could even go so far as to say that that is its objective. In fact, the patient moves too quickly from the one pole to another; in these she has invested opposite affective intensities (as Turner notes: "The symbols and their relations...are...a set of evocative devices for rousing, channelling, and domesticating powerful emotions, such as hate, fear, affection, and grief").[23] At the same time, the interference of contexts leads to a decontextualization or a destructuring that optimizes the conditions for metamorphosis; the movement to a shadelike state and the return to the human and cured state. In fact, as the oscillatory actions take place one by one, the intensities increase from the very fact of the interference of signs and no doubt in expectation of the moment when the shade takes possession of the patient. The intensities also build up because the oscillations take on the appearance of a struggle and often—especially in other Ndembu rituals containing significant elements of sorcery—of a battle quite explicitly taking place between two spirits or two opposed principles.

What brings about the cure? If one interprets tribal cures according to the model of psychoanalytic abreaction, as Lévi-Strauss does—the expulsion of affect attached to pathological symptoms—then it has to be conceded that the process of interference implies a separation being effectuated between the sign (the symptom) and the meaning (the cause of the sickness). By "unknotting" them, affect is liberated and the signs return to their places. In other words, the therapeutic ritual is a meticulous apparatus for allocating signs belonging to different "cultural contexts" (Leach) or "codes" (Lévi-Strauss). We will now proceed to the examination of this aspect of the cure in relation to another Ndembu ritual, which is particularly revealing.

4.4.3.

This is the case of the *Isoma* ritual, which Turner describes in *The Ritual Process*. It is carried out in order to cure women who suffer from repeated miscarriages and are incapable of bearing children. The cause of this problem is an oversight. The sick person has forgotten to honor an ancestor whose shade is now tormenting her.

The ritual takes place in a clearing that is prepared for this purpose in the forest. First the hole of a giant rat or anteater burrow is found; it is dug out to enlarge it and extend it into a tunnel reemerging at another point. The ground all around has been bordered by broken branches and cut and trampled grasses. The gathering and preparation of the medicines follows the same classification into "hot" and "cold" that obtained for the *Nkula*, and Turner shows how several plants used relate symbolically (and explicitly) to the "inauspicious" state in which the sick person finds herself.[24] The ritual will consist of a series of underground trips from one hole to another, from the burrow to the "new hole" and back again. Sometimes it is the husband who leads the wife, sometimes she who leads him. These holes have a very clear symbolic significance: the anteater hole represents death or pain, and the new hole life or health. And furthermore:

> According to one informant, the holes stand for graves (*tulung'a*) and for procreative power (*lusemu*)"—in other words tomb and womb. The same informant continued: "The *ikela* (hole) of heat is the *ikela* of death. The cool *ikela* is life. The *ikela* of the giant rat is the *ikela* of the misfortune or grudge (*chisaku*). The new *ikela* is the *ikela* of making well (*kuhandisha*) or curing. An *ikela* is located at or near the source of a stream; this represents *lusemu*, the ability to produce offspring. The new *ikela* should blow away from the patient (*muyeji*); in this way the bad things must leave her. The circle of broken trees is a *chipang'u*. [This is a multivocal term that stands for (1) an enclosure, (2) a ritual enclosure, (3) a fenced courtyard around a chief's dwelling and medicine hut, (4) a ring around the moon.] The woman with *lufwisha* [i.e., who has lost three or four children by stillbirth or infant mortality] must go into the hole of life and pass through the tunnel to the hole of death. The big doctor sprinkles her with cold medicine while his assistant sprinkles her with hot medicine."[25]

The accompanying diagram shows the ritual ground, which, among other things, is made up of two fires which are lit for the wife and husband respectively, and the place where the red cock is sacrificed. In this space everything is set out according to binary categories. So,

> when the patient first enters the cool *ikela*, she is given the young white pullet to hold; during the rites she clasps it against her left breast, where a child is held. Both husband and wife, incidentally, are naked except for narrow waist-cloths. This is said to represent the fact that they are at once like infants and corpses. The adepts, in contrast, are clothed. The mature red cock is laid, trussed up by the feet, on the right of the hot *ikela*, in fact on the

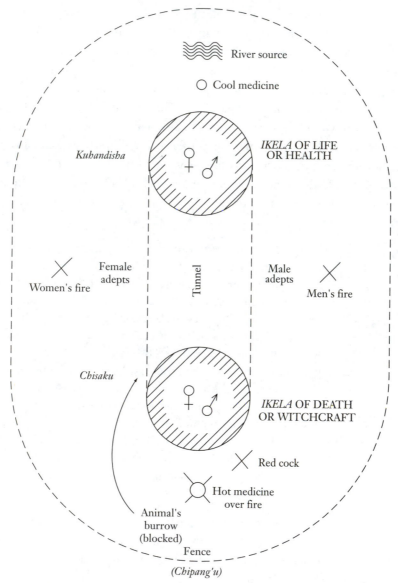

River source

Cool medicine

Kuhandisha

IKELA OF LIFE
OR HEALTH

Women's fire Female
adepts

Tunnel

Male
adepts Men's fire

Chisaku

IKELA OF DEATH
OR WITCHCRAFT

Red cock

Hot medicine
over fire

Animal's
burrow
(blocked)

Fence

(*Chipang'u*)

Schematic representation of the spatial symbolism of the *Isoma* ritual men's side, ready to be sacrificed by beheading at the end of the rites. Its blood and feathers are poured into the hot *ikela* as the final act of the rites, as the antithesis of the reception of the white pullet by the woman patient, which begins the rites. The white pullet is said to stand for *ku-koleka*, "good luck or strength," and *ku-tooka*, "whiteness, purity or auspiciousness." But the red cock, as we have seen, represents the *chisaku*, or mystical misfortune, the "suffering" of the woman. The white pullet, according to one informant, also stands for *lusemu*, procreative capacity."[26]

The rite, as it is carried out, follows

a processual pattern. The first phase consists of a passage from the cool to the hot *ikela*, the woman leading and the man following. At the hot *ikela* the doctors mingle their splashings of medicine with exhortations to any witches or curse-layers to remove their inimical influences. Next the marital pair, in the same order, return to the cool *ikela*, where they are again splashed with medicine. Then they cross once more to the hot *ikela*. There follows a temporary lull, during which the husband is escorted out of the *ikela* to fetch a small cloth to wipe the medicine from the faces of the couple and the body of the pullet. He returns to the cool *ikela*, and after further medication, there is a prolonged interval, during which beer is brought and drunk by the attenders and the husband. The patient herself is forbidden to drink any. After beer, beginning again in the cool *ikela*, the splashing is resumed. This time around, the husband leads the way to the hot *ikela*. They return to the cool *ikela* in the same order. After splashing there is another interval for beer. Then the sequence cool-hot-cool follows, the wife leading. Finally, there is a like sequence at the end of which the red cock is beheaded and its blood poured into the hot *ikela*. Then the couple are swept once more with both types of medicine and cold water is poured over them. In all, the couple are splashed twenty times, thirteen of them in the cool *ikela*, seven in the hot, a ratio of nearly two to one.

While the splashing goes on, the male adepts on the right and the female adults on the left sing songs from the great life-crisis and initiation rites of the Ndembu:[27] from *Mukanda*, boy's circumcision; *Mung'ong'i*, the rites of a funerary initiation; *Kayong'u*, initiation into divining; *Nkula*, a tribal women's cult; and *Wuyang'a*, initiation into hunters' cults. Periodically, they sing the *Isoma* song "mwanami yaya punjila" and mime the contractions of an abortive labor."[28]

In this ritual we should not fail to notice how the representation of a battle between agents of health and agents of illness is made quite explicit. It is likely that the proportion of sprinklings reflects this fact, as well as the final victory of the cold medicines, that is, of health. We can also observe the oscillation between the two poles, and the way in which the polysemic nature of certain medicines adds the element of "turning about," from sickness to health, in the production of the crucial moment. Thus, the *mulendi* tree with the slippery bark relates back to the premature child slipping toward the outside and "exiting" before it is due, but this characteristic of the tree also signifies that the sickness "escapes" from the patient, because "it is indeed not uncommon for Ndembu symbols, at all levels of symbolism, to express simultaneously an auspicious and inauspicious condition. For example, the name *Isoma* itself, meaning 'to slip out,' represents both the patient's undesirable state and the ritual to cure it."[29]

According to Turner, the *Isoma* ritual is constructed entirely around a multiple structure of binary oppositions that extend to space, to the behavior, to the length of time it takes, to the dress code, to medicines, and so on. In the table he sets out these oppositions according to three "planes" corresponding to the same planes of the space in which *Isoma* takes place.[30]

Longitudinal	*Latitudinal*	*Altitudinal*
Burrow/New hole	Left-hand fire/	Below surface/
	Right-hand fire	Above surface
Grave/Fertility	Women/Men	Candidates/Adepts
Death/Life	Patient/Patient's husband	Animals/Humans
Mystical misfortune/	Cultivated roots/	Naked/Clothed
Supernatural curing	Bush medicines	
Hot medicine/	White pullet/Red cock	Medicine roots/
Cool medicine		Medicine leaves
Fire/Absence of fire		Shades/Living
Blood/Water		White pullet/Red cock
Red cock/White pullet		

The relations of equivalence are found between pairs of oppositions of the same plane: The burrow is to the new hole as the grave is to fertility, and so on. Note the presence on all three planes of the red cock/white pullet pair. On this point, Turner asserts:

> In the life/death plane, the white pullet equals life and fertility as against the red cock, which equals death and witchcraft; in the right/left plane, the cock is masculine and the pullet feminine; and in the above/below plane, the cock is above, since it is to be used as medicine (*yitumbu*), poured down from above, while the pullet is below, since it is closely linked, as child to mother, with the patient who is being medicated. This leads me to the problem of

the "polysemy" or multivocality of many symbols, the fact that they possess many significations simultaneously. One reason for this may be found in their "nodal" function with reference to intersecting sets of classifications.[31]

What is a ritual? Is it a series of highly symbolic gestures and aspects of behavior that make up, as Leach says, paraphrasing Lévi-Strauss, "machines for the suppression of time?"[32] The machinery that comes into operation to accomplish a therapeutic ritual has the effect of suppressing irreversibility. First, through the production of an event that is both unique and ambivalent: the oscillation between two symbolically opposed poles offers a way of setting up a controlled irreversibility; at the climactic moment when the event takes place, namely death (irreversible in principle), an about-face happens, a radical mutation that, making the event intelligible, links it up to other models of the same type of event: initiations (see, for instance, songs: the woman in *Nkula* is assimilated to a pubescent girl undergoing the corresponding initiation ritual; in *Isoma*, the patient *also* represents a child being born) or others that take meaning from "birth." At the point where irreversibility should "begin," the event takes on a new meaning, a meaning that goes back over earlier events: irreversibility is recuperated in the reversible event, the cure is a dressing on the bleeding (or flowing) wound of time.

This resumption of irreversibility is accompanied by an overturning of the signs that, up until this point, had been affecting the body of the patient (and through her the whole matrilineal social network as well as her husband): the passages that *Isoma* requires one to complete allow one to think that the symptom achieves the maximum degree of accentuation with the sacrifice of the red cock (which seems to be isomorphic with the trance in *Nkula*). The patient is covered with feathers and drenched in blood: let's say she becomes "totally sick" (or dead); the negative aspect (the symptom that signifies that the woman has been captured by the shade of the ancestor) increases to the point of completely taking over the patient. This negative excess constitutes the turning point; now the signs of health can start to fall into place—and the symptoms begin to disappear. We will see later why it is necessary to go through this absolutely negative stage for things to turn around, and how in this way the signs are reorganized.

In order for the symbolic capture of irreversibility to be possible, for the therapeutic ritual to be able to put time back on track, so to speak, the event that comes about has to have ramifications and implications for meaning in many domains of life. It has to be itself inscribed in a complex and rich tissue, so that the ritual becomes the occasion to reiterate the reversibility that touches the everyday life of the people; social time, the time of individual actions, the time of unexpected or dangerous events, and so on. So it is necessary for the ritual and its activities to function like a huge machine (like the control panel already invoked) that has the capacity to take a generalized disorder and put it all into place.

I have already stressed the fact that among the Ndembu the sickness that afflicts a woman and prevents her, for instance, from keeping her premature children affects the totality of social relations, in particular via the conflict minutely analyzed by Turner, between matrilineal descent and virilocal marriage. In Ndembu society this is a permanent source of tension between these two groups, who vie for authority over the child. When a woman has problems, this has effects throughout the community because these troubles are due, as we have seen, to the "forgetting" of an ancestor, which the sick woman has neglected to venerate because she has been too closely in touch with "the man's side"—and by way of revenge, she is "caught" by a shade and made frigid and sterile.

So, on the plane of social relations and behavior, the trouble, far from being isolated, has repercussions on the collectivity. This implies a whole set of signifying networks that, on the cognitive level, are found to be inscribed in the behavior of the patient—and in the curing ritual. This is how Turner, following his informants, constructs the articulation between the two levels as it is thought by the indigenous people (in the case of *Isoma*):

> Ideally, a woman who is living at peace with her fellows and is mindful of her deceased kin should be married and a mother of "live and lovely children" (to translate a Ndembu expression). But a woman who is either quarrelsome herself or a member of a group riven with quarrels, and who has simultaneously "forgotten her [deceased mother's or mother's mother's or some other senior deceased matrilineal kinswoman's] shade in her liver" [or, as we would say, "heart"], is in peril of having her procreative power (*Lusemu*) "tied up" (*ku-kasila*) by the offended shade.[33]

The relation between the social effect of the illness and its origin, considered also from the point of view of the social relations of kinship and marriage, is articulated to the relation between the individual (somatic) effect, the symptom, and the supernatural cause. It can be seen how the ritual acts on the very kernel of this articulation, even as the cure brings about the reestablishment of the social order.[34] In this sense the ritual is a way of mastering certain social relations at the same time as the illness; doing this, it shuts down the threatening irreversibility on itself.

Reversibility comes about when the relations between things and actions in space weave a texture such that any event, any significant gesture, or any phenomenon necessarily comes to be inscribed there. Anything that escapes is gathered up in this tissue, because only its total disaggregation would allow time to temporalize. Time would then be the endless sands where genealogies, filiations, and broken and abandoned cycles would come to be forgotten and lost. On the contrary, tribal thought fixes time, bringing to it an order, a regularity, and a reiterative rhythm that stem the flow of the temporal wound.

How is this order constructed? The analysis of the symbolism of the ritual allows us to glimpse an answer, given that as a "machine for the suppression of time," it goes well beyond the bounds of therapy as such.

It is useful to distinguish two aspects: (1) The organization of the signs of the ritual, and (2) The effectiveness of the rite. In focusing our attention for the moment on the first aspect, we will see a way to understand the second.

4.4.4. The organization of signs.

The picture that Turner paints of the oppositions between what he calls "symbols" comes from the ethnologist's own deciphering, which has nothing to do with indigenous thought:

> If one is looking atomistically at each of these symbols, in isolation from one another and from the other symbols in the symbolic field (in terms of indigenous exegesis or symbol context), its multivocality is its most striking feature. If, on the other hand, one is looking at them holistically in terms of the classifications that structure the semantics of the whole rite in which they occur, then each of the senses allocated to them appears as the exemplification of a single principle. In binary opposition on each plane each symbol becomes univocal.[35]

The Ndembu who are carrying out or attending the ritual are no doubt not aware of the majority of the binary oppositions nor of the total organization of the space and the signs. As Turner says, they carry out their actions in "living" their polysemy; in any case the totality of their behavior and the global process is perceived as absolutely coherent, even if Turner's informants do not manage to be completely aware of this.

There is a double coherence here: the structure of the organization of signs, which the analysis of the ethnologist restores or constructs, and that of the concrete ritual process in the form that it takes in a particular community. The first is "unconscious," in the Lévi-Straussian structural sense; the second is both conscious and unconscious: it manifests in the action that the indigenous people take for granted (it is not simply conscious because the people—and only a few of them—have only a very limited idea of the meaning of what they are doing, the relations between acts, and so on; and it is not simply unconscious because for them, all the ritual behaviour is meaningful and connected according to a stable logic); it could be said to be "unconsciously conscious."

Now, if it is possible that the logic of the *Isoma* ritual implies the organization of the social space according to Turner's symbolic structure, then how does one negotiate the passage between this unconscious structure and the "unconsciously conscious" level of indigenous lived thought (*vécu-pensé*) (or should we say "belief")? In his interpretation of mythic thought Lévi-Strauss comes to the conclusion that "myths are thought (or translated) among themselves." Here it may be a question of a more complex problem, because not only does discourse come in as a factor, but so do many other forms of communication like songs, theatrical representations, music, techniques of the body, and so on. "Who" is thinking all of that at the same time? "Who" brings together these different registers, some of which are of the order of nonverbal communication? Or, to pursue our question: how can the organization of signs in unconscious structures be integrated in a unique experience on the "unconsciously conscious" level of ritual action?

If we compare the organization of the "sacred" space of the ritual to that of the "secular" space of the village, we notice two differences.[36] (1) The first is built so that gods, doubles, and the dead can appear there; it is the space of epiphany, or as the Ndembu say, "revelation." It is prepared for that, and the appearance of the supernatural presence remains under control. (2) The ritual space has a symbolically overloaded, polysemic topography. Every important site, limit, or place is overdetermined. Unlike the secular space, where the places are marked with a symbolism that coarticulates with functional requirements (kinship structure, economic necessity, defense against enemy incursions, and so on), the ritual space need only follow the requirements for magical-therapeutic action. If there is a "function," then it is now a magical one, and it does not follow the rules of any technical causality. When the couple, in the *Isoma* ritual, make the trip backward and forward from the burrow of the giant rat to the new hole, they are carrying out an action that would be absurd in the secular space. But one should not just see symbolism in this, because it is an action, because these things are done, and their role in the system of signs that the ritual implies can only be understood because they are what they are. In other words, they "signify" particular actions and gestures, and not symbolic "meanings"; they designate realities, they set forces into motion, they are "in the present," and it would be an error to think that the ritual constitutes a pure symbolic representation "from afar." In a sense—and no doubt the indigenous people see it this way—the ritual is truer than life; it is more real because it brings into play more powerful presences, calls forth terrible forces, and stirs up powerful emotions (Turner makes a point of this in *The Ritual Process*).[37] The "symbolism" of the rite is accompanied by a particularly intense affective experience. It has to be taken into account in order to understand how the organization of the signs is also leading to this objective.

Three elements are working in tandem to produce the therapeutic effect: symbolic overdetermination or polysemy, presence of the dead or of the gods, emotional investment on the part of the participants. How are they articulated together? How is it that the presence of the dead is paired up with symbolic overdetermination? And how is it that so many different codes that go into making up the ritual are "translated" onto the "conscious unconscious" plane?

All these questions call for an investigation into the mechanisms at work in the ritual. But let us be satisfied, for the moment, with indicating some possible lines of inquiry.

To begin with, the link between signs and forces, between symbolism and the release of energy, will have to be tackled. Allowing for a moment a working hypothesis that will be enlarged upon in Part II, the relation between signs (symbols) and forces is not one of opposition, but of articulation. If the signs appear to be overdetermined in the ritual, it is *in order that* powerful energies are released that will become the main power source for the cure. On the other hand, we note that the process of cure consists in making forces converge on the body of the sick person that are supposed to come from the dead, or supernatural powers (these are rituals of the "possession" type among the Ndembu). Now, this process can be seen as a cycle of transformation of linked-up signs and forces, or more precisely as a way of decoding and recoding the patient's forces in such a way as to undo the cause of the sickness and make the symptom disappear. So, the body of the sick person is showing a problem that is manifested as a surplus energy relative to known signs.[38] (2) By arranging for this body to be invested with forces that are even stronger (through "possession"), a new balance between forces and signs is obtained, such that the body is once more healthy, cured. (3) But if, on the one hand, the forces that are applied to the body and that come from supernatural powers are overdetermined symbolically, then those which show up in the cured body are in response to the ordinary codings of the symbolic systems that regulate behavior in social life, systems that divide up objects and living things according to well-regulated distances and differences (and which the ethnologist describes by analyzing cooking techniques, regulations for the use of different spaces in the village, behavior on the hunt, and so on). All this happens as if (to use the current ethnological phrase) the overcoded forces coming from the gods and the dead (including those which appear in the body of the sick person and are also attributed to supernatural powers) had been, through the process of the cure, recoded, regulated, separated, and reordered according to the regular logic of the symbolic system. Now, for this to come about, it would have been necessary for the condensed energy, amplified by symbolic overdetermination, to be distributed once more along the networks and systems of signs, a distribution that corresponds to regular, everyday circulation of this energy (which is to say, according to the ideal model currently operating in the group). The process can be represented as in the accompanying diagram.

The movement from one regime of energy (and regime of signs) to another assumes that (1) an operator works on the code and the energy in a particular way, a work that implies the possibility of *separating* energetic fluxes according to signs and, in reverse, the possibility of *condensing* several fluxes into one (this is the illness as the manifestation of raw uncoded fluxes of energy); and (2) that there is a condensation and displacement of energy invested in the signs presupposes that the latter are *translated* from the one to the other. From this point on we can understand that all the codes that come into play in the ritual can act (thanks to the energy they carry) at the same time, immediately and directly on the body; and that the cure

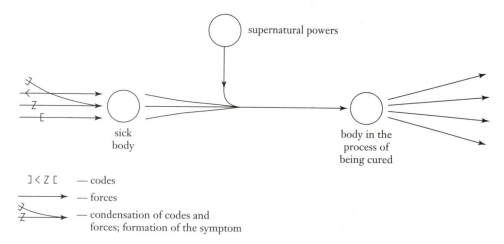

is brought to completion through their regulation and their rule-governed relationships according to the mediations acting in regular life.[39]

The result of this is that the operator translating signs in the ritual is the body—which the Ndembu mark with various codes, which they make drink medicines, on which they apply leaves and herbs imbued with magic powers, which they open up to the presence of the dead, in short, which they put to work in the task of creating a curing process.

This is what leads us quite naturally to enter new territory, at the source of the articulation of forces and signs: the body. Now we know why tribal people have no need to interpret the unconscious meaning of signs and symbolic acts—they carry them in their bodies.

4.5.

The solution of the fourth antinomy rests in abeyance on this examination of the role of the body in ritual. We can look again at its place among the other antinomies of power. We have seen that the solution of the first three antinomies depends on the fourth, and that the last one posed a question that went beyond the statements of the Thesis and the Antithesis, since a brief appraisal of the reasons for the antinomy made us anchor them in the noncorrespondence of space and time. This is where we find the foundation of the antinomies of power. Why is there this separation between space and time? Because the irreversibility of time is unleashed when it is not recuperated into a symbolic tissue. So I asked myself how this symbolic tissue was behaving so that it could produce recurrent time. A therapeutic ritual, such as the one given in the Ndembu example, has the precise function of closing off temporal irreversibility. This analysis opened the way for us to see a body for which a certain "work" on signs and forces seems to be at the heart of its symbolism, and consequently at the hinge of the articulation of time and space. It will also be at the heart of the way of thinking about power for which there are no antinomies. This is what led us to the point of thinking that it is at the moment when the body stops being able to put space and time in relation to each other that the possibility of thinking about power antinomically emerges. Because if antinomies cannot be conceived when a certain relation of space and time is operating, then they can appear in a discourse on power once the link is broken. But in this case, this antinomical thinking about power would necessarily be born of the overthrow of the space-time relation and more profoundly of the relation that subtends it, between signs and forces, symbols and affects. More indirectly, the emergence of an imbalance between political power and social power (and the appearance of nonegalitarian state societies) would have as their source certain events for which the body would be the seat.

4.6.

The ritual eliminates a situation of impotence (as the Ndembu informant stated in speaking of the woman's menorrhagia) and restores power by reproducing the effects of power in all the domains of life. So it is the case that a fundamental power has been exercised thanks to magical-religious therapy: over and above these forces and supernatural powers, the control of which guarantees the correspondence of space and time (thus conditioning the solution of all the antinomies), there are no more powerful ones. In a sense, the gods can do what people can't do. They can make energy circulate freely, since they embody both loose and overcoded energy, the loosest and most overcoded of all.[40] People, for their part, *treat* energy. It is the condition for which they can, in turn, make it circulate.

But in another sense this is what has enabled people partially to control the free and overdetermined energy of the gods (at least enough to assure the survival of the group). In fact, this control represents supreme power, because the cure makes people coincide with gods.

Magical-symbolic thought and practice not only resolve the antinomies of the discourse of power, but also — and it is definitely the same thing — the antinomies of the power of discourse. Is this not to say that this way of thinking provides a solution to the problems posed by the transcendental dialectic of Kant?[41] What was at stake there — in the question, What is it possible to know? — was the power of scientific discourse itself. For magical-symbolic thought there is no obstacle in getting to the noumena, and it is the same for the hypothetical Kantian figure of the *intellectus archetypus*, which knows the unconditioned: magical words are action, thought coincides with being, time and space do not impede the grasping of the thing in itself — because, on the contrary, they are organized in such a manner that they can be transformed by appropriate techniques (such as those at work in the therapeutic ritual) and at the same time remain linked to their normal perception — in order to create from it the conditions of possibility and the formal framework for knowledge of the absolute.

4.7. Note on the Antinomies of Power.

This exploration in the domain of antinomical thought about power has led me progressively to focus the analysis around therapeutic power. This is not by chance. We have seen how ritual brings in all the effects of power: speech, knowledge, political power, and the different forms of social power; and how the solution of the first three antinomies remains suspended on the solution of the fourth. Therapeutic power thus appears as an essential axis around which are deployed all the fields where the effects of power are manifested. As if the question of the potency or the impotence of a given political or economic organization reverberated (and/or found its source) in the mechanisms at work in the therapy. It is certainly not by chance that the *Anti-Oedipus* of Deleuze and Guattari has "Capitalism and Schizophrenia" as a subtitle, and that the movement of this work is a constant coming and going between the therapeutic field and the field of social and economic power. It is because at the center of the question of power one finds the question of the potency of the body, of its energy, and of the circulatory regime to which it is submitted according to the different organizations of power with which it is involved. Not forgetting that there is power only with and over people, the result is that whenever one wants to evaluate the power of such and such a system, one has to ask about the power of the bodies involved: what can a body do there?

Besides, the essential role of rituals in the question of power relates no doubt to the possibility of capturing the free forces that traverse bodies. Power thus becomes, first of all, the power to control the effects of such forces—which leads us to the problem of "causality." The tribal therapeutic ritual constitutes a way of thinking and acting on a "free" or "haphazard" causality. From this point the other causality—be it economic, political, or social—can be included and overcome. Here we are in the sphere of the "noumenal." Let us not forget that Kant's whole effort in the *Critique of Practical Reason* consisted of the reconciliation of the subject's free causality (in another sense) with natural necessity.

On this subject I would like to make one last point concerning the reference to Kant in this exploration of the antinomies of power. If one has to take the transcendental dialectic as yet another effect, in a particular domain, of antinomical thinking about power (being here the power of knowing), then we should be able to find the same explosion of thought about time that is found at the heart of the antinomies of power at the root of Kant's antinomies. The analysis—which does not enter the scope of the present study—shows in effect that there is a certain conception of linear and homogeneous time already at work in the Aesthetic, which is still at play in the Theses and Antitheses of the antinomies of the Dialectic. So that, on quite another level of knowledge, the failure to understand how to know the "thing in itself" appears from afar as a counterproof, or the negative proof, of the success of magical-symbolic thought in capturing fleeting time in the links of its spatial representations, making it a recurrent or a cyclic system.

Metamorphoses of the Body: Prolegomena to a Theory of the Symbolic Object

By "symbolic object" I mean the object of symbolic thought. In order to inquire into the conditions of possibility of this object, I have adopted a method that goes counter to the usual perspectives dominating research into symbolism. Far from beginning with manifest symbolic functions in content or form (from dreams right through to myths), I have tried to come to terms with the mechanism for the development of symbols as it is being born. This type of approach is deliberately distanced from that of semantics or semiology, even as it assumes them, but it does not concern itself with the way in which the sign signifies, or what it signifies. This is taken as given — especially, from our point of view, since the work of Lévi-Strauss on myths. But on the other hand the relationship between signs and the forces that underpin them has not been sufficiently studied, and yet, whether it is a question of stories, rituals, art, or raptures, their signs appear to be shot through with particularly intense investments of affectivities, to the point where one is tempted to take their affectivities as their characteristic traits. Whatever the case, one cannot neglect, for the unique signifying function of "symbols," their relation to the buildup of energies that carry them and are carried by them, in other words the relationship between semiology and an economic theory of signs.

This is where the body comes into the picture. From the economic point of view, it plays a major role in symbolic logic: we have found a trace of it in the description of a tribal therapeutic ritual.

But the study of the body should be embarked upon with caution. And the first temptation that one should be equipped to resist is that of making a language of it — straightaway there are a million discourses on the body that want to be "liberated," or that need to be allowed to express themselves. Now, all the attempts that have been made in the direction of constructing a corporeal language — especially in the domain of the gesture — have failed. We have to know the reasons for this failure and draw lessons from it. The second danger is to introduce into the study of the body premises that will crop up again in the results. So, for example, if one begins with anatomical or physiological structures as they have been revealed to us by medical science, then it is almost certain that one will reduce oriental knowledge on the body to the expectations of the Western model. Or, if we look for analogical foundations in bodily forms, we will end up making the body and its forms the paradigm of all other natural forms, whereas it is in fact the case that one needs to know why the body (1) is so often on the receiving end of analogies, and (2) never functions as a complete and total model for (linguistic, pictorial) analogies. This shows that the corporeal forms of the body as such are themselves taken to be objects of analogical relations, resulting from previous mechanisms. In short, the care one should take in the study of the body is merely a methodological principle that protects one from false leads. The body, this "object" that is not one, seems to be subject to radical indetermination as soon as one tries to define it. And yet it is neither a set of organs, nor an organism, nor a machine, nor the body as such that one can observe among other peoples, nor the lived body, nor the scientific body with its dead objectivity. This "object"—through which death comes to us—seems to lend itself, always with the same docility, to a range of objective procedures.

There is no end in sight to the violence one can do in order to recover the body from the violence that has lost and scattered it among signs, in writing and in science, in institutions and in war. We begin the process with an act of violence. First, what I wanted to discover, at the point where all trace of the body disappears under the litter of signs and logical relations, was the token of its life. Alone, placed on the periphery of symbolic codes, it remains ignored. Lévi-Strauss gave it a major role, but in the same way that Pascal characterized the action of God in Descartes's system: one flick and it starts up all the signifying codes; then, as soon as it is no longer touched, it disappears. It is designated in any case by a term that is imbued with evanescence: signifying "floating," signifying "zero."

It was from this signifier that we characterized the function of the body in the tribal regime of signs. This function remains somewhat—but not always or entirely—an exemplary reference for the analysis of the life of the body among other regimes of signs. I hope it is understood that this is not a matter of forcing things into line; all cultures of all "historical" societies have lived in a nostalgia for cyclical temporalities that they tried, for good or ill, to bring back again. This appears most clearly in the functioning of the "regime of signs" underpinning them.

We followed the transformations of the floating signifier in other regimes of signs, assuming that this itinerary had no matching chronology: this thread led us to the dawn of Western medical science. Where there are regimes of signs there are formations of power. The other idea, not too subtextual, that ran through this inquiry returns to the examination of the transformations imposed on the body by the installation of certain types of power. Here again tribal systems have served as a reference, to the extent that they assume a relation between signs and forces that aims to impede the formation of despotic meanings.

The perspective that gives this study its unity is a double one: a typology of regimes of signs with a typology of formations of power. And in the center there is always one question: what has become of the body and its life? This is a question that can be posed otherwise, more critically, by asking, In the name of which signs have certain types of violence been imposed on the body? What operation has it had to undergo for power to be installed?

So my approach, on this plane, takes up its position in the simple analysis of certain mechanisms for the transformation of bodily energy—and leaves to one side everything to do with real repressive or disciplinary behavior, which authors like Michel Foucault and Thomas Szasz already began to work on some time ago.

O   N   E

The Floating Signifier

WE CAN observe, in the symbolic universe of tribal societies, a strange occurrence, which is found in other guises in any society. First of all, as people attempt to render the world comprehensible, they arrange signs according to the divisions that they use in the real world. They classify, rearrange, and define. This is the way we identify living things and objects, establishing precise relations between "signifiers" and "signifieds." However, since "the universe signified long before people began to know what it signified,"[1] everything that people knew had a meaning was not necessarily identifiable or locatable in the systems of correspondences already established between signs and things. From this a paradox emerges: there is *some* meaning, *something* signified, but it is impossible to assign *a* meaning to it that is precise and recoverable (which would make the thing not only signifying but known); in the same way, some signs (especially in language) remain free-floating, without being anchored by signifieds.

This situation is dangerous because, in order to maintain the inadequate relation between signifier and signified, the symbolic codes—which are interchangeable, translating each other as they go, producing fixed signifiers—would lose the power to function, since there are no identifiable frontiers or limits that would be in place to separate the unknown from the known or the unidentifiable from the recognizable. This, by the way, is what comes about in certain pathological states in which the breakdown of these frontiers is translated into linguistic abnormalities.

How can this danger be avoided? When Lévi-Strauss asked this question, the answer he provided was the following:

> So, in man's effort to understand the world, he always disposes of a surplus of signification (which he shares out among things in accordance with the laws of the symbolic thinking which it is the task of ethnologists and linguists to study). That distribution of a supplementary ration — if I can express myself thus — is absolutely necessary to ensure that, in total, the available signifier and the mapped out signified may remain in the relationship of complementarity which is the very condition of the exercise of symbolic thinking.[2]

So, besides the complementary relations between signifier and signified, there are strange semantic functions for certain signifiers that do not have any precisely corresponding signifieds or "points of reference" either as "things" or "meanings" determined in a homogeneous context. Next to the order of the signifier that various symbolic codes impose on the domain of the signified, there would be a kind of indeterminate zone, which would initially come about because of this fundamentally "inadequate relation" between the two orders, and subsequently because of the fact that people find themselves being forced to distribute the "supplementary ration" of the signifier among things that are in any case already mapped out in the orderly frameworks of the symbolic codes. In this way, according to Lévi-Strauss, all the semantic strangeness of certain tribal notions like *mana* would be explained: it seems to have a place in all codes — objects have a *mana*, but so do plants, people, the dead, food, and so on — which mean both everything and nothing, "a simple form, or to be more accurate, a symbol in its pure state, therefore liable to take on any symbolic content whatever."[3]

So these *floating* signifiers do not designate anything in particular, they would simply have a "zero symbolic value," but they would have a basic function in that they allow "symbolic thinking to operate." In this case one can imagine that the zone of the signified that the floating signifier corresponds to is found in the space that separates the codes, or it is their hinge — because, in spite of the fact that this "zero symbolic value" can be reduced to "a simple form," when it is filled with a content, it always belongs to these semantically disordered zones, straddling two or several codes, two classes of objects, or two worlds. In short, it is not by accident that the floating signifier is always found on the boundaries of the social order that certain institutions and practices of tribal life occupy — like magic, the art of fortune-telling, curing, and in general any field that escapes symbolic coding. Nor is it by chance that the energetic connotations accompanying various floating signifiers that Lévi-Strauss uses to illustrate his point — from ideas like that of *mana*, *wakau*, *hau*, and *orenda*, which he takes up from Mauss's work, to the contemporary examples of "whatsit" (*truc*), "thingummy" (*machin*), and "oomph" in American slang.[4] Even Mauss himself suggested the definition of *mana* as "the quintessential force."[5] It seems to be necessary to develop Lévi-Strauss's idea in this direction if one wishes to fully grasp the function of the floating signifier.

It always designates an energy or a force — which is impossible to see signified in the codes, since these are concerned with objects and their relations, and not with what makes them possible. The floating signifier is also an explanatory principle for indigenous thought. It denotes the fringes of semantic disturbance that are the signs of any taboo-transgressing activity, attacks of sorcery, the practice of shamanistic rites, or the behavior of someone who has gone mad: energy and the spaces between codes often go together. As soon as there is disruption of some order, or the breakdown of a structure, liberated forces can be seen to arise. Any passage from one state to another — birth, marriage, death, initiations, or expeditions — sets into motion energies that the rites liberate and utilize. If one is able to say, as Mauss did, that witches and shamans occupy a distinct and separate place in society, carrying out their ambiguous, symbolically ambivalent, trades — blacksmiths, gravediggers, or shepherds — it is for this very reason. Even if this idea is widely contested today, there is no doubt that the activity of witches and magicians as "agents" of the symbolic differs considerably from the ordinary experience of the indigenous person.

This means that the floating signifier does not function only as an element of a semantic structure, that is "opposed to the absence of signification,"[6] fixing the relations of reciprocity between signifiers and signifieds given in the established codes. It is only structuralist rationalism that leads Lévi-Strauss to assert that "the notion of *mana* does not belong to the order of the real, but to the order of thinking, which, even when it thinks itself, only ever thinks an object"; the only real is the signifier, and since signifiers are only found in "language," everything outside of structure does not exist.

Nevertheless, these energies exist, and in a sense they exist even more than the fixed signifieds of the symbolic codes, because we must add to the floating signifier's semantic function that Lévi-Strauss speaks about, the further decisive function of mediator or interchanger among codes. Mauss no doubt had an inkling of this when, in analyzing the function of *mana*, he took it to be the synthetic agent in the case of certain a priori synthetic judgments, such as "the smoke from the aquatic grasses produces the cloud," a magical judgment that would be equivalent to "*mana* smoke = cloud."[7] Mauss was certainly well aware that the sorcerer's language opens up the passage from one code to another, and that this enigmatic movement is also the result of a certain force.[8] But being unable to consider the two levels—the level of codes and the level of forces—separately, he fell back on considering them together, ending up by asserting that "thanks to the notion of *mana*, magic, as the domain of desire, is full of rationalism."[9]

The shaman, sorcerer, or magician is precisely the one who, in a tribal society, has the special task of making the individual or the group move from one code to another, one state to another, or more exactly to make multiple codes traverse the bodies of these individuals or groups. He or she thus makes a body of sign *translatable* by (and in) another, creating a relationship between the stars and food, animals, or plants. How exactly do they do this?

Here we find ourselves at the very source of the signifying function—the problem of translation at the heart of linguistics.[10] How can we understand the transfer of signifiers from one code to another, how can we make sense of this passage from difference to identity with its gaps and redundancies? Especially since each code keeps its secrets, its principle of untranslatability, and its separate individuality.

Codes are in the first instance sensual, they have an immediate relationship with our senses: colors, smells, forms, and sounds. As Leach said in referring to the general problem of translation between codes:

> Thus we can visualise what we hear in words; we can convert written texts into speech; a musician can transform the visual patterns of a musical score into movements of the arms, mouth and fingers. Evidently, at some deeply abstract level, all our different senses are coded in the same way. There must be some kind of logical mechanism which allows us to transform sight messages into sound messages, and vice-versa.[11]

In the rite (of the shaman or the Ndembu medicines) this logic is in play, producing what Leach calls a "metaphorical condensation":

> But what actually *happens* is that the participants in a ritual are sharing communicative experiences through many different sensory channels simultaneously; they are acting out an ordered sequence of metaphoric events within a territorial space which has itself been ordered to provide a metaphoric

context for the play acting. Verbal, musical, choreographic, and visual-aesthetic "dimensions" are all likely to form components of the total message. When we take part in such a ritual we pick up all these messages at the same time and condense them into a single experience which we describe as "attending a wedding," or "attending a funeral," and so on. [12]

There is no doubt that this "metaphorical condensation" is only possible if the codes are all translated, not into a singular language (which would have its own lexicon and grammar) but "among each other," as Lévi-Strauss says about myths. (In fact, rites have sequences that one day it will be possible to divide into "ritemes"; but they do not produce specific "signifiers" in the same way as words, musical notes, or even colors or clothes.) And since in rites the role of the floating signifier seems quite fundamental—since the forces that subtend the rites are stimulated, awakened, and manipulated—it is possible that it acts directly on the translation among codes that every ritual implies. The fact that it occupies a position between the codes should be an indicator that goes in this direction. This is what two other writings by Lévi-Strauss, essays that take up the problem of shamanistic cures, help us to understand.[13]

We know that among those tribal societies that have a shaman, he or she plays various roles, among which that of medicine man[14] is not the least important. Whether psychic or somatic sicknesses are involved—tribal classifications generally provide sets of categories within these groups that are fairly subtle—the cure comes about during a series of events that bring in three types of participants, which compose what Lévi-Strauss calls the "shamanistic complex": the shaman, the patient, and the public, which actively participates in the cure. The event is made up of several stages that differ according to the type of illness, but one in particular, the trance, usually always appears.[15] In seeking to come to terms with phenomena that happen during the events and that result in the cure, Lévi-Strauss sees a way in which to make good this inadequate relation between signifier and signified, which the *Introduction to the Work of Marcel Mauss* describes at length:

> In a universe which it strives to understand but whose dynamics it cannot fully control, normal thought continually seeks the meaning of things which refuse to reveal their significance. So-called pathological thought, on the other hand, overflows with emotional interpretations and overtones, in order to supplement an otherwise deficient reality. For normal thinking there exists something which cannot be empirically verified and is, therefore, "claimable." For pathological thinking there exist experiences without object, or something "available." We might borrow from linguistics and say that so-called

normal thought always suffers from a deficit of meaning, whereas so-called pathological thought (in at least some of its manifestations) disposes of a plethora of meaning. Through collective participation in shamanistic curing, a balance is established between these two complementary situations. Normal thought cannot fathom the problem of illness, and so the group calls upon the neurotic to furnish a wealth of emotion heretofore lacking a focus.

An equilibrium is established between what might be called supply and demand on a psychic level.[16]

The shamanistic cure offers the opportunity for signifier and sig-nified to coincide. The sickness — like any event that brings about the emergence of meanings loaded with risk, danger, the unforeseen, or chance — causes an overflow of signifiers without objects, signs for which it is impossible to find corresponding things; the event offers these signs a way of being "put to use." They are attributed to some evil being, a god or a "spirit," or a "monster," which in tribal thought always refers to a supernatural code. The ritual of the cure is often accompanied by the recitation of a myth, in contrast to the system of thought that underpins modern science, where

the relationship between germ and disease is external to the mind of the pa-tient . . . the relationship between monster and disease is internal to his mind, whether conscious or unconscious: It is a relationship between symbol and thing symbolized, or, to use the terminology of linguists, between sign and meaning [signifier and signified]. The shaman provides the sick woman with a *language*, by means of which unexpressed, and otherwise inexpressible, psy-chic states can be immediately expressed. And it is the transition to this ver-bal expression — at the same time making it possible to undergo in an or-dered and intelligible form a real experience that would otherwise be chaotic and inexpressible — which induces the release of the psychological process.[17]

But how does this passage come about? In what way does the shaman make the sick person understand his language — this secret and esoteric language that is expressed in the chants of the Ndembu doctors carrying out afflic-tion rituals or in the funeral ceremonies of the Dogon,[18] or the language that the *kadag*, Georgian shamans, call *dzhvart ena*, the language of the gods?[19]

Let us first note that this language is lived by the patient in his or her body, as Lévi-Strauss himself shows as he attempts to come to terms with the "symbolic effectiveness" of a shamanistic chant of the Cuña indians.[20] This song, designed to relieve the suffering associated with difficult childbirths, retraces the steps of the shaman and his protective spirit helpers as they approach the house of

Muu, a power, responsible for the fetus, that has run away with the soul of the patient.[21] But this voyage in fact describes the itinerary via the vagina and the uterus of the sick woman in such a fashion that the song acts directly on the muscles and organs of the person initially "conditioned." How then is "transition to the verbal expression" brought about? What symbolic agent has allowed the reorganization of the signifiers of the illness into a meaningful language?

We have already seen this in practice: the body.[22] In effect, if it is not the spirit it must be the body. But how would the spirit, all by itself, translate sensual codes relating to "empirical concepts" like "high," "low," "left," "right," "red," "rough," "hard," or "soft"? As Maurice Merleau-Ponty says, there is no "high" for a pure spirit.[23] How can a pure spirit, all by itself, construct a "concrete science," with its taxonomies and differential gaps, which are founded above all in the sensual, and which Lévi-Strauss showed to have such subtlety and rigor?[24] The verbal expression given to these "unexpressed [psychic] states" is only possible if an initial differentiation is drawn at the signifying strata of nonverbal signs, which then permits language to anchor the signifieds. This is a differentiation that is realized at a "deeply abstract level," as Leach says, and all the more abstract in that the material is the most concrete of all — the sensual. In fact, if "the relationship between monster and disease is internal to [the] mind," it is thanks to symbolic thought, and if this link is tucked away in the "interior of the mind" to the point where the mind itself can only be thought about as a relation of this order — this is the meaning that must be attributed to Lévi-Strauss's formulation — then it is because there is a "logic" "preceding" the mind that forces it to think according to these types of (symbolic) relations. Now, given that these relations depend most closely on the sensual, that they have an organizing and almost immanent role in the sensual such as it is conceived of by the symbolic order, then the agent of the "logic" that underpins them can only be the body. It is the body that carries the symbolic exchanges and correspondences between the different codes that are in play, and it is in the body that the exchanges and correspondences that the sickness disorganizes and that the cure reestablishes in integrating the patient into the group once again are carried out in shamanistic cures. The body is the exchanger of codes. It is the body — and its energies — that the floating signifier refers to. This is not surprising: on its own the body signifies nothing, says nothing. It always speaks only the language of the other (codes) that come and inscribe themselves on it.

If it signifies nothing, then it allows signification to come about. Thus, there is a double scene going on in a trance: one is about the decodification of the body that is "worn" or "sick," and the other is about the revival of this same

body as healthy and cured. The first corresponds to the setting loose of signification, necessary for the recodification that is under way. This setting loose is obtained through pushing the codes and languages, for which the body is emblem, to
the point of extreme confusion—music, incantation, hallucinogens and drugs, dance,
and the whole atmosphere pervading the event join forces in obtaining this result.
This is a process that favors the progressive irruption of the uncoded body, which,
significantly, can only exist in a state of trance or possession.[25] It is only on this surface of inscription, rendered virgin, that new meaning can burst forth. And if it is
true that the shamanistic event repeats the personal experience of the "call" that
shamans hear and that decides their vocation, and that they induce in their patients,
and if we know that this experience is that of madness and cure, then on each occasion the whole group relives the origin of meaning as the origin of normality—an
origin that coincides with the production of a new body, newly coded and diffusing
meaning. Thus is the order of symbolic codes reestablished, at the price of a per-
ilous journey to the regions of the uncodable.

      We can understand how certain particularly spectacular shaman-
istic events include metamorphoses of the body. In Java, the *dukuns* (shamans) "transform" their patients into boars, into monkeys that they make jump from branch to
branch, and into beavers that they oblige to go fishing in the river. In Haiti[26] or
among the Ethiopians from Gondar,[27] possession is interpreted as being the incarnation of a spirit (a *loa* for the Haitians, *zâr* for the Ethiopians) in a man who thus
becomes a "horse." With certain Ndembu therapeutic rituals, the state of sickness
of a woman who has menorrhagia is likened to that of a sterile man (who bleeds
during battle), and the cure implies a complete transformation to the state of a man,
then a return to that of a woman.[28] The voyage outside of all codes signifies the
crossing of a cultural boundary, or going outside of culture, and the "pure" uncoded
body, traversed by free energies, must go over a threshold (or return to nature) in
order to play the role of code exchanger.[29]

      The floating signifier certainly designates this initial force, which,
in the tribal world, circulates among diverse worlds, putting power, possibilities,
and life into objects and living things.

> This world view is man-centred in the sense that explanations of events are
> couched in notions of good and bad fortune.... In such a universe the ele-
> mental forces are seen as linked so closely to individual human beings that
> we can hardly speak of an external, physical environment. Each individual
> carries within himself such close links with the universe that he is like the
> centre of a magnetic field of force.[30]

These forces, whether personified or not, act directly on the behavior of individuals engaged with trees or the country, in communication with plants, their bodies receiving and expending energies that travel the universe. Mary Douglas believes she is able to generalize the notion of vital force, which Father Tempels discovered among the Bantu,

> not merely to all the Bantu, but much more widely. It probably applies to the whole range of thought which I am seeking to contrast with modern differentiated thought in European and American cultures.
>
> For the Luba, [Tempels] says the created universe is centred on man. The three laws of vital causality are:
>
> (1) that a human (living or dead) can directly reinforce or diminish the being (or force) of another human
>
> (2) that the vital force of a human can directly influence inferior (animal, vegetable, or mineral) beings (forces)
>
> (3) that a rational being (spirit, dead or living human) can act indirectly on another by communicating his vital influence to an intermediary inferior force.[31]

Let us retain from this classification, which (if we deduct what she has ethnocentrically added to the meaning of the indigenous terminology) is in effect valid for the whole magical universe of tribal societies, the fact that she places "man" at the center of all symbolic systems, taking for granted the appropriate linkages that allow the circulation of energy from one system to another. It is in the body that these movements take place, it is here that the power of a thing, a place or a death is received; it is because the energy that goes from one object to another is also the energy of the body that it has a meaning.

1.1. The residue between the thing and the symbol.

The floating signifier is often found in the company of a kind of residue of what it denotes (a certain energy): this can be a piece of skin, a bone, a hair, a scrap of dried meat, or a tooth. Even today in southern Italy, a witch will recommend to a woman who wants to attract the love of a man that she should drink a drink in which she has tipped some drops of menstrual blood or a little powdered pubic hair.[32] In general, everything that is of the nature of the discarded—saliva, excrement, nail parings[33]—carries internal powers, poised on the threshold of several pairs of conjunctions: between nature and culture, between the living body and its inert parts, between the inside and the outside, since secretions and excretions come from inside the body. Amulets, talismans, gri-gris, elixirs, and relics hold tamed energies inside them.

It is interesting to note that these traces of the floating signifier are insignificant in themselves: their lowly stature calls forth the potency of the energy put into play; and there again the contrast is expressed between the absence of signification of the floating signifier and the presence of the power it has hidden away. As pure rejects, remainders, tiny bits unrelated to anything whole but removed through sudden separation, these residues symbolize nothing, not a body, not a force or spirit, but present themselves rather as the outcome of the dissolution itself of the symbolic function. These little bits of something contain an energy stored away that is intimately associated with them, and, because of their very nature, they are positioned as mere stages to the reserves of energy that circulate beneath the symbolic.

This process of dissolution of the symbolic function, for which the residues are these "little things," demonstrates the necessity, inasmuch as it can be imagined, for a material base for the floating signifier. And this, by the way, would make the sorcerer able to manipulate it. The little things would thus be the points of convergence for two series that disappear into it: a semantic function and a set of gestures. In this way the residue becomes the practical operator during a rite, a connecting lever between a number of energy apparatuses, as well as the store of memories of meaning and experience used by the person officiating. So they are not things, signifiers, or meanings, but they can in turn be any of them or all three at the same time, like the human body that they are immediately related to: the energy they carry is transmitted by contact, incorporation, and assimilation to the great sign exchanger.

Maurice Leenhardt discovered, unknown to himself, certain stages of this process. In trying to come to terms with the way in which the Melanesians live with and understand their bodies, and finding that the body is "identified" with trees in Kanaka thought, he came up against the problem as to whether this was "real" or "figurative" identification. And so he briefly reviewed the various stages of indigenous "tree" symbolism. First one finds a "pure" symbolic function in certain behavior, like planting a tree on the day of birth in the hole where the umbilical cord is buried, or what a man does when he wants to build a hut:

> A young man [goes] into a forest to find the ancestral tree or another tree of the same species. He throws his ax at the trunk and it doesn't catch. "This is neither my father nor my mother," he says. So he goes on to a similar tree. He balances his ax and swings it. It holds in the trunk. He hears a man's voice coming out of the tree: "Are you my younger brother?"

"Yes. I came to call you. I want you to make me a house."
This story leads us into mythology.[34]

But at another stage:

It is not always easy to tell how far tales are from reality. Here, for instance, is a new-born baby. The meconium falls onto his first swaddling clothes of bark cloth. This pleases the midwives attending the baby. By this action the child has assured them of his power to live. The meconium is a bit of old bark, like the moist and rotted pieces on the forest trees which come loose and fall. The child has rid himself of this fibrous remnant of his early existence in his mother's womb. Now only a fresh bark remains inside, a bark which is essential to his life and health. If it is ever discharged, in a final hard stool, life ends and the man is doomed.[35]

We observe the symbolic function progressively evaporating in favor of the energy that it encodes—the act of passing the first stools relates symbolically to a movement, but already these collected and dried "barks" are goping to retain a special force: all the children who left the village to go to Leenhardt's mission carried some at the bottom of their baskets:

They showed an infinite respect for this scrap of wood that attached them by so many fibres of their being and all of its own fibers to the tradition of the life-giving maternal ancestors.[36]

Leenhardt discusses the "equivalence of substance" and "structural" correspondence between the human body and the plant world:

The human body is composed of that substance which turns green in jade, gives form to foliage, swells every living thing with sap and bursts out in shoots and in the eternal youth of new generations.
And because the native is filled with the world's pulse, he does not distinguish the world from his body.[37]

It is this last stage—of zero symbolism—to which the function of the "bark" corresponds, this residue that means nothing because it is above all a haven for material energy; and in its very materiality it is full of strong affective forces: respect, love, desire, fear.
So any trace, residue, drop of blood, knucklebone, or piece of wood represents a limit of the symbolic function, beyond which it ceases to signify or designate anything. As signs they must follow ambiguous laws, since they do not

connote anything precise, framed, or referenced, at the same time as they denote that which escapes the semantic function — forces in movement.

But these things nevertheless have a determinate role to play in symbolic thought. They allow symbolic thought to carry out whatever classifications and divisions it needs to function. Because this "surplus of signification," which Lévi-Strauss speaks of in connection with pathological thought, is distributed among a number of codes only by bending itself to certain symbolic laws, this distribution must follow a logic. The apparatuses that control "distribution" of energy (that is, classing it in different categories) must be able to be assigned to certain places. If to symbolize means above all to take control of signs distributed in space by gathering them into codes, then the floating signifier must also bend itself to this rule, otherwise its functioning inside spatial codes would become incomprehensible. It is for this reason that among the Dogon, for instance, the eight seeds that play the role of transducer of codes transmitting the *nàma*, the vital force — that is, "a specific, impersonal, unconscious energy spread among all animals, plants, supernatural beings and natural things,"[38] in other words, the floating signifier — have their place in the collarbones. These seeds, which constitute an apparatus to relate multiple symbolic codes — speech, farming, individual spiritual principles (*kikínu*), the human body — are there so that a place can be assigned to the energy distributor.

Nonetheless, since the floating signifier belongs to no particular code and has no meaning, its material trace should also reflect this aspect of its functioning, which is outside meaning and space. In fact, the space it occupies appears to us only to better disappear, the Dogon not knowing exactly the position of the eight seeds in the collarbones[39] — every time a place is given to the floating signifier, or to its remainder, the site blurs, loses its bearings, becomes invisible.[40] Or it is the residue that becomes the site of exchange and accumulation of energy, and in this case it is a place moving from one spot to another or from one body to another.

In all cases we notice both the necessity for coding and its exclusion. The floating signifier thus makes codes work: in certain cures, when the medicine man[41] extracts from a sick person's body a leaf, a piece of flesh, or a strip of bloody cloth, it is a matter of showing the observers and the patient that the sickness has been taken out. This action has both real and symbolic values. By exhibiting this unsubstantial, though unique, sign, stripped of all symbolic charge, the curer holds the material proof of his effectiveness: an empty token that gives all the meaning to the other signs and actions used in the course of the cure. The bit of cotton designates neither the cause of the sickness (which is always a "spirit"), nor just the sickness itself (which is caused by what the spirit does to the patient), nor its object (the sick person's body). It symbolizes none of these terms, rather the very experience that has put them together and structured them, and for which it constitutes the significant residue. Although on the other hand, the material trace can come to be located at the other extremity of the signifying function: it has the possibility of telling all, explaining everything, blowing out the symbolic function so that it seems to be situated at the source of its own content. Now the foundation of this doubly functioning schema remains to be found: how can the floating signifier mean multiple things, how can it be all at the same time "force and action; quality and state; substantive, adjective and verb, . . . abstract and concrete, omnipresent and localised"?[42] How can the Dogons' *nàma* claim to be mineral, vegetable, speech, the sea, and human? From where does the floating signifier get its "plasticity" (on both expression and content levels)?

T   W   O

The Body, Transducer of Signs

2.1. Mime and Infralanguage.

THE FLOATING signifier relates to the body, this crucible of energy mutations. But what goes on there remains unknown—and will remain so until an adequate semiology (one that can take account of transsemiotic fields) is established. In particular, it would be important to make a large part of this deal, not only with the capacity of the body to send and receive signs and to inscribe them on itself, but also with its capacity to serve as a base for all communicative activity.

       Take a simple fact: when mimes speak with their bodies they exert a certain fascination on their audience. The audience is held in a continual "suspense" due to an unconscious anticipation of a "failing," in which the performer might suddenly lose the ability to continue his or her discourse. Because of this fear of broken communication, this art walks a tightrope. The performance of mime continually involves the effect of making the signifier adequate to the signified. This suspense indicates a dual capacity on the part of the body, both the capacity to elevate itself into a sort of special "metalanguage" and, at the same time, the very limits of this possibility. Apparently the mime's language makes the body a means of communication that can be compared, in its range of expression, to articulated language. Mime seems to be a metalanguage capable of speaking all other modes of expression, succeeding in abolishing many of the ambiguities that language brings with it: inside a given culture the gestures, the corporeal expressivity, the signs of the body, obey a code that is immediately understood by the public. In other words, the lack of available signifiers also allows for the most direct and least equivocal communication. Where does the fascination that the mime exerts come from? It comes from the inversion of a natural hierarchy, using the body as a system of signs to signify the same signifieds as in articulated language: the body is erected into a metalanguage even though it is not its vocation. It seems to impose on the body the power to say all the other languages—and at the same time the spectator clearly feels the limits of this power: limits that allow analysis to show that it is something other than a metalanguage at work.

Mime dismembers the body: we know that the training of mimes takes them through this basic exercise—separation of the limbs in such a way as to completely remove the connections and make the parts they join independent from each other, thus abolishing the rigidities and stereotypes that cultural coding has imprinted on them. Their bodies thus become the best possible sources of signs, the richest signifying system allowable with a reduced number of corporeal articulations. In this way they *strip the flesh away* from their bodies, seeking to make them into pure signifying material. At the same time the body itself resists this work, setting up a limit, a limit that derives from its natural role in the signifying process. It is the evidence of the spectators' constant uneasiness at seeing the body used, with its gestures and flexibility, as signifying language, while one normally lives with one's body as a support for meaning. The signs produced by a mime unsettle us because they cannot be detached from the signified inscribed in the body itself. The uneasiness comes from what they are using the body to signify—and what it signifies (through articulated language for example) is, in the final analysis, related to the body. Mimes thus follow a perverse path with their bodies; they go from body to body, from their signifying body to our "signified" body, from an abstract to a concrete body that underpins all meaning. The mime's body is as disjointed as that of a robot, but there is no doubt that it is flesh and blood that we see there in front of us breaking apart and joining up again to form a "sentence." It is certainly more than a set of signs from some artificial code: it is also the irrefutable presence of the very base and source of communicable meaning that strikes us most directly. This is a magical body because, though lifeless, it can move by itself; without signification, it can convey a meaning; disarticulated, it can spontaneously articulate; without its own order, it creates order. A bloodless god—like a robot—each gesture originates from a void, moving jerkily, with cause and effect, like hiccups; it imposes on us who observe it the job of creating, with the help of our body-grammar, the sentences it necessarily leaves incomplete. We who understand it are thus brought back to the very origin of the signifier, like demiurges who reconstruct the meaning of life by joining end to end scattered parts of speech. How? What work do we provide as spectators in order for the mime's movement to take on a meaning? We provide them what they lack: the clarity of the movement of one sequence of movements to the other: its "spontaneity." But this is only possible because the body gives off more signs than usual. How do mimes show us that they are drinking a cup of coffee? The movements are not simply the reproduction of the usual way an arm is extended, fingers picking up the handle, the hand moving up to the level of the mouth; the articulations are multiplied, each gestural sequence is exaggerated, now including an infinitude of microsequences that were not there before. The act of drinking is amplified and becomes baroque, the hand almost becomes a little windmill in order to show that the cup is tipping toward the lips. Mimes thus economize on language; their microscopic articulations take the place of words, but do not speak in the same way as words, because "the pantomime is not only a silent art, it is the art of being silent, expressing what emerges from the depths of silence. The gestures of mimicry of pantomime are not an accompaniment to words which are spoken and which we cannot hear, *but the expression by means of gestures of the profound experience of music*, the music which lives in the depths of silence."[1] Like a cinematic close-up, the mime uncovers "the territory where small beginnings prepare for momentous events, the most violent landslide is nothing other than the result of the movement of little pebbles and molecules."[2]

But the mime's gestures present the whole event all at once. Béla Balazs has the feeling, despite his tendency only to see the expressive side of mime, that the kind of communication understood here is one that is, so to speak, subexpressive. It is not an affect or a signification that is essentially imparted to us, rather it is the way in which the body sits in space that allows a signification to be grasped.

So what the observer provides, the observer as decoder of the messages delivered by the amplified gesture, are neither words nor significations belonging to certain sequences of movements that have become visible. Mimes do not speak to a verbal intelligence, they aim directly at the body of the observer. And if the latter comes to perceive a meaning in the message, it is above all because the microgestures sketch out forms that are immediately understood ahead of the precise meaning of the gesture.[3] This relates to the material possibilities of the body in space, not only of course to its anatomy and physiology, but also to its desire. The shape of the mime's movement, which we grasp as the action of drinking, is first of all understood as being able to have a meaning as the form of a bodily action — this makes a gesture out of a movement of the body, but not just any movement. And the multiplication of the microarticulations and their morphological amplification replace the absence of "context" (speech, setting), which is reduced to a minimum in mime. Thus the movement of the arm permits an interpretation and the assignment of a precise meaning to the gesture. We must accept that the appearance of microgestures awakens in the observer the capacity to attribute a meaning to something that otherwise (i.e., if it were only the silent reproduction of an ordinary movement) would be meaningless. Now, the amplification of movement does not just create a form; if this form can be grasped as the possible form of a human action, it is because each of its "elements" and all of its microsequences are themselves charged with a particular investment. If it were only a question of the *figural* in this form, mime would be reduced to a technique of reproducing known forms. But, let me stress, this form is not usually visible in the action of drinking: nevertheless it is certainly contained within this gesture, since its emergence allows us to grasp the "truth" of the gesture. Dance, in a certain way—or certain forms of expressive dance—can be seen as the restitution of the global figures of certain ordinary movements.[4] But in mime, there is no music. It is therefore music that accompanies dance, or there is something equivalent to it that takes the place of the microgestures of mime. Each of these, or each microsequence, plays a role comparable to that of the notes of a score: Balazs also spoke of a music of silence. Global form and microgestures: these are invested with affect, emotions, and feelings (or with microemotions and microfeelings), which come no doubt from the fact that the body is first of all an expanse from which desire spreads out everywhere. In order to understand the affective charge of these microgestures, they can be seen as partial objects (in the sense understood by Deleuze and Guattari):[5] they can be taken out of the whole sequence, they belong to other gestural sequences, they have no meaning in themselves, but are always articulated with other microgestures through the formation of different sequences.

There is also a false expressivity in mime. It reverses the order of expression: it seems to employ expressive means to signify the least expressive, most banal, things to us, like the movement of bringing a cup of coffee to one's mouth or simply walking. It doesn't reveal the hidden depths (the "psychology") of the person acting, but what acts invisibly on the gestural surface itself.

I think we have got to the point where we can say that if the microgestures of the mime replace (partially, but effectively) the usual context of the message, which reduces its ambiguity on the one hand, and on the other presents, in a given situation, a confusion of codes (sensual, cognitive, social) that are simultaneously grasped as the meaning itself of this situation—if, therefore, having abolished as much as possible of this context, the microgestures partly restore it, it is because they carry with them the possibility of translating codes among themselves. This does not mean, of course, that mime is capable, like a poet, of translating a color into a sound or a taste. But it knows how to translate each sensual code into gestures: to show that a color is bright or dull; that a sound is deafening, aggressive, or harmonious; that a taste is agreeable. And if this corporeal translation, as well as including expressive elements, is founded on the microgestures of the body, it is because it is in the body that the codes find their point of convergence and their first point of application: the very one that will allow language, and in particular symbolic language, to translate codes among themselves. This property of the body to be the home or the agent for the translation of signs can be designated by characterizing it as a *infralanguage*. Of all languages, only articulated language fully realizes the role of code translation; it is the only one that can render a color by a shape, a gesture, a sound, a taste, or a smell; or a smell by an idea; or an idea by a color. Because it is a metalanguage, it can handle all the codes, create metaphors, move from one domain to another, assemble them and pull them apart. No other language can do as much. The arts (with perhaps the exception of music), with the help of one or several limited codes, open a middle way, articulating on one side segments, "partial objects" of a code, to emerge, on the other side, in a domain of affective forms or desire that form part of the infralanguage. This latter, reduced to the greatest level of abstraction, also joins up with all the codes — not on the expressive plane, but on the one that permits its production.

In this sense, as we have already noted, the body does not speak, it makes speech. Inasmuch as it is itself articulated, it provides language with a virtual and silent "grammar" ("*langue*"), a potential "infrastructure." On its articulations and microarticulations are founded its own flexibility, mobility, and possibility for self-reference — and the fix that symbolic thought has on the world.

2.2. Gesturology.

Nevertheless, couldn't the body be seen following a linguistic model, with its grammar and lexicon? Then there would be gestural units ("gestemes," according to the terminology of certain authors) comparable to phonemes.

Attempts to establish the base for a "gesturology" find their roots in a long tradition of research into systems of notation of body movement, especially in dance and acrobatics. In 1599, for example, Arcange Tuccaro published his *Three Dialogues on the Exercise of Jumping and the Flying Trapeze*, where he set himself the task of "replacing a global, metaphoric and magic designation by a scientific description" of acrobatic movements and leaps, since, if one makes a dangerous jump, "those who see it done have no other opinion of the said, other than it be done by diabolic art." But the body resists this desire for scientific description: even today, advanced notation systems—so useful for the description of gestures in ethnology—seem to relate to a strange paradox: setting out to translate all the movements of the body through a determinate code (the musical code, in the system of Pierre Conté). We would not know how to translate the result into articulated language without running the risk of becoming "approximate, metaphoric and global,"[6] that is, reintroducing the same problems that Tuccaro was trying to avoid. Any system of notation necessarily imposes constraints on the description of movements. Artificial limits will be imposed (the body as seen by another, for example) or, in a more significant way, a different code (like that of dance) is the starting point.

This is the nature of the difficulties facing the establishment of a science of "gesturology": how can the body's own system of signs be imagined? The two tasks to be accomplished would be

1　to divide the dynamic continuum into discrete, objective, and measurable elementary units; and

2　to grasp, independently of the linguistic divisions, the syntagmatic units formed through the combination of these constitutive units.[7]

The aim presupposes a "basic postulate, . . . the homology between the gestural level and the linguistic level."[8] So, the latest attempt to construct a model for the language of gesture hopes to find in the idea of "volume" ("all movement described in the space of a volume") and of the "intersection of volumes,"[9] which would define the "gestemes," the principles that make possible the mathematicization of the gestural and the description of "dynamic behavior in the form of entities owing nothing a priori to linguistic or semantic divisions"; such that "any dynamic sequence can be studied in the form of an ordered series of volumes, *independently of the body which has described them.*"[10] One thus arrives at a cybernetic model of the body as a "machine for producing volumes."[11]

This is the problem in a nutshell: can the body be reduced to a language? At what price? Kenneth Pike, who also put forward a theory of the movement of the body, arrived at the conclusion that

it is impossible to state exactly where one segment leaves off and another begins. The first reason for this indeterminacy is that the physical movements of a particular moving body part glide or slur from one to another, so

that often at no one instant could one cut the continuum...when the motion of two body parts produces a sequence of two segments....This results
in an overlap of segments.[12]

In short, no gestural unit can easily be isolated, to the point where
it seems to be more difficult to set up a "gesturology" than a linguistics. These
overlapping movements, which sometimes make the gestural continuum indivisible,
make it difficult to speak of "distinctive gaps" that are only made up of minimal homogeneous elements distributed over the same surface (sound, in the case of articulated language), while the dynamic sequences of gestures presuppose articulations
of heterogeneous elements, some imbricated in each other: phalanges, fingers, fore-
arms, arms, and so on. In any case, if the intersections of volumes in the different
sequences were to define the unit "volume," it would have to be the case that the
sequences come first, that the "syntagms" define the "gestemes"—how then is the
syntagm defined? One turns again to a model—of the acrobat or the dancer—while
not allowing oneself to move to a more originary level.

But there are two more reasons that make the task of isolating
gestural "units" even more arduous. First there is the fact that if, for us, the intersection of "volumes" can individuate a segment of the gesture, for the "natural language" of the body such as we can see it at work among tribal peoples, it defines, on
the contrary, a polysemic space. Then (and this reason follows from the first) one
cannot, in the case of the signs of the body, separate the signifier from the signified
except, precisely, at the price of gathering up and ordering these signs in a determined *language*, a corporeal language like that of dance or mime. There lies the difficulty in isolating the signifier units which in themselves remain nonsignifying.

The space where "volumes" intersect in fact defines the very possibility of metaphor, and through that the possibility of the functioning of symbolic
thought. But then one should speak of infralanguage rather than of "gesturology,"
which would be the corporeal counterpart of "linguistics."

When a Melanesian says, "See these arms,...they are water" in
order to show that his child's arms are like shoots of a tree "first watery, then, after
a time, woody and hard,"[13] he assumes, of course, a symbolic relation between man
and tree. In the metaphor, the signifiers swap, and the signified, while remaining
the same, steps aside because a new meaning comes forward. Linguists say that there
is an intersection of statements, or rather "semic intersection," according to structural linguistics.[14] Now metaphor is at the heart of symbolic thought. If one signi-

fier can be replaced by another (for example "arm" by "new shoot"), it is because there is an operator capable of carrying out the substitution. On the other hand, the "semic intersection" assumes it is applied at identical points, something like the space, cut out of the mass of the signified, that is precise enough in its *langue* only to allow certain substitutions—metaphors do not result from arbitrary semic intersections, nor from symbols—and fluid enough so that the semantic difference belonging to each utterance has sufficient play in identification. The zone where metaphoric meaning is born evokes a domain outside of the semantic field: it is the body, as an infralanguage, that will provide it. Then signifiers and signifieds will no longer be relevant; there will be something else that is not directly concerned with signs, but rather with the possibility of their interconnection.

The Melanesian example has the advantage of leading us to the threshold of this domain. The man who says, "See these arms, they are water" is not, of course, identifying arms with tree shoots to the point of being unable to distinguish them. He maintains their difference but adds a few elements: first he creates a new meaning, what the metaphor essentially has to say. This meaning reinforces the initial meanings in all their singularity, while at the same time offering a space of mutual semantic impregnation. How is difference maintained in identification? Through retaining the initial signifiers in the metaphor. And how does the space of semantic impregnation emerge?

If we look on the level of gestural language, we notice that the intersection of "volumes" brings back the idea that aligns itself with semic intersection, inasmuch as each "volume" forming a "gestural unit" always implies the presence of the whole body. Gestural sequences can cross paths and do so all the time. The same gesture—with the global meaning of "gather"—can serve to communicate different things: a multiplicity of movements for which the combinations among the multiple sequences establish their relationship to objects. The latter are therefore linked back to the sequences: "flax" relates to "gather," "weave," and so on. These verbs define actions. But each of these actions, like "gather," for example, relates to other sequences, like "gather mushrooms," for example. Each gestural unit is therefore inserted into a range of sequences of other units.

So far so good. But these units, produced by the intersection of sequences, do not come about or become individuated except as signifiers of multiple signifieds, except in symbolic overdetermination. Thus every gesture can have multiple meanings by itself—including of course that which the whole body, as a unitary presence, inscribes on the singular sequence. In other words, each unit, each "gesteme" brings into play each time all the gestemes of the *langue* as well as language itself as the unit of all the units (the body). This is reason enough for it to be pre-vented from taking on the role of linguistic model for any future "gesturology," and explains the overlappings that Pike acknowledges make the establishment of well-defined units impossible.

But this also explains where metaphor comes from. Taking Paul Bouissac's model, it would be founded in the intersection of differentiated gestural sequences. "These arms are water" would imply the substitution of "young shoots" by "arms," a substitution that would rest on the fact that in the (real) sequence that relates our bodies to our "arms" (taken to be things), there are units in the individu-ated sequence that relate it to "young shoots."

There are two disadvantages to such an approach. First, it begs the question in a way. To begin with volumes in order to (thanks to their intersec-tion) extract differentiated gestural sequences only postpones the problem of dis-tinctive gaps, because where does a volume begin or end? Its limits can only be ar-bitrary because it too is subject to slippages. And if one takes the volumes described by the body in space as a starting point, one is necessarily confronted by an infini-tude of basic elements (unless, of course, one chooses special directions in this mass, like "up" or "down," "left" or "right," but in this case one is falling back on another, already constituted element). Second, defining the possibility for metaphor in this way takes us straight away into meaning. It takes it for granted at the same time as its conditions are being studied. One would be quickly led to base oneself on the "special directions" of the body itself, which retain an originary meaning. And from there it is only a short step to refer it back to "being in the world" and "body image."

We have now come to the point where the notion of infralan-guage needs to be clarified. What is this body-infralanguage; is it the body itself, the "lived body," the "body image," or the body as anatomy's object?

2.3. Infralanguage and Body Image.

Ludwig Binswanger's "existential analysis" claims to have a solution to the problem of metaphorization. Metaphor expresses a certain "mutual exchange of modes of expression," but not as a verbal transposition from one domain toward another.

If, employing identical adjectives, we speak of a high tower or a low one, of a heightened feeling or a depressed one, a character who has reached great heights or fallen very low, it is no way a question of verbal transposition from one sphere of existence to the neighboring one, but rather from one general signifi-cant direction that spreads equally to different regional spheres; that is, it carries over different significations (spatial, acoustic, spiritual, psychic, and so on).[15]

Similarly, when we are suddenly let down by someone or something we are waiting for, we might say, "It was like a bolt of lightning," or "it came right out of the blue";[16] we are not in the presence of an analogy or even a metaphor "in the poetic sense of the word,"[17] or of an "analogical transposition of a fact from the somatic domain."[18] But

> a collapse or a fall represents a generally significant direction from the high to the low; it takes "for" our presence a primary existential direction following the "ontological existential"; in other words, spatiality ever increasing outward, abandonment to receptivity (*Stimmung*), or the explanation of the act of comprehension. In the case of sudden disappointment, if there are lightning bolts or things falling out of the blue, this is not because, as Wundt said, disappointment or shock represents an "asthenic affect" that appears as a threat to the body staying upright, like a tottering, a stumble, or a fall, which provides language with real physical models for the imaginary poetic image. Language will instead dip spontaneously into this supposed comparison and pull out an essential feature, specific to the ontological structure of the human being, that is, the power to move from high to low, and it describes it by way of consequences, like a fall. For this, there is no need to go via asthenic affect and its corporeal expression. It is much better to explain the asthenic nature of the disappointment; that our whole existence no longer sits on a solid base, but is tottering or doesn't even stand upright, is because our agreement with the world has been broken, and the ground slips from under our feet and it begins to float. This floating existence does not necessarily imply a downward movement; it can also signify liberation or the possibility of going up. But as long as the disappointment continues as such, we no longer float, but we begin to sway, descend, and fall.[19]

The meaning of a certain presence in the regional sphere is grounded in the ontological existence of the "lived body," that is, in the "sphere of corporeality."[20] The latter is not concerned with the physiological-anatomical body, but with the "unity of the soul and the lived body."[21] This is what provides those significant directions that form the basis for the creation of verbal metaphor. So, for example, in the case of a schizophrenic patient who was suffering from hiccups and had lost all sense of the body, Binswanger detects that "the patient cannot *swallow* the mother's orders [not to go to a dance and to get engaged to her boyfriend], she can neither *swallow* nor *digest* the attack and the offense suffered by her love and her desire to live."[22] Again, this has nothing to do with metaphoric expressions "coming through bodily expression," but with our *existence* always being open to certain signifying directions (*Bedeutungsrich-tungen*), i.e., rising or falling, flying or jumping, *becoming* wide or narrow, full or empty, light or dark, soft or hard, hot or cold, etc. Meanwhile, in our case, it is a case of taking, accepting, absorbing, in short, "*assimilation*" and the *refusal* of the subject, *resistance*, in a word, "expectoration." These essentially unitary signifying directions are distinguished in language itself as modes of bodily, psychic, or spiritual expression. Nevertheless, it cannot *exchange* these modes of expression among each other, and above all, it could not exchange them lightly and with total confidence of being understood if they were not based on a lived unitary form. The knowledge relating to this unity should not be looked for in science, but well and truly in the place where it is conserved and where it thrives, precisely in popular discourse and the accounts it gives of man, where it is cast into proverbs, vulgarities, witticisms, insults, images, and comparisons. In no way would physiological deglutition (a phenomenon already isolated scientifically from the unitary whole of anthropology and even physiology) be compared with the physiological abstraction of anger, revenge, sadness, and despair. But in the two we can only observe particular and specific expressions for one and the same existential fact.[23]

Apparently this is a translation problem, but translation for Binswanger is only an extension and a particularization of a global meaning given in advance. The existence of corporeality presupposes a "global, vital, determinate, historico-biographical *space*."[24] "Lived through the body" should not be understood as "either sensual feelings, or organic feelings, or particular lived corporeal feelings, and above all ('exterior') optical or tactile corporeal perceptions, but the phenomenal state of affairs, absolutely singular and unitary, of having a lived body and experiencing it."[25] In short, Binswanger, as phenomenologist, locates himself both at the origin of meaning and already in it. He starts with "signifying directions," meaning masses, which are then picked up once again in regional spheres.

This conception owes its fundamental allegiance to Husserlian phenomenology. The movement from one regional sphere to another is done by way of blocks of meaning that are always the same and that language has the job of differentiating. Strictly speaking there is no translation. But since there are primary ontological situations, each event, each individual situation, relates back to a definite original signification. In translation one goes from the part to the whole because in ontological domains the unity of the whole surpasses the part, and, in fact, the whole is given in the part. This phenomenological method thus remains imprisoned within a circle when it attempts to describe the mechanisms of metaphorization: why, we may ask, at the moment when we are fooled into thinking we are falling from the sky? Because our whole being "totters," because "the ground slips out from under our feet." But why do we say that "our whole being totters"? Here again, it is only a metaphor. In other words, the formation of the metaphor is explained through a metaphorical meaning, because the problem remains about how to know why the meaning of a "signifying direction" rooted in the ontological structure of corporeality is used by Binswanger to describe an existential situation. The metaphor is explained by another metaphor supposedly more primary, and the origins of metaphorization remain in the dark.

This has a major consequence for the interpretation of clinical facts (e.g., symptoms, medical histories). That is, in one way or another, each element to be interpreted must be understood as coming from an original block of meaning and, in the particular case of lived corporeality, from "signifying directions" and their meaning. We are thus led back, theoretically, always to the same meaning, always to the same referential significations. Those which are parceled and are located in the "regional spheres" relate to an original ontological meaning, but if they appear as symptoms, they manifest that primary meaning effected by a lack. So in certain therapeutic procedures that draw (in at least some way) on Binswanger, schizophrenic symptoms of body images appear as privations, mutilations, disassociations, and disaggregations of this unitary and original body-self, this "corporeal me" or "lived body-self."[26]

When Gisela Pankow speaks of the "dynamic structuration of the image of the body,"[27] it is easy to see how certain fantasies of the schizophrenic relate to being-in-the-world, and how its lived corporeality is understood on the basis of the global significations of the *Dasein* of corporeality. But Pankow's interpretation never stops at this point, it always appeals to the psychoanalytic symbolic, that is, to the unconscious meaning of the fantasy. The simultaneous and alternative use of these two registers allows the psychiatrist to go beyond the sole domain of the conscious and not to be enclosed by an interpretation that is exclusively psychoanalytical/oedipal, and no doubt to use other procedures that elude theorizations of the "dynamic structuration" method. For example, in the case of Valérine, the plaster model of the flower-man is sometimes captured by psychoanalytic interpretative snares. It is a small figure of a seated man, asexual, with two legs, whose trunk, without arms or head, takes the shape of a flower that occupies the whole area of the chest and stomach, the flower being taken as the representation of a vagina ending at the level of the groin with a phallic protuberance, and sometimes it is taken to be the figure of a body that is opening itself up toward the outside, that is to say announcing the structuration of Valérine's body image (she had lost any sense of her lived body) as container/contents; both interpretations need not, in any case, be mutually exclusive.[28] But is possible to see something quite different here, and the notes made by the therapist on the process of the cure lead naturally in this direction.

This fantasy of the flower-man is supposed to mark the stage in the process where the schizophrenic patient is introduced to the symbolic by installing an "opening onto desire."[29] But the modeling of the man-flower can only be understood in relation to its "polar opposite," the "white head" that the patient made after the first model: "a white head seven centimeters high. The neck is set on a fragment of the chest that extends into the inside of a 'white blanket' eight centimeters wide: this blanket is rolled twice toward the inside."[30] The patient, while indicating that this model has a relation to the preceding one, sees the relation as a disassociation, a "hiatus":

> On a surface level, she says to the therapist, you could say this: there is one [the model of the flower-man] that is well-rooted in the ground; the other isn't. (Pause.) On a deeper level, I don't know. (Pause.) I get the feeling that the first will sort things out, the other won't get there. He has a base that the other doesn't have. (Pause.) He has no vitality. No one knows what will become of him. He doesn't even have any organs in his head. He has no eyes, no ears, no mouth. He has no organs.[31]

On the basis of the evidence, Valérine is opposing these two models not as a representation of one body to another, but as two different regimes for the production of her own "body," two regimes of desire and not two "mutilated" images of her own body. The strict use of the notion of body image would prohibit the understanding of the process of "structuration," that is, the way in which Valérine arrives at a sexed female body. What Pankow calls "the dialectic of container and contents" in the image of the lived body would remain totally mysterious if one held to the image of the body as a representation (even "lived"). The flower-man would be fixed without one of the meanings of the corporeal *Dasein* ("devastated body," "devastated world"). Nevertheless, it is not a matter of representation, as the patient explicitly says: "The little man I made the other day has all stuff underneath [the legs], waiting for what he might be. In no way should this represent something. All that sits on his intestines."[32] It is because Pankow explicitly follows Valérine's words that the cure can be accomplished. She will understand "stuff" in its proper sense, no longer seeing a representation there (even though earlier she had described the flower of the first model as an "unreal and fantastic part of the body,"[33] terms that she continues to use in order to characterize the "white head," the second model):

> Thus Valérine has entered into the dialectic between container and contents. "Between these two poles there is a hiatus." This lifeless white man, without organs, "has no base" and "will not sort things out." The only thing he carries inside himself is a blanket that contains "everything." But in reality, the blanket is rolled up and there is nothing inside. The only "stuff" that could "get organized" would therefore be an unreal material. There is no possibility for any development for him, because "he already has with him what he will be": a body emptied of its contents and all possibilities for development. The only organization that could take place would be unreal. The flower-man, on the contrary, possesses a material in a state of anticipation; only he evokes a possible becoming, a notion of lived time in relation to definite future organization.[34]

It is striking that Pankow projects her own categories onto the discourse of the patient, speaking of "unreal material" in the case of the "white head," while the flower-man is said to have "real material." Despite this, it is because she takes the modeling as a "process of *real organization of material*"[35] that the therapy can come to a conclusion.

The problem confronting Valérine, in relation to these two models, can be formulated in the following way: how, in the body without desire (the second model and the legs of the flower-man), can the organs be attached so that desire can circulate? To use the terms of Deleuze and Guattari, how can one join up the sterile body without organs, without desire, and the female sexual organ, which appears on the flower-man as a monstrous, vampiric, flower-"desiring-machine" that relaces the organs, the belly, the chest, the head, and the arms? Valérine's solution—perfectly understood by Pankow—is to become a flower. (Pankow says: like the flower that is rooted in the ground and opens up to the exterior, the patient opens herself to her own body's dialectic of container and contents.) The model of the flower-man is quite precisely a becoming-flower, just as in the processes of traditional cures there is "becoming-animal" or "becoming-woman" (Deleuze and Guattari). If the body without organs of the flower-man (which is the same, just as real and material, as that of the "white head") must be understood as a representation, and not as the production of a body, we would not be able to grasp how the two dissociated poles work together to become associated, and how the body without organs becomes the basis for the organs of desire. Here it is certainly a situation of the same body (with or without organs); what Valérine has to do here is not "unify" her body image in a body with organs. In other words it is a case of not removing the circulation of desire from one's body without organs, to the advantage of an exclusively unisex sexual body that would stop circulation. The following dialogue between the therapist and the patient supports this conclusively:

> Me: These beings that you speak of, are they sexual beings? [Valérine:] No. This one here ["white head"] can become a man or a woman. (Long pause) Deep down we are sexual, that's why all this will not work out.[36]

The notion of body image is awkward for two reasons; because it can only be grasped first as a symptom, as pathological; and second as a representation or a meaning. Now, in the curing process, it is not a question of trying to reach a "body-self," a "total body,"[37] a "reunified image of one's body,"[38] or a "unity of one's image of the body,"[39] even to a lived body and to a recognition of the unity of the body, but precisely to get to the point of dissolving the lived body into the (symbolic-real) play of the relation between the body and objects; to end up not with the self-presence of the body, but to obtain it while dissolving it, in diffracting this presence in the presence of beings and things.

By becoming a flower in a body without organs, by becoming vegetal, other, Valérine "decomposes" and metamorphoses her body without organs, which is what allows her to attach a female sexual organ to it. She produces another space where her sterile body prepares a new production of a body without organs on which (and from which) organs can function and desire can rekindle.

So here we have a problematic different from that posed by "body image," and it is articulated through notions of infralanguage and the translation of codes. On the one hand what needs to be understood is how infralinguistic mechanisms allow for metaphors and symptoms; and on the other hand how, outside of pathology, it functions in such a way as to permit the circulation of desire — which comes back to the operation of a "distribution" of organs on the body without organs.

2.4. The Space of the Body.

The notion of body image brings to the surface clinical material that should perhaps be treated in another way, with other concepts. It is striking, for instance, to notice that Pankow, in the cases that she provides us,[40] sometimes refers to the image of the body proper as it is given in the perception of the body of another, and sometimes she goes beyond this notion when she analyzes the "lived body" and the space that it implies. The image of the body proper plays a double role in her works; it enters into the definition of her method especially when she talks about the "two symbolizing functions of the body image" ("I call them symbolizing in order to stress that each of these functions, as a 'set of symbolic systems,' alludes to a 'rule of exchange,' a permanent law of the body that is implicitly given through the fundamental functions of the image of the body"): "The first function of body image only concerns its spatial structure as a form or Gestalt, that is as this structure expresses a dynamic link between the parts and the totality. . . . The second function of the body image is no longer concerned with the structure as a form, but as content and meaning."[41]

This is a dialectic between parts and the whole, and between container and contents, for which the referent is the image of the body proper. The second role of the body image appears when Pankow treats her patients' symptoms: at this point this unitary image performs only an *inductive* function of a unity that is not characterized by the image of the body proper. In reality the therapist does not want to reach a unitary lived image through the way in which *a* singular body is normally perceived; but the representation of the totality that is perceived of the body proper is only manifested, in Pankow's discourse, as an *analogical referential* of what should be a structured body which is lived nonpathologically. Hence the notion of "body limits": it is by reference to the limits of the body proper that she can say about a sick person that "lived time becomes the time of the loss of the limits of the body. As long as people possess the limits of their body, they can look themselves in the mirror without fear of the Open. . . . Nobody can survive without limits to their body."[42]

So it certainly seems that here it is a question of the limits of the body proper inasmuch as they are reflected back at us by an image in a mirror. Similarly, with the "dialectic" between whole body and body parts, the referent remains the body proper. But when she characterizes lived time and space, she uses metaphors that no longer exclusively concern the image of the body proper: "As soon as the house disintegrates [discussing Solzhenitsyn's story 'Matriona's House'], space is 'unfolded,' and time, 'folded' into the protective envelope that the house represents, also unfolds, and allows a dynamic hidden in space to appear."[43]

In this way the image of the body does not restrict the space of the body, it induces it, it permits an understanding of its pathology ("the model expresses the real body just as it is lived")[44] and plays a referential role for its normality. But what then is the image of the body lived nonpathologically, in which representation can it be "expressed"?

Pankow's method is interesting because it definitely allows her great scope, never restricting the therapist to the yokes of definitions. The notions of lived time and space, the metaphors used in the pathology of body images (stretching or shrinking, folding, breaking, porosity, and so on), show, at the very least, that this image of the body is penetrated by space and time, by a space and a time that invest the outside in the lived body. Why does the model express the real body, why should one see in the flower-man a representation of the image of the body and not simply a flower grafted onto the body of a man? Notions of "identification" and "projection" remain inadequate here to the extent that this flower plays a role (in dynamic structuration or in the desire of the patient) as such, and not simply as a symptom; not uniquely as meaning, but in a relation of the body to space. Now this relation comes about thanks to a flower, that is thanks to the production of a thing that is not the body proper. So then if Pankow's interpretation is correct—that this flower expresses a certain image of the lived body—we have to understand why the model of a thing equals the figuration of a body (while this thing also remains what it is). But, from another angle, we could say: how do we create an economy of the notion of identification, since the real model is not the patient's real body? There is only one way out: accept that space is "modeled" by the body itself. This modeling's relation to the model made from the patient's plaster presupposes an order that is both parallel and inverse: it is no longer a thing that is modeled in space, but space that is modeled by "a thing" (the body); material gives form to the immaterial (space as a set of relations). For example, bodily movements impress in space the traces of essential corporeal form, and create configurations there (in the relation between things) for which the matrices and lineaments are made up from the morphogenetic forms and possibilities of the body. But because the body models space, when it models a thing in space this activity relates back to this matrix model. In this way Pankow's patient, who is supposed to be giving form to a "phantasm," is doing things that could link up with the "first" modeling of space by the body. "Could link up" if, in effect, the "representation of a fantasy" inserts desire into reality, into space, that is, ties it into action and stops letting it congeal in images. This may work, or it may not. It has to go through the fantasy in order to unblock desire, but desire will not be unblocked effectively unless the model of a representation of desire is already overtaking the representation and circulation of desire. Something happened between Valérine and the object modeled as flower-man that did not happen with the white head.

In this way the notion of identification takes on a quite different meaning: the patient does not identify her body with the modeled body, it is the action of modeling that unblocks the modeling of space by the body. It is not a question of identifying a (body) image with a representation, but of the analogical production of spaces. So, when Pankow interprets the model of a temple reduced to a facade as the figure of a body image with one part destroyed, what needs to be understood is not the destruction of a unitary representation of the body or the representation of destruction of part of the body (which, as we have seen, remains mysterious and incomprehensible), but a space really disappearing into the represented thing. Put simply, it is not something that is lacking in the body image, but something that is lacking in space because the body's modeling of space has only come about because of the fact of the nonfunctioning of what, in the body, allows a certain relation between space and the things that occupy space. It is no doubt the rear of the temple that is missing, as it could have been reconstituted in space (which the schizophrenic continually asserts: what is missing certainly belongs to the model, and in the first instance, it relates back neither to the imaginary, nor to the symbolic or their hidden meanings). So it is better to speak of the space of the body rather than the body image. "Body image pathology" actually assumes a relation to space and not, initially, a representation of the body. The disassociated body, the sieve-body, and the flower-man speak of nothing other than relations to space, and of bodily investments in space, and of space in the body, which could go as far as the total spatialization of the body or the complete corporealization of space.

So what do we mean by the space of the body? We already know that it is not the image of the body, and that it is not the space occupied by the body proper. In other words, it can neither be defined as a subjective function nor as an objective property of space. It could be said by way of a rough provisional formulation that the space of the body is the result of the objectivization of the body in space, an objectivization that itself results from the action of the body — of the singular body, organized in a particular fashion — on space and that finishes up by spatializing space.

Let us consider a metaphor like "two things are close to one another." It is obvious that we have a metaphoric expression, because two things are neither close nor far, not having in themselves the determination of distance from each other. This determination is in a sense subjective (far, near) and in another sense objective (distance can be measured). A surveyor has to be brought in in order to establish a relationship of distance between two things. This surveyor is, it would seem, the body that can traverse the distance separating the objects. But if the measurer only had a conventionally fixed measurement standard, then he would have to refer himself back to another standard, and so on indefinitely; such that two things would not be able to be called "near" or "far" in anything but a totally conventional (therefore relative and aleatory) way. Now, when we come to the possibilities of bodily locomotion, two things are "naturally" and not conventionally close. Thus the body plays a role of absolute measurement, of an indivisible unit of measurement. In order for this to be possible, it has to carry in itself a self-measuring capacity, because being its own measure, it relates only to itself as ultimate standard. Thanks to this property the surveyor-body integrates into itself—that is, into its surveying attributes—the "meaning" of distance, without having to relate it to another standard. The sender of information is also its decoder, and in decoding it, it never stops (even indirectly) being a sender of it. Articulations allow the body its movement, which in turn allows it to measure the distance by using the body as measurer (object-standard), but at the same time the body integrates the measure into itself—precisely because it only finds itself to be measurable by relation to itself as the absolute measure of itself.[45] So, with this particular determination of distance, the body is manifested as an absolute measure and an absolute relation; relation of measure because it is a measure of the relation. In the surveyor-body the relation of distance is manifested as, so to speak, that of a nonrelation, as the substantiality of a relation.

This example—which can be generalized to other spatial determinations—allows us to better understand the notion of the space of the body. It is a space "inhabited" by the body. It is objective, in the sense that it designates the correct relations for things, but it is also "subjective," to the extent that it brings about the spatialization of objective space by the body (which is, as we have seen, itself corporalized as a thing in space). The space of the body has limits that are not those of the body image, if we understand by that the limits of the body lived in a unitary fashion.[46] The limits of the space of the body are in things. In movement, for example, the body places changing limits on these things. To the extent that they are "subjective," these limits constitute the end result of the integration into the body of the relations (of distance, form, and so on) that it holds with things in objective space. To the extent that they can be pinned down topologically, these limits are no longer "lived," but are properties of space itself.

This double play of the space of the body can be illustrated in a symbolic space, like the ritual space. Its boundaries are drawn on the ground in a precise fashion, differentiating it from profane spaces. And at the same time the boundaries designate a space for the metamorphosis of the body, a space that it cannot leave. Everything happens as though the objective space were circumscribed in the beginning only to serve as a basis for the spatialization of the space in which the mutation of the body will happen. What emerges in the rite of possession among the Ndembu, the Songhay, or in Haiti remains enclosed in the circle where the trance begins. On the outside nothing should happen.[47] This is a space that, on the one hand, has been objectively prepared in order to bring about the corporalization of the body according to a becoming-animal (as is clearly seen with the *Isoma* ritual of the Ndembu), and that, on the other hand, will be the space of the "horse" (spatial-ization of space according to a becoming-horse), where a body possessed of a *loa* can evolve and deploy itself in its relations to other bodies and things, where the "horse" rides the possessed person outside of everyday space and time. All the free-dom of movement that the possessed body develops in this situation presupposes a relationship to space that would have been impossible to develop somewhere else. Symbolically, or rather in a way not visible to European observers, the possessed person's body does nothing else than reproduce the relations of the body to a space that has not been given, that is not present. But for the possessed, and those who take part in the ritual, it represents a horse-body that has links with a space (on the perimeter of the rite) implying a whole other system that differs from the one nor-mally tying the human body to ordinary space. But it is the "magical" deployment of the space of the body that suddenly betrays the ritual.

2.5. The One-multiple and Forms.

If we think that the space of the body, as an objective "lived" space, is in debt to a topology, this does not mean that one should expect to get configurations in objec-tive space conforming to the model of the body proper. The interest in body image pathology, as much as that of corporeal phenomena that come about in possession rites, as we shall see, is to show us the discontinuities, breaks, and multiplicities that can compose the space of the body. This is no doubt what remains implicit, also, in Bouissac's idea of choosing "volumes" as gestemes for his gesturology of the acro-bat. In this sense, the term "lived space" can lead to confusion, or to a phenomeno-logical attitude that, I believe, is precisely the one to avoid, because, at the most basic level, we are not talking about signs and meanings but about a mechanics of space. I think it is healthy to take a certain distance on semiological and hermeneutic meth-ods when one is describing phenomena relating to the body.

The examples of the mime and the surveyor-body show us that a gesture or a relation of distance between two things presupposes particular spatial relations that do not engage with the whole space of the body. The anatomical di-versity of the body and its various articulations show us that the space of the body is in itself diversified. There is no sole space, but multiple spaces; no sole relation, but a multiplicity of relations. In the same way, if it is necessary to speak of modeling the space of the body, it is useful to understand it as putting a continuous space into a certain form; for example, beginning with a diversity of discontinuous spaces. The body "lives" in space, but not like a sphere with a closed continuous surface. On the contrary, its movements, limbs, and organs determine that it has singular relations with things in space, relations that are individually integrated for the decoder. These relations imply *exfoliations* of the space of the body that can be treated separately. Relations to a tree, a prey, a star, an enemy, a loved object, or desired nourishment set into motion certain privileged organs inducing precise spaces of the body. Exfoliation is the essential way the body "turns onto" things, onto objective space, onto living things. Here there is a type of communication that is always present, but only makes itself really visible in pathological or magical experiences. Nevertheless the ordinary experience of relations to things also implies this mode of communication. Being in space means to establish diverse relationships with the things that surround our bodies. Each set of relations is determined by the action of the body that accompanies an investment of desire in a particular being or particular object. Between the body (and the organs in use) and the thing is established a connection that immediately affects the form and space of the body; between the one and the other a privileged spatial relation emerges that defines the space uniting them as "near" or "far," resistant, thick, wavy, vertiginous, smooth, prickly. The use of these metaphors in order to characterize the space of communication simply shows that it is the privileged ground for metaphorization; because a "petrified space," for example, merely expresses the quality of the relationship between the body and the objective space. Something of the order of a "petrification" comes from things and affects the body. And something of the order of the body (its capacity to qualify space, to transform it through affective investment) comes to affect things. Metaphor is realized through "semic intersection." For a "petrified space" divests the rocks and stones that parallel it of their mineral state, and divests the body of its movement.[48]

It would be a mistake to think of the relations between the body and objective space by beginning with a unitary corporeal whole, on the pretext that the body is an organism or a lived unity. The interpretation of the fantasies of schizophrenics according to this model leads fatally back to the unity of the body in a self and a consciousness. To say that the schizoid does not recognize as his or her own a given organ that appears in a given image of the body is to admit that the "self" is dissociated. Then it would be a matter of understanding how a certain matter pertaining to the body and to space is articulated with the spirit and the self. In other words, the mode of presence of the unity of the lived body is brought back to the self-presence of consciousness.

So it would be useful to set about defining this unity of the body. If we are granted that the space of the body is composed of a multiplicity of exfoliations that compose volumes, polymorphous spaces, leaves, loops; and if, in addition, each of these leaves presupposes a set of relations to things, integrated relations, that is, ones that are decoded in and through the body, it follows from this that the unity of the multiplicity of spaces of the body must be defined by its activity as a decoder. If one wishes to speak of the unity of the body or the presence of "wholeness" in each of its parts, then the "whole" must be understood simply as the action of the decoder-body in each of its organs, because these are not set out as in a painting: they act in (and produce, i.e., spatialize) particular spaces that "link them up" to things. The one (the unitary space of the body) is not present in the multiplicity (the exfoliated spaces), as customs might have basic content; the decoder-body is not in each organ like a language, an absolute code that would translate all the individual languages into one for which the individual languages would only be partial translations. If the one sets itself out in the multiple, it is only to the extent that it dissolves itself, manifests itself each time (as a decoder) in the deployment of the multiple. The unitary space of the body is only, in this sense, yet another exfoliation of the space of the body. It can appear, without doubt, in a representation that takes as its main axis the body proper considered as a whole, but this is then to make of the body proper an individual organ that functions as a totality. We might think that we find ourselves face to face with the decoder-body (as in certain representations of God's body, or the human body as a microcosm), but this is only the product of a copy and an absorption of the spaces of the body by its representation.[49] On the contrary, in the functioning of the body as infralanguage, as decoder, the one is only manifested as the multiple in order to maintain it as such and to dissolve and disappear into it, to not manifest itself.

There is no need to appeal to an ego in order to account for phenomena like the ones a certain kind of psychiatry links to body image. For example, when there is a failure to recognize a certain part of the body as belonging to the whole, what seems to be going on is that a leaf of space is detached because the decoder-body is no longer acting. The representation (of a part of the body or of what takes its place) that presents itself as isolated, without relations to other representations, shows the impossibility of translation, that is to say placing the represented thing in symbolic correspondence with other things in space. This is why Pankow notices a breakdown of the symbolic function at this point. The flower-man model allowed the patient to bring together previously unconnected spaces; the container and the contained (according to Pankow's terminology), the space of the body where organs can be inscribed, and the space of the organ (the vagina). And the access to the symbolic is translated by bringing these spaces together. These interconnecting spaces create the conditions for organs to be attached to the body without organs—and consequently to the production and circulation of desire. Connection is the imbrication of spaces that make possible symbolic relations.

The space of the body is made of plates, exfoliations, surfaces, and volumes that underpin the perception of things. These spaces "contain" the relations of the body to things, insofar as they are integrated in the body itself and insofar as they are translated among themselves. The elaboration of these spaces in the course of the development of an infant's mobility and organic maturity implies their constitution as spaces decodable into other spaces—that is, their constitution thanks to their activity of the decoder-body, or the infralinguistic body, each of which is thus connectable to the others, associating, intermingling, and bonding according to the laws of a specific mechanism.[50]

While dreaming, these laws undergo distortions compared with ordinary daytime perceptions of space. The condensation of two representations can be roughly characterized as the superimposition of one space on another, which makes two images coincide and melt into each other. Something in the mediation that held apart the two representations in their wakeful state disappears, and the action of the translating body comes into play immediately, without any impediment. What Freud attributes to repression must perhaps be understood not as an (unconscious) "intention" to disguise, but as both the result of the loss of a mediator among correspondences and as the end result of the "free" activity of the infralanguage, making the spaces of the body come into play—in other words, as an action of translation, of the excessive production of metaphors and symbolic substitutions. What is lost is also a matter for body spaces, to the extent that there are spaces that mediatize the relationships among other spaces. It is thought that in dreams heterogeneous spaces often emerge: I go down a vertical staircase and I enter a house that is oriented horizontally, lying on its back. Instead of interpreting these representations by putting them in a network of signs, one can give a greater emphasis to the imbrication of spaces that the dream sets out. It is perhaps not just about—let us suppose, after analyzing the latent material—coitus pure and simple, in which the woman is represented by the house lying down, but rather a reclining house lengthening a vertical staircase can relate to a certain way of organizing the space of the body— which is invested with desire. Two leaves of space, the one vertical and the other horizontal, have become contiguous in the dream, while the body in question moves "without any problem" from the one to the other.[51]

Because the space of the body is made up of multiple exfoliations, the relations between the body and objects is inscribed in forms. This does not mean the perception of the formal properties of given objects, but the form of the spaces that support the relations between the body and real animate or inanimate things. The translation of these correspondences does not come about because of relations that are initially conceptual; analogy, similitude, opposition, and dissimilitude are given in the forms of the space of the body before being thought of as concepts. In the same way as this "concrete science," which establishes classifications on the basis of sensorial differences found in "primitive thought," the decoding-body gathers up, brings together, unites, dislocates, spreads, and separates thanks to the spatial forms that contain in themselves (because they bring them about) the properties of unification and division.

Form has to be understood here in the more general sense of the product of the work done by the body spatializing space.[52] The forms that the spaces of the body take are not perceivable forms. If, in these latter ones, as Gestalt theory has shown, the idea of form already has a degree of abstraction that is like an a priori framework of perception (which is borne out by properties like pregnancy, fitness, and so on), then in the infralinguistic body abstraction attains an even more elevated degree. This appears in the way in which the infralanguage decodes information; information is organized according to spatial-temporal forms.[53] The constitution of a perceived form is a way of integrating information. In the same way, the formal constitution of the space of the body integrates a system of relations at a higher level of abstraction and creates a concrete configuration. But unlike perceptive form, the formal space of the body does not bring sensorial things together, it doubles them up. As the form of the relation of a relation, it is the *abstract figure* of a relation. Now it is this abstract figure that is at work in the decoder-body, making codes interrelate and creating metaphors.

It is only through abstract form that information resulting from the spatialization of space is integrated. Because of its anatomical and physiological structure, the human body encodes information through its sense organs in a particular way. The form that this information takes is not, therefore, that of the perceived object (taken "in itself"), but also depends on the structure of the body. In this sense, infralanguage acts as a primary encoder (we are not yet in need of the soul), organizing multiple and diverse sensuality into a unitary form. For any given object, or for any physical form, perception thus depends on the body organizing space in a certain way. Bodily space is the product of the double investment of the body by space (the information coming from the physical world) and the investment of space by the body (as a certain kind of receiver-encoder of this information). In a way, the space emerging because of this convergence constitutes the channel through which information circulates between the body and the world of objects.[54] As such, and because of its organization into forms, it can only be understood as an abstract form, the form of relations between forms (of the body to things, things among themselves, which relate back to the first type of relation).

So we can see how the body plays the role of a translator of codes. The exfoliations of the space of the body, as abstract forms, integrate the information coming from a perceivable body and make possible its translation into a different object belonging to a different sensual sphere. To take up once again Binswanger's example, why is it that we make deception seem like falling? Disappointment arises with some event like thwarted hope or the refusal of a request. This situation, which can be described phenomenologically, presupposes a set of relations of the body (rather than using the subject or consciousness, I am deliberately restricting myself to the activity of the body) to the object that is supposed to consummate one's hope. Once the object disappears, the set of anticipated actions ceases to be present in the field of possible bodily space, the affective investment undergoes a certain reversal, and so on. The description of the situation of a body falling would deploy similar lines of force: the ground slipping away under the influence of the vertical, loss of the body's potential grasp on things that surround it, affective reversal. The metaphor in "it hit me like a ton of bricks" ("*je tombe du ciel*") is based on the decoding of two situations in which the same abstract form that allowed for vertical falling is encoded in the same manner as for a sudden absence of a hoped-for response; for the loss of a grip on the relation of the body to objects, coded identically in the two cases; for the "forms" of affective investment to follow the same abstract lines, and so on. The metaphor is thus constructed through the transposition of the content of the information in one situation (a ton of bricks falling on you) toward another (disappointment). This transposition is made possible through the similarity of the forms of bodily space in the two cases; a similitude obtained through the abstract rendition of the information encoded (always following an abstract figure) by the infralanguage. The metaphor can be built up because the two exfoliations of bodily space are able to coincide in their common abstract form. It is obvious that this ultimate level of formal abstraction depends, once again, on the existence of a unique encoder, an exclusive operator that possesses its own anatomical and physiological structure. —

We can note the difference with perceptive form. A tune has a recognizable perceived form, as Christian von Ehrenfels showed, when it is played one octave higher. But this same tune can be represented graphically; it has a translatable graphic form (like its transcription onto musical staves). When we translate the form of the tune into marks on paper, this is done on the basis of its abstract form (and not its perceived form, which links things received through the senses), which is like the form of its perceived form.

I think it would be better to investigate, first, the "topology" and the mechanics of the space of the body rather than semantic analysis in order to describe the operations of metaphorization because, if we move from meaning (to describe, for instance, the relation between things and the body), we will run up against the same meaning and get caught up in a tautology.

The space of the body is not imaginary, or symbolic, or conceptual, or "representational." And it is not objective space either, as mathematically definable Euclidean space. It is rooted in the anatomical and physiological structure of the human body; it is induced via the organs, the limbs, the forms of the body itself; and it allows for symbolic thought or, in a more general fashion, for "symbolic function."[55]

2.5.1. The notion of infralanguage: rhythm and exfoliation.

I have described the infralinguistic functions of the body in several ways, which seemingly relate to different methods. I have, for example, defined infralanguage as a "preverbal meaning matrix," which presupposes a phenomenological outlook, while on the other hand I have stressed a definite desire to distance myself from this, by insisting on the "mechanics of space" and on the transducive function of the body.

These two perspectives should not lend themselves to confusion. It will be better understood what is meant by "preverbal basis for meaning" when it is firmly grasped how infralanguage works through the exfoliation of the space of the body.

We should be more precise on the notion of the abstract figure, or form of forms. *Gestalt* theory is quite insistent that form is necessarily perceived along with context, and the example of the figure/background demonstrates a vacillating gaze focusing alternately on the one or the other. Now let's consider a very sophisticated example, in which the gaze cannot hold steady either on the figure or the background: what then is the *form* of this figure/background? We are no longer in the presence of figures, but a kind of scansion between two forms that have the tendency to appear and disappear. Considered globally, these forms make up a whole, they therefore have a form that is no longer a representation, but is something we could tentatively call a "rhythm," the rhythm of the appearance and disappearance of each of the figures. We now have time in addition to space.

Henri Maldiney has analyzed this process of the appearance of forms in the field of art. He defines rhythm as "present time," the "rhythm of a form being the articulation of its implied time," that is to say not a time that is "explained" in terms of past, present, and future, but time that the verb brings with it, "inherent in the process indicated by this verb.... The process implied by the verbal idea and the action that it connotes may be on the rise or in decline (in diastole or systole), or be on the rise against the background of its own decline."[56]

In this way the rhythm of plastic forms introduces time into space. What is the difference between the photograph and the work of art? The photograph has no implied time, it refers rather to an explicit time; it shows no process of appearance, but rather gives an already constituted reality. Photographs have no rhythm.

Now let us consider that "power of simplicity" that art is said to possess:

Where then does the strange "power of simplicity" in a work of art come from? Its first appearance is as a negative power. Compare one of Cézanne's Sainte Victoire mountains with any other painting or etching of the eighteenth or nineteenth centuries on the same subject. In each case it is the number and richness of the details that make the second style work. *But* Cézanne's painting is better than all the others, in the light of the shadows and the naked and irradiating presence of his space. Having said *but* I must say there is no but. The two facts are linked. What picturesque or diligently descriptive works show *in addition* seems in Cézanne's painting to be *excessive* because they are struck by inertia and reduced to the state of dead elements.... In contrast, Cézanne only allows in elements to the minimal extent (and how minimal in his watercolors) that they move to make the surface become an energetic plane, a spatializing energy. This energy is as great as the contradiction between its elements is striking. Art gains in terms of keenness of detail and in power of resolution (contrary tensions) what it gives up in terms of richness and immediate satisfaction. When what is needed is to link up heterogeneous moments in a rhythm that articulates interior space and time, to make them communicate in the unity of a work of art, the most efficient channel of communication is neither the simplest nor the most complex, but the most unforeseeably necessary one.[57]

What this wonderful extract from Maldiney in fact describes is the process whereby abstract figures come into being. The only difference between art and the body, here, is the fixing of a rhythmed space on a canvas and the same type of space in the concrete action of the infralanguage. But it would be better to say *rhythming* space than rhythmed space, because it is the space thus constructed that rhythms the things that are held there. Henri Maldiney shows how from the very start a painting is leading to a certain "abstraction." One can even assume, initially, a figuration from which more and more features or accessory details are removed. This pruning is part and parcel of another type of "figuration": what was in the first instance represented by a form is replaced by rhythms, movements, which are created among pure luminescences, shadows, spots of color and shapes. There is less and less of a representation of the thing in question and more and more of the very *reality* of it as presented in the painting,[58] because, as Maldiney says, the rhythm *presents* the thing, offers it in the genesis of its appresentation.

We can see how rhythm makes space abstract. If, as we have already stated, the body *molds* space (and the canvas is nothing more than a particular effect of molding, the disappearance of the represented form and the making-present of the thing thanks to the spatial rhythms resulting from the transformation brought about by the painter on the surface), then the exfoliation is carried out according to rhythms, the sheet of space vibrates according to the rhythm of the form. Just as the surface of the painting is an "energetic plane" with "critical instances" (Maldiney) filled with energy,[59] exfoliation contains critical points and is presented *in toto* as a space traversed by energy.

In this way, exfoliation is a form or abstract figure, not a gestalt, because the figuring rhythm appears as a result of the disappearance of the form as figure. This figuring rhythm represents, in relation to the latter, a higher level of abstraction. What the form once circumscribed is now presented on the basis of departures, *gaps*, between visible elements, colors, lines, and luminescences.

Infralanguage is capable of translating codes or contexts thanks to its exfoliation capacities. Take a simple example. Imagine a man learning to throw stones with the aim of acquiring a technique that is so refined that at the end he will never miss his mark, whatever distance he is from it. He might begin by learning to throw the stone at a given target at a distance of x meters. When he no longer makes any errors, he tries to do it at a distance of $x + 2$ meters, then from a point $x + 5$ meters away, and so on. It is obvious that this series has a limit. At a given point his training must finish, when he is capable of throwing the stone at a target placed at any given distance, $x + n$ (taking into account, naturally, the limits imposed by the body). Now we are faced with a strange phenomenon. All this happens as if the body possessed a capacity to generalize, allowing it to transpose a set of activities (a stance, with all the implications of muscle tension, respiratory rhythm, and so on) from one situation to another. It is as if the learning process for stone throwing has as its aim the integration of the $x + n$ distance into the body, that is, to make it acquire something like the ideal posture, which would correspond to $x + n$. So there would be a kind of "ideality" of the object (distance) in the body, as Edmund Husserl might put it.[60] And in fact even though this point sitting at $x + n$ meters does not exist as an ideal point, we can say that the process of learning to throw the stone has brought to the body the capacity to move without change from the stance necessary for $x + 1$ to $x + k$, and so on. We cannot pretend that in the process of learning there is something like an "induction" or an interlocking movement from $x + 1$ to $x + k$: there is no interlocking, because each situation is singular and "heterogeneous" vis-à-vis the others. On the contrary, each of these concrete postures appears as a variant of an abstracted posture, which corresponds to $x + n$. This is not to say that a posture relative to $x + n$ exists, that is, can form itself in the body. This, by definition, is impossible. But it is undeniable that each of these concrete postures ($x + 1$, $x + 2$...) also "contains" the abstract posture ($x + n$). This is because the learning process, even if it began with trials on $x + 1$ and $x + 2$, had in mind the acquisition of a general competence, that of knowing how to throw a stone at a target located at any distance. Once the learning process is over, this competence allows one to hit targets at $x + 1$ and $x + 2$. How can we understand the fact that on the one hand there is no ideal posture, and on the other that one would have to allow for a general knowhow that would presuppose, at least, a plasticity of the body that, with the same approach, will throw the stone from all possible distances?

If there is no ideal posture, there is an abstract posture in the same sense that I have characterized the abstract figure. This abstract posture is not a form (but each concrete posture has one, which can be described in terms of the position of the body before the throw, cardiac rhythm, degree of concentration, and so on), but a "form" of forms, which enables it to move from the one to the other, from one concrete posture to another.[61] So how can this abstract posture be acquired? What learning process leads to such know-how? It is not really any different from the process described by Maldiney. It is somewhat like the way Zen Bhuddism teaches archery. For example, it is necessary for an exclusive relationship to be established between the body and the thing in its sights. In order to do this, everything that might interfere in the relationship has to be eliminated, everything that is of an accessory nature in each concrete situation (this is the whole idea behind the trials at $x + 1$ and $x + 2$). This elimination has the result of concentrating energy on the *spatial plane* linking the body to the point in space. The aim is one of making the point belong to the body, and the body to the space of the point. There is no room left for calculation (or trial and error), the posture of the body "contains" the point situated at $x + k$ meters. But in this case the body-point relation is established via an exfoliation, a leaf/lamina of the space of the body. This is not just any lamina and not just any surface. It is built up progressively with the elimination of contingent and heterogeneous contextual factors. In concentrates its own energy, it is rhythm, because instead of an objective space around a point, only the point exists; instead of aleatory corporeal and psychic elements, the abstract posture implies the reduction of any other thing that relates to anything apart from lining up the point. This exfoliation is a rhythmed space that results from two forms being placed in an energy-based relationship: the body and the space of the point. It is a form of forms and a rhythm of forms.

So if the notion of abstract posture is generalized, if all relations that could thus be made between the body and objects are considered, then we have an *abstract body*. For example, there is an abstract-green-of-leaves, just as there is an "abstract-wave,"[62] which is a rhythm that the green of all leaves possesses.

The infralanguage is the abstract body. We have seen that it translates codes or contexts. In the same way that an abstract posture allows the passage from one point to another, the abstract body, capable of elaborating abstract rhythms or figures from different contexts, allows the translation of one context into another. And this, in an even easier way than the condensation of energy on an exfoliated surface, brings about the extreme abstraction of form.

The examples I have just given could allow for some ambiguity concerning the notion of infralanguage. Is it a biological fact, a given, or does it come about through training? It is both learned and given. It has to emerge just as a rhythm makes abstract figures emerge, but it is uniquely on the basis of its physiological and anatomical structure that this "formation" can happen.

We can begin to get a better understanding of what is meant by "preverbal meaning matrix." There is, between bodily forms and the form of things, a *complicity* that the exfoliation of the space of the body is going to make good use of to bring about the abstract figure. Now this relation of complicity conditions and directs the way in which contingent factors are suppressed to form the unity of rhythm, or even better, it is the corporeal forms that "objectify" space by imposing themselves as such on natural forms. On the other hand, infralanguage as abstract body translates as it follows the totality of abstract figures, that is, the rhythm of the forms that compose it. It is in this sense that it can be said to be the "basis" and "matrix" of meaning.

2.6. Return to Ritual.

Significant advances have been made in the understanding of the phenomena, especially therapeutic ones, that surround the role of trance in rituals in tribal societies. It has been shown, for instance, that being possessed derives from a training;[63] that the gestures, words, or cries of the possessed are coded; that the beginning of the crisis is governed by a set of rules. Today, all this has become quite clear for ethnographers. Indeed, a fairly recent ethnomusicological study has provided an exacting analysis in a particularly difficult field, that of the relations between music and trance; the clarity and the categorizations brought to bear look as though they will remain definitive for the most part.[64]

And yet, the author himself admits that there persists a "mystery" in the trance of the possessed (as far as music and dance are concerned): how can it be explained that "a certain conjunction of emotion and the imaginary is all-powerful" for the body?[65] But my aim here is not to "explain trances" but to show how the notion of infralanguage can contribute to the understanding of ritual processes, especially in their therapeutic aspects.

After the description of the *Isoma* ritual in Part I, 4.4.4, a question was left hanging. How is it that the different codes, which Victor Turner's structural analysis so clearly delineated, were exchanged? Where is the operator that changes one code into another and vice versa? It now seems to me that the answer to these questions should be sought at the same operational level as the infralanguage. I have no intention of replacing the structural analysis of rites with another method of interpretation.[66] It is not a question of hermeneutics here, but one of grasping, in the actual activity of the ritual, what makes it more than a text, more than a semiotic structure, and in fact an action.[67] In order to do this one has to keep in mind the link that unites forces to signs, and the investment of energy that the body imposes on symbols. It is here, basically, that infralanguage enters the picture.

Let us take up again two other questions that were left somewhat open in Part I, 4.4.3. (1) The ritual order, the carefully prepared disposition of highly symbolic structures that condition the ritual process: Why do the following obey a certain type of "symbolic structuration": an organization of space and the choice of adornments and ceremonial objects? (2) "Symbolic efficiency": How can a discourse act on a body and its organs? How is this "remote control" possible?

The first question is about the singular activity of the body in a space where the places and the signs are specially arranged and constructed. This is not simply about the role of the body as an instrument of the passage from one symbolic plane marked in space to another, as can be seen in certain profane situations,[68] and as it might seem at first, given the spatial divisions Turner made of the *Isoma*. Here, the "symbols" relate to sacred spots in a topography where everything is set out in such a way that movement from one place to another must occur without the usual symbolic mediations. Being symbolic, these places are polysemic.[69] Simple observation of the ritual shows, of course, that the body is an operator in the passage from one place to another, and consequently is the translator of the codes in play. It is the patient and her husband, in *Isoma*, who are repeatedly going backward and forward between the holes; the three spatial levels set out in the structural analysis cut up the directional axes of the body; the ritual acts (such as pouring of medicines) converge on a focal point where all the symbols come together—and it is still the body. But all these facts and activities remain enigmatic precisely because the connection they effectuate between symbolic codes is produced outside of ordinary mediations. One does not, normally, go from "death" to birth, from "hot" to "cold," from sterility to fertility via a direct route. These paths presuppose, in the life of a community, a whole series of mediations (symbolic, for instance, which are translated by specific ways of doing things, daily events, coded know-how, communications); and the individual finds him or herself involved in permanent "mediatory" actions. But in the context of ritual these mediations fall away; in their place the body acts according to unusual rules. But the disappearance of the mediations happens at the same time as the transformation of everything that is supposed to be mediatized—if it is normally the case that the movement from sterility to fertility (from prepuberty to maturity) presupposes concrete rule-governed situations (e.g., appropriate behavior for different age groups), then both beginnings and culminations are now reduced to "symbolic" gestures. The whole ritual domain seems to be the result of the upending of the normal symbolic domain. How then does the therapeutic ritual return the patient to a "regular" codification of the body?[70]

We can establish the following. On the one hand, either the topography or the mythic account or the two (when they coincide) are overdetermined symbolically. The myth, narrated or sung, is an esoteric language, the language of the spirits, a metalanguage. It relates directly, in its metaphoric richness, to several domains at the same time (kinship, economic, physiological, and so on).[71] On the other hand the body acts by embracing this topography and by conforming to the symbolic account. But parallel to these two levels, two others emerge progressively in the ritual process. The symbolic account of the myth can become completely incoherent, being reduced to onomatopoeia, shouts, or inarticulate sounds,[72] and the gestures of the adepts, as the moment of the trance approaches, increasingly depart from the norms, the dance becomes less articulate, the gestural and rhythmic cadences accelerate, culminating in the lack of physical control of the body in the "crisis."

Ordinary behavior is banished from these two planes of discourse and action. Between extreme symbolic overdetermination and its evaporation there is no place either for an ordinary discourse or for ordinary actions.

Now why does this ritual, having a therapeutic trance as its aim and end point, proceed in this manner? It is a way of obtaining the maximum intensity of forces circulating in the body, and by doing this, translating codes in such a way as to abolish the symptom and the cause.

We know how symbolic overdetermination brings about an accumulation of energy; we know that mythical accounts become charged with forces on ritual occasions; we know also that the breakdown of norms and codified behavior brings about a liberation of energy. The twin contradictory action of symbolic overdetermination and decoding of the body will bring about the crisis. In accordance with the tendency toward maximum codification of the ritual gestures, the energies are intensified following the "condensations" corresponding to symbolic condensations, and they are concentrated in a centripetal direction. In opposition, with the destructuring movement that begins with the decoding of the body,[73] the intensification of energy goes in the other direction, toward dispersion, in a centrifugal sense. This will lead to an untenable conflict for the adept or the patient, one that brings about the crisis. The crisis would not then be the result of two opposed tendencies for the intensification of energy: it arises when the possessed individual can no longer put up with the tension.[74]

From the point of view of the space of the body, the two processes, overcoding and decoding, correspond respectively to the submission of the body to a space organized in advance and to the escape from this submission. On the one hand the body is overcoded: it is the surface of an inscription of signs, of symbolic overmarking. The already organized space, the discourses, the ritual sequences submit the body to a spatial discipline. It does not *translate* codes, codes are translated in it; it does not exfoliate, exfoliations are already given in space.[75] Ritual action, on this level, consists in forcing the body to go from one space to another, to follow a translation already realized in myth and space (symbolic relationships are "purified," the signification of medicines is related to that of places or to the color of decorations, and so on). In short, it is a matter of transforming the body in a *translation* of symbolic relationships. So this translation has a tendency to be an incarnation—this would be one aspect of "possession," or the other-becoming of the body.[76] The overcoded body moves about, ingests medicines, and dances like a metalanguage.

On the other hand, the progressive movement toward decoding runs counter to the first tendency. With the "abstract" dance that accompanies the "figurative" or codified dance, the body is engaged in something other than ritual symbolization: it engages the infralanguage.[77] In addition, phenomena of muscular and nervous release show that as rhythms gradually intensify, then bodily control escapes the normal bounds.[78] The space of the body tends, therefore, to unfold and open out in a way contrary to what is produced in the movement toward overcoding. The body, shot through with fluxes of energy brought about by the mixing up of codes, tries to find spaces that coincide with the infralanguage. In this sense it stops lending itself toward the translation, or incarnation, that all the spaces of ritual and mythic discourse have made meaningful for it. On the contrary, by the very fact that it has to move from one coded space to another, at the very moment when the overcoding movement tries to fix it as a pure surface of passive inscription (an overcoded inert god), released energy revives its organs, limbs, and joints.[79] And because the inscription of codes in the body forces the latter to be more than their translation—quite simply because the body cannot be this, because, in order for there to be a translation (and not a translated body, an incarnation) and not just an inscription—the body itself has to bring about the operation required of it, and the other tendency, that of infralinguistic exfoliation, begins. The norms of ritual behavior require the body to move from one symbolic space to another, that it ingests or assimilates medicines with opposite effects, and so on. Were it to remain passive, conforming completely to the mythic account, it would itself become a kind of incarnated body-sign. But because it has to *traverse* different spaces in order to undergo this overcoding, it is obliged, *even before this translation comes about*, to translate codes, to juxtapose exfoliations given in space, to bring them together, to separate them, break them up, inflate and shrink them—in short, to *exfoliate* in order to coincide with (and make coincide) the exfoliations that the prepared space of the ritual offers for its activities. But doing this means bringing the infralanguage into play: only it can work in such a way that the given spatial forms overlap, interpenetrate, and traverse each other. The infralanguage operates as if it were creating passageways between heterogeneous spaces.

Let us sum this up: (1) It is the movement of overcoding itself that brings about the opposite movement—the extremely codified dance leads to the uncodified dance, signifying music to nonsymbolic rhythms, the overmarking of the body to the necessity to translate codes, the body's submission to symbolic spaces to the work of the body on these spaces. In fact, it is really the same spatial mechanism that is involved at both poles of the rite: where there are outcomes in given symbolic spaces, and where something emerges in the exfoliations triggered by the infralanguage. (2) The two movements are at the same time contrary and convergent: contrary because the first tends to make the body into a kind of meta-language incarnate, while the second dissolves images of the body in exfoliations of the space of the body; convergent to the extent that both have the aim of restoring the function of the infralanguage in the sick body. We should not lose sight of the fact that a therapeutic ritual is involved: the sick body is the (partial) disruption of the infralanguage. In the double movement of overmarking and decoding to which it is submitted, the sick body is unable to respond adequately to the opposed pressures: neither conform to overmarking (which would require at the very least a healthy body), nor exfoliate "normally" (which would imply the correct functioning of the infralanguage). This adds even more to the emergence of a conflict "in crisis."

How is this conflict going to be resolved? Through possession, which is to say becoming-other, becoming-animal, becoming-warrior, becoming-woman, becoming-thing. Incarnation and exfoliation converge here. How does the body escape from the danger of incarnating the symbolic in a metalinguistic body? By becoming another body: no longer the body of the adept herself or himself (the human sexual body), but the animal-body where the spirit or supernatural power is incarnated. In this process, the tendency to oversymbolization is both brought about but diverted from its original destination: animal, woman, thing, other-body is the incarnate body, but metamorphosed; it has taken a form that escapes from overcoding because there are unchained forces circulating within it at their maximum intensity ("savage" forces). And how does the tendency toward exfoliation (contradicted at the same time by submission to the ritual "text" and by the pathological state of the adept) happen without the body completely losing control? In becoming other the body itself becomes complicit in its exfoliation. Here we have an obscure but otherwise incomprehensible phenomenon. The horse-body of the voodoo *loa* that undertakes the trip to the mythical place of Ifé is suddenly in a space that it totally embraces: it does not exfoliate, it is itself exfoliated in a corporeal form, it is confounded with the heterogenous spaces that it traverses. Code translation happens immediately: the horse-body *is* the abstract figure that goes from one space to another and that allows them to meet up, it *brings into being* the metaphors that are the very texture of the mythic spaces. The Ndembu patient who receives the shade in *Isoma* translates all the symbolic relations, all the binary relations of signs from one level to another, without even having to be prepared for it.[80]

Now it is possible to understand certain aspects of "symbolic efficacy," or in other words, the therapeutic effect of discourse on the body. Ethnologists have shown that the mytho-esoteric discourse of sorcery and magic is charged with forces through the manner in which its apprenticeship is acquired, and thanks to its place in the general economy of the ordinary discourse of the community.[81] Let us take the case[82] of the symbolic efficacy of the *historiola* recited by a Corsican *signadora*.[83] The words, which should not be understood by those present, including the person who is ill, and which cannot be conveyed to anyone else, except to a debutante *signadora*, and then only at midnight on December 24, are held under a prohibition that charges them with forces. A kind of complex energetic condensation is produced here. The prohibition, linked with magical beliefs in the evil that will befall the transgressor, condense in the words of the *historiola* all the affect associated with the possibility of the realization of these evils; but the *historiola* is only a series of incomprehensible, broken-up syntagms, which are the result of multiple linguistic operations (mostly metaphors and synecdoches);[84] and all these procedures have also charged the recited words with forces, in a way that resembles the way in which the prohibition was placed on them. How did the *historiola* emerge? One could speculate that it comes from a whole and complete text (this would only be a working hypothesis: it is known that no such text exists),[85] through a procedure of an increasingly compacted production of metaphors and synecdoches. But such operations on language imply a displacement of the affect attached to the "original" words: it is both detached from the metaphors that remain inscribed in the *historiola* and directly linked to them, since they (the words) are their "signifiers." The affect is even linked in a more intense way, because it is condensed, accumulated by the very fact of having been reduced to two or three metaphors as signifiers[86] — the latter become "explosive" because of their energetic charge. Such an operation could be called an energetico-semantic condensation.

Thus the *unconscious* underpinning the *historiola* comes about. It is a "sacred" or "magic" unconscious, since, while it is normally forbidden, it emerges under strict rule-governed conditions, in ritual. The question of symbolic efficiency can now be put in this way: how can the recitation of a myth or magic formula act on the sick person in an unconscious manner? The efficacy of symbols is the efficiency of the unconscious of metaphoric language, of metalanguage. In order for the unconscious of the mythic account to "hook into" that of the patient, we need (1) particular conditions to be created, on the patients' side, so that they can receive the unconscious message of the myth; (2) the recited words to have an effect on the sick part of the body.

Seen in this light, the ritual can be understood as a machine for producing the unconscious. The affective energy, for which the myth is the ultimate metaphor, must be reinvested on the body of the adept. Given that the ordinary symbolic mediations have been abolished, this reinvestment is going to happen directly.[87] How? On the exfoliated body of the possessed, without mediation.[88] Energy will cover the sick person's body as on an exfoliated space: in this sense spatial exfoliation replaces absent mediations, its use is the substitute taking the place of the linguistic operations that, on the level of language, were necessary for the construction of the mythic narrative. The latter discharges (brings into the present, makes return) condensed affect; and to the extent that the body embraces the spatial exfoliations that underpin metaphors, the spaces of the body are charged with liberated energies. Speaking becomes an action because the object of words is found in the spaces of the body—and it is the body as a whole, in its metamorphosis, that receives the message and conforms to it. It becomes the field of action that the story uses.[89]

One thing remaining to be understood is how discourse works on the organs of the body. The very mechanism of ritual, such as we have developed it, gives us the answer: if, in ritual, the body exfoliates in restoring "original" functions that are found at the basis of metaphorization, if the organs as elements of infralanguage (i.e., as agents of exfoliation) open real spaces, it is obvious that mythical discourse can have a direct effect on a given organ. Everywhere, disseminated in language, are the metaphoric counterparts of organs.[90] Liberating the energy in the exfoliated body of the sick person (body-animal), the "knot," which is symptom and witness of "bad translations" of codes, is undone by the deployment of spaces of the body where intensities circulate according to the basic mechanism of the infralanguage.

Symbolic efficiency therefore consists in "remote control," magical action of words on body parts. For this action to have effects, words must release forces in the body; these forces must react directly on organs, on their physiology, and the body has to offer itself as a receptive surface of forces. The mediator between organs and discourse, a mediator that must necessarily articulate paths for the circulation of energy in discourse (forces) with paths for the circulation of energy in the body (affect), is the infralanguage, since, let me stress, the mechanism of the spaces of the body comes from exfoliations beginning with limbs, organs, and other body parts.

So into the notion of "symbolic efficiency" has to be introduced the idea of "efficiency of techniques of the body," giving to this expression the sense of types of know-how (of the magician or the priest, the magical know-how implied by the whole ritual) that produce particular exfoliations of the space of the body.

2.7. Metamorphoses of One-becoming and the Image of the Body.

Infralanguage operates by using a multiplicity of exfoliations. It might be useful to indicate once more the one-multiple relation that characterizes the space of the body. It is in the nature of infralanguage to be multiple at the same time as one, in each individual exfoliation, letting each come into operation according to the specificity of each space of the body. But, as we have already said, the presence of the one in the multiple is not that of the whole in the parts. To the contrary, the one *disappears*, as a whole, in each exfoliation and in each multiplicity, which nevertheless retains its singularity. This is one of the fundamental properties of infralanguage, distinguishing it from the image of the body, the lived body, the organism or the body considered as a whole, the result of the sum of the parts.

This capacity to disappear, to be able to be absorbed in each exfoliation, defines the *metamorphosis* of the body. Metamorphosis is the condition of the activity of code translation: each exfoliation is the metamorphosis of all the other forms in a spatial *one*. Thus the other (objective) spaces underpinning the codes and corresponding to different spheres of the spatial universe (stars, animals, plants, and so on) are placed in an immediate relation with the things concerned with the exfoliated space. It is the same body-space that now develops a form embracing the different objects. It is the same body-space that is capable of creating forms for heterogeneous objects—it is the same *one* that is found everywhere, moving from one sphere to another, always multiple and indivisible. The one belonging to the infralanguage body is not in place *before* its exfoliations, it is not their initial foundation, it is not the totality present in each of its parts: it only appears when (and because) it divides, multiplies, and unfolds itself in the singularity of its exfoliation.

So there is no unified image of the body as such. On the contrary, this image both develops, and is set to work in, the activity of the body; these correspond to a loss of its infralinguistic capacity. It is not by chance that the body, as a *global and unitary* representation, is not used, in the language of tribal peoples, as the model for the creation of all sorts of metaphors useful for the "interpretation" of things ("eyes of the house" for "windows," "feet of the tree" for "roots," and so on). Thus among the Sàr (or Sara) of Chad, houses have "backs," pots a "belly" or "trunk," the village a "forehead"; certain logical or temporal relations are represented by parts of the body:

> The world of (artificial or natural) things is represented on the model of the human body. But from among all the diverse and structured labels of the body, the only ones used for things are a limited number of oppositions or isolated terms, organized according to the particular structure of each object. In relation to the different partial systems of the "corpus" of objects, the human body plays the role of a universal and polyvalent model, a little like a master key in relation to the set of different locks: even though each lock has its own structure, the master key opens all of them.[91]

The partial body-model is found everywhere (it goes everywhere like a master key), but not a unitary representation of it. If the unified image of the body were to function as universal key for metaphorization, then translation among codes would become an immense tautology. The absence of this key shows that the infralanguage is neither an object nor the unity of a totality. If the body is used as a partial "master" image, it is because it is also thought of as an object, but only as an image inducing meaning and metaphorized in some of its parts. No doubt it can be said that arms are "young shoots" and that the branches of a tree are arms. But if one wants to make the singular and totalizing representation of the body itself the pivot of metaphoric representation, then one has entered into another regime of signs, that of a supreme signifier.

Now we can understand better, in the ritual of possession, the why and wherefore of becoming-animal. Because at the moment of godly epiphany when the body tends to become the basis for a global form, a representation incarnate—which would usurp the place of the infralanguage—the risk of energies being bottled up emerges, that is, the opposite effect from that being sought by the therapy. In fact, to the extent that the infralanguage reflects on itself, takes itself as its own object (to be translated), acts on the body—to that extent it must translate the world in the body. This is the meaning of the work of mythic metalanguage, the effect of medicines, and so on: its exfoliation becomes inhibited (an overcoding movement). The tendency that then develops aims to make a global *image* of the body appear, closed in on itself, only allowing energy to circulate within the space of this representation. The unbottling of tied-up energies, which can only be achieved thanks to exfoliation toward multiple "exterior" spaces, becomes impracticable. And out of this, as we have seen, comes the necessity for metamorphosis, a becoming-other that stops infralanguage being fixed in a closed image of the body itself. I have just described the process (2.6); it goes hand in hand with the development of the intensities of invested energies. Becoming-animal thus constitutes a particular sort of exfoliation of the space of the body, because energy circulates directly in space, rather than from the body to things, as in the usual situations, but directly from space to space. With becoming-animal the encoding-body becomes the decoding-decoded-body: the one-body of becoming-animal, as we know, no longer exfoliates, it is entirely exfoliation, it *is* a new space, the space that spans new forms; it is space become form, the form of spaces traversing all spaces.[92] On the one hand becoming-animal conjures the menace of the representation of the singular body image, yet on the other it brings about the absolute exfoliation of body space.

The global representation of the body comes from the opposite movement from that which results in becoming-animal. Overcoding succeeds in incarnating the representation of the body itself. The body becomes the inscriptive surface for all possible codes (it is like the microcosm that *represents*, or translates in representing, all things. The one-multiple regime changes. The multiple is unified in the one image. It is no longer the body that, in metamorphosing itself, translates codes, but vice versa. No doubt some part of the infralanguage remains, since the microcosm is still the *axis* of metaphorization, the meeting point for the exchange of all codes. Nevertheless, on the one hand the space of the body is reduced to the space of representation—therefore the figure of the microcosm represents the moment of passage of the infralinguistic body of magico-symbolic cultures to the new stage, where the activity of code translator will be transferred to the *mind*, tipping to the side of representation. On the other hand, the role now imparted to the body is no longer the same: it is going to translate relationships where the image of the body is built up into this *structural* representation. The body image will therefore acquire a structure of relationships that, in turn, will serve as a basis for the metaphorization of things in the world, and for their understanding. A study could be made of this topic. The body image is built up as a structure and will serve as a basis for functional metaphors in particular.[93]

2.8. Kafka as Ethnologist.

Kafka's "Metamorphosis" illustrates in a surprising fashion what can happen to the body when, instead of undergoing the process of becoming-animal, it becomes fixed in a global and unitary image of the body itself.[94] This short story presents so many aspects of direct interest to my approach to becoming-animal and the differences between therapeutic regimes in traditional societies and those of "historical" societies that we would never complete the analysis. I will limit myself to a rough sketch, concentrating on a number of points.

What is "Metamorphosis"? Something like the inverse of a therapeutic possession ritual. We know the story: "As Gregor Samsa awoke one morning from uneasy dreams he found himself transformed in his bed into a gigantic insect."[95] What insect? We will never know: one day the maid calls it "old dung-beetle"; we have a vague description of his body ("hard, armour-plated back," "dome-like brown belly divided into stiff arched segments,"[96] lots of small thin legs, waving with continuous vibrations and secreting a sticky substance, jaws), and that is just about all. He has the greatest difficulty rising from the bed; he becomes disoriented and can no longer continue his work as a traveling salesman. The members of his family (the father, the mother, the sister), when they become aware of Gregor's new state, are totally disgusted by him. They shut him up in his bedroom and feed him. They are obliged to work, since Gregor was their sole financial support. Their lifestyle goes into a decline. They rent out a room to three boarders. One day these people discover Gregor's existence. Indignant, they decide to leave. Gregor, who hasn't eaten for weeks, dies. The father throws out the boarders. The whole family is relieved. The story finishes with images of future happiness for everyone, with a marriage for the sister being planned.[97]

If we compare the story of this long illness that Gregor suffers from the day of his metamorphosis to the day of his death to the process that unfolds in possession rituals, we are struck by the correspondences. These establish relations of opposition. Setting them out we find (1) In trances, becoming-animal is only a temporary stage leading up to the cure; with Kafka, becoming-animal is definitive and leads to death. (2) Becoming-animal is the manifestation of the circulation of intense levels of energy in the body; Gregor Samsa shows low levels of affect only in the beginning (worry, not about the way he might look, but about being late for the train), which gradually disappear to finish in complete atony. (3) Becoming-animal is the beginning of the cure; the body undergoes the accumulated action of both pathogenic and curative factors—the body inhabited by supernatural powers; Gregor's body is not inhabited by anything, he is said to be simply "sick," "monstrous." (4) In trances the exfoliated body moves freely through space; Gregor is more and more shackled to his body, and the space of his bedroom, more and more cluttered with furniture and dirt, becomes a sort of prison. If we think that the space of the bedroom was that of his metamorphosis (therefore comparable to the sacred space of ritual), then we can gauge the distance between the two.

Let us push the analogy further: (5) In ritual, there occurs a sort of direct communication (with appearances of mimeticism, attraction) between the public and the adept; "Metamorphosis" shows us repulsion, repugnance, and aggressivity toward Gregor on the part of the family, the maid, and his boss. (6) The priest takes particular care of the possessed person; the sister, who plays a similar role to that of the priest ("with her parents she had taken on an authoritative role in matters pertaining to Gregor"), neglects her brother more and more, and shows increasing hostility toward him. (7) The spirit leaving the body of the possessed is the sign of the cure; the departure of the boarders, who could be considered as the equivalent of spirits,[98] brings about Gregor Samsa's death. (8) The person about to be possessed takes magical and sacred medicines, which are given a higher value than regular food; Gregor is only fed "old half-decayed vegetables; bones from last night's supper covered with a white sauce that had thickened; a piece of cheese that Gregor would have called uneatable two days ago; a dry roll of bread," in other words, scraps ("as the fresh food, on the other hand, had no charms for him, he could not even stand the smell of it and actually dragged away to some little distance the things he could not eat"). (9) The rebirth of the sick person reintegrates him or her into the group, which reties its bonds; the death of Gregor consecrates his exclusion from the family group, which emerges stronger for this.

We can see that the metamorphosis of Gregor Samsa follows a path that is opposite to that of becoming-animal. We could even contrast two more poles: trances are in general accompanied by "voyages," departures giving free rein to "nomad" intensities (to use Deleuze and Guattari's expression); Gregor Samsa stops his life of (false) nomadism (commercial traveler) to become immobile in his room and in his insect body. The ritual process[99] seems to be misplaced, the bodily change into an insect precipitates the arrival of a scenario that is the opposite of that of therapeutic rituals: it is the same people and the same spaces, but the relationships are inverted. Nothing that happens helps Gregor get over this "unfortunate accident," as he says, but crystallizes his metamorphosis as a body image and, finally, helps him die. Kafka's "Metamorphosis" does not go from illness to cure, but from illness to death, following a path that inverts that of possession rituals. It shows us an aborted or petrified animal-becoming. There is neither becoming-animal nor transformation of the animal body into a human body.

This intermediate, indecisive state emblematizes the failure of the metamorphosis, and this state is due to the fixing of corporeal mutation in the body image. In fact, the weirdness of Kafka's story and its power to fascinate come from

Samsa's double identity: is he man or insect? And why can't the matter be resolved? Because Gregor remains a man in his thoughts and feelings, and is only a horrible insect in everything else. Nevertheless, as far as he is concerned, while he is well aware that the form and structure of his body have changed, his body remains human. Because, in order to survive, to overcome the difficulty of having an insect body, he has recourse to his human "body plan." This happens from the first moments of his metamorphosis right through to his death:

> He would have needed arms and hands to hoist himself up; instead he had only the numerous little legs which never stopped waving in all directions and which he could not control in the least. When he tried to bend one of them it was the first to stretch itself straight; and did he succeed at last in making it do what he wanted, all the other legs meanwhile waved the more wildly in a high degree of unpleasant agitation.[100]

How does he try to control his body? In constantly referring back to the image of his previous body, his human one. He wants to treat his insect jaws like a mouth, his little legs like human legs, his shell like a back. It's always *his* mouth, *his* legs, *his* back. In fact nothing has changed in Gregor's body image, and it is for this reason that he does not manage to give himself a new body. The latter is reduced to a foreign sheath, a "tool" that is difficult to use at the beginning:

> He thought that he might get out of bed with the lower part of his body first, but this lower part, which he had not yet seen and of which he could form no clear conception, proved too difficult to move; it shifted so slowly; and when finally, almost wild with annoyance, he gathered his forces together and thrust out recklessly, he had miscalculated the direction and bumped heavily against the lower end of the bed, and the stinging pain he felt informed him that precisely this lower part of his body was at the moment probably the most sensitive.[101]

Similarly, his voice, which sounds normal to him, only sounds to others like incomprehensible growling. The unitary image of the body remains the constant reference. Even if he learns "better to use the resources of his body," he cannot undo the impression of possessing a strange body. In short, it is because he cannot succeed in becoming animal that he remains petrified in this monstrous body. In a sense, one could even say that Gregor is monstrous because he will not give up wanting to adjust to the unitary image of the body proper. This image underlies Kafka's story, rising to the surface as a defense against becoming-animal, driving it into fixity. Without the ability to acquire and master infralanguage — that is, the power of self-metamorphosis, the power to give one's body its own space — Gregor Samsa is stuck between an older body image and a current one that the others remind him of: he will die because he is neither animal nor human, and because he does not know how to move from the one to the other.[102]

T H R E E

The Body and the
Traditional Community

THE BODY'S articulation to the world is only possible under two conditions: it has to be oriented, if we understand the world as divided up into categories, domains, spaces; and it must allow for the circulation of the body's energy into the world via specific apparatuses, which owe their own existence to different social spaces: this applies to the bow, to the spinning wheel, and to shamanistic procedures for communicating with the animal world.

The space of the body allows energy to circulate. It is the nature of the floating signifier to manifest life in its unpredictability, diversity, and spontaneity. However, in order for everyone's particular form of power to be expressed, in order for there to be inventiveness and creation, the metamorphoses of energy must follow regular rhythms. In this way all cultures impose on their members not only models of correct behavior, but implicit spaces where creativity and individual expression are developed. These zones fall under the domain of the floating signifier, which is supposed to be "the pledge of all art, all poetry, every mythic and aesthetic invention."[1] Here a subtle economy of particular forms of power and collective signs is established for which the aim is once again to let the body play its role of a basis for coding and accumulation of energy. Any disruption of this economic equilibrium will be translated by hypertrophy either of the sign or of the representation of the body.

There is a simple illustration of these two tendencies in the figures of the caricature and the monster. The first represents signs taking hold of the
body under cultural conditions—a particular trait (like "character") absorbing the
whole body, coding it to the point where only its meaning can emerge. Caricature
reduces the expressiveness of the body to a single sequence of gestures that swamp
its representation. Gestures cease to be gestures and become individual signs. The
second figure, on the contrary, manifests the tendency for the signifying function to
evaporate in favor of the presence of the non-"coded" body, the invading, amorphous
or proliferating body—each time the differences, articulations, and signifying gaps
are stamped out, the expressive microsystems express nothing that is recognizable,
whether it is the hermaphrodite having two sexes coexisting in the same body, the
goat with two heads, where the same sign is repeated to the point of losing the
point (one's head...), or the extraterrestrial alien whose incredible size, whose undifferentiated mass of flesh, eclipses any articulation and homogenizes differentiations—it is always the same process of swallowing up signs in some vortex of meaning, the body itself having become avid for signs, parasitical on all linguistic signs.[2]
In this way caricatures and monsters both express in their opposed ways the limits
of expressivity in individual and collective exchanges. With caricature we laugh, as
social beings, to see what happens to the individual body when it exceeds, in the name
of culture itself, the limits culture has imposed on its use. In short, this is what happens when individuals are made, by the act of ridicule, to occupy a position where
they should not overstep the limits of their social place at the expense of the community. Monsters touch us for the opposite reason. Here it is the irruption of the
individual asignifying body in social space that worries us; it is the sign-devouring
menace threatening our cultural being that horrifies us. Caricature is like a cultural
monster, the monster is like a caricature of nature. The first presents the despotic
sign monopolizing the body, infecting it like an illness. The second shows nature—
the body—setting itself up as a signifier without the help of (and against) culture: it
signifies too many things and nothing at the same time.

Between these two a space opens up that allows for the develop-
ment of singularities, the space of the life of the body. This is a space that, incidentally, brings with it a structural opposite: the place where the body ceases to be the
asignifying foundation of signs, the infralanguage, to become itself supported by a
code. Guiseppe Arcimboldo's portraits reverse the functions of signs and the body,
turning the former into surfaces of inscription...of the body itself! "Composed
portraits" of fish, octopuses, crabs, and shellfish as in *Water*; mammals as in *Earth*,
books as in *The Librarian*, or even, with *Fantastic Face*, turnips in place of the nose,

piles of carrots to simulate wrinkles on the brow. These provoke a kind of nausea, a strange sensation of too many signs and things. Hovering between the caricatural and the monstrous, Arcimboldo's figures present only a masquerade of the human body; false connections and sections proliferate while leaving intact the representations of each vegetable or other element. But in infralinguistic terms, the body could still be said to be taking its revenge—while it is certainly no longer the body that is translating the signs of the world, but the world that is translating the body in a rough way: turnips for the nose...is it a body or a pile of plants? There is a formal irony. It is still the body, when the gaze flips suddenly to the side of the gestalt that welds the elements together; and it is only a pile of things, since it undergoes a vegetable takeover, the gaze returning to the accumulation of signs of a code for which there should be a meaning somewhere decoding them, but, on the contrary, all signification is lost here: these dozens of vegetables, animals, and flowers suffocate the character thus rendered stiff and inarticulate.[3] Each time a code translates the representation of the body. But as if to show that an infralanguage is still at work here, the body resists forced interpretation, in agglutinating plants and animals in a single form, a face that negates these things, a face that refuses to be interpreted according to codes. And yet: the strangeness of Arcimboldo's painting lies in the fact that we have a definite feeling that there is some secret commonality between the human body and sign-things, between it and trees and flowers. But where is this commonality hidden away? Certainly not in the fact that one can put together hair with the help of leaves, or a human eye with a fish eye. Nevertheless in this way a distant, enigmatic analogy of forms is suggested. It is impossible for the viewer to trace this enigma to its source. It alone opens up a poetic space in these paintings and it remains indefinitely open. Viewers can only laugh at it and move on. Unless, through some quirk where their black humor might coincide with Arcimboldo's irony, they see a reverse metaphor (in the manner of a glove turned inside out) of the hypochondriac. These signs would be organs on the outside, and each painting a proposal to devour them.

Whatever the case, Arcimboldo is located at one extreme, where, contrary to that of the caricatural and the monstrous, and in opposition to that of the spontaneity of the infralanguage, the "body" has lost all relation to the living body and has neither a signifying nor foundational function. Arcimboldo's bodies are neither social nor singular—they resist functioning in any language. They cannot be used for communication.

Now in this domain too the body wants to have its say. If, at the very basis of human communication there is *identification*, which consists of "the global apprehension of men and animals as perceptive beings," which "precedes the awareness of oppositions,"[4] a theory of identification could not avoid the part the body plays in it. The psycholinguistic study of the genesis of phonemes in a child's language, for example, has to take into account the fact that "the basic mechanism for the assimilation of language is imitation."[5] "Identification" and "imitation" constitute, of course, generic terms for the complex processes studied by psycholinguistics.

When we speak of "communication" with nature, when the shaman makes out that he or she can understand the language of animals, when traditional artisanal techniques refer to materials (wood, metals) as if they were living beings that one has to "understand," we find ourselves in the presence of a kind of communication different from spoken language and from any other explicit code. And what is the medium used? It is the body, but inasmuch as it enfolds and traverses all individual bodies; it is a body that carries within it the heritage of the dead and the social tracings of rites.

Today as we observe everywhere the demise of traditional and ancient communities — and, from another perspective, efforts aimed at building up, in a whole range of domains, from psychiatry to the organization of working groups, a type of social cohesion founded on communitarian communication — we pose the question, which assumes primordial importance, as to how this type of communication is possible. (A related, more general, question is how can there be, today, communities that are analogous — i.e., with the same cohesion, the same internal dynamics — to those of traditional societies?) I will give a single example. There can be no doubt that these societies have solved a problem with which the West is still grappling. It is that of singular-collective relations. It is clear that they have found a quite remarkable balance between the development of individual singularities and social "pressure." That relates to the fact that the traditional community would leave open the space where the floating signifier can circulate; in other words, in the domain of the communication of signs, as in that of their apprehension and translation, what allowed for codes to be transmitted and understood was a certain function of the body.

There is thus a "tribal" corporeal communication where the principal role is played by "imitation, . . . manifest behaviour, social suggestion, which are informal communications in themselves," language only acting to "articulate and rationalize these communications. But many of these remain unverbalized, if not unverbalizable. It is precisely the function of the artist to provide a vehicle for the subtle intentions of a society."[6] From the artist, the shaman, the dancer; through attitudes, songs, scarifications, tattoos, paintings, ornaments, clothes, masks. Here we are not dealing simply with corporeal signs that are the result of collective encodings of the body, obvious in all these techniques of the body that reflect what Marcel Mauss called "social idiosyncracy,"[7] but above all with a type of specific communication that is found at the basis of symbolic thought. We know that in Africa certain cicatrices mark the individual with an indelible social seal. Signed with group belonging, one's body will reflect for others an exclusive territory. This raises the question of how recognition of identity and exclusion works. Scarification and tattooing assume a deeper communication, because the system of classification implied by these signs acts only on a unique basis, an "incestuous" body that spans all individual bodies. Each sign of recognition is only effective if it is itself recognized as identical in its semiotic materiality; in other words, scarification, signifier of group identity, does not relate back to a signified that, having been grasped, will permit recognition. To the contrary, it is because recognition of the identical comes first that it counts as sign of the Same. This is shown in the despairing mockery of the tattoos among the prisoners in the gold mines of Kolyma, as described by Anatoly Martchenko.[8] When they write on their foreheads, etching deeply into the skin, "slave of the USSR," they are using the same means of torture as those running the camps use on their bodies: the signs of group belonging and recognition can only act if their imposition is demanded by the body itself; if it refuses it, the tattoo, in opposition to tribal societies, signifies their deliberate exclusion from the group and becomes the living proof that the body — which power wants to domesticate — cannot be taken. This shows, *a contrario*, that an artificial corporeal sign only imposes a meaning if there is a transformation of the relation to the body to that of the body of the group (the "communal body"). Scarification allows Africans of the same clan to recognize each other because the *very ritual* of scarification is already a group act; in other words, it is not the meaning of the sign that allows for the definition of group belonging, but its genesis as a sign from among that set in the community presiding over the production of signs. Thus only the sign gives priority to the recognition of what is given in advance of it, and what gives it all its value as a sign.

In traditional societies, and also in those rural communities of the Indo-European area, there is the notion of the "rule of blood," the "vendetta," for example, which translates a phenomenon whose roots plunge into the heart of the clan linkages that assume this very type of corporeal communication, where the sign and the symbol are not detached from the reality they designate. It is not, in any case, by chance — we have observed it in the case of infralanguage being based in the "gesticular" — that in indigenous theories language and speech are always related to the body, to its organs and physiology.

The body that tribal peoples speak of is nonetheless not the individual "body," because the latter is at every moment invested with other community bodies—whether it is through speech, gestures, affective expression, through the eyes, by touch, caresses, or any other social activity (like delousing, which LeRoy-Ladurie discovered in fourteenth-century communities of shepherds in the Pyrenees)[9]—which involve the body directly, before language. This is also the special domain of magical practice, from the reading of fortunes—through yawning in traditional Corsica—right up to the casting of spells. This latter, by the way, represents the moment when, the usual mediations established by language having fallen away, bodies enter directly into contact with each other.

So we are now led to the idea of a communication that would have as its medium the "community body." More than a medium, this term would also cover the zone where "the distinction between the medium, the code, and the communication itself, without dissolving as such . . . can nevertheless . . . become clearer.[10] In each traditional community the link that unites all the members is based in this community body. All the other cohesive factors, the differences and the categories that are erected on the social surface and that determine, inside a community, oppositions, alliances, intersections, and divisions into groups and subgroups, depend on this first body. Here divisions usually considered very deep are at play. People's most immediate and vital functions—like nutrition, reproduction, excretion, perception[11]—flow together and reproduce the Same, where each individual body, fragment, and link in the community body forms and reforms its rhythms in allowing itself to be traversed by the rhythms of all the others. Here is found the environment where the floating signifier really circulates, connecting individual forces to those of the group, transmitting energies of animals to people, and from people to the heavens and earth. In sum, this "community body" does not define an exclusive "social entity," rather its dynamic implies all the presences of a traditional universe.

Now, to isolate a part of this operative domain for purposes of analysis, let us indicate a way it might function. This function opens a space where each singularity is developed, while offering the community its cohesion. This is the space of the individuation of the body, that is, the space of singular rhythms. It plays a role comparable to the one Freud and Lacan assigned to castration in the psychical construction of the child—without using the same vocabulary, like the interiorization of the law of the father or the formation of the "I" in the modern sense of the word. But to the extent that Freud's idea of castration brought in the notion of the symbolic, we can sketch out a functional analogy with the community body, which has a double antimonial role. (1) Short-circuiting the dual relation of child and mother by introducing a third term—which is not that of the order of the Father, or that of community Law, with its prohibitions and constraints. It is rather the presence of the multiplicity of bodies of all the members of the community who are interposed between the two terms threatened by dual capture. The forms of education one encounters in tribal societies show how from a very young age children come into contact with crowds of other bodies, are touched by many hands, nursed by ten women, confronted with a thousand parental images, identified with a thousand other children and adults.[12] This play of a swirling multiplicity liberates infantile singularity by breaking the capture that would result from primary identification to a sole image. The body of the child becomes a sort of articulatory receiver where other bodies are imbricated and disentangled in a dynamic plurality of connections and corporeal influences. In this way the children learn their proper rhythms by learning to modulate those of others in themselves. One only has to see and hear an African storyteller to gauge to what extent his gestures and his expression, which mimes mythical characters or animals or simply a member of the community, follow a "mimesis" quite foreign to the forms of identification of our modern theater, for example. (2) Far from implying the atomization of Western societies, the singularization effect presupposes an extremely powerful social cohesion. If, on the one hand, while always keeping open a gap between two terms of a dual relation, the community body allows "access to the symbolic," on the other hand it preserves the contiguity of bodies, their communication without language, their immediate branchings; and above all else, far from crushing individual potency—as was the case for the whole history of submission to the disciplinary techniques of the West, as Michel Foucault has taught us—it keeps them alive, making them a primary condition for the life of the community.[13]

The community body implies a lived singular body that is not separated or isolated from objects and other bodies. The "body as such" that phenomenology has erected into a concept is a product of the West—isn't this what the Chistianized Caledonian meant when he was interrogated by Leenhardt? " 'In short we introduced the notion of spirit to your way of thinking?' 'Spirit?' he replied, 'Bah. You didn't bring us the spirit. We already knew the spirit existed. . . . What you've brought us is the body.' "[14]

The singularity of the "individual" is not that of an "I" or a distinct body—with its organs, skin, affect, and thought separate from the rest of the community—but that of a body in communication with the whole of nature and culture, and all the more singular to the extent that it allows itself to be traversed by the greatest number of natural and social forces. The community body thus assures a subtle and precarious play between the symbolic and the imaginary, these two categories not having, in any case, the relevance they are supposed to have in modern society: the imaginary is so tangible, underlying and implied in the symbolic, that it rises very easily to the social surface in traditional communities, even in its extreme manifestations, such as madness.

We have already referred to Marcel Mauss's enigmatic text *The Gift*[15] in relation to the Maori notion of *hau* (parallel to that of *mana*), spirit of things and the forest. What is involved is an indigenous theory that explains the "requirement to return" the gift. His interest is such that I will reproduce the whole text. The indigenous informant says:

> I shall tell you about *hau. Hau* is not the wind. Not at all. Suppose you have some particular object, *taonga*, and you give it to me; you give it to me without a price. We do not bargain over it. Now I give this thing to a third person who after a time decides to give me something in repayment for it (*utu*), and he makes me a present of something (*taonga*). Now this *taonga* I received from him is the spirit (*hau*) of the *taonga* I received from you and which I passed on to him. The *taonga* which I receive on account of the *taonga* that came from you, I must return to you. It would not be right on my part to keep these *taonga* whether they were desirable or not. I must give them to you since they are the *hau* of the *taonga* which you gave me. If I were to keep this second *taonga* for myself I might become ill or even die. Such is *hau*, the *hau* of personal property, the *hau* of the *taonga*, the *hau* of the forest. Enough on that subject.[16]

Mauss notes that there is an inexplicable element in this text, the third term of the exchange, apparently useless in the quest to take into account the "obligation to return." However, if one looks more closely, one perceives the contrary. It is in the third term that the *taonga* (necklace, bracelet, or other article) acquires, curiously, *for the second term of the exchange*, the *hau* of the *taonga* of the first. If there were no third term, there would be no exchange, no differentiation between the object given and the object received, therefore absolute equivalence, so absolute that the exchange would become useless (we would then be in the presence of a sort of imaginary capture in a dual relation). Where does this slight imbalance in the exchange come from then? This imperceptible disjunction between the received *taonga* and the returned *toanga*—which makes the swap entirely worthwhile? It comes from the way in which each term in the exchange occludes the others. So, because there are three terms, I (second term) play the role of a screen between the first and the third. The latter does not know that what I give comes from the third — were he or she to know it, there would not be any real exchange between us since I would be a simple intermediary between the first and the third. Since he or she does not know it, I am in the process of taking over the place of the first, I occupy that place in relation to the third term. Now, for the balance to be restored, I therefore have to give back to the first what the third is about to give me, otherwise I will be at fault, having with someone else's object obtained something else (in other words I would be interrupting the circuit of exchange equivalences for my own profit, to appropriate a surplus of goods and power). Now we can understand why the Maori did not say, I receive an object from you and I give another one to someone else, but rather: and I give *it* to someone else. But when I return to the first term the *taonga* the third one gave me, I occupy the position of the latter vis-à-vis the former, who does not know where the *taonga* comes from. So what role have I played in this exchange? What have I gotten out of it? Apparently nothing; but in fact, I have played a decisive part. By introducing a screen between the first and third terms, I have broken the absolute equivalence, and I have created the difference. As "third term" (and each term becomes "third term" when its turn comes around) I have occupied all the places in the exchange, and I appear to others as other than myself — as first giver to the third term, and as first to return something to the first term. Now, this screening game that the disjunction between the given thing and the returned thing creates is also that which permits the material (but also symbolic) individuation of the *taonga* — otherwise everything would be equal to everything else and there would only be dual relations: the bracelet that comes to me from the third term carries with it the *hau* of the first — which does not constitute itself as such except via the screening that I have created in giving it to the third-term party as if this *taongo* had acquired the *hau* of the first term.[17]

We have here a model and an example of a way in which the community body functions. If the screening game individuates *taonga*, in giving it its own *hau*, we see that it also individuates agents that exchange articles, since these each have a *hau* that belongs to the agents. Which signifies, by the way, that it is because I occupy all the places of the other terms of the exchange that I acquire my singularity — at the same time as distributing, among others, my own reverberation, my real and symbolic body in the *taonga* that I give and the *hau* that accompanies them. Thus, because the communitary body allows me to "mime" each of these other singular bodies, because it puts me into constant contact with them, the community is made up of a multiplicity of singularities and of a homogeneity that nonetheless excludes all imaginary capture (except of course, in certain cases).[18]

The community body also has an affective investment. The floating signifier is not just situated beyond codes or in intersymbolic spaces, and it does not just designate a force for which the body would be the sole host. On the occasion of certain collective rites or festivals, exchanges or interminglings of several codes are charged with energies. The constant overdetermined presence of symbols means that every gesture, every individual behavior engages the concrete life of the body, in its relation with other bodies. It is enough to read Mauss's *The Gift* to note that these ("total social") phenomena, spilling over with meaning, symbolically overdetermined, are lived with a remarkable intensity by traditional peoples—whether it is a birth, a circumcision, a funeral rite, an economic exchange, or a game. Commenting on Malinowski, on the question of the circulation of *vaygu'a*, "a kind of money" (bracelets made out of a shell, necklaces of mother-of-pearl), Marcel Mauss writes that the relation that the Trobriand Islanders have with these objects defines

> ownership of a particular kind. One might say that it includes many legal principles which we moderns have isolated from one another. It is at the same time property and a possession, a pledge and a loan, an object sold and an object bought, a deposit, a mandate, a trust; for it is given only on condition that it will be used on behalf of, or transmitted to, a third person, the remote partner (*murimuri*).[19]

With *vaygu'a*, economic, juridical, moral, mythic, religious, and magical codes intersect. This invests them with such emotional power that

> to possess one is exhilarating, comforting, soothing in itself. Their owners handle them and gaze at them for hours. Mere contact with them is enough to make them transmit their virtues. You place a *vaygu'a* on the brow or the chest of a sick man, or dangle it before his face. It is his supreme balm.[20]

The *vaygu'a* are bearers of life. Overdetermined symbolically, they resemble, in an opposing sense, the signifying "residues" that were described earlier.

In the same way the Balinese fighting cocks of the famous study by Clifford Geertz are part of a game that strongly engages the feelings of the members of the community. A true image of the "social matrix . . . [which implies a complex system of] villages, kingroups, irrigation societies, temple congregations, 'castes'"— they put in play symbolizations coming from very different social contexts. The cock symbolizes the Balinese, his social status, but also the animality that he risks and fears more than incest, honor, and sometimes fortune. "We're all cock crazy," says a Balinese to Geertz, who notes that some spend hours stroking their feathers, fixing up their spurs, gazing off into the void, and the spectators at the fights move "their bodies in kinesthetic sympathy with the movement of the animals, cheering their champions on with wordless hand motions, shiftings of the shoulders, turnings of the head."[21] Here, too, energy circulates at the heart of an "institution."

The normal functioning of society brings with it practices destined to decode any energy that has become stagnant by the very use of codes, such that one can say that the culture of tribal societies, different from most historical societies, aims to render the life of the body possible: it is a culture for the body. Here everything contributes to looking after the singularity of each body, its power, its capacity to decode and recode; and in the margins of normal institutions and codes, underpinning symbols, filling them up with forces, an energy circulates under another regime, which will be engaged with by certain practices that are located on the periphery — but also in the interior of the social domain. The shaman and the witch are found here in order to stitch up symbolic articulations in recoding bodies, allowing for the translation of codes. What they do — like any other practice implying a process of decoding-recoding — contributes to the restoration of bodily life by reinvesting force in symbols. In this sense they battle against the kind of primitive entropy that leads to the homogenization of all senses/meanings, leveling out all the symbols that relate to each other in cyclical structure and time. Against this tendency of codes and of bodies — the latter becoming progressively coded by fewer and fewer signs, marked by the reiteration of the same gestures everywhere — traditional peoples discovered the display of their own bodies. They will know how and when to decode them to make themselves quite new ones, where, once again, the gaps and differences would allow the flux of life to pass intact.

F   O   U   R

Dance and the Laughter of Bodies

WITH HISTORICAL time, a whole new destiny for the body is inaugurated. Serious ruptures break up the social equilibrium of traditional and archaic societies. The cyclical or recurrent time that scanned their lives breaks open and becomes historical. New social formations will forever after be attempting to patch up this crackling breach in traditional temporality.

People's attitudes toward signs change. Previously, when the organization of codes was at the service of the body, symbols did not have independent or "transcendent" existence: people lived in familiarity with signs. If they were signs, then all things—in their function, their usefulness, their use—had no distance between their meaning and their materiality.

In this way we can explain the attitude toward the sacred that so many ethnographers have reported finding among tribal peoples: they mix seriousness with levity, they are totally implicated in their rites, and yet seem not to attach to them the importance that we (Western or Eastern), with great state religions, would like to see them dressed up with.[1] They would thus live through a double belief in the meaning of symbols, combining the closest concentration with the most frivolous detachment (the "unconscious conscious" meaning).[2] There is no doubt that for us symbols relate to corporeal attitudes that traditional peoples do not know about. For them, respect is not necessarily expressed through silence, with restricted movements, as in our religious cults; their ceremonies are accompanied by laughter and all sorts of activities that we would readily qualify as "sacrilegious" or "pagan." When, during a religious ceremony in a rural Mediterranean community, a man farts, everybody laughs, often including the priest (although he may get angry immediately afterward). Bodies are freer than the signs imposed on them.

This change in the regime of signs—and the relation they have with the body—is reflected in dance. While in traditional societies, dance—individual or collective—is always linked to a symbolism (a rite), this does not imply a rigorous submission to the imperatives of meaning.[3] The dancers' energy, their flair, their singularity, their self-investment, give life to the symbols being danced. In the end, symbols are only a pretext for dance. Dancers' gestures do not sketch out representations in space, these are born of the mimetic power of the body. No doubt some being or thing is being signified, but first there is play—that is to say, a play translating the logic internal to the production of meaning into movements: playing rhythms for rhythms, forms for their own sake, infralinguistic articulations in a pure state. As Gilbert Rouget said: "No matter how important its nature as a sign may be, or its symbolic function, esthetic power or ascetic possibilities, dance is still a motor activity that finds an end in itself."[4]

Contrary to mime, which leaves infralanguage (the "infragrammar" of gesture) in the dark, the dancer, especially one from a traditional society, brings it out into the open. Whenever one or more symbols are reproduced by the body, the whole system of corporeal logic they imply is set in motion: it analyzes movements, decomposes them, breaks up rhythms, puts new groups into place. This is why this dance is in itself so "liberating"; it does not have to obey a predetermined meaning.[5] The movements are, on the one hand, exercised for themselves or removed from their usual functions (which they mime, as in certain folkloric dances); on the other hand, this freedom of the infralanguage constitutes the "story" of the dance itself.

The following describes the dance movements in the *ndöp* possession ritual from the Wolof of Senegal:

> Usually, a dance begins with a slow sequence in which precise, well-timed movements predominate. The feet advance with small steps, the shoulders sometimes lifted, sometimes lowered, the stomach is pushed quickly forward and backward, the head traces a jerky round motion. The position of the hands varies: most often the dancer grasps the hem of her dress or loincloth, lifting and lowering according to the tempo. In other cases the arms are bent, then extended laterally, one after the other or at the same time. As the

tempo accelerates, the path followed by the feet becomes more and more complex, the dancer lifts in turn her left or right foot, kicks them to one side, in such a way that in the highest position the thigh is almost horizontal and the foot hangs laterally at the height of the knee. At the same time the arms are carrying out a circular movement whose path is hard to describe. At this stage, individual variations are numerous. The sequence can finish simply with the final beat of the drum of the lead drummer, which coincides with a characteristic movement from the dancer: she makes a vigorous pelvic movement while at the same time lifting and letting fall, in the blink of an eye, the front of her dress or loincloth. After this demonstration she either leaves the stage and initiates a "crisis" or participates in ritual behavior.[6]

The ethnographer notes that this is only an "inadequate and rough outline" of a "complex physical activity." It is clear that even codified, the greater part of the gestural sequences are not symbolic (except those concerning the loincloth, which are probably erotic).[7]

It would be appropriate to carry out an analysis at this point on the relation between music and dance. Let us just note one aspect, in order to show the role of infralanguage:

> Even in its most immaterial aspect—sound totally isolated from its source—music is perceived as movement which is being realized in space. This is even more true when it is made simultaneously with dance, or to make people dance. To dance is to inscribe music in space, and this inscription is realized by means of a constant modification of the relations between the various parts of the body.[8]

In other words, musical inscription in space constitutes a first *translation* of musical sensorial stimuli (which are not just perceived through the hearing, but through the whole body, the belly, the chest, the limbs, the skin)[9] into spatial forms, the translation being carried out by an *abstract figure*, starting with the musical form, transposed into acted-out corporeal movements and gestural movements. Here begins the exfoliation itself of the space of the dance, which, like the music, modifies "the experience of *being*, in space and time simultaneously."[10] But in the exfoliation thus produced in the conjunction of music and dance, something very strange happens. The space deployed by the movements does not extend beyond the limits of the space circumscribed by the evolution of the body. To the extent that the gestural is not symbolic, and that the movements have no other goal than themselves (no take on things, no play with other living beings), it is produced as the work of the body (a "technique of the body") on itself: it plays alone, without attachments, it plays its "play," as it were, that which makes of it a body attached to things; the body plays the body, it projects an arm, lifts a leg, turns a head. What is it playing? It plays infralanguage, it inscribes in a space (without things) whatever allows its own ordinary inscription in the space (of things). But to inscribe in "empty" space is to reconstruct this very space, not in symbolically reconstructing things (which also happens), but in creating a "pure" space. This is precisely what I have called body space. We know that dance is one particularly effective way to get into a trance, at the same time as it initiates all the destructuring effects ethnopsychoanalysis talks about (loss of the sense of direction through confusion of the balance mechanism, disorientation and distressed feelings of space and time, and so on). Dance exfoliates the body space itself, it dissolves the body in the physical space it occupies, thus preparing the body for a metamorphosis for a becoming-other that will be possession. The latter will thus result from a quick restructuring of these exfoliations in a unique spatial form, according to the shape of the incarnated spirit.

In producing a body-space detached from real time, dance creates its own "intemporality": all dance is "divine" because it is intemporal, evolving in a space without inertia or hindrance. But while tribal peoples' dances get this liberatory virtue from their independence from symbols, by the activation of the infralanguage, other social formations see in the sacred meaning, in the "spirituality" of danced symbols, the "divine" character of dance. Hindu tantric iconography represents Shakti, the "wife" of Shiva, and principle of power and energy, dancing on his immobile body; or even simply Shiva's dance, with the multiple arms symbolizing freedom from all conditioning, detachment from all linkages. Here the representation orients the movements of the body so that they signify a certain state (of the mind as well as the body): in this sense Shakti's dance represents what happens to the yogi when he reaches a state of individual liberation. This freedom and the nature of absolute play in the dance are only obtained at the price of stripping away all bodily attachments. In opposition to African dances, any "decoding" of the body, any dimension of free and gratuitous play, is obtained by rooting the body even more firmly in the world and its energies and rhythms. One would like to reduce the body to a sign or to a machine for producing signs; the other would like to dissolve it into a pure form of energy. The first would aim to abolish all material reference; the second, to accentuate corporeality to such an extent that it would become "abstract," liberated of the weight of symbols.[11]

No doubt this distinction is too cut and dried.[12] Even a dance that is the most regulated by conventional norms has the inherent task of displaying the pure gesture. Indian classical dance, for example, as it is codified in Bharata

Muni's treatise, *Natya sastra*, is made up of three parts: *natya*, which combines dance and theatrical representation; *nrtta*, which designates "pure dance, . . . movements without any particular meaning used to show pure technique and the complex interrelations of musical measure, rhythms, positions and work of the feet";[13] and *nrtya*, which includes movements that have meanings and that form the "discourse of dance." This discourse, coming from an alphabet of hand gestures (*Hastas*) and eye and eyebrow expressions, itself implies the confluence of other bodily movements that have no meaning, because each hand gesture is polysemic. For example, the first sign in the "hand alphabet" called *Pataka* (the Flag)—palm of the hand turned outward, the four fingers and the thumb extended together—"is used to designate clouds, the forest, objects, the belly, softness, peace, a river, the sky, bravery, moonlight, strength, sunbeams, waves, entering, silence, an oak, the sea, sword, a palm leaf."[14] To reduce this polysemy and fix the meaning of a gesture one needs "well-established conventions defining the positions of arms, fists, the body, and combined with facial expressions [which] determine a particular meaning for the available significations linked to this gesture, meanings which represent the interpretation which is best adapted to this precise context."[15]

This context is based on a position (*karana*), and the dance consists in going from *karana* to *karana* to make up *Angahara*, or meaningful unities. All of this classical dance thus seems to put the body and the grammar of gestures in the service of a text (quite often a sacred one). And of course a rule determines the context, which in turn fixes the signification. The representative or mimetic elements seem to dominate and work in such a way that the dancing body marries the sacred text; the movements and the gestures being themselves so "artificial," so "conventional"—the gestural sequences implying such a divorce from the usual bodily gestures—that one has the impression that the dancer's body is writing, stopping, picking up the pen (the body), again making up sentences in an exotic language, spinning out quite elaborate contexts. Knowledgeable Indian dance seems more truly like a writing than a representation.

Nevertheless even here a great part is given over to pure gestures. Dances generally begin with *nrtta*, in order to "accentuate the importance of musical measure and rhythm;[16] these too play on their "infragrammar."

If dance always has a "divine" character it is because it locates itself beyond all syntax, whatever the grammar or lexicon that it might use on each occasion. Basically dancing means confusing lexicon with grammar, such that gestures do not relate back to any meaning outside of corporeal movements: everything is displayed in expression, there is nothing hidden, no background. Dance is a sort of levitation that is sufficient unto itself, with its own space and time; it carries within it and presents to everyone the key to the intelligence of the body. Dancers are at one and the same time paper, pen, and graphic, the space that their bodies use being the place where, eventually, the sign is inscribed, which is none other than a figure of the body yet again. Here expressivity does not relate back to an emotion, as in "emotional space," or to a meaning coded by a gesture. Rather, the forms of body space are outside of meaning, the exfoliations developed offering themselves sometimes as pen-bodies, sometimes folding back on themselves and dissolving; the body extends along its space then drops, contracts itself; there is only a point left visible in the space.

Dancers make up "stories" with movements that retrace the purely formal "structure" underpinning them. And how can this be reconstituted if not through employing this same "structure"? How can the infralanguage (or infragrammar) be played on without having recourse to it? In this way a tension is produced between infragrammar and expression, the second appearing bizarrely, emerging both suddenly and progressively from the profusion of dancing movements, the latter combining a precise code (with a grammar and lexicon that permit the expression of a motif or a theme) with the infralanguage. The symbolic gesture—such as the attack of a lion in an African dance—is both long in preparation in the preceding and concomitant movements, and surges suddenly—like the attack itself—in the form of a separate unit, having always been distinct from the other gestures, which did not have the aim of signifying it.

The impossibility, as we have already seen, of reducing gesture to a language (in clearly defining the indivisible elements and the laws of their composition) demonstrates the existence of a limit to the absolute "formalization" of gestures, as well as the emergence of infragrammar in the system. So all dance, even the most formalized, coded, or academic, lets escape a residue that is not formalizable. The very continuity of a dance spinning out its "story" rests on this "sliding" of corporeal movements over each other, as Kenneth Pike has suggested.[17] The "articulation" of one dance movement with another and the passage from one sequence to another are, by definition, unanalyzable. Dance would thus be the expressive form of the impossibility of reducing the body to a "gesturology." It is like an act of defiance, or a transgressive device keeping signs from being too serious. In a parody of linguistic systems, and in the flash of immediate liaisons, it wipes out at one blow laborious constructions like "figures." Dance is the quintessential mockery of signs and forms that set themselves up in the place of meaning or the body.

Today, with the progressive fragmentation of the Western symbolic cultural context, dancers can become Fred Astaires who deconstruct meaning and space, dancing on the walls and the ceiling, upside down—thanks to special effects that cinematically extend dance's own logic.

The lightness of the body leavens once again the symbols of traditional communities. Symbols speak to each other, leaving people to get back to their own business, namely their bodies. The function of symbols and gods was to guarantee the life of the people. As for the rest, for all that concerns how one lives in the world, people have to figure this out with their own bodies. Because gods are born at the same time as people, because they live with them on a daily basis, and because, above all, their unfathomable transcendence is *exchanged* every time a ritual is carried out, never getting to the point of becoming set as a deep object, the life of tribal peoples, however impregnated with symbolism it may be, never reaches the degree of seriousness of "historical" societies.

On the contrary, there is a profound laughter there, a belly laugh—the laugh that early travelers and European ethnologists were so struck by that they sometimes took it to be a sign of the "humanity" of the savages. An endless laugh, without premeditation, as undefinable as a rhythm, it plays a part in the community and creates a social link and a mode of recognition at the very foundations of the community body. It is there to guard against seriousness and the possible heaviness of signs. Like dance it is ready to irrupt and defuse the risk of the petrification of gestures listing with the weight of meaning.

This is so true that traditional societies even provided an institutional means for such laughter. The "joking relationship" of traditional peoples allowed for "free talk" between certain members of a clan, and the mockery, bantering, and humor that resulted created a counterweight to the tendency to seriousness—and acted as genuine antipower devices.[18]

As Bakhtin noted, this social function of laughter was particularly prevalent in the traditional societies of western Europe.[19] Through the whole Middle Ages "comic popular culture" parodied the other culture, that of religious rites, feudal hierarchies, and chivalry. Popular festivals open up this space—often during three months of the year—where all is allowed, where laughter inverts social statuses and undermines the power of institutions: the "fools' festivals" (*festa stultorum*), the "donkey's festival," carnival.[20] "Pascal's laughter" developed popular creativity in this sense, from public amusements with exhibitions of clowns, jesters, madmen, dwarfs and monsters, idiots and giants, right through to literary works, like parodic homilies (*sermons joieux*) and skits on liturgy and biblical scenes, which were part of the *parodia sacra*, often composed by the monks themselves. While the hierarchy was consolidated in "official" festivals, with the deployment of signs that marked the various places to be occupied—flags, coats of arms, dress, decorations—the popular festivals overturned this order and created an upside-down world.

In this way the representation of the "grotesque body" was elaborated, and Bakhtin opposed it to the "classical body," the latter obeying the rules and calculation of proportion, ever since Polycletus, in the fifth century B.C., set them out in his "Canon." In the classical body there is no excess, everything is balanced and measured. It is a "complete body, rigorously delineated, closed, shown from the outside, un-mixed, individual";[21] whereas in the grotesque body, where the movement of life bursts forth, disorder dominates: being neither closed nor complete,

> it outgrows itself, transgresses its own limits. The stress is laid on those parts of the body that are open to the outside world, that is, the parts through which the world enters the body or emerges from it, or through which the body itself goes out to meet the world. This means that the emphasis is on apertures or the convexities, or on various ramifications and offshoots: the open mouth, the genital organs, the breasts, the phallus, the pot belly, the nose. The body discloses its essence as a principle of growth which exceeds its own limits only in copulation, pregnancy, childbirth, the throes of death, eating, drinking, or defecation.[22]

There is a whole study of the grotesque body of the Middle Ages to be done, taking it as an infralanguage. There are precise relationships between the emergence of the "grotesque" in statuary and pictorial representation and the sociocultural changes Europe was going through at the time. Suffice it to note that all the extraordinary fauna that, especially around the twelfth and thirteenth centuries, appeared in manuscripts and in Gothic cathedrals, and for which Jurgis Baltrusaitis has revived the lively abundance,[23] occupied particular places, like the floating signifier. In cathedrals the fantastic bestiary does not haunt the broad surfaces of the walls, or the shafts of the columns, or the altars or reredos. They are instead in the corners of the columns, the friezes, the capitals, the misericords, the choir stalls, under the consoles, at the corner of the gargoyles, at the end of the cornices, in the cornerstones between two figures of saints that monsters leap out of, covering the cracks, spying in the crevices, hiding in the shadows all the better to surprise us. Like magical beings—and because they are part of that world—they are placed on the hinges between two worlds, on the edges of two well-defined spaces. In manuscripts their place is also characteristic: they are set out in the margins of bestiaries, the Psalms, books of hours, Romans. They extend the capital letters that begin paragraphs and fill up the white spaces at the ends of lines. These are also place limits, marginal places that surround the text, which is the sacred, ordered, "symbolic." The inventiveness, the extraordinary movement of the fantastic figures is opposed to the rigid immobility of the letters that make up the *right*-ing (l'*ortho*-graphe). In the same way that "weirdos" and grotesqueries interrupt the medieval order, cathedrals also swarm with griffons, hermaphrodites, two-headed monsters, and sirens, and the sacred text is overwhelmed with monstrous figures — an overwhelming that, as we know, confirms in other ways the solid architecture of the real world.

F I V E

Seriousness of Symbols
and Incarnation

IF, AT a certain moment, the regime of signs changed in such a way as to subjugate the body, it is because the mechanisms put in place by traditional societies (without State apparatuses)[1] to avert this danger had been destroyed.

For example the "reversibility" that Jean Baudrillard speaks of would have the precise aim of stopping the process threatening the transformation of the symbolic.[2] Potlatch[3] would aim to restore to symbols their former lightness—if we understand it in the following way: in destroying goods, wealth, food, stores, and precious objects in an agonistic type of exchange that demonstrates the power of the clan or the community, tribal societies that incorporate this institution (like the Kwakiutl of North America) arrested the development of a space that, in the very interior of the social domain and in opposition to it, ran the risk of absorbing it.[4] In this space certain processes took place that were able to control the equilibrium of social exchanges. From a chieftain's accumulation of goods or women, where he refuses to give recompense to the community for his privileges, through to the inevitable proliferation of powerful objects of the *vaygu'a* type in the Trobriands, there is always a certain mechanism whose elaboration tends to break the equivalence of exchanges, creating a fixation, a surplus of things for which the quantity, in the hands of the clan, a chieftain, or a group, exceeds their usual symbolic value. Disequilibrium can arise when there are too many women for a chief, or too much *vaygu'a* in the possession of an individual. As amply shown by Mauss in *The Gift*, the great obsession of traditional societies is nonreciprocity.

Potlatch acts in the opposite way to a bank. It consumes instead of conserving and accumulating, it destroys the surplus that will grow until it ends up destroying society with its fatal weight. The normal functioning of codes can be upset by the quality[5] of things as well as their quantity.[6] These things run the risk of being affected with a symbolic value that is not their own in the habitual circuit of exchanges.

It is in this way that values can get inflated: "Each of these precious things has, moreover, a productive capacity within it. Each, as well as being a sign and surety of life, is also a sign and surety of wealth, a magico-religious guarantee of rank and prosperity."[7] For example,

> the notion of "*logwa*" (generic title that the *Kwakiutl* give to precious objects, spoons, dishes, and coppers used in potlatch) is precisely that of *mana*. For our purpose it is the "virtue" of wealth and food which produces wealth and food. A discourse on the *logwa* calls it "the great past augmenter of property." A myth tells how a *logwa* was good at acquiring property, how four *logwa* gathered to it. One of them was called "Making property accumulate." In short, wealth begets wealth.[8]

If one considers that "richness" and "property" mark symbolic value, then it is certainly from a surplus of this value that things being exchanged can be affected. How does this surplus emerge?

Ideally, normal social exchanges postulate perfect correspondences on the two levels of symbols and things, such that with a real action, function and result coincide with symbolic value. Thus, tribal societies, which do not have harmonious correspondences everywhere, produce compensatory devices for the inevitable imbalances. Their practices constitute, as Mauss says, "total social acts," with multiple and overdetermined values and effects — religious, magical, juridical, economic, and so on. Under these conditions, if a surplus crops up in the social domain, it can remain without a correspondent in the other domains of exchange.[9] Thus the danger emerges that this surplus of things could be affected by an absolute symbolic surplus (in relation to all the symbolic values of exchangeable things) — an eventuality that is all the more formidable because it is inscribed in the very logic of the process.[10] As long as this does not happen, this surplus of things, which cannot have a symbolic value equivalent to that of the normal quantity of things in circulation—since there is nothing to swap with—possesses in itself a "neutral" symbolic value (which at the same time becomes frustrated, overdetermines itself, inflates itself enormously, and eliminates itself in potlatch, which is the way of bringing about this value in transforming it, in destructive exchange, from the absolute to nothing). This is what leads it to occupy, unlike the case with the symbolic, the same arena as the floating signifier. Like the latter, it is inexchangeable, threatened with symbolic emptiness and available for all sorts of applications. The fact that it is placed in reserve—a potlatch reserve—gives it a particular character compared with other things; it is no doubt not by accident that in potlatch it is attributed with power, recalling in this way the "material remainders" of the symbolic function, real traces of the floating signifier. In the end potlatch puts into play, besides all these goods in excess, innumerable precious objects of the *vaygu'a* or *orenda* type.

We can therefore assume that at a certain moment of the production of this surplus of things, their available symbolic value (neutralized, in suspense) is identical to that of the floating signifier, in other words, zero. This assimilation is found to be confirmed in the fact that, as Mauss insisted, potlatch gives off a power: there is the prestige, honor, and pride of those who are destroying, in rivalry with goods, wealth, and various objects charged with forces. A sort of transfer of powers operates between these objects and the participants, as the process of furious destruction takes its course. So what are these chiefs of traditional communities destroying, since these things have lost their utilitarian function and their symbolic exchange value? They ward off a menace: the incarnation of symbols.

This surplus of goods is full of forces that are the same as those which designate the floating signifier and which the body harbors, so naturally the symbolic neutralization (decoding) that affects them makes the same decoding appear in the body. It is in this way that, under certain conditions of social life,[11] it can emerge that all the symbolic meaning of bodies and things can be stripped naked, so that bodies and things can evolve outside of any sociocultural coding, virgin and empty. They can even define a space of social exclusion (pariahs, failures, fringe dwellers). If at the same time these bodies are related to an empty ("floating") signifier, but are ready to be filled again and positioned, in such a way that actions (techniques, practices, ritual, and corporeal disciplines) carried out on them bring about the emergence of a despotic signifier (and Meaning), the whole regime of signs and codes is disturbed: these techniques, these disciplined gestures, are now taking the place of social manners (the only manners really valued).

5.1. Fixing the Floating Signifier.

How can this be done? Whoever holds the potencies of bodies, in the social domain, holds power and, in particular, political power. So all one has to do is to make bodies work under another regime of signs to monopolize power, to transform the floating signifier that governs the circulation of energies among codes into a supreme signifier and frame it in another system to which all the signs are submitted, in order to have control of the bodies. Here is without doubt one of the basic mechanisms of power formation. The witch and the shaman manipulate the floating signifier; so too does the priest and the political leader, through the despotic signifier.[12]

Transforming in this way the empty signifier means giving it a separate place, at the center or above the system. Its meaning cannot be grasped or decoded by other signs. Its meaning (which now presents itself as full) is reduced to that of a practice, a technique, a way of dominating the body. The activity of translation of codes is partially transferred from the infralanguage to the metalanguage for which the supreme signifier becomes the detainer and the carrier. The latter conceals an absolute symbolic value, if we think about it in relation to bodies, because it indicates the only way of liberating the potency contained in bodies, and it draws its power from the very forces that it overcomes — forces used against bodies, for the production of the Signifier in bodies.

The practices of esoteric sects exemplify this process of domination of bodies. This example may have more general relevance, perhaps contributing to the understanding of the formation of "voluntary servitude," which political and religious repression use to different degrees.[13]

The sect's first principle is renunciation of "mundane" life, the aim being the search for spiritual liberation. In this way Hinduist sects, or modern groups, often exploit members, making them work for huge corporations.

Renunciation is an asocial principle.[14] The whole practice of the sect begins with the avoidance of contact with the world. This implies a practice of the body accompanied by multiple techniques designed to prepare the body for coding by the supreme signifier: techniques of fasting, group work, games in which all libidinal investment is banished, bodily hygiene, and so on. So in a way that is both individual and collective, the person reaches a state of clearing "the conscience," going hand in hand with passivity and the neutralization of the forces of the body.

Obedience is therefore not the result of a discourse, of the force of its conviction. But, on the contrary, it is the strength of submission that develops on the basis of the void in which the member is immersed: he or she emerges to obey; they find a calling in obedience.

The structure of the sect can be imagined as enclosure in a specific place, in the manner of the cure in traditional communities where the sick person is isolated in a sacred space. Renunciation is accompanied by social enclosure. A space is thus created that enfolds all those involved in renunciation (not just the sick person, or the sick person and the therapist). But, the aim of the sect is not to cure someone and return them to normal life, but to take them away forever. It is a matter of grouping this set of people who have made the vow of renunciation into a "society" (which in fact disowns society). And since the ideology of the sect preaches renunciation in the first place, rejecting the world as false and illusory, the sectarian group will try to structure itself according to the "truth." What does this mean? That the relations between the members of the group, and the rites and "institutions" it creates for itself, must not pass through or be based in ordinary symbolic mediations; that no screen of this type should obscure the relation between words and acts, between what one thinks or what one says or does; that between the subjective feeling of truth and its objective evidence there will be no hiatus, rather a total agreement. How can this type of structuring work in a group, unless it is by eliminating all possibility of individual conflict, creating unanimity of will and desire? By at least eliciting passive consensus, or a collective agreement that engenders complete obedience. Obedience to what? To the truth (and the leader who incarnates it); to the text of truth that tells you how to behave, how to live so that all lies are eliminated from human relations.

All this is possible because of renunciation and enclosure, and initially because of the practices that aim to cut one off from the world. Thus an energy is released that remains floating, without anchor, as long as the text of truth is not there to direct its flux. This would be more or less how one could summarize the logic of the sect's discourse of truth. I renounce the world because nothing in the world helps the path to freedom and access to truth; on the contrary, everything there is a hindrance, because the meaning of everything is illusory; and since all discourse—all positive discourse—is condemned to utter false meanings about things in the world, the only true discourse is my own. In other words, the discourse of truth resembles that of a negative theology. It does not tell the truth because it is not able to be told; it says one cannot tell the truth, and that that is the truth. In this way a circle is closed, a circular discourse that speaks only to deny, to say: the truth is neither this, nor this . . . no sign. The world, reality on the outside of the sect, becomes everything that has to be denied. And it is this discourse that will "hook" the floating energy of the members.

It will hook them through the intermediary of their bodies. Since nothing that is said or sayable is true (except for the discourse that says this), since the rule of truth and transparency of the sect wants there to be absolute agreement between speech and act, then each completed act must reflect and become the incarnated truth of the text. Here in these moves there is a fundamental ambivalence, which serves the aims of the sect perfectly. On the one hand the members will work, doing extremely laborious tasks, and all that is put in the category of the inessential, since it is still a kind of "sign"; and on the other hand, in the sect's own religious or esoteric rites the body shows the presence of the truth. The body speaks in place of the sign (speech); the body is transformed into a living language, an incarnated signified of the truth of the text. In the same way that sick people, thanks to therapeutic trances, transform their bodies into the "language of symptoms," members of sects offer their bodies for the text of truth to expropriate. The rites make their bodies exhibit "true signs" (not visible in the text). In this way a believing body is constructed. It does not work as an infralangauge, but as the presence of the truth of the metalanguage; it is only a relay for this major truth and makes up a ring with the other individual bodies. The discourse of truth is uttered by a chain of bodies, a chain of symptoms that have become language and truth. Unlike curing, in which this process only lasts a moment, here it changes into a structure and guarantees the links of the group.

The text of truth always has someone to utter it and to interpret it (or produce it): only he or she knows the hidden meaning of the words. This person will have the status of leader, and will possess authority and power. A social group is formed, founded on a despotic relationship of power, where the mechanisms of voluntary slavery are out in the open. The power contract works full bore because it is inversed. Nothing is asked; everyone believes they are only giving. The relation of group member to the leader is one of pure donation. He or she gives over everything, completely, even to the point of sacrifice; family and homeland are abandoned, all of one's resources are handed over to the sect. Members work to the point of exhaustion; in any case work indicates yet another sign, it has no value, truth is not there, and since one is working for truth, it has a maximum value. Everything is given to truth so that truth will arrive. The power contract comes to its final conclusion: obedience is perceived as commandment, servility as the supreme value of freedom. One works in order for work not to count, to give it up. One acts for the production of truth, to protect the sect, in other words to maintain the conditions that push ahead the work of maintenance. The circle of meaning is closed, thanks to the docile bodies asking for more. The body does not close the meaning, it does not close anything, it is only a signified of the chain that travels through the bodies. It is the set of the circle of bodies that enchains it, it is its identification with this set (which is the despotic body) that makes it believe it possesses total meaning. Under these conditions, the surplus value of the power collected by the leader is, in a manner of speaking, maximized, absolute.

Because forces are liberated, and because they are only attached to manifestations whose meaning is absorbed by the supreme signifier (the truth), which has no meaning other than that of denying all signs and therefore these "manifestations," energy is produced and reproduced for the negations of these signs and the confirmation of this discourse until the bodies can take no more, and this energy is constantly solicited by the members' desire for truth.

In summary: (1) sects presuppose a closed "imaginary" space, an enclosure. (2) The enclosure allows for the normal reversal of the signs and forces, in the same way as therapeutic processes. The sect's social structure is like the result of a freezing of this exceptional moment, and its transformation into a permanent state of affairs. (3) The formation of sects throws light on the mechanisms whereby certain despotic powers come about, built on the "desire to obey": the surplus value is absolute here, and each act on the part of the leader (a word, laws, an idea) only adds a link to the discourse of truth. This is why they receive immediate conversion from their subjects.

What is the real mechanism for the formation of a sect? It is formed by a Manichaean division between inside and outside, each completely valorized and devalorized respectively; division between the "chosen" and the others, often identified with persecutors. This all begins to look like the structure of the discourse of paranoia. Forces, because they are not worked by mediating devices, only connecting to acts that have the sole aim of releasing more energy, are taken to be laws: in sects, fanaticism is de rigueur. And, instead of producing meaning, power homogenizes the diverse meanings of the world. Each member is the same as the others, their "less meaning" only reinforces the "more meaning" power has. Repression is redundant.

This mechanism is at play in certain types of fascism, in Stalinism, and in secret societies. The individual loses identity and singularity. Should one "save" him from what he believes is his freedom and is really only his prison? Even putting the problem in this way,[15] one has to be aware of the fact that the sectarian group (or any power of this type) can only survive through proliferation, in extending their territory over more and more members. It is their main defense against the outside, which is assailing them and from which they want to escape: absorbing endlessly, gathering into their bosom all that threatens (and the outside is always there, insistent and inexhaustible) their truth and their power, or their very

existence. The relation to the outside is a double one; passive in the sense of para-
noid persecution, active in the sense of aggressive proselytizing. This is in their
logic of enclosure and redundant power: imperialism is their vocation.

Trained in this way, bodies will be condemned to the everlasting
repetition of the rite of conformity to the supreme signifier. From this moment on
they will try to incarnate themselves, in other words to bend themselves to the rule
that will lead them to "appear," in their flesh as the pure presence of the supreme
and despotic signifier. This is the method that Christianity teaches, in the mystery
of the Eucharist, or any practice that, as in Buddhism, aims to reproduce in the human
body the "glorious body" of the Buddha—it is always the presence of the supreme
Meaning which must be incarnated.

What happened in this passage from traditional regimes of signs
to this new despotic regime? Let us say that with history, a certain presence of bodies in themselves is lost, because the presence of the world in singular bodies has
disappeared. And history inaugurates the mad chase for this presence of the world
in bodies and bodies in themselves. This is also the function of the infralanguage
that has been dislocated. The translator now being—in the multiple aspects of life—
a Signifier, the singular body no longer has to deploy its spatial exfoliations to be
cured, to translate, to inhabit space. A part of this body space is taken from it by the
multiple social marking apparatuses that arise with the development of the history
of the State, and that, under another mode of functioning, try to carry out identical
functions while at the same time feeding off the passivity of the body.[16]

From this point the search will take people toward representation and incarnation. Bodies no longer having symbolic value (they are decoded)
will be used to make meaning emerge; they will be filled with absolute value as soon
as this Presence is attained. In this way they will alternate between an empty value
(before integration into the domain of the supreme signifier) and a full value. The
despotic signifier becomes the sole referent for the value of everything (a little like
"general equivalent" money in Marxist political economy). It absorbs all the meaning of the other signs that find themselves affected by a lack when it comes to Meaning. Transcendence is thus fixed in its dispersal from signs, because, whether it is a
matter of God, a Law, or a Name, the supreme signifier never has any meaning; the
impossibility of giving it any is in any case the proof itself of the transcendent and
absolute nature of its meaning. This is its mode of functioning, its perverse way of
showing itself to be full while inflating other signs with lack. Its emptiness is the
condition for the presence of meaning (which is given in a Conscience, in a Soul, in
an ecstatic experience) and of the mastery of the body.

So here begins a new history of power; through the fixing of the floating signifier, its transformation into supreme signifier — into a despotic "index" regulating other systems of signs. The floating signifier no longer designates forces that circulate around the outside of codes, but forces that have been overcome, framed, and gathered up into bodies incarnate that are at the service of new formations of power. Those who have power — the founders of churches and states, priests, leaders — also have ways of training bodies, and in the eyes of those they dominate, they possess the knowledge that allows them to control and manipulate the forces now denoted/connoted by the supreme signifier: they transform these potencies into power over bodies.

And elsewhere, since the links that held together the members of the communal body have been broken, new means will be used to try to recreate them. Communication will happen through a single mediation, that of the body of the Presence (a "God") from whom the Word emerges, and that plays the part of the absolute transducer of all human utterance. So in this new regime of power, communication has to proceed via this surface of inscription, which implies the observation of certain rites, certain gestures, certain corporeal and spiritual constraints. In the case of religion, the true, moral, authentic relation between myself and the other will depend on the truth of the relation of each of us to God, that is, to the carrying out of religious duties. In the place of the "communal body" — and supposedly having the same cultural functions — arises the Law of the supreme signifier: from now on there will indeed be "castration" in the sense that Freud intended. At the point where traditional culture collapses — which was disseminated in signs and things, which was immanent in gestures and functions — religion, with its discourses, practices, community and power, takes the place of culture.[17]

In this way signs and the depth of bodies become serious things. Bodies conceal zones that are charged with transcendence, hiding the soul in regions that can only be reached through appropriate techniques. They have spiritual shadows as copies, or they are repeated in different ways of being with different physiologies (as in Tantrism, where the "vulgar" or physical body is accompanied by a causal body and a "subtle body," real but invisible, its physiology being as "subtle" as it is precise). Gods are in us, having ceased to be among us — does not the *Kula-narvatantra* say "the body is the temple of god"?[18] Separated bodies, separated from one another and from cosmic forces, close in on themselves and their laughter ceases. The most our bodies will be allowed is a little bodhisattva smile. It is also true that throughout the length and breadth of this history — but silently, without a "spiritual" outburst, in little traces, immediately washed away by the sands of time — we have never stopped laughing; laughing about this great masquerade, in drunken or mad bodies, or bodies so desperate to live that they made fun of death; among women or children understanding nothing of the seriousness of symbols, stubbornly communicated with things or bodies; or with the astonishment of someone, who, having seen a flagellation, manages to move away from the crowd and bursts out laughing.

S I X

The Body and the Voice

THE QUEST for presence has marked the history of Western philosophy. One could say that it is its metaphysics.[1] The Orient could be included in this, with one remarkable difference: the East has kept the body as the means of *direct* activity for the production of presence, while the West, from a given point in history, lost all visible links with the body. This is no doubt because the West evolved a civilization that, more than any other, diversified the means for exploiting energies of the body, using it for all sorts of social purposes, institutional or private, and at the same time, more than any other, lost the presence of the self in individual bodies and the communal body.

So every time there is a general movement that tries to renovate society—always at moments of the decline or disintegration of the former social totality, as, for instance, in the year 1000—prophets and revolutionaries expend their energies in the formation of a new collective "body." Here we are in the presence of the activation of "practices" designed to produce the presence of meaning, isomorphic with those which monks or ascetics use. The creation of incarnated energy and new surfaces of inscription for members of a collectivity basically reproduces the same process. Jesus, by breaking the bread and giving it to his disciples, saying "This is my body," confirms, at the same time, that he is affirming a new "union,"[2] his presence in the bodies of his disciples. And whether it is in the domain of the history of societies or that of mystical asceticism, the framing and the "filling up" of an empty floating signifier is always accompanied by the constitution of a new body—which inaugurates the process of the emergence of the presence of meaning.

The medium used in every case is the voice. There is something of a mystery here. How can the voice carry out the articulation between the body and meaning? (Or rather, in Husserlian terms, how can the voice be the medium capable of restoring the presence of the object in its very ideality?[3] This question will have to wait its turn, if it is formulated in terms of the body; that is, what operations does the body undergo—with the help of the voice—for such a question [about the ideality of a thought object] to be posed? A very specific point about the type of response to give to this question will be given later, with the analysis of the constitution of the anatomical object by Vesalius.)

The voice plays a decisive role in the production of the supreme signifier and, by this very means, of presence, and therefore of the body through which this presence is produced.

What happens with certain phenomena of "correspondence," or of "silent communication" between an audience and a speaker, for instance, or in a more general way between spectators and actors on the stage, between a singer and those in the concert hall? Everyone is aware that at a certain moment, if people are "turned on" (this metaphor is significant both in its meaning and in its motivation necessitated by the object it designates), a new entity is formed, a totality encompassing all the elements into a new unity. We will say (and this time nonmetaphorically; the reason will be clear) that in this way a new voice-producing body is constituted.

When Hitler spoke to thousands of Germans massed in a stadium, with an "electrifying" effect, his discourse was the means, for him, to build up in a few hours a new social body, which in turn spoke. The words of the Führer were then emanating from a unique "organism." How did Hitler succeed at this game?

This question has a broader scope. All politicians must be good orators. Why? Because it is a matter of convincing, of limiting the dispersion of meaning (which would be manifested by the scattering of the listeners, their diversity and noncohesion) to a single surface, from which point each utterance becomes the utterance of any of the listeners. It is a matter of producing collective speech, beginning with the enunciative subject, the orator.

If we imagine that we start with an auditorium with a million separate subjects, then the aim of the discourse is to make everyone stick together, a unanimity out of which something like a "collective will" would emerge. This implies the capture of the listener, to the extent that she will end up adopting the opinion of the speaker. Now this capture cannot take place without a *translation*. A complex procedure, since what is translated is not simply the initial opinion of the individual listening, but his deep motivations, her unconscious desires, and the like; and if the latter are in contradiction with the opinions being expressed, we would have to assume several translation operations — between the unconscious and the conscious of the listener and what appears on the "indicative" level on the part of the orator, and so on. What are the mechanisms for such a translation (because these multiple operations are carried out at the same time in the discourse of the politician)?

Let us pick up Husserl's terminology once again. Let us say that all discourse presupposes an "indicative" layer (made of bodily indices) and an "expressive" layer (language). When an orator speaks in public her discourse is also deployed on a level parallel to that of the words, a level that everyone understands. It is made up of gestures, physiognomical quirks, rhythms of silence, vocal intensities, and so on. It is through the role of these two layers in the speech of the orator that the translation will take place, moving (and capturing) the singular listener into a collective subject of enunciation.

Oratorical technique consists, initially, in arranging for the indicative layer to progressively take over from the expressive one. The message, which has to be got across, is not necessarily argued, the discourse is not addressing itself "to reason." The orator opens the indicative stratum toward the exterior; the rhythm, the timbre, and force of the voice are directed outward, appearing as the very meaning of what is being said, as the expression. So a first translation takes place. The indicative stratum becomes the expression of the expression. The message finds its ultimate argument in the fact that what signifies is that there is nothing to hide, since any "hidden motive," dissimulation, or lie (which is screened at the threshold of the indicative stratum and the expressive stratum) has lost its defense — the interior of words is on display.

But the opposite is also verifiable. If expression is now expressed only in the indicative, the indicative is *indicated* in the content of the message. Since the indicative is built on the expressive, it has become the criterion of sincerity, of the truth of the message (the orator's "call," her power of conviction). This works on the expressive layer, intensifying it on the message plane itself, which thus acquires a *hyperclarity*. Expression becomes full of transsemiotic overexpressive content; each utterance is the bearer of a global unquestionable statement, beyond its strict content. Now in the message there is *illumination*, which comes from the transformation of the content carried out by indicative cutting down on the expressive. The indicative is now dovetailed into the expressive, and vice versa. This is why rhetorical figures of speech are important in political discourse. For example, redundancy never seems to be empty, because it is supported by the transsemiotization of the message, by the hyperclarity that it carries.

This double translation has the effect of constructing a body for the voice, as an expressive-indicative ensemble, which is neither expression nor indication, but the *abstract figure* allowing free movement from one to the other. The indicative stratum becomes the form of meaning, and the expressive stratum becomes the form of the indices. Each takes the other's form. The message's meaning—multiple meaning that is not unified by the listeners—acquires a unique form, which is translated and, in a manner of speaking, folded over in the rhythmic continuity of the expressive stratum; and the perceptible configurations of corporeal indices (rhythms) are unified in the unique form of a single meaning for the message.

The translating agent is thus made up of the linkage between two devices: body and speech, voice and message, voice-speech. Speech becomes voice, voice becomes speech in this modality of the body without organs, which is the body of the voice.

How does the operator use this procedure to make the crowd follow him? The capture of the listener happens like this: once the double inversion of the indicative and expressive layers has been accomplished, all of the listener's resistive capacity comes up against the surface the orator is creating. As long as they have no chance of responding, the silent arguments the listeners would like to mount encounter the continuous wave of the speaker's discourse. Once "hooked," they cannot release themselves, since they are entering into the continual flux of the words of the orator. And everything that is indicative in it will find its expression in hyperclarity, the illumination that the message carries, transforming itself into hyperindication: the ecstasy of the crowd. This implies that the vocal body that the orator creates is a collective body. The process of double inversion of indication and expression will also play a part in the leader-audience relation in a complex way. As long as listeners' expression cannot be expressed, they will find their translation more easily in the leader's *indicative*, and the latter will know immediately how to translate the listeners' unsaid; their impotence to speak (back to the orator) will be transformed into power when they see (and integrate themselves in) the effect of the indicative breaking down the expressive: vocal emphasis, sincere tones, the reversion of the (unconscious) corporeal interior onto the exterior of the words heard. All this ends up creating a unique discourse, made out of "appeals" and "responses," out of silent demands on the part of the audience and indicative-expressive reactions coming from the orator. A collective vocal ensemble emerges.

The example of Hitler is revealing on this point. He managed to transfer the whole indicative layer onto the level of the voice before superimposing it on the expressive layer. He stopped having any particular body when he spoke (with its organs, a subjectivity) in order to become a *vocal ensemble* (*bloc de voix*), which transmitted its indicative message all the more forcefully to the extent that National Socialist jargon was intensifying the expressive side. His body passed entirely into voice, he was thus able to induce states of intensity into the Germans who were listening via the simple manipulation of the voice. What went on between them and him—and in a more general way what goes on between any orator and his or her audience—amounted to adaptation, bit by bit; progressive conformity of "responses" to "demands," special respiration, a single rhythm, a single collective body. Once united, this body can produce collective statements—which, in fact, first came from Hitler. This technique of crowd manipulation requires certain conditions, especially from the expressive side of discourse, which must use a special redundancy. But above all it is the body of the voice that creates the unification of the group of listeners. In the beginning there is a multiplicity of listeners, at the end a collective enunciative subject, a sole proclaimed and accepted conclusion. Given the imposition of the indicative on the expressive and vice versa, the conclusion of the message *is reflected back onto* the surface thus formed, in a manner such that the listeners' individual inscriptions on this body imply that they share the same aim.[4]

So the action of the voice does not encounter obstacles, and the indicative side can appear and enter into communication with its complementary dimension among the listeners. In the ecstatic vibration of the National Socialist body composed of tens of thousands of Germans speaking in Hitler's voice, Hitler brought about the "miracle" of presence that Meaning had heralded. There, in the stadium, at that moment, under the lights and flags, the ritual process abolished all signs, all gaps between ideology and reality, in the incarnate presence of the Third Reich.

In order for such phenomena to become possible, the voice has to entertain a special relationship with the body, a relation that oriental techniques of meditation (especially yoga) have long recognized in the importance that they attribute to breathing exercises and control of the breath, *prânâyâmâ*.

Husserl attributed special properties (among other "signifying substances") to the voice. One, which he called the "pure self-affection" of the subject, was the subject speaking and hearing itself speak at the same time. Husserl took advantage of this privilege of the voice, of the *phone*, in order to exclude the mundane and the body from the presence of the ideality of the object: "As pure self-affection, the activity of hearing oneself speak seems to be reduced to the interior surface of the body itself; it seems, in its phenomenality, to be able to deliver itself from exteriority to interiority, to this interior space where we hold our experience or our image of our own bodies."[5] Hearing oneself speak would be an act of "absolute reduction" of space, putting the subject in immediate contact with herself and the object thought about. In the soliloquy of "hearing oneself speak," subjectivity, not coming out of itself, discovers the presence of the object.

One fact comes out of this analysis. The subject hears himself. The I speaking hears himself say "I." From here the possibility of reduplication of articulated speech emerges, therefore of metalanguage. But, in one way, one can see in the result of Husserl's analysis the very presence of what he wanted to exclude, the body. Obviously, the reduplication of *I*, the proximity of self to self, can be understood in this reduplication as the condition for the pure presence of the object to consciousness. The subject hears itself as mediated by the body, and it is in the infinitesimal interval separating the speaking and hearing subjects that this object places itself. But there is something else. Doesn't this reduplication of the subject itself reduplicate the fact that the body can think about itself and take itself as its own object? This follows from the fact that the forms taken in the different reduplications of the subject listening to itself speak will be isomorphic with the reflections of the body on itself, the first reduplications carrying with them (obviously with the evaporation of the body) the distant trace of the presence of the body.

If this is the case, the reduction of the space and of the experience of the body itself in the phenomenon of "listening to oneself speak" can be assimilated to an "infoliation" of the space of the body. Its paths will follow, against the grain, the lineaments of the paths of exfoliation. This seems so true that "listening to oneself speak" is not the "pure" autoaffection that Husserl talked about, but also an experience. There are multiple modalities of "listening to oneself speak" that presuppose diverse infoliations (listening to oneself speak in a murmur, in the strangeness of self to self, and so on).

This ability of the body to reflect on itself and transpose its capacity for exfoliation onto another plane can be noted in the breath, which is more primitive than the voice and is the basic stratum and condition for language.

What is a body? It is speaking respiration. Respiration, breath, *pneûma* — these carry the unity of continuity in time, but not yet the unified spatialization of this continuity. As long as breath is not seen as anything other than in its "indicative" light, it is only the manifestation of corporeal rhythms superimposed on the temporal plane. But being a permanent mediation, a modulating pathway, between the interior and exterior of the body, it contains in itself the very possibility of expression (meaning). Any rhythmic expression, like rapid speech or hesitation, which reverberates there, is made possible, as such, by this property of the breath as a passage. It is found at the hinge of revealed articulation (index)/expression (meaning). Nevertheless, this "mediation" should not be understood as (for example) allowing meaning to manifest itself or even (as Husserl seems to think), at the indicative layer of language, to find its full flowering in expression. On the contrary, not only does it demonstrate the intensities of the body, but it constitutes them as *expressions*. In allowing their emergence toward the exterior of the body, it constitutes them as such, which is to say that there is no expressive sense before its exteriorization, but that the pathway from inside to outside constitutes expression as meaning fully expressed.

It is in this way that breath is set up as a sort of directive principle of bodily rhythms. Because it has something to do with the beginnings of expression on the inside, expression reacts over the entire indicative layer of meaning—and therefore on the body, such that breath—and voice—appears as that which makes up the body as an articulated totality in time. Breath is what organizes a spatial exfoliation in a specific form (given in time). Because it "hears itself speak"—that is, because the fact of "hearing oneself" reorganizes into a whole certain sounds (which form a whole in themselves) for the subject—the human body constitutes itself as a specific totality, which, in its own physiology, is not reduced to a single living material. The body is thus, in a manner of speaking, self-meaning. This means that in its very "organicness," in its being-one, it is differentiated from other organic unities. Because it speaks about its meaning (not to be confused with the meaning of life, or one's life)—and hears itself—we live our bodies in an immediate "nonthetic," unquestionable presence. There is therefore a unity of lived meaning that is not thought, that has no object. Infralanguage presupposes a self-meaning body that constitutes itself through the effect of the voice.

In any case, it is in this regard that the "body" is always used as a specific metaphor when one wants to characterize a certain type of organization of the totality linking different parts—such as the "body of doctors," the "body of dancers at the Opera," the "political body," or the "social body."[6] These "bodies" speak, and in speaking say that they are unities of "spontaneous" meaning, organized in a cohesion extending beyond any uttered meaning, resulting in a double transfusion where life passes into meaning in such a way that the meaning sets itself up as just as unquestionable and immanent as life, and where meaning, impregnating life, brings life into a total self-presence, without separation or transcendence. The body, through its voice, contains this unity of life and meaning.

Nevertheless, when such totalities are called "bodies," the will to add the factor of cohesion, which they don't necessarily have, is put into play. The "body of troops"[7] is not composed of united parts as a human body is, but one wants it to seem to be.

There is a trick happening here, because this disciplined group—with bodies subjected to very rigid rules—has no voice of its own, does not produce collective utterances, it only obeys commands. It is characteristic of the body of the modern army not to speak, unlike tribal warriors and ancient armies, for whom every element contributed (even if just by way of yells and chants) to the collective organization of the self-meaning totality.

Today war requires a particularly fascist discipline of the body. Just as Hitler manipulated crowds by breathing into them the cohesion of corporeal rhythms, military order induces in soldiers automatic and synchronous movements. Where the body was "hearing itself" because it spoke, now, once integrated into the army, it only hears the massive articulation of a body that is basically materialist and crude. Soldiers who obey orders to grab rifles and aim hear their bodies, not their voices. They hear the abrupt sequence of their movements in the echo of the commandant's order; their silent movements reverberate the double deadening of the voice that requires them to pass the weapon to the left. They can thus give themselves the illusion of a personal voice, synchronizing their movements to the rhythm of the voice; the noise of steps, hands on weapons, stocks hitting the ground replying to and extending the order given by the voice. The body "makes a body" with the voice, it hears itself (in the noise of its "articulations") by listening to the other's orders. So war would be easy, because the noise of guns, bursts of machine-gun fire, bomb blasts, are already, in advance, in the soldier's bodies—the destruction of all bodies and meaning responds to this voice now.

It is a major perversion to make a submitted, passive body that has had all speech taken away from it leap into action in a highly dynamic way. A particularly military perversion, this force of the dominated body hides the interiorized violence of the voice that was silenced. Despite being unable to speak and be heard, the soldier will henceforth speak with his killer body, in the deafened after-image of the clamorous, yelled, vociferous disciplinary orders of all the leaders.

Yet these bodies prepared for war and massacre also carry a luminous, mystical and quasi-jubilatory surface. In times of peace, while they parade to the sounds of military fanfare, they really seem to make up a single body. Homogenized and rendered invulnerable with their sparkling uniforms and flamboyant helmets (like those of the English Dragons), they march around and go through their paces, battalions joining and separating, suddenly falling apart, only to join up again all the more effectively. They perform a smooth dance with the articulations of this huge body, they play a gratuitous and inoffensive game; military music takes the place of voices, the better to create the illusion of a collective body. Nevertheless in this body, and in the individual bodies, is inscribed the possibility—the profession—of murder.

S E V E N

The Body in Penal Settlements

ALL DOCTRINES concerning salvation take place within the logic that controls despotic regimes of signs. They remain attempts toward transcendental discourses for which "spirituality" can only be founded on the exploitation of bodily energies—even if, as in the case of state religions, they tend toward the opposite aim.

But salvation is only set up as an aim to be achieved when daily experience is that of irreparable loss, nothingness, and death. This implies a specific temporality—social time and individual duration have stopped being recuperated in the reiteration of the same cycles. The body is no longer acting at the center of the metaphorization of things, and historical time has started to slip away.

This is the process that Kafka takes us through in *In the Penal Settlement*.[1] This short story is not just prophetic. It reveals to us the mechanisms presiding over disciplinary methods when they make use of a supreme signifier, and how oppression that depends on transcendence (Justice in this case) finds its echo in obedient bodies—all those involved, like the officer, like the story's readers—who expect an ecstatic redemption from the cruelty.

Kafka describes yet another machine that produces a metamorphosis of the body. This machine administers punishment to the prisoners who have been condemned by the officer who, among other things, is the the judge, jury, and the person in charge of the machine. The punishment is always the same thing: the prisoner is attached to a "Bed," then a Harrow engraves "the sentence on the skin of the guilty"—for instance, "Honour thy Superiors." The Harrow makes its marks according to the models designed by the machine's inventor; they are illegible because the letters are so overelaborate and elongated with arabesques. Only this esoteric and hermetic language is capable of carrying Meaning.

Before starting the execution, the officer busies himself endlessly, an activity resembling an amorous ritual. Everything in the machine has to be meticulously arranged, the cogs, the harrow's points, the springs, as if the slightest hitch, the minimal "dirtiness" ("its one drawback is that it gets so messy," says the officer,[2] with the blood of the victim), threatens its workings. The machine itself has its bodily techniques, or rather, it is the incarnation of the *practical rule* that guides the mediation between the sacred text and the body. Is it not in the machine that the signs of the sacred code are inscribed, initially in "sleeping," then in an active mode (the piece of paper with the sentence to be engraved is placed in the Designer)? Is it not its "physiology" (its very elaborate workings) that makes the energy (pain) of the body of the victim work, which wakes him in the end to the revelation of the presence of Meaning (of Justice)?

Can you follow it? The Harrow is beginning to write; when it finishes the first draft of the inscription on the back, the layer of cotton-wool begins to roll and slowly turns the body over, to give the Harrow fresh space for writing. Meanwhile the raw part that has been written only lies on the cotton-wool, which is specially prepared to staunch the bleeding and so makes all ready for a new deepening of the script. Then these teeth at the edge of the Harrow, as the body turns farther round, tear the cotton-wool away from the wounds, throw it into the grave and there is more work for the Harrow. So it keeps on writing deeper and deeper for the whole twelve hours. The first six hours the condemned man stays alive almost as before, he suffers only pain. After two hours the felt gag is taken away, for he has no longer strength to scream. Here, into this electrically heated basin at the head of the Bed, some warm rice-pap is poured, from which the man, if he feels like it, can take as much as his tongue can lap. Not one of them ever misses the chance. I can remember none, and my experience is extensive. Only about the sixth hour does the man lose all desire to eat. I usually kneel down here at that moment and observe this phenomenon. The man rarely swallows his last mouthful, he only rolls it around in his mouth and spits it out into the grave. I have to duck just then or he would spit it into my face. But how quiet he grows at just about the sixth hour! Enlightenment comes to the most dull-witted. It begins around the eyes. From there it radiates. A moment that might tempt one to get under the Harrow with him. Nothing more happens after that, the man only begins to understand the inscription, he purses his mouth as if he were listening. You have seen how difficult it is to decipher the script with one's eyes; but our man deciphers it with his wounds. To be sure, that is a hard task; he needs six hours to accomplish it. By that time the harrow has pierced him quite through and casts him into the grave, where he pitches down upon the blood and water and the cotton-wool. Then the judgement has been fulfilled, and we, the soldier and I, bury him.[3]

Here the transformation of energy is carried out through suffering; and at the moment of "turning over" that heralds beatitude, the whole body becomes self-present in the presence of the revealed meaning. How else can we understand this terrible image of a body that "deciphers the writing with its wounds"? And yet this revelation is not just — or especially not — individual. Presence is manifested by a mark, a trace, scarcely a sign: a radiance, a smile, an expression of happiness. How do the spectators know that the man has grasped the meaning of the paragraph that the harrow has engraved on his skin? Because the mode of revelation of presence is definitely not individual, it is collective. The body that is radiant in suffering only reads the meaning of the law because for us it is the obvious writing of presence; what the prisoner is for himself is only translated by the discourse of the officer and the public. His experience is thus transmissible, because his incommunicability constitutes the essential link of the new community of the faithful (commandant, inventor of the machine, new Messiah). One knows therefore through an esoteric knowledge: not being able to say it (not knowing how to say it or what to say), and to make the body speak in silence, this is the communication that everyone crowding around the machine wants: "Many did not care to watch it but lay with closed eyes in the sand; they all knew; now Justice is being done. In the silence one heard nothing but the condemned man's sighs."[4]

The aim of the machine is to produce the signs of this ravishment, "the look of transfiguration on the face of the sufferer,"[5] these sighs that work like a collective voice. It is in the observer that the sign on the body of the other becomes the mark of happiness. The new surface of inscription, the new collective body holds itself at this distance and in this game of reflexions and mirrors, between the sign on the body of another and my belief in the possibility of a presence in my own body becoming a sign for the belief of yet another: there where the gap between the empty sign and the ecstatic experience overflows ("How we all absorbed the look of transfiguration on the face of the sufferer,"[6] in this movement that makes one body into the relay for another body—in the repetition of executions, festivals, public rituals.

This explains why, when this collective chain runs the risk of breaking once and for all—because the new commandant wants to prohibit the use of the machine in the penal settlement—and the officer, the last man to still defend the old methods, decides to bring things to a head by subjecting himself to the transfiguration, the machine goes wrong: "the Harrow was not writing, it was only jabbing. . . . This was no exquisite torture such as the officer desired, this was plain murder."[7] Because there was no one left to keep up the link with the officer, it seemed that this job should have fallen to the explorer. (Did the officer not ask him, before committing suicide, to take his place? "Then the time has come," he said at last and suddenly looked at the explorer with bright eyes that held some challenge, some appeal for cooperation";[8] "he had a feeling that he must now stand by the officer.")[9]

Failure of the metamorphosis of the body, end of one epoch, beginning of a new regime of signs. In the meantime, those nostalgic for the supreme signifier become silent and gather around an epitaph:

> Here rests the old Commandant. His adherents, who must now be name-less, have dug this grave and set up this stone. There is a prophecy that after a certain number of years the Commandant will rise again and lead his ad-herents from this house to recover the colony. Have faith and wait.[10]

In this rediscovered Messianism, they hope to embrace and recuperate history.

Why this horror? Why this nausea that suddenly invades our *thoughts*? The punishment that the machine metes out transforms justice into torture, but why does Kafka's story carry in itself a sort of enigmatic revelation that overwhelms us? What perverse intention pushed the old commandant to want to build an institution, a whole society (colony) around a torture machine?

Nevertheless his aim seemed quite praiseworthy; what else was he looking for, except to correct divergences from justice with a system that was proportionally exact, that made the punishment fit the crime without the slightest lack of correspondence? The old commandant succeeded in inventing what no society has been able to achieve, a judiciary device that eliminated subjectivity (therefore error and miscarriage) in the appreciation of crime, such that an absolutely just verdict could be delivered.

His idea was simple and brilliant. It was not necessary to separate the scale of crimes from that of punishments; subjective judgment was not to be allowed to slide between the two, judgment that, in a natural movement, classes the seriousness of the former according to the weight of the latter, thus inhibiting any protest that might claim that a given punishment is too heavy for a given crime.

To do this one has to make punishment emerge "spontaneously" from the verdict, it has to be inextricably linked with it. The punishment will no longer depend on the quality of the crime and of its situation in the hierarchy of penal transgressions; in a word, it will no longer be linked with the signification of the crime—which is always so aleatory, so arbitrary, so relative to all social and historical conditions. But if the punishment can no longer be attached to the meaning of the crime, how can it be specified so that it can in fact be made appropriate for each case? In relating it directly to the written sign of its meaning, to the graphic formula of the sentence, to the letters and the words "Honour thy Superiors" or "Be Just." The "reading" of these sentences is transformed into pain for the condemned man. The pain remains therefore quite singular, varying according to the length of the sentence and the arabesques of the calligraphy.

So it is a system of correspondences that the old commandant was looking for. Where did the necessity to invent such a system come from? The machine relates writing and the body in such a way that the meaning (of the judgment) is revealed in a corporeal ecstasy, and not in a mental reading. The Harrow, tearing skin and flesh to inscribe its formula, will bring about the revelation of meaning in an ecstatic manner, through an absolute presence, incarnated in the same body that suffered. So there is something that might *escape* in this conjunction of meaning and the body. We have already pinpointed this thing: the injustice inherent in all justice that flows from a power that is there to maintain it. It appears in the subjectivity of the evaluation of verdicts, in the eventual lack of consensus that surrounds all judgments, and finally in the accused's refusal to accept the punishment. When justice serves power, there are always multiple risks that meaning will *escape*, risks therefore coming from forces that are put into circulation outside the domain of state control.

In fact, the penal settlement presupposes a State and a very specific type of power. Kafka writes about the explorer: "He was neither a member of the penal colony nor a citizen of the State to which it belonged" (181). And the officer, when he wants to recruit his visitor to the cause, says to him: "You are conditioned by European ways of thought, perhaps you object on principle to capital punishment in general" (185) and sees him as "a famous Western investigator, sent out to study criminal procedure in all parts of the world" (186). These vague indications make us think of an "oriental" despotic power (or "colonial," exercised, in this case, by some local potentate), which would not be incarnated in a monarchy, but which would have taken the form of a republic (of which one can be a "citizen"). Bringing these two principles together is an apparent antinomy, but the existence of certain despotic republics in the twentieth century only makes *In the Penal Settlement* all that much more prophetic; the story appeared in 1919.

I feel this registers the historical conjuncture of the old commandant's grand plan: to reconcile a "liberal," "democratic" political system with an institutional power of uncontestable and uncontested authority, to which all citizens belong without restriction—and which cannot be found (at least in its "ideal" form) except in totalitarian systems. Certainly, the penal colony belongs to a state where powers are shared, at the moment the explorer gets there ("Although he [the new commandant] is powerful enough to take measures against me, he doesn't dare do it yet");[11] but before, the concentration of power—for some, perhaps not for all—was normal:

> "Did he [the old commandant] combine everything in himself, then? Was he soldier, judge, mechanic, chemist and draughtsman?"
> "Indeed he was," said the officer, nodding assent, with a remote, glassy look.[12]

The concentration of power is countered by a structure of correspondences set in motion by the judiciary apparatus. The convergence of all power in a single man has the advantage over the democratic system of stopping the leakage of meaning, obstructing the vocation of politics, which is to devastate the symbolic. By giving the authority principle a stable and absolute symbolic meaning—which could only be obtained by unifying power—it is stabilized and enclosed. The political principle of the modern liberal state, freedom, introduces into the social domain a factor that overturns the foundations of law[13] and the legislative activity of parliaments aiming to reduce injustice, and only broadens the field where another factor comes in to disintegrate traditional symbolic structures, the economy. The world where "European ideas" (no doubt freedom and democracy) were born threatens the judiciary system of the penal settlement, and we can assume that it is going to destroy not only the "old" world, but also the old commandant's wonderful machine. This is the same world where politics and the economy work in concert, enlarging the social surface of freedom, breaking family, religious, moral, and cultural ties. A completely new type of political power is thus preparing itself on the ruins of traditional symbolic structures—and directly, imposing its state domination on traditional society, without going through the "monarchic" stage, which delays the disappearance of the latter.

It is at the hinge of these two types of society and power that the judicial regime of the *Penal Settlement* is located. Witness of the maintenance of despotic power in the heart of a republic, this regime accumulates overdetermined personal authority, and it also has this already modern element, a normal part of the law of liberal democratic societies that is positive, written, and draws no legitimacy from any divine or (individual) human word. The tension, if not the opposition in principle, between the quasi-religious authority of the old commandant — thought to be a "Messiah"[14] — and the authority that only emanates from the "nation" (as democratic constitutions postulate it) in the modern republic is here resolved through the ingenious process of dispensing punishment. In fact, positive law also contains in itself the principle of its negation and its destruction. Law, because it is written, that is, only existing as written, only gets its legitimacy from the ultimate legitimacy of the representative organ of the nation, the constituted assembly, and because the statements of the assembly only exist as written, consigned on paper, the writing of the law creates the nation as a subject (based on the vote that completes the "work of the parliament") — how else would it speak, with what voice, what body, what mouth? It is therefore not through some historic contingency that the nation speaks its law through written laws, but because it is the only way it has of affirming its existence and its authority. This necessity has another side. If writing, as is the case here, is not the simple reproduction of a voice, the words of a subject, if it emerges of its own accord, so to speak, if it is not accompanied by the presence of a speaker or draughtsperson, it ends up making them abstract, distant and vulnerable. It is sufficient then that a more intense presence arise in the course of history — in a revolt or revolution — for the traditional law and the old principle of authority to be contested, denied, swept away. Others will claim they are more representative of the nation and will draw up other laws, other constitutions. (Those which followed the French revolution at an accelerating pace are a good illustration of this process.)

Isn't this also what happened after the death of Kafka's old commandant? Yet he had foreseen the dangers of writing: he had to be incarnated, given a subject. But since this State was a republic — the functions of the old commandant did not include legislative power — where can the meaning of the law be incarnated? How can it be given the authority of the whole nation and the invulnerability it needs to survive the vicissitudes of historical time? In the very principle of democracy, in the consensus of all the people. In the event, in that of the principle stakeholders, the accused. The accused will be made to own the law they are submitted to. This is the whole process of the production of presence based on the torture the machine installs.

The brilliance of the commandant was thus able to fend off all threats. First the one that opened the arbitrariness of subjective interpretations of legal formulas, then that which sees the law become cut loose from the thread of time, from its main founder, from the initial act that legitimates it. These two dangers relate to the specific nature of positive law. It is a written law that only exists because of the act that makes it such. So it is a question of reviving writing, giving it back the originary presence from which it was removed. The machine manages to do this, by making punishment flow from the very writing of the law, and in inscribing its meaning in the body of the accused.

By setting up foolproof justice as his aim, the old commandant wants to guarantee the harmonious functioning of the whole social edifice. Kafka describes this clearly when he talks of a society "grouped around the machine," or when he indicates that "the organisation of the whole penal settlement is his [the old commandant's] work,"[15] a colony whose calendar is dotted with executions—holidays with "fanfares" and crowds of people—and finally he notes the foundation role of this mythical time when everything worked perfectly: "I know it is impossible to make those days credible now."[16] "Now" everything is going badly, all sorts of glitches are stopping the machine from dispensing justice without error; this certainly seems to be a run-down period, caught in a kind of entropy that has spread its gloom across the settlement: "How different an execution was in the old days! A whole day before the ceremony the valley was packed with people; they all came only to look on; early in the morning."[17]

Entropy means running the risk of dying through a lack of meaning; on the other hand the time at the start of the settlement obeyed a sort of recurrent structure.

This is not yet historical time. But Kafka's story introduces us to the huge upheaval that history caused in human time. Because if the republic is liberty, liberty is time opened up in all directions. The old commandant opened social temporality to immediately close it again. In this sense, the two "moments" that the story refers to as its horizons—and that are often amalgamated—"go back" respectively to the threshold of the foundation of the (despotic) state and to the turning point of the installation of modern republics.

The first brings with it the traces of its past, after those happy days where the old commandant installed penitentiary order with his machine, and he found nothing better to manage it than a system of relations, a system that translates the nostalgia of an era that was no doubt more ancient, where the relations assured the permanence and the survival of the community while leaving the body the freedom to invent and produce the new things. There, symbols and things were at one; language itself was a symbolic act, therefore real, and was able to signify worldly things.

"Cyclical" time in traditional societies traced a spiral. Individual lives pass through the same processes of initiation into collective life, the body molds itself to (and supports) cultural norms; it is born and it dies, and each event relates to a mythical event, situating itself in an originary history that is the basis of human history. The spiral opens and turns back on itself. Each generation believes it lives differently from the former, while reiterating their beliefs. The structure of symbolic relations of all spatial elements and relations between diverse levels of the universe command the pace of time. Social time is molded on sidereal time, cycles of the moon and movements of the stars, and the latter relate to cultural myths—always in space. In this way the recurrent temporality of traditional societies is a product of the spatialization of time. Time passes, of course, and the far point of the spiral at the end of a turn marks the irreversible distance of all temporality, the loss, the toll of chance and entropy that affects any society. This is why permanent adjustment is necessary, brought about by the production of newness, more and more forces, and more and more symbols; but the same gestures and the same rites will reinvest this new content for the benefit of the reproduction of the same group.

The ripping apart of time that opens up the history of the West—henceforth things will be bit by bit detached from their meaning, and in consequence, from their symbolic context. A huge decontextualizing movement hit Europe around the fifteenth and sixteenth centuries. Everything turns backward: time is progressively freed from its nets, and ceasing to measure itself with human life and astral cycles, it tends to become the measure of all things. Now it is space that will be measured by time. Geometry becomes the language of the new objective temporality, both its criterion and its expression, all space will hereafter take its cue from geometry. The truth of the body, say the first theoreticians of perspective, like Alberti who was taken up by Leonardo, is in geometry. The meaning of representation depends on how faithful it is to the real, and faithfulness is determined by geometry. It is no longer the meaning of the represented image that gives value to the space that surrounds it, as in medieval iconography, but the contrary. Now the measure is definitely the measure of a distance, which is to say a time. All of space and nature that unveils itself and bodies are thus impregnated in time. They breathe in time, they live by exhaling time—and they fill up with death. (This extreme sensitivity toward death, which appeared in Europe toward the end of the fourteenth century, witnesses the discovery of the precariousness of time, a discovery that people had just made in their bodies). Later, much later, the imperialism of time would extend to all human activities, and would become the standard of value.

But always in a certain extension of symbolic relations. Even when scientific rationality was in full swing—toward the end of the nineteenth century—obscurities of "superstition" and religion would be rejected, because they thought they had found a new relational form; even when time is the measure of everything—prison time (value of punishment), work time (exchange value), survival time (value of life)—it will still constitute a sort of abstract pivot, a translator-writer of all the codes. Man cannot think without making things correspond to each other. This is the very condition of the existence of the body and of the immanent meaning that it brings with it.

The old commandant perfectly understood the system of correspondences that was aiming to reinject meaning into the body (from the law, in the absence of any suitable infralinguistic symbolic regulation). In inventing his machine he first of all set things up like those binary structures in ancient cultures:

$$\frac{\text{writing (paper)}}{\text{meaning (illegible)}} = \frac{\text{writing (on the skin)}}{\text{meaning (revealed)}}$$

Then, with the workings of the machine, he wrote the perfect circle of reduced temporality, imprisoned in the repetition of the same process, as shown in the accompanying diagram.

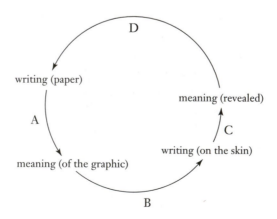

Here the machine carries out the function of exact translator of these successive transfers. In effect, the papers on which the sentences are written—identical to the formulas of broken laws—are illegible. Only the machine can "read" them, only it knows how to translate this "meaning" (in the calligraphy of the words) into a new writing and a new meaning that the accused can eventually read with his body. A perfect circle is formed when the final suffering (sequence D) delivers its meaning, its truth in writing, justifying it totally.

A reversal of roles: it is the machine that puts the various codes together, it is the machine that translates the significance of things (the law, therefore punishment, the trial, power, the whole state system) in/through the man's body. In taking on this function of code translator, it creates a circularity of time that stops meaning from escaping, wearing away or disappearing in decontextualization. How does it do this? In capturing the meaning that, if it is not being translated into other things, if it is not being symbolically transferred, is irretrievably lost in the asignification of time. There are two important breaks that inaugurate the possibility of this erosion, which is the very entropy of history: disjunction, already noted above, between the thing and the symbol, between the meaning and the sign; and the temporalization of time that historical time installs. These two "events" are clearly indicated in Kafka's story.

The first is marked by the old commandant's desire to give writing back its meaning. In the traditional symbolic system, the action of the body reiterates the coincidence between the sign and its meaning, especially through ritual. Writing opens up the threat of distance, it is the sign of a sign, speech. The latter, in this same traditional structure, was not just a system of signs, but also and above all a system of acts through which speech was made to come out of the body. Speech was made up of things, signs, and meanings, all at once—that is, an act and a symbol, intimately linked. In speech, the bodily relation between the sound and the signification is not at all arbitrary, as is evidenced in the energetico-semantic anatomies of traditional peoples. Speech is full of the potencies of the body (liver, entrails, stomach) and of the potencies of the thing named. Now, because writing is the representation of a representation, it contains the menace of an irreparable break between the signifier, which would become totally arbitrary, and the signified. The old commandant wants to prove that on the contrary, one cannot write (the law) without dire consequences. He will bring together, with the help of his machine, the two sides of the written sign. Making writing and representation, signifier and meaning, coincide, he will restore the dignity of action to the movement of this articulation—the machine that adapts itself perfectly to the body of the condemned man ("As you see, the shape of the harrow corresponds to the human form; here is the harrow for the torso, here are the harrows for the legs."[18] And everything in it is conceived like a *meaningful* system of absolute mechanical correspondences:

> Now listen! Both the Bed and the Designer have an electric battery each; the Bed needs one for itself, the Designer one for the Harrow. As soon as the man is strapped down, the Bed is set in motion. It quivers in minute, very rapid vibrations, both from side to side and up and down. You will have seen similar apparatus in hospitals; but in our Bed the movements are all precisely calculated; you see, they have to correspond very exactly to the movements of the Harrow. And the Harrow is the instrument for the actual execution of the sentence.[19]

How can it be otherwise, since they are conceived to do a job that is one of man's supreme destinies, the production of the presence of meaning? This machine is not just one among many, it is not part of a group of manufactured objects, it does not have a function that is written into a greater set of other functions carried out by other machines: it is not a functional object. It is its function to abolish all other functions, its meaning to short-circuit all other meaning, its truth to interrupt the interrogation about truth, to abolish doubt, to stop all reference. Nor is it the realization of the fantasy of the intelligent robot who turns against his creator — because it is totally obedient and escapes human control only in breaking down. It is a modern monster, coming about through the condensation of the meaning of history (of power) in a production of this very history. It is a spiritual object, which holds the key to the essence and the existence of humankind. Something like the "Body of God."

The machine's acts have another virtue, that of transforming time, to stop it in a way, by cutting off the hemorrhaging. The machine, and machines generally, incorporate time. Pulleys, wheels, pistons, rods — their mechanical movement reduces subjective and collective temporality to a homogeneous, quantitative time, by scanning and secreting a linear time. Time produced in this way differs profoundly from that of traditional or ancient societies. The actions of the body or the technical gestures of the artisan disappear and are replaced by programmed movements that are always identical. But for machines to be able to absorb time, there must already be in the social domain something like a temporality that has been stripped of its qualitative attributes, of its symbols, of its weighty spatiality. A neutralization, an asignification of time must already have been produced in the society in order for the machines to be able to appropriate time. And yet, from another angle, they are working this time, elaborating it, giving it a rhythm, so that the output is normalized, disciplined, ordered.

The special feature of the commandant's machine, and in this it is the opposite of most (say, industrial) machines, is that it *takes back* what is escaping from the time "output" in the social domain. Industrial machines "deterritorialize" (to use Gilles Deleuze's term), break recurrent time, insert themselves in a context where historical time opens more and more. In other words, where the meaning (of the object produced) escapes and calls for other meanings (other objects to be produced, other goods) in the future. Kafka's machine, on the other hand, is self-justificatory and self-sufficient.

Nevertheless, it seems that the aim of the old commandant was not attained, since the machine's recuperation of time did not stop the decline of the penal settlement. The machine works time in two ways, as we have just seen. On the one hand it temporalizes historical time, in breaking the loops of the spiral of traditional time; on the other hand it inserts this same historical temporality in a network of symbolic relations that does not itself symbolize time, but uses the fact that a machine has overcome it (through the synchronizations it establishes) to its advantage to make a set of relations (between writing and meaning) work, which would otherwise be very difficult to arrange.

Time obtained like this differs radically from that of traditional societies. It is a historical time, and this despite the efforts of the old commandant to establish a cyclical time. It is definitely historical because the ordeal of the torture ends fatally with the death of the prisoner.

As we have seen, the temporality of the penal colony plausibly presupposes a past where time had already been temporalized, ready to become historical, but still flat and neutral. The old commandant had put a stop to this tendency and made it into a *process* that he wanted to be symbolic, even initiatory, with his preparations, his stages, his ecstatic moments. Why does the tortured person end up being executed? Could we not imagine another judiciary device, another machine, which would limit itself to using torture to achieve the revelation of meaning—selectively punishing at the same time—and which would be the axis of the penitentiary society? Wouldn't the punishments then become identified with initiation rites? Condemned people could possibly "return" for another bout; this would already constitute a favorable support for creating symbolic relations; the stages of the "rite" could no doubt be aligned with other acts and other events in social life; the punishment would become a judicious and redemptive ritual, each member of the community possibly coming under its sway. But the fact that death is necessarily at the end of the process throws the latter out of society; death without rites, without salvation, accomplished in the form of a dirty corpse that is thrown into a ditch, there for the others, the spectators that feed on it.

Kafka invites us to recognize the mortifying aspects of this history, not because the punishment kills (which happens with justice in societies without history) but because it excludes death from the society of the living. In doing this it opens itself to infinite suffering, which cannot be recuperated from the flight of historical time. Yet the old commandant had thought of a trap for this exclusion; salvation would occur just *before* death, so there would be no more death. The body that the machine throws into the ditch is nothing, a cadaver. There is no under-value in diachrony, just as there is none in the system of "synchronic" correspondences; no loss in (and through) time, since there are only living people, there are no dead—no need for funerals.

Nevertheless, in excluding death, history introduces the possibility of radical exclusion of certain members from their own communities. A brutal and absurd exclusion, outside of any meaning or ritual. It is not escape, banishment, or ostracism, but the total dispossession of the self through death. Suddenly the penal settlement throws light on the modern death penalty with an unexpected starkness, this mechanical absurdity, this anti-institution that brings no real good to the accused. After he gets the ecstasy of truth, he dies like a dog. Why is this, since there is no redemptive rite? It is redemptive for those watching and remaining behind, because they are the only living. With his death taken away from him, the prisoner is doubly dispossessed; in life, since the death penalty is "unlivable" (having no power of deterrence—Kafka shows the prisoners to be ignorant of the fact that they are going to be punished); it does not modify any behavior, it always remains like an antimodel for existence, always beyond what one is doing—and yet there; and in death, since it cuts short life, which stops without further reference; a continuity (assured by a rite) can be taken up by those left alive. This is the modern death penalty stripped bare. It is a monstrous asocial institution that has no other function than that of allowing other institutions of power to continue working; it only enters these workings from the outside, guaranteeing the nothingness of death for some, so that the others (and their state) acquire the transparency of immortality: only the living live.

But this despotic power has its limits—it is mined from the inside by the history it would like to abolish and that it is obliged to secrete. Wanting to establish such absolute and close relationships to shore itself up against "freedom" ("European ideas"), it is led to the imposition of death to close this process of closure: to be perfect is to be a despot. But this is possible in excluding death and bringing in the death penalty; in other words, in fact, another remainder of asignificance, of temporalized time, a minimal act that escapes from the network of correspondences — an act that cannot be "translated" — and that, nevertheless, is sufficient to upset the network and inaugurate history. The decline of the settlement starts at its beginnings.

If at the end the machine breaks up, it is because there is too much coherence among all the elements of the judicial device, and it is even in an attempt to save the commandant's perfect life's work that the officer decides to suicide. But maybe his suicide takes on multiple significations. Apart from the proof of the absolute justice of the system (since even the judges undergo it) that would thus be carried out, the final suicidal act also has the status of an act of defiance, a final warning directed at the new power being put into place, and perhaps it is also the beginning of a martyrdom for the new messianic religion whose arrival the epitaph on the tomb of the old commandant predicts.

The death of the officer marked the end of the era in which the body was at the center of relations. The time of freedom will begin, and the body will undergo other manipulations.

7.1. On Écorchés.

The transfiguration of the prisoner involves turning the inside into an outside. With the expression of happiness during the torture, the painful interior is reabsorbed, shed into a transparency for those who see it. The observers see their own salvation in this delight, as in the times of public executions where the crowd enjoyed a sort of salvation through procuration, or one's own death adjourned. The sight of blood spurting from the neck of the beheaded empties the inside out of the spectator's body: the inside of the other's body revealed creates a surface without inside of my observing body, and the shadowy meaning of the death of the other, punctuated by the abrupt noise of the guillotine or the "splash" of Kafka's prisoner's body falling into the ditch, absorbs in its pure asignificant sonority the whole meaning of my death thus mastered, reduced. The metamorphosis is accomplished; the vulgar body of the prisoner dies, but he attains immortality since he is engraved on the surface of inscription of eternal Justice — his "death" will nourish eternity. In any case, this "sweet incomprehensible theft," is it not witness to some consolation received in exchange, does it not evoke some kind of ascension?

Nevertheless, the new regime of signs that the breakdown of the machine announces in the *Penal Settlement*, and that was starting to be formed in the Europe of the fifteenth century or thereabouts, on the level of scientific knowledge, will profoundly disturb the domination of a system tending to impose a supreme signifier.

This evolution is translated, in the iconography of the human body (or Christ's body) by remarkable changes, in particular by what pertains to the representation of the "inside." There is a whole world between the medieval Dead with their chests open and angels flying out toward heaven (or demons toward hell) and the *écorchés*[20] of the Renaissance. The first translate the idea of death as a passage and a transformation of the body; the latter inscribe it in a much more complex context.

Art historians generally classify the flayed under the category of "cruelty, a taste for the horrible, sadism, attraction to ugliness," which emerged at the end of the Middle Ages and reached its height in the sixteenth century. There is no doubt a relation between a painting like *The Three Ages of Woman and Death* by Hans Baldung Grien (c. 1484–1545) or sadistic representations of witches, like *The Old Witch* by Niklaus Manuel Deutsch (c. 1484–1530), or even *The Ugly Duchess* by Quentin Metsys (c. 1460–1530), and the flayed that Jan Stephan van Calcar, Titian's pupil, drew for Andreas Vesalius's book, *De Humanis Corporis Fabrica* (1543). The problem is that this relationship is not clear, because it is not always the same horror one is dealing with.

Let us take another example, which is also a classic from this period, Grünewald's Christ, from the Isenheim reredos.[21] This greenish-colored Christ is striking; almost in a state of putrefaction, it is pain incarnate. The Isenheim Christ would be a kind of *écorché*. Yet it is positioned at an opposite pole from those of Vesalius or Valverde. Their respective functions highlight their differences.

The Isenheim reredos was constructed with a precise intention. Destined to go to the Antonites convent in Alsace, it played a therapeutic role:

> The weekday side was visible most of the year when the altar was closed. The Crucifixion is in the centre, St Sebastian on the right supporting wing, and St Anthony on the left one. The Antonites were an order of hospitallers, and care of the sick their *raison d'être*. As patron saints, St Anthony offered protection against erysipelas, St Sebastian against the plague, and the two St Johns against epilepsy. These four saints were united on the weekday side under the outstretched arms of the crucified Christ as under mighty wings. Patients brought to the monastery hospital were first taken before this side of the altarpiece in the hope that they might be miraculously cured. When this did not happen, medical treatment began. This side thus played an important part in the medical practice of the hospitallers.[22]

Faced with the spectacle of the crucifixion, which by its "dispro-portionate [size is intended] to hit the onlooker like a blow in the face,"[23] the sick person was supposed to react, even to be cured. The key to this therapeutic method is perhaps to be found in the words of Saint John's evangelical text—written on a panel—which Saint John the Baptist (looking very healthy) produces in pointing his index finger toward the cross, at the same time as looking toward the spectator and saying, "He must increase but I decrease."[24] Whatever the relation that Grüne-wald, no doubt under instructions from the Antonites, wanted to induce in this way between the sick person, the vision of Christ, and the words of Saint John the Bap-tist, it is certain that a metamorphosis of the body is proposed: of both Christ's body and the sick person's body. The expected miracle would imply a strong perturbance on seeing the bloodless Christ, flayed, so horrible and so close that he calls forth the emotional engagement of the sick person: the latter should contribute to the ending of Christ's suffering, to his rebirth and his resurrection. The Isenheim Christ is all about this appeal. But for this to happen, for him "to grow," the sick person must "diminish." "He must grow": this representation of a gigantic Christ, a Christ already on the way toward growth, who must still "augment"—here we touch at the heart of the invitation to therapeutic metamorphosis. The "growth" that Saint John the Baptist is proposing is metaphorical, because in fact it invites an energetic ex-change between the sick person—expelling their sickness, transforming it into pu-rified energy offered to the Crucified—and to Christ, who makes the grace of a miracle descend on the sufferer.

From this hypothesis we can retain this much: the representa-tion of Christ situates him *before* the moment of the transformation of his body, of the body that is opposite to that of the flayed in the anatomical treatises: his skin al-lows one to see inside his body, but still hides it, there are only suggestions of death, "massacred" organs, rotting. The dice have yet to roll. This is a waiting Christ, he still has an inside.

Real *écorchés* show their interiors, even exhibit them: muscles, viscera (like the amazing *Hussard* of the *Tabulae Anatomicae* by Pietro Berretini).[25] They take a perverse pleasure in stripping off their skin in order to show us their bodies. They are certainly alive, they think, or they are walking about. Others have an expression of sadness or tiredness, or even suffering, often accentuated by the absence of a lower jaw. This is a suffering that directs our gaze from the face back to the flayed body. There can be no doubt, they suffer because their skin is torn off, like Valverde's *Ecorché Showing His Skin Taken Off*,[26] who is moving forward, pain showing on his face. And what about the "suicides"? Some are still holding the dagger they cut their skin off with, or they are dragging along with their hands the skin that had covered their chest and stomach before, now showing their viscera. Here he stands, Valverde's flayed, brandishing his skin, as if a strange force had obliged him to inflict this torment onto himself. This force exists; it is called science.

The first flayed to appear was in a work by Mondino, a Bolognese doctor.[27] The popularity of *écorchés* is linked to the development of dissection and to the plates in Vesalius's book, which had been reprinted for over a century. These horrible bodies, with muscles hanging off them, are stamped with the mark of the great upheaval that science brought to the former regime of signs, as we shall see later.

These strips of flesh, like terrible rags, these skins on display, this plucked frontispiece from the *Anatomia Reformata* by Thomas Bartholin,[28] hung up like a shooting trophy, are witness to an irreparable process that human life had attained; that which the installation of a science inaugurated in tearing Man's body away from him, to make it the object of this science. What is irreparable is the interior of the body, which can no longer become the site of metamorphosis: it is discovered, it is to be discovered. It will no longer be the body along with its skin that will be a mobile and plastic surface of inscription, in a relationship with a knowledge. The flayed are not naked; they have "taken off" their nudity in removing their skin — they have been skinned, but they stay alive, clothed in muscles that leave tattoo-like marks, simulating uniforms (the *Hussard*) or folds of robes.

Yet they seem to want to say something. Their strange expressivity comes from the fact that they are deaf-mutes who are desperately trying to express what they cannot say in other ways than by the voice. Speech is removed from them in taking away their skin. Is it merely by chance that next to the Vesalius skeleton deep in thought, leaning on a tomb, the speech organs are quite clearly placed on the marble? The flayed can no longer speak because they carry another language in their bodies: the language of science. So, what else do they have to say? It seems that in their silent world their theatrical movements, their way of showing their skin and muscles, only express a cry of astonishment: is this still my body? Why can I no longer speak, why is a discourse coming from elsewhere speaking through me? This other voice will bring together another body on these opened bodies: the "corpus" of medical science.

These are strange execution victims. They live a strange life,[29] an immortal one in a way, condemned to walk forever on the earth like this. No possibility of metamorphosis, of reconstructing or transforming their bodies. Science's job is infinite, it will never be finished. The tattoo that they carry like a uniform is the inscription of scientific knowledge on their bodies.

The only changes that will be allowed to their bodies will be able to come about only via a particular orientation, toward greater and greater detail, the product of observation and analysis — to end up one day with groups of cells or atoms. They are no longer waiting like the Christ of Grünewald, rather they are placed after, or before, the metamorphosis, like an abortion parallel to that of the officer whom Kafka definitely describes as an *écorché*. Having been impaled, his head "was as it had been in life; no sign was visible of the promised redemption . . . the lips were firmly pressed together, the eyes were open, with the same expression as in life, their look was calm and convinced, through the forehead went the point of a great iron spike."[30]

But Kafka's man is dead, even if he never stopped believing, even if death had not transfigured him. The flayed, for their part, extend their inextinguishable mourning, they will never resign themselves to accepting the failure of their false transmutation.

In the way that the movement of scientific change embraces that of history, the flayed represent the stigmata of this failure, that is, of the incapacity of history to produce the metamorphoses, the proper "returns" to recurrent temporality. These muscles, these viscera, these interiors of the bodies of the flayed will remain for a long time, perhaps forever, undiscovered. Here, plainly and simply, the beginning of the modern body begins.

E I G H T

Note on the Frontispiece of
De Humani Corporis Fabrica
by Vesalius

THE IMAGE of the human body that medical science holds today takes root in the huge intellectual upheavals that shook Europe in the fifteenth, sixteenth, and seventeenth centuries. Here finishes—at least on the plane of official knowledge—a multiple heritage difficult to grasp, coming as much from antiquity as from medieval religious traditions and the popular culture (so imbued with magic) of rural European societies.

The movement to set up certain sciences, like that of anatomy by Andreas Vesalius, was preceded by a long process of destruction of former habits of thinking, and it was done in an indecisive, tumultuous, and ambiguous climate—the very one that came to be called "the Renaissance." So, before the classical age, which saw a new "episteme" imposing itself under the aegis of "representation,"[1] scientific ideas and practices were unfolding in an atmosphere that was scarcely saturated with "scientificity." One has rather the impression that the first pathways of science are traced in a permanent tension and amalgam between old resurgences of magical and religious thought and the logic belonging to the new requirements of rationality and experimentation. This is an amalgam that is also an "interrogation": the work of people like Nicholas of Cusa,[2] Paracelsus, and so many others show how one can try to encompass in a complete system (whether it be esoteric, astrological, alchemical, or even theological) the elements that are being inscribed in a radically different, essentially scientific, movement.

A more profound rupture is perhaps hiding behind this tension among several ways of thinking. It is that which works between a temporality that endeavors, through and in spite of the power formation (of a religious type) that exudes it, to keep up symbolic correspondences and historical time, which is really getting under way in this epoch. The worldviews of the Cusas and the Paracelsuses represent a last effort to retain in the links of a closed system — containing knowledge given in advance and used up in the rule-governed relation of its statements to a supreme signifier — time that unfolds, time that always brings new facts that could possibly overturn knowledge.

This is the epoch of correspondences between microcosm and macrocosm, of analogies between codes, where they went back to Aristotle and Hippocrates for a theory of humors — in short there was a general effort to reestablish a balance between all the elements of creation; but it was also the time of experimentation and the submission of the gaze to the observation of nature. Leonardo da Vinci writes:

> Man was called a minor world by the ancients, and they were correct, because he is made of earth, water, air and fire, like the terrestrial body, which he resembles. If man has bones to be used as armatures and to support the flesh, the world has rock to support the earth; if man has in him a lake of blood where the lung grows and shrinks for respiration, the body of the earth has its ocean sea which grows and shrinks every six hours to breath: if veins come from this lake and spread throughout the organism, so too does the sea fill the terrestrial body with countless veins of water: but our globe is lacking nerves, which were not given to it, because they are used for movement. So the world in its perpetual immobility does not die, and where there is no movement nerves are useless. But for the rest, the world and man are similar.[3]

This is something inconceivable in a system of absolute correspondences (like astrology, for example), a weakness, an exception, an exterior element that does not square with the whole thing and yet coexists with it. Already this mode of thought no longer believes in itself.

With historical time disrupting these balances in this way, something in human life becomes forever irreversible, something that will always elude us. In another text, Leonardo makes a point of the rupture between recurrent time and history, and the madness history leaves in people's bodies:

> Here, then, we have the hope and desire to go home and return to one's ini-
> tial state, to go like a moth to the flame; and man, in a continual desire, al-
> ways aspires to a new spring, and always a new state, the following months,
> new years, etc.; and when things arrive, it is too late, and man does not real-
> ize that he is here aspiring to his ruin. But this desire is the quintessence of
> the elementary spirits which are encased by the soul in the human body;
> man always wants to go back to his representative. And you know that this
> same desire and this essence are the companions of nature, as man is the
> model of the world. And man has a sovereign madness, which always makes
> him suffer, in the hope of no longer suffering, and life escapes him while he
> hopes to enjoy the fruits he has acquired in it, at the end of strenuous efforts.[4]

This text, which seems to be inscribed in the tradition of the
memento mori that flourished toward the end of the Middle Ages,[5] nevertheless
adds a note of precision to the simple regret that passing time leaves behind: it is
passing because between desire and the things desired there is a yawning gap impossible to close. Human psychological time does not follow social time, and "when
things arrive, it is too late": thus a certain desire is born. In ancient times things
"did not arrive too late," since they came to each person according to a calendar set
up in advance, and according to his or her place in the community. In historical
time, where seasonal cycles ended up being homogenized in a single temporal flow
of "months" and "years," where people continually put off the satisfaction of their
desire, a gap is established between desire and social time. This desire, as a consequence of desiring that which it cannot enjoy, turns back on itself, leading people to
"aspire to their ruin." As the transformation of cycles of desire in a vicious and
mortifying circle, this "sovereign madness" is the inscription of history in the human body.

This is a prophetic text that announces the other civilization that
science will carry; because science has the peculiarity of embracing opening and
discontinuity in historical time, of integrating a nonrecurrent temporality in the internal movement that animates it: epistemophilia is indefinitely opened toward the
future. Nothing in knowledge will ever be able to stop knowledge.

More especially as the model for this rationality (mathematics)
incorporates two absolutely new characteristics, which it will convey to all the sciences: it proposes anonymous signs, by rights useable and comprehensible for everyone—contrary to the hermeticism of closed systems, under the sway of a supreme
signifier that cannot be grasped by reason. No more esotericism, no more secrets in
sacred texts accessible only to initiates. The new science is democratic. In any case

it is not based on any constitutive knowledge, no tradition, no revealed truth: it carries in itself the origin of knowledge, and has the vocation of knowing everything.

Nevertheless, science, unlike formations of a religious type, does not propose a system of individual or collective conduct. Humans run the risk, for the first time, of finding themselves without culture, a risk all the more likely in that science's very program inscribes its primordial task: the analysis of the contents of all thought, therefore of all cultural codes. In this way the whole world becomes, in principle, the object of science. This scientific "imperialism" will make up for the lack of culture—aided in this by the parallel development of the history of techniques, which will impose new activities.

If science does not erect a supreme signifier for all other codes to rotate around, it nonetheless does not neglect to build its specific terrain on a certain mechanism of extortion and of transformation of energies of the body. The floating signifier does not have to change itself into a despotic signifier; it is to be reduced through the progress of scientific knowledge.

I will show, à propos of the frontispiece, which will take on an allegorical value, for the major work of André Vesalius, *De Humani Corporis Fabrica*, how it comes about that there is a transfer of energy from the body to the benefit of science in a particular (and privileged) domain: that of the medical knowledge being introduced in the sixteenth century.

8.1.

The transformation of the image of the body that culminates in that of medicine takes its origin in Galen. The Renaissance doctors rediscovered Galen first to use him against Christian doctrine and the medical practice of scholastic teaching. From the fourteenth century, a professor at the University of Bologna, Mondino di Luzzi, who wrote the first anatomical treatise, began dissecting bodies with the exclusive aim of verifying Galen's lessons. The novelty was that he tried to observe the body and not just expatiate on it, as was the habit of medieval theologians. Mondino's dissections broke from those of doctors of the Middle Ages in their observational intention.

Galen's teachings were known and followed at the time, because they were passed on and kept up—despite the difficulty in finding his works—thanks mostly to Arab masters, like Avicenna. In the fifteenth and sixteenth centuries, Galen's writings were translated into Latin, notably by Guenther (the *De Anatomicis Administrationibus* appeared in 1531), and made accessible to students of medicine.

For these students, Galen's medical work brought an extraordinary collection, which included a coherent physiological theory, in relation to an anatomical description of the skeleton and the viscera (the fruit of numerous dissections carried out on animals and perhaps human bodies); a pharmacopoeia and a diagnostic art; and a philosophical theory of life, of Stoic origin. Here scientific thought is combined with a metaphysical rationality and the remains of magical beliefs. The body image produced by Galen is the result of these three factors. In this body reason dominates, but it is in immediate contact with natural forces that it can only imitate. It borrows from Aristotle the doctrine of the four elements, to which correspond, in the human body, combinations of four qualities—hot, cold, dry, wet. This allows him to welcome into his pharmacopoeia magical conceptions that are energetically rejected from the anatomy.[6] In the name of the principle of similitude, which attracts the similar and banishes the dissimilar, he asserts that the crab is effective against hydrophobia because it is an aquatic animal, river crabs being even more effective because sea crabs soak up moisture with their salt; and he believes in the work of certain amulets, which have the virtue of "antipathy" in relation to certain sicknesses. Galen, who is trying to set up scientific anatomy, who bitterly decries sorcerers who believe that crocodile blood improves eyesight, admits beliefs that come from other parts of this same magical system of thought. And if one considers that in his body image the microscosm reproduces the macrocosm, it is no longer surprising that his work was the melting pot from which, in the fifteenth and sixteenth centuries, scientific anatomy emerged. Humanity was the center of occult energies, hidden virtues, antipathies and sympathies, and the locus of correspondences and analogies, and it was also the object of a medical experimentation that served as the basis for scientific reasoning. Galen's body participated in the same polyvalent and ambiguous thought that was current at the time.

Galen's anatomy, as it was understood in the Middle Ages, was subordinated to a philosophical-religious text of Stoic and Christian inspiration. This sacralization of the text prohibited any experimental research. Perception—of partially dissected corpses—was submitted to a textual meaning that controlled the gaze. Any dissections carried out were limited to illustrating Galen's knowledge. Anatomy lessons were dispensed by a *magister* who read the work of the Greek master, while a *demonstrator* showed the organs to the students.

Andreas Vesalius, a Dutch doctor teaching in Padua, initiated another practice that revolutionized these habits in the first half of the sixteenth century. As the frontispiece etching of his book *De Humani Corporis Fabrica*[7] indicates, it is now the *magister* himself who is dissecting (it is Vesalius who is shown), submitting the explanation to proof, the text to experimental observation.[8] The gaze no longer has to bend itself to the meaning dictated by the written work; on the contrary, it will henceforth have the task of discovering what the scalpel will reveal of the human body. Is it not this which is illustrated by all these faces leaning toward the corpse that Vesalius has already begun to open? Doesn't their immense curiosity come from the desire to know what the surgeon's practices promise to reveal?

Vesalius is no doubt a man of his time. His work is still shot through with that quite peculiar sense of the "Renaissance." But Vesalius will inaugurate observational laws to counter the medieval gaze. The path that leads to the new scientific gaze had been traversed for a long time by the representational technique that painters had discovered: perspective. In overturning medieval iconography, it introduced precise tools; perspective analyzed space, separated bodies, desacralized nature. The exactitude of the plates in the *Fabrica* are instances of the powers of the new gaze. These plates are not just illustrations, additions to the text; rather they bring an irreplaceable dimension to scientific work—more than a "reminder" as Vesalius says, they are an instrument of analysis, and, as such, they contribute to the installation of a knowledge.

It should be noted that before Vesalius's *Tabulae Anatomica Sex*, published in 1538, only Berengario da Carpi and Charles Estienne had represented anatomical figures and diagrams.[9] Sylvius and Fernel were even opposed to it, alleging that this was a sign of vulgarization and amateurism. This certainly shows that Vesalius's representations, and initially those in the *Tabulae*, corresponded to the desacralizing imperative that the new knowledge maintained in relation to the ancient texts. The discovery of the printing press played a decisive role here, and its repercussions were even felt in the very history of Vesalius's plates: these inaugurated a new method of representing etchings in books, which were henceforth printed like letters.

Where did this practice of representing the body in plates come from, a habit that the *Fabrica*, in systematizing the procedure, will transform into a requirement that anatomical knowledge will no longer be able to do without? In the introduction to the *Tabulae*, Vesalius explains that on one occasion, when drawing veins for students, he noted the pleasure that these drawings elicited. And yet at the time he had little regard for the usefulness of plates: "I am convinced that it is very difficult—if not vain and impossible—to obtain a true anatomical knowledge on the basis of simple figures...though one cannot help but attribute a great significance to them as reminders."

Why did these plates give so much pleasure to the students? Here, one factor is no doubt the general imperative toward representation, and its importance in this period. But, in this particular case, it is more a question of a phenomenon that is at the heart of the very possibility of the anatomical object. Vesalius's plates make possible the constitution of this object, to the extent that it is thus removed from the real corpse.

In fact, the corpse was, in the Middle Ages, totally steeped in magical and religious traditions; the ancestor cult, funeral rites—pagan, then Christian—are all evidence of the "life" of the departed among the living. The dead were buried with their goods, tools, clothing; the repugnance toward the rotting of bodies was such that important dead people were painted immediately after death. In the eleventh and thirteenth centuries, "if a person of rank died far from his country, the body was often cut up and boiled so as to extract the bones, which were sent home in a chest, whereas the rest was interred, not without ceremony, however, on the spot"[10]—a custom that Pope Boniface VIII called in 1299 and 1300 "an abuse of abominable savagery." The dissection of corpses, for reasons other than medical or legal ones, was prohibited up until the fourteenth century.

This whole atmosphere surrounding the dead contrasts so markedly with the medical practice that Vesalius is introducing that one can say that his plates are responding to a clear necessity: to break with tradition at the same time as establishing a new balance. One only has to look at the plates in the *Fabrica* to see that they represent *living bodies*. The anatomical drawing has had to slip between the practice of dissection (still enveloped in sacrilege: Vesalius narrates, still in the *Fabrica*, the "heroic" adventure that led him to spend a night outside the gates of Louvain, after having stolen a convict's corpse from a cemetery) and the master's text to constitute the dead as a cadaver, while at the same time displacing life toward representation. One only has to see these magnificent *écorchés*, full of vigor, in Vesalius's plates. They allow for a *life of science* in removing sacred forces from the dead, in ceasing to see death as a sign of corruption and as the end. From this point on dissections will be carried out on inert bodies, where the "negative" is exorcised, that is, the frightful potencies that corpses bring with them—and thus impeding the compunctions of science. Representation detaches the dead from their bodies, allowing medicine to constitute itself by excluding death from its domain. At the same time, a new relationship to the living—to their bodies—is thus installed: the living whose life is detached from the forces of nature, whose bodily functions will be progressively assimilated to physiochemical processes.

So it is false to assert that the object of medicine is the corpse.[11] On the contrary, it is a representation of the human body that is neither dead nor alive, but that is built up through the separation of death from the body; the body goes on to find an independent life breathed into it. This is a partial transfer of forces of the dead toward another level, scientific knowledge.

Consider the famous series of three plates in the *Fabrica* representing skeletons: they are "muscled," full of life, "filled out," and even elegant as they seem to go about a funeral rite. The first, like a grave digger, is getting ready to dig a tomb, the second is leaning on a tomb meditating, the third is lifting his hands to his face expressing his grief on a tombstone. Who would cry like this? The *death* that Vesalius's science has stripped death's energy away from, to turn it into the representation of a neutral corpse. Is this not the meaning of the inscription on the tomb in the second plate: *Vivitur ingenio, caetera mortis erunt*? "One lives through the mind, all the rest belongs to death"? In other words, from this point on death will no longer participate in life. Anyone who dies, whose decayed body ends up underneath the tombstone, is *saved;* he or she lives in this representation. A funeral rite, a rite of passage, these three engravings describe the transfer of forces of death toward the represented corpse (the skeleton): a metamorphosis of energy that is going, in another way, to animate the very movement of medical knowledge.

The floating signifier that denoted death in the former medieval culture provided the base for the creation of a new object of knowledge. The opposite of the living dead (i.e., "vampires," who never stop dying), these bodies in Vesalius's plates, these skeletons, will never stop living an artificial, procured, silent life, a life borrowed from that of science in the service of which these representations are set up.

Another etching in the *Fabrica* captures the special moment when anatomy is established through the transfer of forces from the real body to the "body" of science: the frontispiece, showing an anatomy lesson. In the center, Vesalius has just dissected the corpse of a woman whose stomach is open. He is getting ready to incise the uterus, as several things indicate. First the fact that the figure of the woman in the frontispiece is exactly the same, on a reduced scale, as that in the *Fabrica* and bears the caption: "However this figure has been mainly shown in order for the situation of the bladder and the womb to be in view in such a manner that it appear in this woman before we had in any way touched the womb."[12]

The corpse in the frontispiece reproduces the "Prima figurarum" of the chapter devoted to reproductive organs. Next, the audience shown in the frontispiece surprised commentators on the *Fabrica*, since anatomy lessons, even given by well-known masters, would never attract such a crowd. Yet is seems that in this particular case it could well be a faithful portrait, precisely because Vesalius is getting ready to open a uterus. The master himself makes a note of this plentiful crowd in a passage where he contrasts his practice to the vain discussions of doctors: "quibus frequentior de genitalibus et semine quam medicis disputatio est quosque quum generationis organa in scholis ostendimus freuentissimos habemus spectatores."[13]

In this way the frontispiece is a good indication of this special moment where forces (here life forces) are captured and transferred toward a new level of knowledge.

It is a matter of energies linked to the reproductive function. According to Freud, the question "where do children come from?" is the foundation for the desire for knowledge, epistemophilia; on the other hand, one of the potencies — if not the major potency — denoted by the floating signifier is that of life (*mana* is the force of life). From this, woman's body appears as the very home of free energy. This moment captured by the frontispiece of the *Fabrica* is that of the capture of the free energies of the floating signifier and of the desacralization of their place of origin: the open womb of this woman will now hide only organs, the vital potency that was lurking there having passed entirely over to the side of this crowd, swarming and straining with their extreme thirst for knowledge. Students, monks, gentlemen, bibliophiles — all are squeezed around Vesalius, perhaps hoping to finally decipher the meaning of life. Yet this belly only shows organs, and the open womb will only bring out . . . the *Fabrica* itself (hence this frontispiece), that is, medical knowledge. The corpse lies there, with its skeleton that looks like it is welcoming the potency of death by working like a memento mori, lies there like a deflated sign, its stomach emptied. It has given birth, by Caesarean section, to a science. The frontispiece bears witness to this mysterious transmutation, and stands in the place of a universal allegory.

Knowledge is built on the emptying out of the body. With the reduction in the energies of the body, what also disappears are the material traces, the residues that condensed precise powers, such as those for passing from one code to another or for translating one register into another. Vesalius records a medieval idea about a certain bone existing in the human body, an incorruptible bone that served as the seed for the resurrection of the body on the day of the last judgment. After having left the discussion of this belief in the hands of the theologians, he adds: this bone — the one described by the magicians and followers of occult philosophy, and which the Arabs call Albadaran — is better known to the superstitious than to students of anatomy. He tells the story of three prostitutes from Venice who had murdered a young child to obtain this bone and its heart, which they tore from its living body.[14] This bone, the residual code-exchanging material, assured the passage from the human to the divine world, from death to resurrection. Henceforth, there would no longer be an everlasting bone — but an everlasting science.

The Body and the Origin of the State

Why is it that, among all the domains in which power makes itself felt, politics is considered the most important? Because the political sphere privileges the power relation, because it is in the political sphere that power really shows itself for what it is, to the extent that it has the peculiarity of soaking up, in its historical development, all other power relations; the end result is that the command-obedience relationship emerges in all its purity. This is not to say that the political establishment has no aims, use, or effect outside of its domain, but by "politics" we must understand that beyond its aims relating to the organization or the well-being of the city, there is the space where power, no longer being submitted to a particular function (technical, magical-religious, or social) takes on a life of its own as pure power, power over power(s). Here, the obedience relation does not only emanate from this simple hold on power, independent of any aim or special competence; it is here also that, paradoxically, all the other aims of the forms or modalities of power find their convergence and synthesis. Thus, at the very summit of what seems to be the most extreme, subtle, and knowledgeable version of all powers (including competencies and know-how in all areas), emerges the crystalline gem of political power, free from the cancer that submits the other types of power to constraints that are exterior to their "essence." And the essence of political power is to produce the obedience effect, independently of any particular competence.

Nevertheless, one shouldn't see in the normal command-obey relationship the nucleus of political relationships. Obedience can be obtained in many ways, and it is present in numerous links that are not political. We have seen, for instance, how prestige, exceeding any particular competence, can lead to obedience. While this is not yet politics, prestige certainly constitutes one of the breeding grounds for its emergence.

There is a study to be done on obedience, and the way in which it becomes reinforced when prestige is transformed into power. Were this study to be specifically ethnological or "ethnopsychological," it would have to make explicit the mechanisms of the desire for power in asking why, in the social domain, this desire becomes a desire for political power, monopolizing, in certain individual or collective cases, all other desires.

Let us take, for example, the relationship of "belief" (to an ideology, to the legitimacy of a power). Where does the necessity for belief come from? From the need for consensus. And how does power manage to obtain consensus? It is not ideological discourse that achieves this, because we would still have to explain how it "takes." It is rather in the very building up of political power that belief is formed, as a power resulting from the absorption of many other little bits of power. One example will illustrate this process.

        To obey is also to be recognized. "Voluntary" obedience is also a desire for recognition and singular identity. The study of the devices that allow for individual recognition show how political power establishes its preeminence over other powers. At the level of politics, leaders no longer have a need to be recognized. They have the right to universal recognition. It is for this very reason that they keep the authority and the legitimacy of their status. On the other hand, the others, the subjects, demand recognition from the leader. When we know that in a traditional or ancient society everything is put together (from the genealogical system and the naming of kinship terms to the spatial materiality of the village) so that recognition of individual identity can be assured—on all levels: recognition of rights and goods, recognition of the place of the individual in kinship and age classes, recognition of one's place in an ethnic group, and so on—the force that political power in state societies contains can be measured where politics has quite often kept up the connection with traditional social structures. With politics, the system of diffractions thanks to which individuals acquire and maintain their identity tends to become vertical and polarized at the top. Political obedience is thus partially explained by this tendency to polarization: the reciprocity of recognize–to be recognized that was at play in an immanent way in sociocultural mechanisms in the social domain is displaced in favor of a sole location; from now on, individuals or groups, recognizing political power (to be recognized by it), find themselves caught up in another type of relation, by virtue of the very fact that the reciprocity of recognition is broken (it is the state that "recognizes"—determines—individual rights, and so on, in the first instance). Obedience insinuates itself insidiously into the recognition relationship, appearing to be its natural element: to be recognized means becoming submitted to a new system of public recognition imposed by power (to be recognized today, in the media system, for example, is but yet another way of acceding to a power by submitting oneself). The obedience relation thus appears as if inherent to the political relation—without the need for recourse to beliefs in ideological discourse. It is therefore not belief that procures adhesion to power; rather conditions for the emergence of political power induce belief in its legitimacy.

        But if the obedience relationship pervades political connections, doesn't its existence signify a relationship of imbalance or division, at the very heart of society, between lords and subjects, oppressors and oppressed? This is what Pierre Clastres's theses are striving to deny—while at the same time confirming, thanks to the impotent state they assign to the political chief of stateless societies, the unequal vocation that inhabits the political relation. It seems to me that Pierre Clastres's analyses could have taken another direction. In fact, in the places where he isolates anti-power devices, one should always take into account a factor that he seems to neglect and that is at the heart of the matter: the play of forces that work to get power or to banish it. Whether this is in the functions of traditional chieftainship or in the irresistible rush driving the tribal warrior toward his death, the mechanism stopping the formation of particular sites of power as lasting and transcendent is made clearer through the notion of force. The very logic of exchange, inasmuch as there is reciprocity in the balance of power, necessarily includes this idea.

I have traced this idea over a wide terrain, but have limited it in particular to two domains, juridical process and traditional political power. This is an uncertain enterprise, and I have to add up the risks. For example, when we refer to an exchange between goods and forces, wouldn't it be necessary to quantify the notion of force, in one way or another, so that the idea of *equivalence* between forces and goods attains a working consistency? In reality, this is what Marx did, when he established a relation between the working time socially necessary to the production of the merchandise and its exchange value. In the case of traditional societies, it turns out that the quantification of force has an incredible complexity, given that "use value" is included in "exchange value," and functions of "representation" or "symbolic value" are included in the economic function (as is the case with economic goods anyway). While measuring the difficulty of the approach attempted here, I have simply drawn from it a general proposition toward an "anthropology of forces."

It seems to me, in any case, that this attempt allowed for clarification on a number of aspects of political anthropology or legal philosophy that tradition has systematically left in the dark—in particular, the fact that in the treatment of notions like law and justice, the history of juridical doctrine has always neglected the notion of force, always taking it as their negation, their opposite—an obliteration on which this history has been built.

*   *   *

If the solution to the antinomies of power is founded on a certain exercise in symbolic thought, such that the latter brings about the necessary matching between time and space, then it also relates, and in a more profound manner, to the possibility of exfoliation of body space that this thought presupposes. There is a close connection between the emergence of a power that transcends (society) and the reduction of the capacity to exfoliate that is inscribed in individual bodies.

With the ancient regime of signs, body space established, thanks to exfoliation, immediate bridges and branchings between people and things. When the regime of signs changes, the exfoliation regime also changes. The two upheavals go together: whether the body no longer exfoliates, or whether it only exfoliates in folding in on itself (and it is only in the *soul* that "expansion" happens: but this would no longer be the space of the body, simply its afterimage in real life, as in mystical experience), then this is evidence both of the transformation of this space and of the mutation brought about in the relation of body (of forces) and signs. At this stage body image emerges, and the role of the transducive infralanguage is transferred to the despotic signifier. Body space becomes objective, and is marked by economical and political constraints. As a working tool, it becomes a (particular) object in space; as instrument for the production of the symbolic in the new regime of signs it is enslaved to the requirement to furnish another body (that of a god, or a king) the burden of meaning that it will be stripped of later. Now techniques appear that are appropriate for the production of translations of codes via the mind. The history of the soul begins (because the mind traverses the traditional body from top to toe).

Thus, in the framework of symbolic thought there is a necessary relation between exfoliation and the solution to the antinomies. As a foundation for symbolism, the space of the body allows magico-symbolic relations with the earth. The earth is not limited by a border that has precise contours tailored to the needs of the military, administration, customs, taxation, or politics. The earth is the magical territory perceived in the extension of the community body in its relation to the ancestors. It constitutes the ancient solution to the fourth antinomy: limited surface, since the Others (strangers, nonhumans) live elsewhere, it nevertheless exists in its own symbolic stability, presenting itself in this way as absolutely limitless. Not having geometric borders, or those bands of empty land that surround great empires, it is finite on the outside and infinite on the inside. And according to the myth of origins, this earth certainly had a beginning, but not *in* time, since time also began at the same time as it.

As I showed earlier, the solution to the fourth antinomy entails the resolution of the three others. The recurrence of time allows specific exchanges between the dead and the living, such that an equality can be established among the latter (third antinomy), an equality whose social effects are manifested in the relation between singular unities and the totality of the social body (second antinomy): the condition for society to have power is that each singularity has plenty of it. The "social contract" does not imply a division between dominators and dominated, between possessors and dispossessed, between detainers of power and subjects, but assumes the possibility, for each particular social unity, of exercising its rights without hindrance, and public rights are even founded on this very capacity.[1] Last, all this implies, in turn, the circulation of the floating signifier, which is to say the infralinguistic activity of the body that, as a transducer, modulates the relation between forces and signs (first antinomy), not allowing any of the latter to elevate themselves to the position of despotic signifier.

Now I would like to show how this whole ensemble totters when the State arises and installs the principle of the primacy of the political relation over all other social bases, and, in particular, how the supreme signifier intervenes, with the figure of the body of the king, in the upheaval of the regime of signs.

In fact, in the East as in the West, in Africa as well as in America, the body of the king appears in the form of the pivot of the representation of power, a pivot that has a real and primordial function in the structuration of power. Why this representation? If we refer just to the history of the edification of the State in Europe, Ernst Kantorowicz showed that the doctrine of "the king's two bodies," which emerged with English jurists of the sixteenth century from canonical law, founded the legitimacy of monarchical power.[2] And the whole history of Western law up to the French revolution remains impregnated with this model; the variations to it following the process of development of the modern secular State. The model of the body was also used to conceptualize civil society. From Seyssel's "mystical body" to Seyès's conception of society as an automaton,[3] the movement toward the autonomization of power and the parallel construction of the idea of "nation" follows the modifications of the model, the split between the two bodies of the king,[4] and in the end their desacralization.

I will not pause to retrace this history. It is sufficient to interrogate the logic of this process, which demands that the figure of the body of the king accompany the first state formations. A surprising phenomenon: why does power, since it is constituted as transcendent and as an apparatus, represent itself in the image of the body of the tyrant? Why is this fact so common as to take on the appearance of a law? Why the body, why not some other representation, some other sign?

O   N   E

Anthropology and the Problem of the Origin of the State

THE PUBLICATION of Pierre Clastres's *Society against the State* in 1974 was an event that went beyond the bounds of normal ethnology.[1] The author took on board one of those questions that summon up specters like the one that Marx said haunts humanity: the phantom of a society without a transcendent power, without a state apparatus that is in opposition to community life. Clastres's analysis, unexpected heir to the lowest ebb of May '68 utopianism, breathed new life into the ancient dream of a society without class, power echelons, or the barriers that political hierarchies set up between people. *Society against the State* proved the existence of such societies by unmasking their political structures. If such societies existed, they were therefore possible, and it would be possible for there to be social formations of this type once again.

Pierre Clastres had the merit to draw attention to a fundamental aspect of political organization in tribal societies, namely antipower devices. While political anthropology traditionally stuck to the description and definition of political systems according to functional models that were in a way closed and perfect, analyzing institutions in relation to a Western mold (state organization), Clastres heads off in a radically opposite direction. It is true that from the fifties and sixties Anglo-Saxon anthropology had begun the study of conflictual dynamic processes in tribal societies, but it remained a subtheme of the major ideas (cohesion, order, coercion, judicial power) used in the analysis of state power in Western societies. Pierre Clastres's originality lay in reversing this perspective, in changing its ground rules: some of these conflicts, some of these dysfunctions, could henceforth be understood, not as weaknesses or faults in a complete system, but as devices tending to halt the formation of concretions of political power imposing themselves on society. In this way South American Indian chieftainships are not institutions that present the image of a weakened or diminished political power (for which the perfect model would be the state), but in fact are mechanisms conceived to ward off the danger of the emergence of state power. These so-called rudimentary institutions, these "embryos," these "preorganizations," these "protopolitical" systems turned out to be real institutions, as complete and as adult as ours. Here Clastres should no doubt take credit for giving speaking rights to an insider perspective (in tribal societies) in the domain of political anthropology; in short, for taking "*seriously*, at last, the men and women who live in primitive societies."[2] His contribution to the intelligibility of political phenomena was thus doubled, with another nail in the coffin of ethnocentrism.[3]

What remains is to investigate the way in which Clastres set out these problems, but sometimes he falls victim to their broad categorizations. If on the one hand they bring a certain light to fundamental questions, they carry the incidental risk of obscuring others that no doubt require more subtle analysis. But it would be unseemly to reproach thinking as sensitive as that of Clastres for not doing what it set out to do: the elucidation of the movement from societies without states to state societies.

1.1. Before the State.

Having shown that the political institutions of tribal societies are sufficient unto themselves and suffer from no lack, Clastres takes up arms initially against an ethnocentrist prejudice of classical anthropology concerning the definition of political power as a "typical social relationship: command-obedience."[4] If tribal societies do not admit coercive political power, does this mean, for all that, that they should be denied the political dimension? It is clear that Indian chieftainships, which give no power to the chief, are political, and yet no coercion is exercised through these chieftainships. From here Clastres derives his first operative classification:

> 1 Societies cannot be divided into two groups: societies with power and societies without power. On the contrary, it is our view...that political power is *universal*, immanent to social reality (whether the social is defined by "blood ties" or social classes); and that it manifests itself in two primary modes: coercive power and noncoercive power.

2   Political power as coercion (or as the relation of command-obedience) is not *the* model of true power, but simply a *particular case*. . . .

3   Even in societies in which the political institution is absent, where for example chiefs do not exist, *even there* the political is present, even there the question of power is posed: not in the misleading sense of wanting to account for an impossible absence, but in the contrary sense whereby, perhaps mysteriously, *something exists within the absence*.[5]

It would seem that Clastres's thinking does not manage to make up its mind here, and that it is vacillating between two requirements. On the one hand he wants to affirm the existence of political power in tribal societies against those who would only see their embryonic forms of (State) power, and on the other hand he wants to reject the idea of political power as an obedience relationship, against those who would deny the political dimension to those societies where this relationship is absent. In fact, what is this "something" that "exists within the absence"?

There are other texts that set it out clearly for us: it is the phantom of the State, which tribal peoples strive to exorcise with their antipower devices. One can no longer envisage what a political relation means for the author if it is not molded on a command-obedience one, unless it is the opposite relationship, rejecting this one, a rejection that entails different political relations—but that, in the final analysis, returns us once more to the coercion relation. Since societies without states, like Indian societies of South America, do not attribute any power to their chiefs, how can we still entertain the idea of a "noncoercive power"? For want of analyzing the positive (power) aspect of Indian chieftainships, it seems that Clastres has been led to this mysterious status of a "presence in absence" that would define a noncoercive politics.

Paradoxically, Clastres's thought does not therefore escape the problematic of the State in the analysis of the political organization of tribal societies. Does not the lack of precision come from the fact that he would have needed to answer the question, Is a political relation always a relation of power? And can political power totally exclude coercion? There is something of a lack of definition of terms as important as "power," "politics," or "State," which seem to take several glosses. For instance, sometimes all social inequalities and all political divisions are assimilated to the State; sometimes the State has the quite precise meaning of powerful apparatuses such as those which appear in African royalties or the Incan empire. Sometimes Clastres sets up, as in the text cited, a noncoercive, nonstate power; sometimes he identifies power with the State, as in this passage:

> When, in primitive society, the economic dynamic lends itself to definition as a distinct and autonomous domain...what has come to pass is that society has been divided into rulers and ruled, masters and subjects—it has ceased to exorcise the thing that will be its ruin: power and the respect for power.... The emergence of the State determines the advent of classes.[6]

With the last chapter, which dates from 1973 or 1974—while the first, "Copernicus and the Savages," was first published in 1969—the notion of political power systematically accompanies that of the State. On one side tribal societies are placed, without states, without history, without political power, nondivided into masters and subjects, dominators and dominated, possessors and dispossessed; and on the other are state societies, ancient despotic societies, monarchies, capitalism, divided societies where time is historical, where the private accumulation of goods takes place, where political power arises.

Despite this woolliness—between classifications that are too broad and glaring and a lack of definition in concepts used—Clastres's thought is far from being as simplistic as has been made out. In particular, the major objection: how does a tribal society ward off an evil (the State) that it is not aware of? How does the haunting of an absent unknown power (Clastres rejects the idea of stateless societies resulting from the breakdown of state societies, i.e., ones that had already a familiarity with the State) drive or regulate actual, concrete political organization of society? How is this brought out in the many analyses of how chiefs are tempted by power? Some ways of putting it allow, in fact, for the understanding that tribal society would be haunted by the image of the State, as if it already had the idea before trying it out:

> In fact, it is as though these societies formed their political sphere in terms of an intuition which for them would take the place of a rule: namely that power is essentially coercion; that the unifying activity of the political function would be performed not on the basis of the structure of society and in conformity with it, but on the basis of an uncontrollable and antagonistic beyond; that in essence power is no more than the furtive manifestation of nature in *its* power.[7]

And yet, the author of *Society against the State* makes it abundantly clear that tribal societies have the constant experience of attempts at seizure of power on the part of their chiefs; their warriors, who want to take advantage of the prestige they get as a result of their forays; or their shamans. And in a deliberate way he takes up the objection in another text, "Liberté, malencontre, innomable," in connection with La Boétie's *Discours de la servitude volontaire.*[8] Here he makes it very clear that what is involved is not prior knowledge of the State, but a "desire for power." These societies reject the state in order to hinder this desire's fruition. This would assume that the formation of the State finds its source in this desire. So we would then have to ask how the State—which is an institution—can be born of an individual drive, and it seems, one that has an initial psychological nature.

It is in a chapter titled "Philosophy of Indian Chieftainships" that the conception of a tribal political power that would in fact be an antipower appears more precisely set out. Four fundamental features characterize Indian chieftainship. The chief is a pacifier, an appeaser of conflicts and quarrels; he must be generous, distributing goods among the community; he is a good orator, using his words to keep the traditional ways in mind, criticizing some people, scolding others; and finally he has polygyny privileges.

Analyzing the meaning of these features in relation to exchange structures, Clastres notes that generosity, the gift of oratory, and polygyny do not enter the circle of gifts and countergifts: the chief receives women and gives nothing in return; gives words and receives nothing in exchange; squanders goods without getting the equivalent back from the community. He concludes from this that "the political sphere" is formed outside of that which founds society itself: the circulation of goods, women, and words. This relation, from the community to power, "institutes the political sphere not only as external to the structure of the group, but further still, as negating that structure: power is contrary to the group, and the rejection of reciprocity, as the ontological dimension of society, is the rejection of society itself."[9]

And now this way of ejecting the political function from society "is the very means of reducing it to impotence."[10] This rejection allows society to oppose the chief's desires for power and to render them quite ineffectual. In any case, the tasks that an Indian chief is supposed to take care of illustrate his total dependence on the "will of the group," in short:

> The advent of power, such as it is, presents itself to these societies as the very means for nullifying that power. The same operation that institutes the political sphere forbids it in the exercise of its jurisdiction: it is in this manner that culture uses against power the very ruse of nature. That is why the one called chief is the man in whom the exchange of women, words and goods shatters.[11]

The very thing that constitutes power as exteriority and transcendence, with all the threats implicit in these attributes, also situates it in the impossibility of concretizing these threats against society.

As cunning as this interpretation of the facts of the organization of tribal politics may be, it remains unsatisfying, because the obscurities begin to pile up. Let us enumerate them:

1. The regulation of power (controlling any possible excess, thanks to its immediate annihilation by antipower) seems to take *feedback*[12] as its model without restoring its mechanism. In fact, it is not because (or when) the chief's power grows that the self-regulation that would require him to go back to his original "level" is started up. Why is it that when the chief wants to "play the chief,"[13] he has to give it up? Because the group would stop obeying him. By establishing a more or less absolute exteriority between the political sphere and the one where exchanges take place, Clastres makes behavior incomprehensible in the former. Any passing fancy for power is condemned: "it never works."[14] One wonders how the desire for power could exist at all in such a society. The exteriority of the political sphere, the formation of the political domain of power as exterior to society, allows its exercise against society. But, because it finds itself removed from the circle of exchange, power can derive no benefits from this circle, it can't profit from it, accumulate surplus value, or exercise any domination over it. Nevertheless, the identity of all these reasons is a purely formal one. Power in tribal societies does not form and become negated for the same motives. Because, if it is formed in order to be negated, it is useless: shouldn't one then admit that it is formed in order to negate the transcendent power that is haunting society? We fall back on the difficulties already raised. In reality we do not know why it is formed, or, according to Clastres, why it is needed, while he asserts the universality of the political fact and asks the basic question: "Why is there political power?"[15] But, in the absence of an answer, which he does not claim to give, long shadows are cast over the problems he has at hand. For instance, why do tribal societies have need of chiefs who have no power, who don't exercise it, who, apparently, are only there in fact to ward off the peril of a real coercive power forming? We thus arrive at the opposite end of the earth from the classical models of political anthropology, but in the same logical system. Here is a society (even if one denies a "teleological metaphysics, according to which some mysterious will would employ devious means so as to deprive political power of precisely its quality as power")[16] in its "initial intention" at the level of its "sociological intentionality,"[17] this being the place where the structural model of the relation of the social group to political power takes form, being constructed in opposition to nature

on the one hand and power (as nature repeated) on the other.[18] In the absence of an explanation that would exceed the teleological contradiction that he has himself articulated, he takes cover in the classical nature-culture dichotomy (which tends to become a catchall), which in any case only picks up the contradiction at another level.

The feedback model of antipower that Clastres presents is unsatisfactory. The best hypothesis one can imagine is that the political sphere was created to provide a space for the expression of desires for power, delineating them all the better to neutralize them. Some parts of the text allow for this assumption,[19] but the fact remains that the initial saddling of tribal power with impotence makes it difficult to see how the political sphere could encourage the rise of desires for power.

2. This separation between society and the sphere of power makes the chiefs' desire incoherent. Why would one want to be a chief? Clastres says it is for the prestige, since the burden of chiefdom does not bring any material advantages to justify this desire. But this means recognizing: (1) that the political sphere carries with it an increase in prestige; (2) between the political sphere and society there is not just exteriority but a common base. By becoming a chief, he who was already enjoying the prestige that comes with technical competence[20] finds that his prestige is justified (it is the "official" and recognized confirmation of his gifts) and, in principle, can pursue further gains in prestige. This is what places the chief both on the same level and a different one vis-à-vis the other members of the community. Given that, one can understand political desire and the formation of the political space as a system of antipower in an egalitarian society and, following the internal logic of the effect of self-regulation of power, in determining the common source both of the desire for power and of the antipower device that is stopping it from freezing up and creating inequalities.

The most "refined" example of the self-regulation mechanism that Clastres gives is in a way too "brutal" and self-destructive (but in itself no doubt perfect) to serve as a model: the warrior who is condemned to death through an escape into the fray in a quest for prestige and glory.[21]

3. The possibility for the emergence of a state power remains obscure as long as one allows for the separation between the political and the social. Because on the one hand, where there are societies without states, a system has been set up that is in the end without fault ("it never works"), one cannot see how, *from the inside*, one can move from one type of society to another. It is true that Clastres has not given an answer to this question, limiting himself to drawing attention to

the demographic aspect and the Tupi-Guarani prophet phenomenon. One can nevertheless insist on the fact that even if political power and the State have arisen under the influence of events or factors "exterior" to the politicosocial relation, there must already be some sort of territory, principle, or basis for the possible division of society into masters and subjects so that such a relationship can be overturned *in a certain manner*. Otherwise it could only remain mysterious. In fact, it is difficult to understand how an institution, Indian chieftainship, for which the aim is to block the road to the formation of power, can be transformed to the point of becoming its contrary, to totally change its telos. One cannot see—unless it is in the formal character of the exteriority of the institution vis-à-vis the social domain—how the workings of chieftainship, in its four characteristics set out by Clastres on the basis of Lowie's work, can suddenly begin to work backward:

> Primitive societies are societies without a State because for them the State is impossible. And yet all civilized peoples were first primitives: what made it so that the state ceased to be impossible? Why did some peoples cease to be primitives? What tremendous event, what revolution allowed the figure of the Despot, of he who gives orders to those who obey, to emerge? *Where does political power come from?* Such is the mystery (perhaps a temporary one) of the origin.[22]

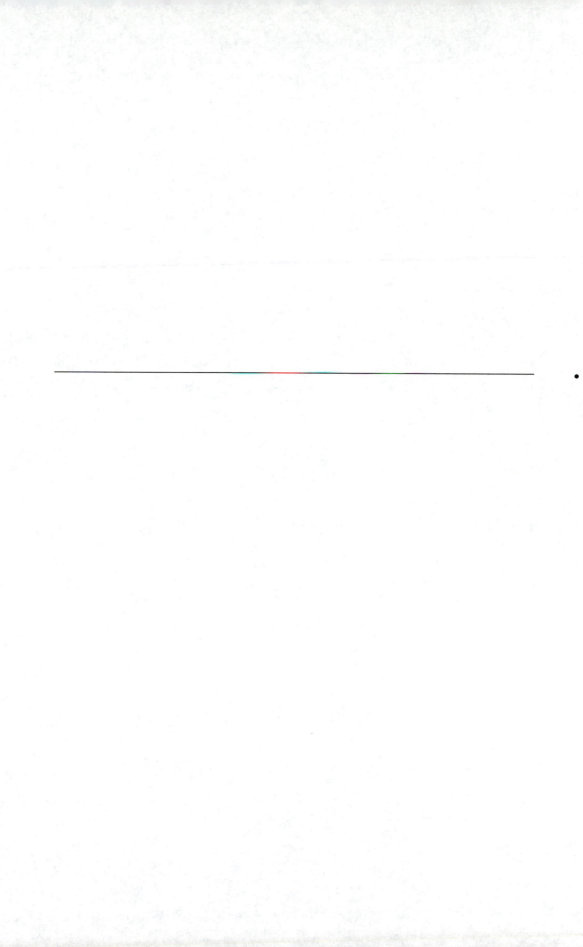

T	W	O

Conditions Under Which
Societies without States Can
Become State Societies

2.1. The Nature of Politics.

LET US pick up Pierre Clastres's problem at its source. The political establishment has to be interrogated at the point where it displays its minimal functions, as in Indian chieftainships. He puts it this way: why politics? "Why is there political power rather than nothing?"[1] Clastres's thesis—that in tribal societies the political sphere is installed in order to ward off the menace that the fantasy of state power holds over society—leads, as we have seen, to difficulties and circularities. It helps in this discussion to stick to the "positive" roles of Indian chieftainships (and by extension societies without States). Of all the major features of tribal political organization, one common point emerges: the chief acts in a general, public way, addressing one and all, and never singling out a group, family, or individual. When he distributes goods in times of want, when he welcomes starving families into his home, when he leads into battle or organizes hunting bands and community work, when he establishes the preparations for a ritual or makes speeches to the people in his group on the necessity of following inherited and ancestral norms, he acts for the "common good" and sees things from the perspective of the whole community.

In looking for a way to establish an idea of the political that cross-checks and elucidates anthropological facts, Marc Swartz, Victor Turner, and Arthur Tuden write: "First, a political process is public rather than private.... The second generally accepted quality of politics is that it concerns goals,... public goals,... goals desired for the group as a whole."[2] Finally politics "involves some kind of focussing of power,... a differential possession of power."[3] Which leads them to a definition: "The study of politics, then, is the study of the processes involved in determining and implementing public goals and in the differential achievement and use of power by the members of the group concerned with these goals."[4] This definition tries to take into account new tendencies that came about in reaction to the study of political "systems" such as those touted in *African Political Systems* by E. E. Evans-Pritchard and Meyer Fortes. It is on the side of political processes, of their disparity, their conflicts and incoherencies. And finally it tries to distinguish political processes from other processes (e.g., ritual, economic, while at the same time leaving open the possibility of the examination of the strictly political aspects of these). From this definition one essential characteristic can be retained: politics concerns the common good, as such. This is what makes it different from the judicial; the latter covers the domains of both the public good and the distribution of power. But justice is said to be private to the extent that a State apparatus is not involved, with laws and tribunals; and the regulation of conflicts, even if they are public, as in village assemblies, do not initially have any link, *directly*, to the common good, but to the *différends*[5] among contesting parties. It is often only a short distance, with an indeterminate border, between the political and the judicial (later I will identify this as *protopolitical*). But because the authors of the definition in question were reacting to a systematizing orientation, they speak of "objectives" and are careful not to suggest that they are unified. Yet this is really the internal vocation of politics: the unification of aims, the organization of all the activities involved in it into a unique whole that is in accordance with the other social aims. In this sense politics is, by definition, unificatory, so that as soon as a tear appears in the social fabric (and there are tears and runs appearing all the time), one can say that there is a hiatus on the political side (and they always exist; it would be inconceivable for it to be otherwise). When anthropologists make classifications among different types of political organization, for instance by dividing them into centralized and decentralized, between those which have different centers of decision-making power and those where this power is found to be concentrated,[6] it is clear that in those places where there are several centers of power there are also several social units that are self-sufficient under certain conditions and in certain contexts. But these groups constitute minimal unities where political power plays a unificatory role. In this sense Schapera is right to think that a band of several dozen Bochiman hunter-gatherers in Southern Africa constitute an "independent" group analogous to a nation under a state,[7] even if there is no statelike political organization, but only a chief whose attributes scarcely differ from those suggested by Clastres in relation to the Indians of the South American forest.

So, in short, there is the unification of aims and public activity. The other characteristic concerns the division of power. According to Clastres, the establishment of the political sphere has the consequence of prohibiting an unequal distribution of power among members of the community.

Let us consider once again the circuit (interrupted, according to Clastres) of exchanges that is established between the community and the chief: the goods received by the latter that, elsewhere and not via exchange, give the community goods and gifts, and words. Now, whatever the nonequivalence between these two fluxes of gifts from one side to the other, it is certain that a reciprocity has to be created, if only because "being chief" constitutes a function that assumes roles, the accomplishment of which becomes the object of approbation or criticism from the members of the community, such that the community knows that the chief *owes* it something, and he owes because he also *receives* something from the community. What can be the type of exchange or the "contract" that is established between the chief of a society without a state and the whole group? It is not a contract of power or obedience, such as can appear in a society with statelike power; it can only accord a power (or an overpower) to the chief in exchange for benefits that he is supposed to bring to the society. So what does the man who becomes chief obtain? We know: prestige. Or rather: prestige consecrated. One becomes chief through some competence — war, hunting — and even when the post is hereditary (as with certain nomads of southwest Africa), it is necessary for the incumbent to demonstrate gifts that are superior to those of other members of the group. When he takes on the position of chief, he acquires the capacity to, as it were, "freely" increase his prestige. This position, this political space, these new functions, do not bring him any personal advantages other than that of being recognized as the most competent, clever, and prestigious of men. In exchange for what he must accomplish for the community — considerable burdens that give him no rest — he gains prestige. Here then is the exchange that is established between the chief and the community. The latter gives (allows for the growth of) prestige and receives from the former goods, services, and so on.

But these forces that are part of the prestige of the competent man transform when he accedes to the position of chief. Not only does the prestige that he previously enjoyed obtain a universal legitimation, a consecration that gives him a perpetuity no longer attached to a given specific competence; but by the same route he acquires a hyperprestige, a surplus of forces that exceed his own domain. Or, at the very least, since it is still only a question of prestige and not power, the political domain is the one where it is legitimate, for an individual or group, to try to increase their prestige. Why? Because this is the specific domain precisely *made for* expressing prestige. This is why it is necessary to create antipower devices to regulate the domain. In fact, the circuits of women and goods are stopped here, in the chief's domain. They are broken because prestige must not depend on one competence, which it would run the risk of developing in accumulating women and goods. The growth of prestige must not come from a real social activity, because then the surplus of forces can be transformed into power. There would be something like a *legitimate* overthrow of power, since the skill and competence of one person would bring about the poverty and dependence of all. So the surplus of prestige would correspond to a real surplus of forces, goods, and women, without return; whereas in the tribal chieftainships the chief enjoys a hyperprestige that he cannot "cash out" socially, that he cannot transform into advantageous social effects, since the exchange circuit has become short-circuited. If these exchanges were of such a nature that they allowed individuals' natural gifts (or acquired competences) to develop without hindrance, inequalities would arise with fatal consequences, as would a social division into dominators and dominated. This is the reason why prestige changes its nature when one goes from the case of a specific competence to that of political prestige. By becoming chief, the competence of the individual ceases being specific to become "general." The politician (and this is as true for the chief of a group of hunter-gatherers as it is for the head of a modern state) is the person who has a unique incomparable competence, that of unifying all the social dimensions. Their knowledge is no longer concerned with technique or know-how, but is displayed as the knowledge of all knowledges, the competence of all competencies. Here, on the rock of politics, each competence is infinitely multiplied and elevates itself to universal knowledge. This is why politics, not knowing how to do anything in particular, knows, above all, how to speak.

If this is the way things are, we can understand how the establishment of the political brings about a real feedback mechanism of power. The conditions under which this can happen are found, no doubt, in the exteriority of the political sphere in relation to society, such as it is manifested in the rupture of the exchange circuit. Women are given to the chief; he does not get them through his skill or competence. And the goods he produces, he has to get rid of. His competencies, which got him the position of power, can only be used outside of the social domain. But here we see that to maintain and increase his prestige the chief has to divest himself of his goods, has to make his women work to produce them. In addition, given that his chiefly functions oblige him to accomplish certain general activities designed to guarantee the community's cohesion, and that these activities could only be effective through the consensus attached to his position as chief, this position necessarily implies the use of prestige. The chief therefore uses his prestige to be a "chief" (a function), without which nobody would believe what he says, nor would they follow his instructions in hunting or war. But what does he use his prestige for? To strip himself *individually* to guarantee the *collective* good. The more goods he gives, the more the community benefits; the poorer he is, the more he deserves his position as chief. And the more he merits it, the better he fulfills it (if he is mean and negligent he will be the object of criticism), and the less he will be able to use his prestige for his personal ends. The chief is therefore reduced to always battle to increase his individual prestige, and to always see it "stolen" by his own community functions. In the end all he can do is retain the simple hyperprestige that his position accords him. So, in always desiring more prestige, the chief is caught in the trap of the *political illusion*, since he is carrying out a function conceived to take away from him the possibility of realizing this desire.

The self-regulation of the institution of tribal chieftainship is therefore carried out on two levels. The first is the one that Clastres analyzes — the accumulation of goods and women by the chief ends up short-circuited by the interruption of exchange between the chief and the community. But this rupture can only be understood because it assumes a more subtle exchange between the two terms; between the surplus of forces acceded to the chief by the society and its utilization for collective purposes, removing all possibility for personal prestige to be transformed into power. In continuing to want to deserve his position, the chief reiterates the reasons why he became what he is, and thus believes he is working on his prestige, but now what is in play is another recognition and another prestige. The more he works on looking after the prestige acquired because of an individual competence, the more he alienates himself from the possibility of increasing it. He is not recognized as an individual among other individuals; he does not possess prestige linked to his person — rather he becomes the object of a (consensual) recognition attached, like his prestige, to his position. He is no longer an individual, and this is why he is unhappy; he is a function.

The self-regulation mechanism consists of a transformation of the nature of prestige, which will allow for the *equivalence* of this unequal exchange established between the chief and the community. Because the first receives prestige that he only gives back to the latter in the form of personal dispossession, he is in line to receive personal compensations, especially in the form of women. But these women, who are only compensations, will not be good for the prestige of the chief and its transformation into power because, as soon as he enters the political sphere, the prestige is destined to change its nature: it becomes "general," it escapes individual monopoly. And the women whom the chief receives from the community, he can keep, because they serve the precise purpose of carrying out the mutation of personal into collective, statutory prestige (and from this into services rendered to the community).[8] In this sense the chief's polygyny is the very image of his impersonal and social function. And the exteriority of the political sphere in relation to society is now understood not as being fundamentally a rupture of social exchanges, but as what allows the political to be what it is, that is, being able to possess the positive collective functions and purposes vis-à-vis the community. Seen in this way, tribal chieftainship looks like a model of the constitution of the political sphere, a constitution that, in turn, founds the very possibility for the constitution of society. To the extent that the latter is other than a set of individuals, that is, to the extent that society consists of exchange and reciprocity, the collective, *global* regulation of the surplus of goods and forces that these imply is brought about, at an immanent level, by the political sphere.

2.2. Politics and the Magical-Religious.

Why is it that State power, especially in its most archaic forms, depends on, or is bound up with, magical and/or religious power? From African royalties to European states, by way of American empires or oriental tyrannies, the emergence and the establishment of the state apparatus is always accompanied by the magical-religious phenomenon, which it seems to match with quite naturally. It is easy to understand how magic or religion serve the aims of political power, at the superficial level of coercive *functions* of the state, but it is harder to understand how the state, as a political institution, could borrow its structural form from religion or magic. It is not self-evident that the way in which a magical African royalty is governed should be ritualistic, and this sets up the problem of the relationships between the political establishment and the magical-religious one. Why did the state, at the time of its emergence, take on the magical-religious mantle? Why did it not set itself up in the first place as a profane state, especially as the political institution that "preceded" it, tribal "chieftainships," did not entertain, it would seem, any special or structural relation with the religious establishment? What intimate kinship is there between the political and the magical-religious that they can so adequately serve each others' ends?

In an article that sets out to answer this question, Marcel Gauchet notes that "the foundation of the State is the same as that of religion."[9] In attempting to resolve the problems left open by Pierre Clastres's problematic—and in particular the "mystery" of the move from undivided societies without states to state societies that are split internally by a division into masters and subjects—the author proposes looking at an earlier basis for the political division in ancient society: the one dividing humankind from the gods, or the "powers up above" from the here-on-earth. This first religious break—depending, of course, on equality among men—establishes a first inequality: the gods hold people in bondage. The subjection that this break implies between the living and the nonliving is the mold in which political division will be cast:

> At a certain moment... the religious break with the "up above" will come to... *justify* the division in humanity. On the one side the person or the people who can delve into the essence of the powers from above; on the other the ordinary mass of those who must bow down before the supernatural truth materialized in some way in the heart of society. The Man of power is born; a figure from the inside, but imbued with the sovereign difference of the outside, and in his very nature set apart an infinite distance from the common people.[10]

So "religion was historically the condition making the State possible" (23). The original religious division would assume a "radical alienation of meaning" in society: people owe the gods their being and essence, reason and the knowledge of their customs, practices, and beliefs; and the law governing their lives comes from somewhere other than among them, it comes from the gods. Here is the "meaning deficit" that the power of the state is going to add to its account by reversing the order of subjection.

Marcel Gauchet's article asks fundamental questions. By interrogating the close relationships between religion and the State, he shows "how the major characteristics of tribal religious thought can be explained by the political imperative of the indivisibility of people."[11] Thought about origins, as it is presented in myth, "is required by the essentially political plan to maintain an equal dispossession among members of the same community."[12] And the exteriority of the origin's past, like its immediate relation to the present, assumes "that what is involved is the rigorous banishing... of the very idea of human creative intervention in the domain of their social life."

Peoples' impotence in relation to their society is "established, produced, instituted" by the exclusion of the possibility of human action contained in the myth. And finally, the necessary plurality of figures and religious powers stop anyone—person, subject—from occupying *a* single site of power, and puts everyone in the same boat.[13]

What is surprising about this analysis is that everything hangs together, everything is right, and yet one has to ask if Gauchet's idea does not incorporate assumptions that are perhaps imputable only to a specific "theoretical enthusiasm." For example, he sometimes gives the impression that the egalitarianism of tribal societies reduces these people to submission under an exterior (religious) law, and they are all equal to each other because they are crushed by this law, and that the dispossession brought about by the split between humans and gods transforms the former into the playthings of a "liberatory illusion"[14] while in reality they refuse to allow themselves to take a "hard look" at the true reasons for the existence of political power. We can ask whether the author is not unintentionally allowing himself to bring into his analyses the idea of a relation between people and gods that essentially comes down to the same one people have with the state, because this impossibility of coming to terms with the real reasons for power "would have continued to irritate human communities in the defense of what was still providing, despite the real division between masters and subjects, an essentially cohesive picture of society, and which at least avoided having to look at the true origin of the split among people."[15] This vision of tribal peoples as equal among themselves because they are equal before the gods they submit themselves to, coming after having warded off unequal power at the price of religious alienation and of the refusal (if only ideological) of the "human creative intervention in the domain of their social life"—wouldn't it assume a utopian image of a self-evident, free society, having its meaning definitively reappropriated because it has recognized the basis for its alienation? This is the origin of the feeling, despite the pertinence of the author's central idea, that calls for the necessity of a more extended analysis, in societies without States, of the link between people and the beyond. Certainly the author seems to analyze the ideological *discourse* that tribal societies maintain on themselves, rather than the reality, which would in itself be inegalitarian in its "content."[16] So what is one analyzing, then? What these societies are or what they believe themselves to be? Or what they are because they have conceptualized themselves as such? What is the reality of power? Having failed to distinguish clearly these two levels, the impression remains that the tribal peoples are sometimes victims of their beliefs and sometimes the beneficiaries. What is missing here is an analysis of the individual-community link.

What is it about these "proud" peoples, like the Nuer and so many others whom "religious alienation" seems not to have sufficiently "flattened," that their behavior is not always attributed to mere "illusion"? What would then be a nonillusory gaze, which would bring to the building of society a "truth" that knowledge could hold about power—if it is not yet another Hegelian utopia? Maybe it is necessary, instead of tying up social relations with the problematic of "truth" and "illusion," to ask if this split with the gods is not the condition for an active, insubordinate, rebellious, egalitarian tribalism that is the source of the intense dynamisms, breaks, dysfunctions, and conflicts that constantly arise in such societies. To a lesser extent than us moderns, they "leave it up to someone else" (41), when they pretend that through magical practices they can control social and natural forces, cosmic powers, chance, and time. Finally, it has to be explained anyway why this "meaning deficit" that seems to weigh so heavily on the tribal people does not seem to affect them too much, and even seems to give them unknown certitudes on their being, origin, and the meaning of their existence—in other words, a "meaning credit"—which we in our cultures and societies are far from possessing. We can admit that all this may be possible through illusion, although on the condition that it has to be explained why this illusion reveals itself to be so operative and efficient that it perfectly fulfills the role of "truth."

2.3. Toward an Economy of Surplus Value of Power.

If we analyze the relation between political power and magic and/or religion, we notice that a series of correspondences is established between the two. Here we will look at the political establishment of stateless societies, as has been determined earlier:

Magical-religious establishment	Political establishment
Makes use of nonunified forces, has recourse to multiple and diverse powers	Unifies social forces in an individual
Must, in principle, neutralize the capacity to increase the goods (of each social unit)	Must, in principle, allow (the chief's) goods to increase
Reservoir and producer, in fact, of forces	Neutralizes, in fact, the capacity to produce forces

Magical-religious establishment (cont.)	*Political establishment (cont.)*
Each social unit gives the surplus of goods to the gods (sacrifices, offerings), and the community receives the surplus of forces	Each social unit gives forces (e.g., recognition of prestige) to the chief, and the community receives goods
Sacred	Profane

The parallel is striking. The characteristics of the political establishment seem to be symmetrical and the inverse of those of the magical-religious establishment. In a general way, one could say that the chief plays, on the "profane" level, the opposite role to the one played by magical-religious powers on the "sacred" plane: the latter give forces, the former receives them, and so on.

I am even in a position to reply to the question asked earlier: why does politics often rely so heavily on the magical-religious? In fact, it is not by chance that this parallel exists between the functions of the magical-religious establishment and those of the political one (this parallel could be extended to other domains: both establishments contribute to group cohesion, ancestors and chiefs retain certain forms of authority, and so on). Nor is it by chance that so many functions in tribal societies (with or without states) are at one time or another carried out by one or the other establishment. Let us take an example. There are societies in which social conflicts are regulated by mechanisms relating exclusively to the magical-religious, which has taken on the judicial function. Among the Azande of Evans-Pritchard, the control of litigations springs from a whole system in which divinatory practices, sorcery, and magic occupy the whole judicial process (from the search for the guilty party to punishment). The chief Zande, who has centralized political power, holds the most powerful oracle (the poison oracle), which decides all the doubtful cases.[17] Elsewhere (e.g., like among the Ammassalik Eskimos of Greenland, who have no chiefs or any differentiated political establishment), the regulation of disputes goes through the *angakok*, a diviner, who detects the perpetrators of crime, and ends either with a session of public confession, jousting with insults, or a vendetta.[18] In yet other societies (like that of the Trobriand Islanders) judicial processes are partly handled by the magical-religious establishment (theft is punished by supernatural sanctions) and partly by a "profane" apparatus, public opinion and the village assembly (for minor charges).[19] These examples bring to light the overlapping of the domains covered by the two establishments and make us think that they constitute two different answers to similar, if not identical, problems. Why is it that in certain societies, certain conflicts are resolved with sorcery and magic rather than through courts or other judicial institutions? Putting the question this way (as Jeanne Favret-Saada did)[20] means going back to the assumption that sorcery and magic take care of problems that are also the province of politics—for all that the judiciary is by nature protopolitical and that, in all state societies, it represents one of the principle functions of power.

Given this fact, it is necessary to specify the nature of the political in order to grasp its relation with the magical-religious. If you will grant me that, in a sense, these are two systems involving beliefs, practices, and institutions that aim to provide answers to the same problems, the question is one of knowing: (1) what problems we are talking about, and (2) in what way the two types of responses differ.

In a general way, one could consider that the two systems function to give a solution to the problem of chance or risk; natural risk (involving sickness, birth, death, and the unpredictablity of natural phenomena), which the magical-symbolic system will integrate, and social (or cultural) risk, which will be "corrected" by politics. Two modes of causality correspond to these two types of risk. The causality assumed by magical beliefs—whether it relates to natural phenomena or to the judiciary conflicts that it is supposed to motivate—is of a supernatural order. The force that pushes the sorcerer toward killing is, when all is said and done, of supernatural origin. The opposite applies when one notices that where the litigation is taken in hand by public judiciary processes, through assemblies or tribunals, the causality can be imputed to humans themselves, without reference to the order of gods or the dead. It seems that this is a question of a radical difference, separating the magical-religious moment from the political one, at least as far as the regulation of litigation is concerned.

Why is political authority so often confused with the status that emanates from certain social positions, such as those of priests, ritual chief, shaman, or "elder"? Here again, we find ourselves in a territory where the political domain encroaches on that of the magical-religious.

Looking at the comparative table of the two establishments, we notice that the fourth characteristic presents "exchanges" between gods and people and people and the chief, respectively. These are exchanges that are not about goods and forces, but are about surpluses of goods and forces. We are not dealing with an ordinary exchange system, but with an "economy" of surplus value.

One of the functions of the gods is to guarantee fertility and abundance, thanks to an exchange system (both symbolic and real) that ends up regulating the surpluses produced by different social units. Sacrificial rituals, potlatch (which relates to ancestors), consummation of goods during festivals and ceremonies—all have the effect of "wasting" the excess of richness that could accumulate in the hands of certain individuals or groups to the detriment of others. In this sense one can say that the magical-religious moment constitutes a system for the regulation of surplus value (or of "abundance"). It guarantees natural fecundity with equitable redistribution over the whole society of forces that are going to allow people to produce goods (natural forces of animal, vegetable, or human fecundity, force of health, and so on). The redistribution of "abundance" indirectly concerns goods and directly concerns forces. I think that the magical-religious moment regulates an excess of power at the heart of society.

From another point of view, if we examine the corresponding function of the political establishment, we perceive that it also guarantees a certain "economic" regulation of the social domain. Except that it is no longer a question of abundance; we are dealing with insolvency and penury. The different roles of the tribal chieftain show that he is there to overcome a possible lack in social exchanges. His generosity also regulates the distribution of goods, especially in periods of want. In the same manner, when he organizes hunting expeditions for the whole group, he procures from everyone (and redistributes in advance) whatever is necessary for the feeding and the needs of the society. His role as war leader guarantees the community against the living defaulting (dying in war), an inevitable defaulting if he doesn't carry out his function properly. His mission to uphold civil peace, to serve as arbiter or "wise man" whose counsel is listened to and followed, translates a social lack that he is trying to overcome. There must be insufficient control or insufficient self-regulation of exchanged solidarities for conflicts to be reduced; his reminders of customary norms aim to sharpen the memory (which was running the risk of fading) of what makes for the smooth running of social life.

In every case, the political leader "manages" a lack rather than an excess. This lack relates directly, in opposition to the excess that the magical-religious establishment "manages," to goods and to forces (of work, production, war, and so on). It could be said that the job of politics is to regulate a weakness of power at the heart of society.

Now we can understand why the political establishment (in societies without the State and in state societies, but much more in the former than in the latter) always finds itself to be *in default* in relation to the demands and needs of society. It is because its nature is precisely to manage a lack in social power (which appears unexpectedly, "by chance"). We will see below how the emergence of the State will make of this political vocation a way of appropriating for itself an *excess* of power, which was supposed to compensate (according to the ideological discourse of the State) for the equivalent lack in the social domain.

In this economy of the surplus value of power (i.e., the excess and the lack of goods and forces, the usage and possession of which procure power), we assume, therefore, three spheres, which are distinguished here solely from the point of view of the production of the surplus value that circulates among them. The first is a sphere of social exchanges controlled by reciprocity and self-regulation. But since the exchange necessarily includes (as Sahlins showed in *Stone Age Economics*)[21] an imbalance producing excess, the second, magical-religious, sphere has the function of establishing a regulation of this surplus (produced by each social unit, family, group) by distributing it in society, that is, in this first sphere of social exchanges. Elsewhere, in the third sphere, this excess is repeated in a lack: global society alway finds itself in a state of insolvency when it comes to the possibility of natural catastrophe, or in general when it comes to its material needs.

So much for goods. The three spheres come together on the level of the exchange of forces. At the heart of the sphere of social exchanges, the specific social units secrete an excess of forces that will be absorbed (managed) by politics (e.g., in recognition of the prestige of the chieftain and the authority of the elders), so that one would have to distinguish, inside this sphere, two types of units, specific social units and the whole community. Now we notice that the excess always arises on the side of the specific units, and that the lack is always on the side of the global society (excess and lack of goods and forces). The circuit from one to the other can be represented as in the accompanying diagram:

M-R — magical-religious establishment
Pol — political establishment
S — specific social units
G — global society
g — goods
f — forces

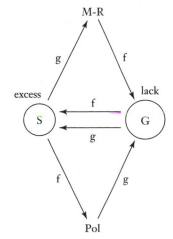

The two establishments, magical-religious and political, appear as two great "transformers," the first of goods and forces, the second of forces and goods. This diagram only provides a simplified version of the reality. There is no doubt that the circuits of forces and goods are complicated by the very fact that the two establishments overlap, according to the type of political organization in each society.

So what is politics? It is the establishment that takes care of the distribution of public power, to the extent that this is seen as emanating directly from each social unit (with the difference that the magical-religious establishment neither manipulates nor distributes publicly social power and does not consider it as coming from humans). In society "all is power": so politics, that is, the political relation, is contained potentially in every other type of social relationship. Man to man, man to woman, parents to children, a man to his cousin, neighbor, ally, opponent, enemy; from one group to another and from the individual to the group, all social relations are accompanied by the possibility of a relationship of forces. Or even better, it is this eventuality, maintained in the tenor and tension coming with each particular social relation, that subtends and situates this force relation in the set of human relationships. Love, hate, desire, envy, friendship, generosity, jealousy—in short the "passions," all bring with them (as psychoanalysis has shown, long after everyone knew it already) the possibility of domination and violence. Because power can result from an imbalance in social relations, its distribution is the first condition for every living thing, every group, each social unit to be put in the right place. The distribution of power at the heart of society is the condition of possibility, not only for civil peace, but also for the intelligibility of the social order. Power, or rather potentiality and the possibility of power, run through the whole of society. Society necessarily secretes excesses, and also finds itself lacking power: social dynamics takes its cue from this. To deal with the dangers that this excess and lack represent, appropriate responses have been built up, thanks to the magical-religious and political "apparatuses." If they resemble each other in some of the ways they work, it is because they are "working" the same object: power, in its two main ingredients, goods and forces.

T H R E E

The Origin of the State

SO IF the first forms of state organization resulted from a process of transposition of certain attributes from the magical-religious sphere toward the political sphere, this does not yet tell us anything about what allowed such a transfer. My approach here could be neither historical nor exclusively anthropological. We can certainly find an origin for the state *in* history, and show, for example, how the state took shape in Europe at the end of the thirteenth century, but we would not know any more about why it *took*, that is why, at this time, the convergence of certain troubles (war, penury, political instability) brought about the development of diverse factors (centralization, national feelings, the breakdown of the empire, administration, and so on), such that a progressive refinement of the (political and juridical) definition of the institution ended up triumphantly and definitively imposing itself and replacing once and for all the former medieval institutions. As long as one does not have a model for the logic of state formation, historical intelligibility will always be clouded by chance. In the same way the anthropological approach seems disarmed—and this, despite the illumination that it has been able to shed on this question: it is certain that Pierre Clastres's idea (which he was unfortunately not able to develop) to root the State in prophetics helps us a lot in seeing how history (which prophetics both "rejects" and displays) can penetrate societies that are ignorant of it and force them to invent new forms of power that prefigure the State. But since anthropology is not supposed to concern itself with history, the origin of the State could not be studied with anthropological method alone, but must take into account the new temporality that comes with it. In a way the problem seems insoluble: when did the State establish itself? If a chronological origin is asked for, this assumes that history has already been created, which allows this origin to be put back indefinitely. Isn't history the history of the birth of the State? When was the State formed in Europe? One can partly answer by restricting the research to the "modern state," whose origin is inscribed in the feudal State of papacy and empire. Yet with the modern state a whole other historical temporality began in Europe. Here, historical research lacks a conceptual framework.

One can say that the State comes from the outside, through war (as Deleuze and Guattari do in *Anti-Oedipus*), or that it has always existed (as they do again in *A Thousand Plateaus*). In both cases the question still remains "how it worked" when a State imposed its own type of power on a nonstate society. The problem of origins comes back. Even if the State always existed, even if there were always societies organized politically in states, why did their domination over other nonstate societies *also* allow these latter societies to keep going? What is it that went on in these (even if it came from the political supremacy of the conquering society) that made them "accept" a new organization of power foreign to them? In short, even if it is possible historically to identify states forming — and history provides numerous examples — after wars (on the basis of the *outside* therefore), it remains to be understood how *internal* social and political transformations led a society to "correspond" to the political form of the state. The question of the origin of the State remains — a question that, incidentally, hails us from beyond history, from the very foundations of our social being. If it is true that the State is always accompanied by social misfortunes — even if one admits that its aim is to avoid them, or reabsorb them — the origin of the State sets up the question of its meaning, and of its possible liquidation, that is, of the liquidation of the non-sense that is the existence of misfortune and injustice.

But the question about the origin of the State must be carefully posed. It is not about looking for a basic key for social dysfunction, but of describing the mechanism that allowed the upheaval of a certain social function. Any origin problem is immediately limited by the type of approach one adopts. It is clear that it is not a question of a "metaphysical" origin that only myth can account for (because the origin story delivers meaning). What is needed then is to locate the essential axis around which the whole archaic regime of exchanges is balanced.

There are usually two ways of setting up the problem of the origin of the State. Either one looks outside of the sphere of political power to locate a decisive factor that would take control of the organization of this power (war, justice, economy, law), or one explores the zone of pure politics, that is, politics as a specific power. In the first case one assumes a general doctrine of relations of subordination between a particular domain of social activity and the sphere of power: the whole difficulty then consists in articulating the two domains by determining the fields of influence belonging to each of them.

In the second case the origin of the State can be looked for in the political sphere, as a moment or a specific product of several changes within that sphere. So one has to clearly distinguish the form of the state from other types of political organization. Here the difficulty lies in the fact that the transformation that these pre-State forms attained can only come from domains outside of the sphere of politics. The analysis no doubt relates to changes in this sphere, set up as it is as the territory where the State was built: but how can one understand these changes without being interested in what causes them? This leads to the necessity of taking into account the articulation between political power and other domains of social activity.

I will take this criterion as a starting point. The important thing to remember from the commentary just made on the ideas of Pierre Clastres is that the State only began when political power changed in nature: this power that was occupying a region on the perimeter of the social field, not participating directly in any exchanges, but establishing a different circulation with the community, moves to the very center of society as the State form arises. This characteristic is essential in understanding the nature of the State. Even if at its beginnings the State does not engage in a significant and omnipresent way in social life (limiting itself often to fiscal activity, or when there is a need, to the organization of wars), it already contains the conditions — de jure and de facto — for this engagement. By right because it holds the principle of power; by fact because its nature is such that it exists *in order to* intervene in the heart of society (by way of the law, justice, police, and so on).

If this is the case, the extraordinary upheaval that transformed the pre-State political sphere into a State implies as profound a change in the relations between the social and the political. For example, what happened for the political power of the modern State to give itself the brief to *organize social life itself* (and not just to look after it, as in tribal chieftainships or in the case of feudal power)? So we have to assume that as soon as the State began, it had in it the seeds of this demagogic task, the effects of which are obvious: rework society from top to bottom, create it as God created Man (as Hobbes says), dissolve ancient and traditional human relations to establish in their place quite new relations. Now, if this State task was to emerge, it is because a "fundamental lack" appeared in the social fabric, a lack that the action of the State only increases in size. The existence of the State is born of this lack, which only becomes fundamental because of its very existence. All of a sudden the State, in building itself, occupies a place so important in the society that it soon appears indispensable. Not only can one no longer conceive of society without the State, but its absence would really bring about its disorganization. What is this "fundamental lack" that is there at the birth of the State? Gauchet's analyses will remind us of the determinant role that magical-religious potencies, in relation to society, play in the origin of the State.

I will begin with three statements that stand as conditions of possibility for the existence of the State. For it to exist there must be

1   a political establishment that holds on its own the monopoly on legitimate violence or the primary rights to use its potency;

2   a political relation of obedience that takes an institutional form, in other words, that it is created and founded in law; and

3   a political organization whose authority is founded in a "representation" of a whole society.

These three statements can be checked against the three classical domains of the definition of the State: potency, power, and authority.

From this point on the problem of the origin of the State is put according to a series of three questions: (1) What is it that was transformed on the level of social exchanges so that such a huge amount of potency appeared concentrated in the political establishment? Whereas previously this potency was spread around the social body (either in particular social units or in nonpolitical systems), it now turns out to be collected, with the emergence of the State, in a specific apparatus, with well-determined functions. (2) How was the State constituted as a powerful institution? How is this power founded in law? These are questions that underpin classical problems posed by legal philosophy, specifically the one of knowing if State law is the result of throwing out more fundamental rights or if, on the contrary, it is the actual realization of them and their guarantee. (3) What is it that founds State authority, its laws and its agents? What is consent, what is obedience to the State?

I will not answer these questions here, confining myself to two special domains, which seem to be instrumental in the problematic of the birth of the State, the ground, as it were, on which the answers to these questions can be elaborated. The first domain is that of justice. Here we have to show how the monopoly on violence brings about a mutation in the functioning of archaic judiciary institutions, such that the monopolizing of political forces by political power brings about symbolic loss at the level of singular social units. The second domain is that of the formation of the image of the king's body, a formation that, as we shall see, is inscribed in the very logic of the edification of the State.

3.1. The Monopoly on Violence and Tribal Justice.

It is important to be clear about the approach I am taking. I assume along with Pierre Clastres that it is the changing of political relations that brings about the mutation in the regime of economic exchanges; the State form is hence to be sought in the first instance inside the political sphere, and not in economic or other changes. The mechanisms that impede the accumulation of wealth in societies without the State are of a political order. It is their destruction that allows the unleashing of the process of economic accumulation.

So I will attempt to show how a slight displacement in the structure of political power can bring about an upheaval in social relations, in particular how the monopolizing by politics of the principle of the legitimate exercise of violence leads to a different regime of economic exchanges and, in consequence, to the possibility for the accumulation of goods for some to the detriment of others.

As soon as the State arises—and one of the criteria for establishing that it is in fact being born is certainly the following—it appropriates the principle of the exclusive use of potency. As Max Weber says, in a definition that has become famous: "Today, however, we have to say that a state is a human community that (successfully) claims *the monopoly of the legitimate use of physical force* within a given territory. Note that 'territory' is one of the characteristics of the state."[1] We can generalize this characteristic of the contemporary State to all forms of state, understanding that Weber's definition has the monopoly on legitimate violence containing within it the principle of exclusive usage of political potency, assumed under the principle of State sovereignty. This signifies, for example, that any demonstration of potency (whether implying violence or not) on the part of a particular social unit that conflicts with the interests of the State is considered illegitimate. Henceforth any other subject (faction, family, individual, party) that thinks it can get away with exercising its force in public runs the risk of seeing itself confronted by the apparatuses (army, police) of State potency.

On the level of justice, the consequences of this monopolization of force by the State are well-known: the creation of courts of law with administrators in charge of delivering justice; a capacity for the State to hand out sanctions and punishments; the appearance of an arsenal of laws and codes that become the templates on the basis of which magistrates measure the degree of responsibility of infractions, and so on. But there is one in particular, among these consequences, that has been less explored: the difficulties the State gets into when it is a question of repairing social tissue torn by conflict, in giving the injured party ways of reacquiring its potency. This incapacity traces a whole other destiny for justice. Since the State has the exclusive right to violence, all other subjects cannot but find themselves dispossessed of it. The existence of a center where forces are located and accumulated throws into disarray the exchange economy assumed by justice in egalitarian societies without a State. As we shall see, at the center of the notion of justice there is a particular type of exchange (of goods against forces according to a specific modality), which compensates and redresses by restoring their rights to the two parties in conflict, and especially their right to deploy their individual potencies. With State justice, on the other hand, redress becomes a way of calculating equality on the basis of an equivalence in goods or the elimination of potencies (punishments, prisons, and the like). This calculus implies the necessity for the infinite proliferation of domains where the law can be applied. Since there is no longer a principle for the unification of blame, responsibility is distributed, diversified, and modulated. The criteria presiding over magistrates' verdicts presuppose that equality has been shattered, that it can't be found, since it is lost in the legislation envisaging cases that are more and more circumscribed and objectified. In its primary task to reestablish equality, State justice remains a tributary of the law and its norms. So it is enclosed in a circle: judging according to its laws, it also necessarily judges according to the State, since the laws are devised by state organs, reflecting its nature and the equilibrium of forces at its heart. Now if the State really worked with the first major inegalitarian division in society, state justice could not judge according to equality, or reestablish equality, except in very limited spheres of law. It would not be able to correct this fundamental inequality, which makes up the separation of State and society. If State justice were to follow its internal vocation, it would have a double mission to carry out: correct inequalities that show up in infractions and crimes on the spot, and fight against the primary inequality that any State law incorporates and rarely makes visible. A contradictory and infinite mission: mission impossible. The equality that justice has in mind represents an ideal that is impossible to attain: restoring the potency that each singularity has lost would mean dispossessing the state of its own potency.

Why is justice blocked like this? Because of the State's monopoly on force, which is translated into state law via the principle of the exclusive use of its potency, which is to say, in the final resort, through the legitimate use of violence.

The State acts, on the level of justice, like a center for the accumulation of forces. In societies without a State, conflicts are resolved either by sacrificial rites, recourse to sorcery, or magic—the surplus of force, which the conflict is evidence of, being "consumed" in the act of reparation, in the form of a gift to the gods—or by judiciary apparatuses conceived in such a way that the excess of force that brought about the conflict returns to the victim, by way of, for example, a public shaming of the aggressor. There is never any accumulation of forces for the benefit of the sorcerers, priests, or arbitrators. In State justice, on the other hand, the surplus of force—which marks the beginnings of inequality and is always possible, in the social relation—is going to be monopolized by the State apparatus. The State's ability to apply punishments and make taxes payable to the courts is evidence that the judges' ruling must necessarily be obeyed.

3.1.1. The space of justice.

The definition that Bronislaw Malinowski gives in *Crime and Custom in Savage Society*, of "civil" tribal laws (second group of norms)[2] includes the feature that these laws exclusively have: they are *justiciable*, with the kind of amenability that Kantorowicz has pinpointed for the attributes of the law;[3] in other words, they are susceptible to interpretation during a trial or judgment. At a deeper level, this assumes that these norms, far from prescribing rigid or stereotyped behavior, delimit an arena of freedom, or rather an indetermination of behavior.

The space for indetermination that the rules of the second group imply differs distinctly from that of the other norms. One can always desist from observing the rules of the first and third groups, and be sanctioned for it; but those of the second group can not only be transgressed, but also affirmed beyond standard behavior. This characteristic of tribal norms, which Malinowski found so striking that he keeps coming back to it in his text, does not seem to have been really picked up by his successors (who perhaps saw only "psychology" in this). Here is the most telling passage:

"Civil law," the positive law governing all the phases of tribal life, consists then of a body of binding obligations, regarded as a right by one party and acknowledged as a duty by the other, kept in force by a specific mechanism of reciprocity and publicity inherent in the structure of their society. These rules of civil law are elastic and possess a certain latitude. They offer not only penalties for failure, but also premiums for an overdose of fulfilment. Their stringency is ensured through the rational appreciation of cause and effect by the natives, combined with a number of social and personal sentiments such as ambition, vanity, pride, desire of self-enhancement by display, and also attachment, friendship, devotion and loyalty to the kin.[4]

Malinowski deliberately attaches the "latitude" of these norms, the space of indetermination that they open up, to the expression of all these individual and social traits that he lists. Elsewhere he writes:

The rules here described are essentially elastic and adjustable, leaving a considerable latitude within which their fulfilment is regarded as satisfactory. The bundles of fish, the measures of yams, or bunches of taro, can only be roughly assessed, and naturally the quantities exchanged vary according to whether the fishing season or the harvest is more abundant. All this is taken into account and only wilful stinginess, neglect or laziness are regarded as a breach of contract. Since, again, largesse is a matter of honour and praise, the average native will strain all his resources to be lavish in his measure. He knows, moreover, that any excess in zeal and generosity is bound sooner or later to be rewarded.[5]

In this way these laws allow certain forces to be expressed with both negative and positive margins exceeding their prescription: "the real savage, keen on evading his duties, swaggering and boastful when he has fulfiled them . . ."[6]

"Personal honour,"[7] "ambition,"[8] "vanity and self-regard, . . . their love of self-enhancement by display"[9] can not only appear in this space, but constitute "motive forces" for obedience to laws. These laws are not in place to repress these motives or to find compromises among several self-interests. On the contrary, "the binding force of these rules is due to the natural mental trend of self-interest, ambition and vanity, set into play by a special social mechanism into which the obligatory actions are framed."[10]

This quotation from Malinowski gives two characterizations of the juridical space of tribal law. It is the space where individual potencies are deployed, "potencies" (in the quasi-Nietzschean sense) being understood here as designating the set of forces that work with those attributes having a moral or psychological tone, such as "pride," vanity," and the like. Potency thus understood represents the social expression of these forces, that is, their action inasmuch as it has an effect on someone else.

The other characteristic of juridical space flows, in fact, from the action of these potencies. They have variable intensity (since their deployment occurs in an indeterminate space); they can push individuals to carry out their instructions over and above simple egalitarian reciprocity. In this way Malinowski defines exchanges through debt, and, machinelike, connects them to potencies.

The juridical space where goods are circulating and where potencies are deployed is a public space. Norms apply to modes of behavior, and all imply a social relation. The surface where conflicts and litigations show up corresponds to the arena covered by norms; since these norms allow for a margin of freedom, certain control mechanisms act on this space that come neither from a public force nor, strictly speaking, from the community considered as a transcendent entity weighing over all individuals. More exactly, in the case of stateless societies like Trobriand society, there must be means of assuring the smooth running of social exchanges, correcting any deviations that might occur, without for all that crushing individual potencies. Now one of the most generous of these means is inscribed in the very function of the public space. It is open, and in such a way that it maintains social control without standing over the members of the community.

Malinowski puts publicity at almost the same level of importance as reciprocity on the scale of constraint mechanisms. Where does publicity get this force from?

The first example of crime that Malinowski discusses in his essay is that of a young man who had broken rules for exogamy by committing incest with his maternal cousin, his mother's sister's daughter. The young girl's lover, feeling rejected in all this, decided to take revenge; "he insulted the culprit in public—accusing him in the hearing of the whole community of incest and hurling at him certain expressions intolerable to a native" (78). This drove the guilty party to suicide.

Malinowski observes that "public opinion was neither outraged by the knowledge of the crime to any extent, nor did it react directly—it had to be mobilized by a public statement of the crime and by insults being hurled at the culprit by an interested party."[11] In other words: "If the affair is carried on *sub rosa* with a certain amount of decorum, and if no one in particular stirs up trouble—'public opinion' will gossip, but not demand any harsh punishment. If, on the contrary, scandal breaks out—every one turns against the guilty pair and by ostracism and insults one or the other may be driven to suicide."[12] The ethnographic literature is full of examples of this type.

The news about the incest spread from the level of chatter (gossip), where the message can be transmitted without making contact with the accused, to the public level, where it no longer has any need to be spread since it is common property. Incest does not become a crime until it attains this public surface, and there is no real law, obligatory norm, except at this level: where the obligation becomes imperative and the norm justiciable.

It is at this surface that insults can be exchanged. It is here that *yakala* can take place, a "special legal arrangement," a sort of protojudiciary, quasi-institutional device. Trobriand Islanders thus get their quarrels off their chests in the form of an "exchange of public expostulation in which the two parties assisted by friends and relatives meet, harangue one another, hurl recriminations back and forth."[13] Likewise the Eskimos sing their song-duels, a peaceful way of resolving certain litigations. And again the Tiv, for similar reasons, sound out their drums.[14]

Here we have societies without the State and without courts that, in addition to using particular devices, make extensive use of joking, mockery, and ridicule to reinforce the constraining force of customary norms. The public space constitutes without doubt the primary terrain for tribal justice, if not for justice pure and simple. Village assemblies or tribunals are only the result of transformations that this open surface has undergone. Here the perception of social balances ceases to be individual or isolated to become communitarian.

3.1.2. Conflict, exchanges, and debt.

Judiciary processes intervene when the normal course of social exchange is interrupted by an individual action that deviates from the behavior prescribed by the norms. The intervention has the aim of resolving the conflict that has thus appeared, and bringing back the situation, as far as possible, to the prior state.

All conflicts are translated into a break in the exchange cycle. Or more exactly, by a break in the link that underpins the exchanges. In fact, if the conflict interrupts the exchanges of goods and beings, something more profound is occurring at the level of that which the norm is the effect of: an infrasymbolic link (since all exchanges are symbolic) that concerns the circulation of potencies in the community.

The social fabric formed by these links allows for the exchange of all things (speech, services, goods, beings) according to circuits regulated by norms of reciprocity. Now, the very possibility of conflict is inscribed in the indeterminate space defined by these norms.

If we recall what Malinowski says about the exchange of fish with agricultural produce from the interior, in order to have equitable exchange, all circumstances — bad fishing trip, poor harvest, and other aleatory factors — must be taken into consideration, and "only wilful stinginess, neglect or laziness are regarded as a breach of contract." In other words: (1) if the reciprocity norm delimits a zone of indetermination, it is so that a margin can be given to chance; and the correction of chance relates to justice to the extent that, for the exchange to be just, all the aleatory factors have to be taken into account; (2) the care taken in correcting chance allows exchanges to vary quantitatively, the norm not specifying any figure to which the parties will be held. One can thus say that tribal norms give primacy to quality over quantity, as is shown by the will to always give more in order to obtain "honor and praise." Flexibility is the expression of any fixed quota being exceeded, that is, the assertion of the singularity of everyone's honor and prestige, in a word, singular potencies; (3) in fact, there is no numerical or objective equality in the exchanges, in the sense that the potencies (in their plural diversity) find themselves in the sway of constraining monetary barometers — which elsewhere would abolish the "egalitarian" exchange dynamic by introducing surplus values.[15] The zone of indetermination is not only used so that exchange quantities can be modified (according to calculations that take chance into account), but to allow debt to creep into exchange. Now, debt (the surplus of a gift in relation to a countergift) is an exact translation of the singularity of individual honor, the hidden inalienable (inexchangeable) aspect of all potencies. So there are thus two levels to the exchange: that of goods ("values" in juridical terms) and that of the debt that translates potencies (or "persons"). There is an inversely proportional relation between the two: the more I give, the more my potency appears to increase; the more I owe, the less my potency is assured.

Thus an egalitarian circuit of exchanges is established, which differs from the simple "tit for tat" measured by quantitative equivalence of goods. The exchanges take place in a fundamentally agonistic context where the first concern is to create a debt with the party who is receiving the gift. But, paradoxically, it is the context that produces the equality of exchanges and, initially, the equality of the right to take out debts; then the circuit of debts — which began in one generation and cannot be closed except in a subsequent one, to begin again on a new footing and so on — denies the accumulation of goods, disallows potency to found itself on such accumulation; on the contrary, it is the surplus of the goods given that becomes a surplus of potency, it is from the debt the other has taken out that I get my prestige ("In the giving of gifts, in the distribution of their surplus, they feel a manifestation of power, and an enhancement of personality").[16] This is a fundamentally egalitarian circuit, since it founds the value of individual potency on the capacity to rid oneself of the greatest number of goods (when this logic will become overthrown to the point where potency will depend on the accumulation of goods, then this potency will change into a type of state or prestate power drawing surplus value from the rest of society). In addition, equality is here defined negatively, as the equality of *not being able to accumulate:* the equality of not-having, which allows the inequality of potencies to coexist as unique singularities.

This then summarizes the general framework for exchange in tribal society. This is a framework that will be broken by conflict, establishing imbalance and inequality that were not there before.

First, the very nature of the zone of legal indetermination allows conflicts to arise, because it is a zone of variation of the intensity of potencies. As Malinowski says, only laziness, negligence, or the like can break a contract: the infrasymbolic level erupts into the exchange level. Someone appropriates, in one way or another, another's goods. Whether this is intentional or not, this action runs the risk of being seen by the other as a reinforcement of his potency, but without any symbolic counterpart (of goods). Now this is equivalent to the opposite of a gift received: the person committing the act has forced her victim to "give" her something without any obligation for return accompanying the act and, on top of that, no debt to absolve, and no possibility of opening a circuit of debts). There is a conflict because the victim has been denied his exchange capacity for giving or deploying potency (on the basis of the item that has been "taken" from her).

The agonistic exchange context thus finds itself overturned. This victim sees his or her own injury as a surplus of potency in the aggressor that comes to him or her through an accumulation of goods. At this point she or he can only counter the illegal action by reinforcing his or her potency outside of any symbolic reference: a violence that is in reply to an initial gesture itself seen as a violence against one's rights (to potency, in the exchange circuit). So conflict breaks out.

Now an extraordinary situation is created in the social order with the interruption of the exchange of goods and the risk of violent confrontation. Another situation will respond to this one, and it is no less extraordinary: the one that establishes the judiciary process, which has the aim of reestablishing exchange.

It should be noted that the conflict will break out in broad daylight; injustice is in the public arena. And the injustice is nothing more than running away with this false gift, without any return, since it does not reinforce the potency of the victim (who "gives") nor create a debt with the receiver. This aberrant gift removes any chance of a countergift. Here lies the real injury that the felonious acts brings, as it sets up a barrier to reciprocity and is incapable of founding a social order.

3.1.3. The judiciary process.

Exchange implies a removal, a break, and the birth of another link—in giving one's daughter, one receives another into the house; one takes products grown in the earth to swap them with goods that have come from far away. On each occasion there is a rupture that threatens to disorganize social life. The moment of exchange represents a particular moment in which the social fabric finds itself to be totally changing, and during which other activities are suspended. Important exchanges are also accompanied by ritual ceremonies. The network of prior relations is momentarily paralyzed, and this allows for a new regime for the functioning of forces inside the community. At the moment of exchange a certain energy is gathered up and produced by each individual or each party who accumulates it as they offer gifts. At the end of the exchange, the energy put back into circulation can be reinvested in the new social body.

This is a precarious and vulnerable moment, rendered all the more unstable by the prestige battle that starts up. Nevertheless, because of the conflictual risks that such a situation implies, ritual prohibitions reinforce social pressure. Ceremonial exchanges thus represent a dual process of rupture and linking up again—at the level of goods and potencies. In the regime in which these two factors function, four major situations can be distinguished: (1) Exchange of goods, circulation of potencies—this is normal social peace; (2) exchange of goods, retention of potencies—agonistic ceremonial exchange; (3) no exchange of goods, no circulation of potencies—isolation, conflict; (4) no exchange of goods, clash of potencies—war.

In opposition to ceremonial exchanges, which reknot the link voluntarily broken, without there ever being the separation and isolation that conflict implies, the judiciary process assumes a real break in the exchange process and aims to reestablish the connection beginning with the current situation. Justice thus seems to be a mechanism correcting the unexpected interruption of exchanges, and takes place between situations 3 and 4. In peacetime, one would try to restore communication in ways other than an exchange of goods—by using potencies that would be "exchanged" in a sort of agonistic ritual. In a reverse situation from 2, there is an exchange of potencies in the mode of an exchange of goods, with the goods being retained. This is the case, as we shall see, with the Eskimo duel songs.

But first of all I would like to note two things. The first perception about the functioning of tribal justice shows that its aim is the reestablishment of exchanges by taking up once again the link broken at the level of potencies. The judiciary process relates especially to this level. What has to be done is the reconstruction of the link that underpins the possibility of exchanges, by reknotting the interrupted communication. This signifies that the work of justice consists also in reconfiguring the indeterminate space where each singular potency is deployed. An essential condition of tribal justice emerges from this, namely "face-saving," conserving the honor of both parties, particularly the one in the wrong. If the end point of the judiciary process were dishonor, the broken link would never be reestablished— which can happen when the process fails, ending up in war, or even in the case of those crimes that require death or exile in order for the link to be tied again.

The second thing to note concerns the space of justice. We can now understand the necessity to arrange a special territory in the heart of the community space (which will become the place for the tribunal). If the judiciary or protojudiciary process corresponds to a sort of agonistic ceremony, one where the roles of goods and potencies are inverted, it necessarily requires something of a "ritual" space, but without the magical or religious charge of magical-religious ceremonies. This space will be at the same time "profane" and quite different from the rest of the communitarian space. One of its features will be a desacralized seriousness, of the order of a "nonreligious mystery." It has been prepared so that a ceremony can be celebrated there for which the agents and forces are, according to Malinowski, "deprived of all mystical character": the singular potencies that circulate normally in the public space.

The analysis of a protojuridical process among the Eskimos confirms these results. Eskimo society depends on diverse procedures—which vary among different groups—to control litigations: vendettas, hand-to-hand combat, fights with the fists or slaps. Often the blows and the slaps are accompanied by another practice that can exist in an autonomous fashion: singing duels. The weapons used are words, "as pointed as the splinters of wood flying off from my axe." These duels regulate all sorts of litigations, except for murders.

Here is a conflictual situation that ended up in a singing duel: E had married K's divorced wife, K being an old man. Once she was gone, K wanted her back. E not being in a mood to give her up, the duel took place (this is normally decided by a challenge to duel, launched by one of the parties). Here is the beginning:

K—:
Now shall I split off words—little,
sharp words
Like the wooden splinters which I
hack off with my ax.
A song from ancient times—a breath
of the ancestors
A song of longing—for my wife.
An impudent, black-skinned oaf has
stolen her,
Has tried to belittle her.
A miserable wretch who loves
human flesh—
A cannibal from famine days.

E—, in his defense, replied:

Insolence that takes the breath away
Such laughable arrogance and effrontery.
What a satirical song! Supposed to
place blame on me.
You would drive fear into my heart!
I who care not about death.
Hi! You sing about my woman who
was your wench.
You weren't so loving then—she was
much alone.
You forgot to prize her in song, in
stout, contest songs.
Now she is mine.
And never shall she visit singing,
false lovers.
Betrayer of women in strange households.[17]

The joust can go on for hours, sometimes years: "He who is most heartily applauded is 'winner.'... The sole advantage is in prestige."[18] Hoebel asserts that the song duels are juridical instruments insofar as they do serve to settle disputes and restore normal relations between estranged members of the community. One of the contestants receives a "judgment" in his favor. There is, however, no attempt to mete justice according to rights and privileges defined by substantive law. It is sufficient that the litigants (contestants) feel relieved—the complaint laid to rest—a psychological satisfaction attained and balance restored. This is justice sufficient unto the needs of Eskimo society as Eskimos conceive it.[19]

Each improviser tries to make the audience laugh—with mimicry, farce, mockery—to the detriment of his adversary, although the accusations of incest, bestiality, murder, avarice, adultery, failure in hunting, lack of virile force, or having a wife who wears the trousers[20] do not have to be true—while at the same time serving to start the battle off again. These duels follow certain rules, like the one of not showing that one has been wounded by the words of the other; one cannot win if one shows one is susceptible. Another rule to never make reference to personal griefs: it is not a matter of being sorry, but of accusing.

It is the job of the audience to make sure the rules are kept, and it also makes the final decision, which becomes progressively clearer since it is the consequence of the greater and greater support given to the future winner.

In relation to these rules, Gluckman, in criticizing Hoebel's interpretation, writes "But is it possible that truth and rightness affect the audience's support, as Hoebel quoted? Then the songs might punish the defaulter by causing him to lose the match."[21] Now, as we know, exaggerations and false accusations are allowed. The verdict does not depend on evaluating evidence in order to establish the truth. Something else is more important for the Eskimos.

The rules I have cited keep the combat happening at the level of discourse–sustained by forces, in particular by the force not to resort to violence (incited by verbal attacks, false insinuations, insults) or to give way to vulnerability. One has to be above all that. And the combat is not settled by the loser being crushed or humiliated: all the sources insist on good relations, a joyous atmosphere that prevails at the end of the match, which finishes in a communal meal.

In this case the conflict began with a contestation at the level of exchanges of goods (an ex-husband who wants to impede the marriage of his former wife with another), which leads to a rupture at the level of potencies. Once the link between the latter is broken, the exchange system can no longer function: this symbolic system is now dependent on the noncirculation of forces. Now, in a normal situation, it is the system of exchanges that regulates the distribution and the circulation of potencies in the social field. Since the exchange of goods (of women) is in paralysis, it can no longer start the circuit of potencies up again, a subsitute for "goods" will be sought: this will be speech, which, incidentally, carries potencies in it. So they will exchange words, at the same time as "exchanging" potencies, making them circulate in a peaceful mode.

During the duel each accusation carries with it the desire to make the balance tip to one's own side — a trial of force between parties who want, in turn, to turn themselves into communal speech. In this way potencies are exchanged, crashing into each other in the form of words (reproaches, insinuations, allusions). The circulation of potencies, through the communitarian establishment of the open space and the audience's presence, is progressively reestablished. Having made anger, bitterness, and resentment pass over into words, song, and laughter, the symbolic level has been liberated (of goods, the cause of the conflict) from that of potencies (affect). From now on infrasymbolic circulation can begin to function again, since what stopped it (an inequality, an "injustice" among the exchanges) is symbolically rewoven through words and songs taken as goods, in a logic of the same type as the one that controls the exchange of goods.

Laughter and scorn actively contribute to the process, in "disarming" potencies, in removing brute violence from them, to liberate the autonomy of the symbolic (and of language, which risks at any time becoming contaminated, overcome by too much anger, too much affect). Dry mockery creates the separation between the two levels, at the same time as they are brought together by the sarcasm in the songs. At the end of the contest, it becomes possible once more to exchange things because the link of potencies is restored, resituated in their communal circulation. Peace is signed at the symbolic level of goods with a dinner or collective celebration.

As a desacralized ritual, this regulation of conflict is a good example of a protojuridical process. Were one to take it as an originary model of justice, then justice according to this model would contain two essential aspects: the reestablishment of the circulation of singular potencies in the communal circuit and the recommencement of the system of exchanges, interrupted by a point of conflict.

It goes without saying that these two aspects are themselves in such a relationship that the first controls the second. This is what clearly emerges if one looks at the question from the perspective of "laws."

Tribal norms do not fix laws, in the sense that our law is in black and white. They do not apply except in determinate zones of social behavior (corresponding to diverse types of laws), and they do not constitute a model to which in-

THEORY OUT OF BOUNDS

dividual conduct must be molded, and which would allow for an exact calibration of illegalities. On the contrary: another consequence of the existence of a space of indetermination allowed for by norms is the impossibility of a unique and rigid interpretation of their prescriptions. This is where the characteristic that has so struck certain anthropologists of law—namely elasticity—comes from. The incertitude of tribal norms that allows them to be used in very different situations is a characteristic that contrasts with the dogma of the certitude of law in our modern societies. If the tribal norm does not rigidly fix laws, in what way are they asserted in a concrete and precise fashion? Because of the potency (which is expressed in certain signs, especially speech in the judiciary process) that is applied in the evocation of customary norms.

Note that the incertitude of these norms, and consequently the margin of indetermination that they leave, allow both the deployment of potencies and verbal expression. These attributes of the rules of tribal law are only, in any case, the result of the absence of writing. Unwritten norms are spoken, affirmed in the course of the judiciary process. This is so true that, as recent analyses of judiciary processes in African societies—having, nevertheless, state power and tribunals—show, the norms involved in the course of the trial serve to carry images of "good behavior," each part using the same rules to affirm different and even opposed laws.[22] The judges' determinations impose their own model, but it remains possible to build different models with the same bundle of norms. These particular models affirm the laws of each part, and only do it once they are constructed. And these singular laws are supported in discourse and carried by potencies.

In short, norm systems in tribal societies do not so much fix individual rights as they open up a space for the expression of potencies. The image of a *corpus juris*, oral and frozen, imperative and categorical, is incompatible with the reality of juridical processes in societies without States. On the contrary, rules here are elastic because they are oral, and they only fix (bring into being) individual laws at the moment where a singular force affirms them.

So, tribal justice reestablishes everyone in their rights, but rather than "formal" or specific rights—economic, moral, familial—these are rights to affirm potencies that are in play in each litigation. What does justice do, in repairing broken social relations, except accord to the victim the possibility to once again exchange, create debts with other people? The sanction imposed only represents the obverse of the absence of debt at the origin of the conflict. This conflict implied an aggressor who was accumulating goods and potencies without any obligation to return them (no debt vis-à-vis the victim). Justice will correct this movement by reversing its orientation; it restores equality at all levels—there will be reimbursement at the level of goods (or a punishment, a fine for the "damages") and a sanction at the level of potencies (pain taking the place of the debt inflicted, or, with modern disputed claims, this is translated into "interests").

If this is the case, if justice is first of all the right to singular potencies—which depends, of course, on the global functioning of potencies in the community according to the egalitarian system of exchanges—does it not act on the very formation of the social relation? According to the example of the Eskimo singing duels (others would be just as revealing), the judiciary process seems to condense in itself the originary image of this relationship. If justice recreates social links with the same solidity (or the same fragility) that they had before the conflict, is this not because it puts into action originary mechanisms of the general social relation? Otherwise, what can it do, except pick up the path along which this link is edified?

Gluckman's whole analysis on the diverse procedures for conflict resolution in tribal societies, and in particular his interpretations of the Eskimo duels, tends to show that litigations generally set in opposition adversaries who occupy precise positions in the kinship system or in the structure of social groups. The frequency of certain types of conflict along some relations, and their absence along others, leads us to believe that there are preferential lines for conflicts, directions in social relations that are more fragile than others. Not just any relationship is broken, not just any conflict comes about—because not every link is generally social (it can be primarily religious or familial and not, initially, a regulator of social exchanges). This idea is perhaps subtextual in Malinowski, who equated tribal "civil law" with social rules for reciprocity; he predicted the autonomy of this domain vis-à-vis customs and the penal, the autonomy of the social. Indeed, *Crime and Custom* does not spend much time on the judiciary process, but to the extent that the law embraces the set of norms that the juridical process looks to in order to mend the social fabric, the alignment with justice was going to happen anyway.

This alignment is such that it might throw light on classical questions touching the social function of justice, especially in its relations with power. Political power aims to impose itself, and impose social relations as if they were generic; justice is the expression of the generic social relation to the degree that the process by which it can work is generic to the social relation. We can understand that justice can never achieve its aim in a society where power is concentrated in the State—when we know that the aim, affirming everyone's right to have potencies, is booby-trapped by the fact that the State builds itself up by feeding on the energies that it monopolizes (only it has the right to deploy its force). The exercise of justice depends obviously on political power, which in turn conditions social organization, modulating its different imbalances—which justice, under the thumb of the state, tries to counterbalance, at the same time as aiding the global functioning of this society that itself "serves" the State. In this case (of a tyrannical power imposing an unjust social order), the judiciary apparatus contributes to the best possible functioning of this regime (without conflicts or setbacks), even though, at any given point, it works according to "justice."

In order to fully understand the workings of such a social system—equilibrium in disequilibrium, allowing for justice that is both just and unjust—one has to take into account the type of political power that is at the helm. Here we have to clarify another question. It seems that the idea of justice is not just the bearer of ideological elements; it seems that under all the juridical-political doctrines set up to justify one conception of justice or another, be it that of a political regime or a particular social class, something else apart from ideological discourses is hidden; it seems that the very notion of "justice" resists its complete absorption into ideology. Why, for example, do people keep crying out for "justice" while, in one way, the history of judicial systems has been the history of their failure—especially when confronted with the imperatives of power? Where does the perennial requirement for justice come from?

From the fact that it has the "natural" and internal capacity to organize social relationships—which is just because these relationships make people into social beings. The requirement for justice, hardly founded in natural law, or in positive law, finds its origin in the emergence of people into society. The protojudiciary processes of certain stateless societies would only be the return of mechanisms at the origin of the beginnings of social relations. It is in the nature/society connection that justice is born.

All the literature in legal philosophy says the same thing, from Plato's *Gorgias* through Locke, Rousseau, and Nietzsche: the justice problematic revolves around the nature/society or the force/law connections. And how, except in this perspective, can we understand Marx's observation that the bourgeois class, having become, in the eighteenth century, bearer of the ideals of justice for the whole society, can identify itself for a moment with the very image of humanity? Let's be clear. Because justice is fundamentally generic to the social relation, those who defend it against various forms of oppression can, from time to time, appear as models for the whole society. By a strange irony, the part of justice that resists ideology is also that which favors the production of ideology in other domains (especially politics).

But justice is not immanent to society. As an apparatus that corrects disorder, it cannot be reduced to a simple relay in the system of exchanges; it must be able to oppose itself to and control the source of conflict—in short, it must impose itself with a certain authority. This second characteristic makes it a *protopolitical apparatus*. Thus, to the extent that it is generic to the functioning of the whole social order, it approaches social organization itself; and to the extent that it plays a corrective role in relation to this order, it approaches political power. It is therefore sited between the organization of society and political institutions.

The protopolitical nature of the judiciary often means that the call for justice is confused with the call for control of power. There is more: the aporias of juridical thought on the theme of justice and politics come from this point, too. Especially the question of knowing whether there is justice independent of political power, if "real" justice should (or can) stand up one day against the power of the State, if judiciary power can tip the scales of political power, if magistrates can hand down their judgments based on "equity" rather than on "law," and how justice can be given all the means it needs (relations with the police, for example) without tangling with the interests of the State.

One can usually say that justice in societies without a State contains a dual mechanism: one slows down the domination of political power; the other can enhance it. The latter (which makes the judiciary a protopolitical instance) filters and controls desacralized social forces, facilitating the birth of State power.

The controlled circulation of potencies brought about by judiciary procedures like the vendetta lend themselves particularly well to being manipulated and appropriated by individuals or groups (in the case of vendettas it is often the arbitrator who initially sets himself up as "judge" and then lays down the law), upsetting its economy: potency will now only circulate in submission to power, in obeying its political aims, in nourishing its forces, which are themselves in circulation following networks legitimated by state laws.

Judicial institutions are not only protopolitical. As generic to the social relation, they are also antipolitical and work in this way against the edification of single centers of political power.

While unraveling conflict, justice spreads the forces that were in conflict around the social organization: this is antipolitics. Conflict on this level is nothing other than a two-way process of disinvestment (or withdrawal) of the singular forces previously associated with social beings and things, and of direct, violent reinvestment on other forces (in collision). Conflict thus liberates energies, making them available (uncoded by ordinary exchanges). The judiciary process acts on forces, making them undergo a treatment the aim of which is to redistribute them along habitual social channels — in other words to set them loose in the social field by obliging them to reinvest themselves. This aim means stopping these forces from stabilizing in the "pure" state they were in before, as well as stopping them from being mastered by mechanisms tailored to control and use them (political mechanisms). In tying up the link broken by the conflict, and eliminating it, justice works against the production and automatization of politics.

So it is useful to think about the functioning of the judiciary institutions from two directions. These institutions are not only trying to staunch the breaches that break out on the surface of social life, but also those which its own existence can make happen. The risks of rupture with society are contained in the gaps that separate them (this is valid, of course, for state societies). It has to return to society the surplus of power that it holds, unless it wants to see it turned into political power and itself into a transcendent and unjust institution. It is thus that, in the history of justice, the most diverse judiciary systems were endowed with specific antipolitical devices, which governed their internal functioning — like the Athenian city with its removable judges, chosen by lot, and a whole judiciary organization that seemed to be in charge of politics,[23] like any society without permanent courts of law, where the institution (village assembly, mediators chosen by the parties involved) only exists for the time of the conflict.

3.1.4. Justice and State law.

It appears that the regime of applied justice changes with the emergence of the State, although this is not a radical and sudden upheaval, bringing into being all at once the characteristics of the modern judiciary apparatus more or less complete. While it might be possible to set out a comparative list of similarities and differences between the judiciary processes of societies without States and state societies, it is more difficult to draw precise conclusions from it. There are societies (African royalties, for example) where the power formations presuppose an actual State, with courts and judges who are able to create new laws, but where the vast majority of the norms remain customary ones, norms that people fall back on to resolve conflicts, thanks to judiciary processes that still depend a lot on the regimes of stateless societies.[24]

There is no actual example of pure state justice. Even today in Western societies easily recognizable aspects of archaic societies persist. Multiple levels frequently coexist in the social organizations that make up a State, but still function in a manner following tribal culture, and not the culture that the presence of the State produces. There are courts, but the judges only exercise their authority on questions having to do with power or the authority of the king, for example; procedures belonging to private justice—such as the vendetta—remain legal even though they are limited to certain crimes; whereas for other types of crimes, punishments that can only be applied by a State force live side by side with communitarian apparatuses—such as public censure—that retain a high degree of potential disincentive. It is not possible to draw a clear line between judiciary processes before and after the birth of the State.

This is because the State did not suddenly appear. In a way it has never stopped forming, and its whole history is reducible to a permanent effort to make its existence more and more real. So, for example, the classical judicial controversy about the definition of the State (the State is the society, or it is an institution opposed to it) can only be understood in the context of its history. Clearly a primordial institution, it was destined from the start to control the whole of social life; however, this does not make it any the less, in its beginnings, an offshoot of traditional structures; its power only works effectively on this or that cog in the machine, it is only heavily felt in insular domains (war, economy, administration). In societies with unified political power under a supreme signifier (God, emperor, sovereign), large areas of social life are very often kept in an archaic mode of operation: it is the nature of this type of State power to preserve them almost intact. On the other hand, with the modern State and its industrial societies, the upheaval affects all areas of social structure; historical acceleration spares none of them.

Now, through the various forms it takes on in the course of its history, the State acquires functions that used to devolve to groups or institutions, or possibly to structures (like the family, groups defined by age, or to community judicial procedures), such that it begins to replace society itself. The natural calling of the State would thus be to put itself in the place of the whole social organization. As bit by bit its history destroys archaic and traditional formations, it increases the scope of its rights and competences, it provides for the needs it brings into being, it controls its own devouring body, it stamps the process of absorption and self-reproduction with its own dynamic style. Society disappears by being reabsorbed into the State, but the latter withers away as it becomes confused with society as a whole. A Marxist-Hegelian convergence that defines the essence of the State.

This aim defines its internal telos, so that history becomes its very texture; it is the history of the State that prevails over and commands social aims. It is therefore the essence of the State never to be completed, and one of its perennial sources of power takes birth in the permanent and growing hold that it elaborates on the movement of history. Its lack of completion is useful for the ideo-logical messianism that serves to better anchor its power over society (in particular on the exploited social classes).

If the State is made of history, if it built itself up gradually as history expanded and accelerated, if it tended to become society itself, then its con-struction must be understood through the history of its incompletion. This is a move-ment that sketches the progress of the State based on its failure, because the history of its construction is also that of the progressive enlargement of this task. But this is a movement that also represents the gradual reinforcement of the power of the State and its control of social mechanisms.

All this explains the apparent inconsistencies in the history of the judiciary institution. It accompanies the State, depends on it, does not necessar-ily embrace it — but, in its contours, it reproduces the same hesitations, pauses, and sudden power grabs that punctuate the history of the State and its law. There is perhaps no single criterion that marks as a clean break the birth of the State, and, in addition — given the antipolitical calling of justice — that of State justice. The exis-tence of courts and codification of law does not seem to be a decisive criterion, since there can be state formations with simulated courts and no codes at all.

But if the inventory of characteristic features of tribal justice does not offer a solution to the problem, it may be that the examination of the functional domain of these same characteristics before and after the State might help to solve it.

The first difference that the arrival of State law brings with it concerns violence; state power cannot exist unless it holds the ultimate and exclu-sive right to force. Even if it does not use it in the end, only the State has the right to force. The principle of this right is absolute, and allows the flow of the history of the State, the development of its power, and the reinforcement of its authority.[25]

The monopoly on violence is translated, historically, in a specific situation: the repression of the vendetta, this form of "private" justice that manuals and law books still refer to as barbarous revenge, without rules or laws.

Now for a long time ethnology has shown us that the vendetta, so common in tribal societies and in use among a good number of western Euro-pean peoples who would be Christianized by Church and Empire, constitutes a ju-diciary *system* subject to norms and rites. In addition to this, the vendetta is a device that *regulates* social violence. While Paul Bohannan asserts that it is a defective ap-paratus, letting reprisals get out of hand, leading to endless massacre, the vendetta actually makes violence circulate, it channels it, restricts it to certain groups and above all acts as a dissuasive device.[26] The analysis of certain particularly "tough" vendetta systems (tough because they are operating in permanently dysfunctional societies)[27] reveals the vendetta's social role (the circulation of women, the magical-religious system), that is, its supportive function for the social order.

With the appearance of the State, one of the first steps it takes is the prohibition of private wars. By doing this it eliminates the role of vendetta arbitrators, taking this role for itself at the same time as exercising its exclusive right to violence.

This principle also guarantees the capacity for the organs of the State to produce laws — thus contributing to the transformation of society. So the point where new law appears is a suitable place to begin changes to the workings of the judiciary apparatus.

The principle of exclusive right to violence (a right contained in the sovereignty of the State) opens a territory on which the law will develop that will slowly legalize the monopolization of social potencies. The State thus invests the social surface that history has overturned, destroyed, and left empty. Of course, it reinstitutionalizes customary norms (Bohannan) in its courts, cabinets, and parliaments, but in reaffirming them as laws, it reinforces its own power over the individual potencies, which, for their part, were once the fundamental wellsprings for the assertion of laws.

The whole operation of the judiciary system can change now, thanks to one factor being displaced (potency that is no longer distributed along "just" and egalitarian lines, for which the function is to keep any disparities from being frozen in the social fabric). From now on justice will always find itself in the position of overhanging a society that is now made up of a center for absorbing potencies and a noose that is tightening on the circulation of social and individual energies, the system of exchanges and debts. To the extent that it plays a part, the judiciary also contributes to the domination of State political power, with permanent courts, judges appointed by power, imposed laws. There will be irrevocable decisions, sanctions applied against the violence of the parties, without taking their "rights" into account — nothing can oppose the law that is crowned with the fetishism of its authority and infallibility.

The exclusive right to potency allows for a certain orientation in the evolution of the law. Because singular forces (or the value of global persons) will be taken less and less into account, the accent will be placed on the value of goods. The separation of the juridical ideas of contract and misdemeanor, between the civil and the criminal, assumes a double process for the shrinkage of potencies. First, the isolation of a social space as the province of all contractual freedom independently of the State; this domain will be opposed to both the public and the criminal, where misdemeanors and crimes would be directed toward society or the State. But, in fact, the litigious domain is all that is left of the quasi-civil tribal sphere (Malinowski) that was concerned with the exchange of goods, after one has taken away any relation to potencies. And reciprocally, the criminal domain becomes what is left of the circulation of potencies when it has been relieved of any symbolic link to goods—which was formerly a matter for private litigation; now peoples' infractions are crimes against the State, since there are no mediating exchanges.

Paradoxically, in the first case—which will depend on "private law" in our juridical terminology—it is a zone of public social relations that will be covered by state law. This "private" is only such because it represents no threat for the "public": a social space on which State law has a power that prevails over that of individuals, where the latter no longer have any use for their potencies, which they have abandoned in order to engage in their "acts" with their material consequences (torts, damages). This is an inculpable area because it has been devitalized by the State; there are no misdemeanors because only goods are involved, the circulation of which must be guaranteed by the main stakeholder, the State (considered here as a "private person," which, through a historical irony, enables the exercise of "true" justice, but putting the State at the same level as any contractor). In this way this domain is extracted from the living community to be placed under the jurisdiction of the State, wearing a "private" mask.

Potencies are submitted to radical treatment in the criminal domain. The whole field of legal indeterminations—cast in the negative because of the form their normativity takes, in opposition to the positive prescriptions of customary norms—now submitted to political power, becomes the space of an essential culpability (of religious origin). In the reverse of tribal justice, which considered misdemeanors, or at least conflict, as a sort of normal illness in the social body, all violent acts are henceforth banned from society. A dual culpability will weigh on this domain, that which deals with the damage caused and that which is attached to the right to violence. The main culpability is to have violated the exclusive right of the State (i.e., to have stolen violence from the State), which makes everything prejudiced, guilty of being guilty.

A strange process begins. Because potencies are deprived of symbolic counterparts, surfaces for social investment, they *disappear*, buried in the ideological bazaar of fantasies and the discourse of the state: it becomes a matter of "instincts," "animal drives," "passions," "vices," "bestial nature"—in short, the criminal body. Elsewhere we see emerging little by little the search for intention as the principle of responsibility (which is put there with the help of theology in Western Europe). Here where honor used to control violence came to be placed the whole arsenal of evil and the crimes of a now profound conscience, an abyss, a well of guilt for having failed to remain vigilant over the body.

Now the aporias of justice also begin; so Kallikles, in Plato's *Gorgias*, having opposed legal justice according to natural justice, the latter being the just and legitimate one because the mark of potency is stamped there (from "the man worthy of the name"),[28] ends up defining nature through the frustration of desires, through unlimited enjoyment, through sensuality, intemperance, and license (491e). While Trasymachius can, in the *Republic*, define justice as an institution established by governments to serve their interests without taking into account its egalitarian calling, and Glaconius can expose the doctrine of justice compromised between the greatest good, which would be to commit injustice without punishment (stealing, killing, committing adultery without risks, "like a god"), and the worst evil, which would be to submit to it.[29] In each case there is a radical opposition between law and desire or interest, between State or society and nature—no longer any agreement between norm and potency. In these works is founded, then, the tradition of a discourse on the law that has still not ceased going around in circles.

F   O   U   R

The Body of the State

SUBMISSION, FORCES monopolized, tributes payed: the state seems to occupy the place reserved for the magical-religious establishment in stateless societies. If we refer to the table on pages 253–54, we can understand how the monolopoly on legitimate violence will overturn the regime of exchange. We could be led to believe that this "division" that magical-religious potencies installs between gods and people tends to reproduce itself in the heart of society, and this would be partly true, but it does not happen without some essential changes.

In tribal chieftainships natural potencies, or rather, the forces they embody and squander on people, are not to be found in a closed and unified system. On the contrary, the *form* of the political establishment, although empty, stripped of potency, has the aim of unifying society in giving it special goals. The State puts itself forward as a form full of potencies. This means, first of all, that the existence of the State, to the extent that it monopolizes violence, implies the unification of its own potency; then that the nature of this potency is, *in principle*, profane.

We have seen how politics in tribal chieftainships locks into a circuit of exchanges within the community such that it becomes impossible to transform the forces that the community gives the chief in the form of power (because recognition of prestige is stopped, the chief is caught in the trap of the antipower device). In other words, the forces he receives from each social unit are entirely converted into work for the community.

In the State system, this regime changes. The State receives forces, but uses a part of this potency to make the community work. Because there is a power apparatus without a counterpart, the entire conversion of forces no longer happens. The surplus of forces seeks another direction. How did this happen?

If we take into account the fact that part of the mystery of the origin of the State is in this sort of overbearing of the magical-religious on politics filling out the empty form of the latter, we can assume that the unification of centers of forces (e.g., magical-religious) contributes to the "seizing up" of the tribal antipower system and that, in this very manner, the way is open for the accumulation of a surplus of forces and merchandise at the heart of the State.

In order to understand this double process, we have to resort to the notion of the "body of the State." It is not by chance that the first forms of state power, in the West as well as the East, have been represented by the figure of the king's body, or the body of the tyrant. Here we have more than a metaphor, and more than a way of conceiving the unified power of a chief.

Why a body, and why the body of the king? Let us recall: the magical-religious crushing down on politics implies a transformation of forces in the latter. More precisely it becomes a force-center. Where previously there was only impotence, a pole of power is now created. This overbearingness fills the political sphere, not the other way around: it is not the magical-religious establishment that, because of being overcome by politics, unifies itself and begins to exercise political functions. In this case, we would have a spiritual power with temporal functions, without the structure of the first having radically changed, the political role being but one among many that priests or cult leaders would have to carry out. What happens is different. If the magical-religious quells politics, the latter keeps its special character, which remains that of a profane and public power. No doubt with the arrival of supernatural forces in the public sphere, the profane character transforms and almost disappears. Meanwhile, it remains, in a way, if not "profane" and "human" (since the king becomes "divine" or a "magician"), at least social and political. The king's magic is pertinent to social and cosmic well-being; he is like a god, but a god on earth, an incarnated god, in charge of "national" functions (as the Swazi in southern Africa say in relation to *Incwala*, the harvest ritual accompanying the enthronement of their magician-king). Now, everything about the function of magical-religious power changes in societies without States. This power is unified and becomes totalized. Magical potencies gather together in the body of the king and have global effects on nature and on the community as a whole, that is on society.

We can understand why this magical-religious power is incarnated in the representation of the body of the king. It is political, it acts in its internal calling on society (through the magical-religious, of course). That is to say that the emergence of these first state forms also transforms the community and the image that people have of it. How, under these conditions, could a State power be conceived via an inverse domination, the political over the magical-religious? If the latter had to retain or accentuate its supernatural character it would remain without a unifying "terrestrial" pole where the new image of the human community could be reflected; a purely divine power would relegate its political functions to second best, or would absorb them into religious functions. It would lack the necessary support for the specific exercise of its political power. Now this support is the body of the king. This body becomes a representation a represented body — but it also reflects the representation of the community, the "social body," which thus acquires another type of cohesion.

There is another reason for state power to be represented by a body (rather than by an emblem or some other symbol). This is that power is nothing other than the capacity to translate forces (into other forces and into signs).[1] Here lies the general function of the body as an infralanguage. As a pure transformer of energy, it is capable of transferring a qualitative load of forces from one context to another, from one set of signs to another, without, for all that, itself becoming in turn a privileged context or sign. This translating activity, which in the case of ritual Edmund Leach says must be performed by a "very abstract" agency, is taken in hand by the body.[2] In archaic societies, the body is neither the image of the body nor the body itself nor the anatomical body in the way we figure it. It is, in fact, an "abstract" body. It is that which, as we have seen, brings about the translation of Leach's "contexts" or Lévi-Strauss's "codes." It is the body that makes it possible to place into direct relations the different symbolic spaces in a possession ritual (movement from one world to another carried out by the *action* of the body) and the correspondences between colors and sounds, minerals and plants, temperatures and shapes. In the ritual where all codes are translated one into the other, the translating agency is not a language (it would be a metalanguage in any case) but in fact a preverbal support for meaning: an "underlanguage," in which gestures, rhythms, and the anatomical and physiological constitution of the body "preform" the different languages in which every sign is written. This body can intensify or diminish force without loss. It can modulate the potency of forces according to the invested signs; it singularizes them in always investing them with the necessary charges. In order to do this it does not have to become a signifier itself. Precisely because it is a pure translator of forces, producer and consumer of energies, it dissipates itself each time in its own activity. And since, through its function as preverbal matrix of meaning, it only "launches" forces in the direction of signs, these forces do not coagulate in it, they escape it because there is no territory (sign) to settle in. Attaining maximal intensities (especially in trances), these forces decode signs, mix them up, put them in direct contact, and then (at the end of the ritual) recode them, replacing them in the original contexts.

I have called this body an *infralanguage*. I have shown that it enjoys special properties such as "exfoliating" the space of the body to enter into a direct relation with an object or another (symbolically different) space. So we know now that the body can move, in possession rituals, for example, from the village space to the "spirit" space or the space of the dead. Thus we can explain certain experiences described by possessed people, like the feeling of ubiquity. The exfoliation of the space of the body signifies the diversification of the space where the body molts, in leaves or scales that allow the direct branching of the body with things. We will revisit this exfoliation of space in looking at the attributes of the king's body.

Paradoxically it is these same properties of the infralanguage that constitute the basic pivot for the transformation of the archaic regime of signs. The king's body sets itself up as the supreme signifier because it can take itself to be a sign, and it concentrates power to the extent that it appropriates the capacity to translate forces.

First I will try to distinguish the function of the body as infralanguage from that of the body of the king. James Frazer, talking about the taboos applying to the divine king, notes that the king acts like a

> dynamical centre of the universe, from which lines of force radiate to all quarters of the heaven; so that any motion of his — the turning of the head, the lifting of his hand — instantaneously affects and may seriously disturb some part of nature. He is the point of support on which hangs the balance of the world, and the slightest irregularity on his part may overthrow the delicate equipoise. . . . His whole life, down to the minutest details, must be so regulated that no act of his, voluntary or involuntary, may disarrange or upset the established order of nature.[3]

And, to illustrate these remarks, Frazer cites a text describing the life of the Mikado, spiritual emperor of Japan, in the seventeenth century:

[The Mikado] thinks that it would be very prejudicial to his dignity and holiness to touch the ground with his feet; for this reason, when he intends to go anywhere, he must be carried thither on men's shoulders. Much less will they suffer that he should expose his sacred person to the open air, and the sun is not thought worthy to shine on his head. There is such a holiness ascribed to all the parts of his body that he dares to cut off neither his hair, nor his beard, nor his nails.... In ancient times he was obliged to sit on the throne for some hours every morning, with the imperial crown on his head, but to sit altogether like a statue, without stirring either hands or feet, head or eyes, nor indeed any part of his body, because, by this means, it was thought that he could preserve peace and tranquillity in his empire; for if, unfortunately, he turned himself to one side or the other, or if he looked a good while towards any part of his dominions, it was apprehended that war, famine, fire, or some other great misfortune was near at hand to desolate the country.[4]

As Frazer notes, similar descriptions abound in the literature on those systems of power that today we usually call magical royalties.

Thanks to this example we can see the new regimen under which the king's body is placed. Here the infralanguage is, so to speak, doubled back on itself. Taking itself as its own object, translating itself into itself, it makes its image appear;[5] the body is not only a transducer of forces, it becomes a symbol, a magical "machine," and a surface of inscription. The body of the king has a meaning, while the infralanguage had none. And each of its parts symbolizes (and acts through symbolic efficiency on) each part of the world. Gestures and physiological functions cease to be preverbal "forms" (or matrices) that allow infralinguistic translation, in order to become universal symbols. The meaning of the world is condensed in the body of the king, which changes into a surface for the inscription of everything that there is. Each movement repeats the order of the cosmos, instead of giving it form, in weaving the correspondences while fading away. And in the inverse: the world has taken the form of a body, the king's body has the consistency of a representative whole, and this representation is the very being of the king.[6] His movements are no longer movements, but sentences that nevertheless possess powers: a movement is the same thing as an order; he is a rainmaker when he turns his head, he fertilizes the earth when he spits, he guarantees good crops when he eats the first products of the season. His whole body has become a language, which speaks the language of the world. This is a basic language, with a vocabulary and a grammar that allow the formation of a minimum number of statements in which the metabolism of the world is condensed.

How does this body translate forces and signs? The infralanguage has been reduced to a point of accumulation of energy and meaning. It has become a powerful symbol that absorbs cosmic forces. Everything that exists only lives and takes its meaning from it. As the sole gathering place of natural forces, the king's body looks after the health and prosperity of the kingdom. His illnesses threaten every single person's health; these are social illnesses.[7] I must underscore the fact that all this (the tyrannical absorption of forces and meaning from the world by the body of the king) could only happen because a parallel transformation did not happen on society's side. Now society allows into its midst a privileged element, the shape and internal order of which not only constitute the model for social functioning, but participate in it in a decisive fashion. People cease to think of themselves as a group whose cohesion depends on the deployment of forces belonging to particular social units, but as a whole submitted to a transcendent order.

But if the king's body translates these forces into signs, it is because he has become a huge crucible of energies. I have already stated it: the necessary condition for the translation of signs (or codes) is the intensification of the energy that is conducive to the exfoliation of the space of the body. Now the king's body seems, quite exactly, to possess a magical space, an exfoliated space. The actions this body accomplishes bear on a social and cosmic space that constitutes the space of the king's body itself. East and west, the directions in which the Swazi king spits to build up the land, are not only "symbolic," but belong to his space of activity, where he molds himself, which he reaches and crosses, on which he acts without hesitation; in short, these directions and the places they indicate are a part of the space of his body.[8]

This property that the king's body has of presenting itself as exfoliated from the start leads us to consider it as a variant of the body of the possessed, which then, in turn, leads us to think that all these enthronement rituals of the magician kings are the result of transformations brought about in therapeutic possession rituals, seen here as paradigmatic.

Such a hypothesis might be fruitful. The analysis of certain African rituals—like those of the Moundang from Chad and the Swazi in Swaziland—bring to the surface a common logic and throw new light on some points that had remained obscure. It would be even better if the enthronement ritual could be considered as a particular case among possession rituals. Then we have a way through to the genesis of the formations of body images (of the king), if not to the logic of the transformation of the infralanguage into the image of the body.

A brief description of the Swazi *Incwala* will bring out some points that are of immediate concern.[9] In Swaziland, when the king dies, a big ceremony is prepared to enthrone the successor. The ritual concerns all the people in Swaziland, who consider it to be the main national ceremony. Its aim, according to Hilda Kuper, is to deliver forces and to assure the health of the king. The "national priests" belonging to the most powerful clans are in charge of the ceremony; the princes and hereditary chieftains who do not belong to the royal clan (the *Dlamini* clan, in the thirties when Kuper worked there) are subject to prohibitions; and the national troupe, set up in the three principle royal villages, actively participates in the various stages of the ceremony.

The ritual begins with a period in which ingredients and medicines are prepared. This involves two expeditions, one to the sea, where the cortege led by priests (*Belwandle*, sea people) goes all the way to the coast of Mozambique in order to fill gourds with sea water; the other toward the rivers of the interior, with the same aim, is led by the *Bemanti* (water people). During these expeditions, the priests plunder the populace, taxing them abusively, with arrogant attitudes in order to provoke friction. The king and the queen stay at home. He is accompanied all through the ceremony by *tinsila* (the king's blood brothers), who are like shadows and whose role, from our point of view, takes on a primordial importance.

After the expeditions have returned, the date for the beginning of the ritual proper depends on the positions of the sun and the moon. It is not supposed to begin until the precise moment of the solstices (21 June and 21 December) and when the moon is "dark," that is, when the position of the sun and the moon coincide, the first disappearing into its "hut" behind the horizon, the second hiding there to "die" at the moment the sun covers it. The symbolism of the sun and the moon is determinate.[10] Kuper says, "The king is not only connected but even identified with the sun and the moon."[11] Once the exact date is set, the ritual begins. It is divided into two major stages, the Little *Incwala* and the Big *Incwala*, separated by a period of transition.

The Little *Incwala* essentially consists of a group of rites and chants during which veteran warriors utter words of hate against the king, with the result that the *Incwala* has been mistaken for a ritual of rebellion. The king stays in his sacred enclosure (*inhlambelo*), where he carries out several ritual gestures (such as spitting through holes to the west and the east to strengthen the land).

This is followed by a neutral period, lasting fourteen or fifteen days, where the Little *Incwala* is "played" in the four corners of the kingdom.[12] This period is also devoted to the preparation of medicines and costumes.

The first day of the Big *Incwala*, young people go to look for the sacred tree (*lusekwane*), which has special properties. It grows at a surprising rate and keeps its leaves green during many long months, even after they have been picked. "Quick growth, greenness, ever-recurring fertility characterize most of the ingredients of the Incwala."[13] This force will spread to the whole nation: "The nation's life, soul, and well-being hang in the faith and belief that the rebirth, rejuvenation, and purification of the king ushers in a new life, added virtue and strength and national unity, bound up in the life of the figure-head and sovereign," notes a Swazi ethnologist.[14]

The first day is that of "leaves" and the "bull."[15] The leaves belong to a tree used for royal medicine and for constructing the roof of the sacred hut, in order to "hide the royalty's secrets." The stage of the bull is very important. The veterans start the ceremony with a chant, the herds of the capital are mustered, and the warriors of the whole nations are there; the women are also present.

The king is being cared for by priests in his hut (*inhlambelo*). He drinks and eats medicines. A black bull (stolen from the communal herd) is brought, released, taken by the young people who had collected the sacred tree, and then put into the *inhlambelo*. While the old people chant hymns, the king hits the bull with a ritual wand. And "though it may have been one of the most docile animals when it entered the *inhlambelo*, it comes out as vicious and as wild as a buffalo."[16] The young men throw themselves on it, one grabs its tail, the others try to subdue the animal. It is a sort of ordeal. If an "impure" young man (who had had relations with a married woman, for example) had, despite this, gathered the *lusekwane*, his failing would appear, because the bull would throw him to the ground. The bull is killed by the priests in the sacred hut. His spirit is "transferred" to the royal whistle. He is dismembered, and the organs that "have power" (the ear, tongue, lower lip, and others) are taken away, as well as the gall bladder. The rest of the bull is put in "the shrine hut of the nation," and will be used to "put strength into the king."[17]

The next rite is also important. A black cow is brought in, which the king mounts to be washed with the sacred waters. This cow has special prerogatives, over and above the other animals in the royal herd. It is never mistreated, never used for a profane duty, and never killed. The cow is made to lie on the ground, and the king, completely naked, sits on her. The two *tinsila* (the king's blood brothers) wash him, the "right-hand" *insila* washes his right side, the "left-hand" one his left side. The water used "is powerful with foamy medicines [like those given to bulls] to make them strong and quick to climb the cows, and to men to stir virility. The ox [the Swazi call this cow an ox] is so powerful that all those who touch it must wash their whole bodies, and when [it] dies it is ritually burnt by old men, and people should not go near the smoke lest by inhaling it they go mad."[18] While he sits on the cow the king is made "the bull of the people."

The fourth day is that of the main *Incwala* ceremony: "On this day the king appears in all his splendour, and the ambivalent attitude of love and hate felt by his brothers and by his non-related subjects to him and to each other is dramatised."[19] Before dawn the people begin singing and dancing for the king. These are the sacred songs of hate already sung during the Little *Incwala*. As the sun rises the king is bathed by his *tinsila*. Afterward, he goes from his sanctuary to the sacred hut, down a path bordered by people, warriors, women, and children. He is naked, wearing only a glowing white penis cap of ivory. The women cry, while the songs of hate continue. The king spits a powerful medicine toward the east and the west to "awaken his people. In this rite the king reveals his potency."[20] This rite repeats that of the royal marriages. The king is now sufficiently strong to bite the most powerful of the new season's crops. He also eats the meat of the sacrificed bull. The young people must partake of it, too. After the king come the queens, the king's children, his sisters, his brothers, his counselors, and the priests who bite the new season's crops.

"Towards midday the command is given for the people to dress in full *Incwala* clothing."[21] They get dressed and prepared during the whole afternoon, and medicines are brought to the *inhlambelo*. Then a wild song erupts. The women cry, the warriors stamp their feet on the ground, the princes come closer, driving the king in their midst, leading him to his sanctuary. The crowd grows frenzied and the king is forced within. The priests follow. When the king comes out again he is transformed into "nameless" monster, *Silo*.

On his head is a cap of black plumes that cover his face and blow about his shoulders, and underneath the feathers is glimpsed a head-band of a lion's skin. His body is covered in bright green grass and evergreen shoots that trail on the ground. In his left hand he holds a shield smeared with the fat of the sacred herd, the *mfukwane*. His right hand is empty and as he moves it gleams with lines of dark medicine. The fatty tissue (*umhlehlo*) of the [sacrificed bull] is tied cross-wise on his chest and the blown-up gall bladder lies on the costume. Round his loins is a belt of silver monkey skin.

Each item of the costume has meaning and ritual association. The green grass is the *umuzi*, razor-edged, strong, from which are made the mats in the shrine hut that are kept from one reign to another, a symbol of the life and continuity of the nation. The *mfukwane* are the sacred animals of kingship that have the tip of their tails cut off to brand them for work of kingship. They are rarely killed, and those that eat of their meat cautiously lean forward so that no drop of fat may touch the body and cause madness; "their milk is red and they have human feelings." The king, his mother, and the great ritual wife, *Matsebula*, smear themselves with the fat. They alone are powerful enough to withstand it and are made more powerful by using it. The silver monkey has the power of life—"no one has ever seen it die." It is used as a sling for an heir apparent to the throne; it is "his health."

In this powerful costume the king appears reluctant to return to the nation. He executes a crazy, elusive dance with knees flexed and swaying body. The movements are an intuitive response to the rhythm and situation, a dance that no ordinary man knows and that the king was never taught. The teachers who trained him in all his duties explained, "We do not know it; we are not kings; it will come to you at the time." Suddenly he crouches low and disappears into his hole, and the *tinsila* follow close behind, picking up any bits that drop off the sacred costume, lest they be used by enemies to ruin the nation. The princes spring forward crying, "Come out, king of kings." They draw back, pause, sway forward. At last he responds. At his approach they retire, enticing him to follow, but after a few steps he turns back and they close behind him again.[22]

This scene is repeated several times. Now everyone is dancing vigorously:

Here more than at any other stage they keep their king alive and healthy by their own movements. The mime goes on with increasing tension, each appearance of the king making a sudden startling and unforgettable impact. His eyes shine through the feathers as he tosses his head, his face is dark with black medicine, dripping down his legs and arms are black streaks—he is terrifying, and as the knife-edged grass cuts into his skin he tosses his body furiously in pain and rage.[23]

Other rites follow, then the king withdraws definitively. He is undressed, but the paints are left on the body. He is said to be *cungiwe* (painted in blackness) and *emnyameni* (in darkness). Now he undergoes a period of seclusion in which he is considered unapproachable and dangerous for himself and others.

The taboo state is extended to the whole population. Ordinary activities and behaviors are suspended and sexual relations prohibited. No one can touch themselves or wash or even scratch their hair. The king sits all day naked, on a lion skin in the ritual hut. "On this day the identification of the people with the king is very marked. The spies do not say, 'You are sleeping late' or 'You are scratching,' but 'You cause the king to sleep,' 'You scratch him (the king),' etc."[24] If a prince has sexual relations in this period he is said to have "soiled the nation."

Finally the sixth day is the day of final purification. The objects used for the ritual are burned — the remains of meat, the costume worn by the king on the Great Day, and so on. The king walks around the fire, completely naked, while the paints on his body are washed. The water that falls on the ground is supposed to "help the rain."

The last day is mainly made up of festivities and rejoicing. All the taboos are lifted. The warriors go off to weed the queen mother's largest garden. Throughout the country the local contingents serve their local chiefs. The division of the harvest of the new crops is made among the heads of the homesteads.

Several aspects of this ritual are of special interest here. We first notice a specific characteristic of this rite of power: the two types of violence are mixed. Symbolic violence, linked to the condensation of magical power in the person of the king, and the raw violence of force manifested in the acts of pillage carried out by the priests on the population. One would no doubt want to so mark the right to the monopoly on violence.

Hilda Kuper asserts that the main aim of the *Incwala* is to build up the health of the king. But there is more going on here than a simple enhancement of health, because it is not the individual person of the king that is at stake. As certain symbolic aspects of the ritual show (for example, the skin of the silver monkey and the *umuzi* grass that is made into mats passed on from reign to reign), its goal is to make the king immortal. To do this his body has to be transformed, changed into a "body of the kingdom," a deathless State body. For me, the main question posed by this ritual is, How does one transform a man into a god, how does one transform singular, mortal, and human body into an omnipotent, divine, and immortal body?

The answer to this question is given in the logic that belongs to enthronement rituals, which restore the genesis of the formation of the deathless body of the king.[25] From another angle, if one adopts the proposed hypothesis — seeing the enthronement ritual of the magician king as a variant of the possession ritual — the question takes another form: since the model of therapeutic rituals follows a process of death and rebirth, what form should the enthronement ritual take on so that it ends up with a body that never dies? Because in therapy, rebirth is complementary to death. The cured body, if it does not hide away any more illness, nevertheless remains vulnerable, mortal. With enthronement (since we are dealing with the body of the State), the rebirth must lead to immortality. So on the one hand the ritual must follow the logic of the death-rebirth sequence, and on the other it must deny this logic in one way or another since it is a matter of making a deathless body appear.

The solution to this problem is found in what Alfred Adler calls the "splitting of the person" of the king, which I would rather call the "splitting of the body of the king." It can be described such that what is joined in the same body in the therapeutic ritual will be distinct in the enthronement rite: the king's body will be split into a perishable body and an immortal body. The first is required by the logic of the process: one has to die in order to be reborn, and since it seems to be, in the case of the king, an "endless" rebirth, which does not include death as an end point, the complementary mortal body will thus have an infinitely deferred death. This is what happens with the Moundang, whose earth god, *gō-pekworé*, takes on the role of the king's double. He has a sick body, and his death is endlessly put off to another day.[26] In the Swazi case, the material provided by Kuper on the role of the *tinsila* shows that they have the same function as the earth chief of the Moundang. From the blood-brother exchange to the ritual acts in the *Incwala*, they play the part of the king's doubles. Negative doubles, who protect him by taking on the sickness he was supposed to get (redirecting witchcraft attacks toward themselves), washing him, and gathering dangerous dirt, and so on. But, above all, they do not have the right to die as long as the king is alive (their corpses are kept in a hut, and they are only buried when the king is buried). In other words, they are the ones who incarnate the mortal body of the king. So a double complementary function is carried out by the mortal body of the *tinsila*. By really dying, they allow the human element to be integrated into the logic of the deathless king's body (because the "king's body" as a representation requires, of course, the perishable basis in the real body of the monarch); and, by not dying like other men by deferring their own death in the case where their decease occurs before the king's, their body has hidden, as it were, an eternity factor—which corresponds to the institutional reality of the body of the king.

But how is the representation of this body made up? Only a close reading of the *Incwala* ritual can furnish a satisfying response to this question.[27] Unfortunately I will have to limit myself to a few points, which will be useful only in giving directions for future work.

First, the whole ritual can be seen as a process of metamorphosis of a body. At the center of this metamorphosis there is the transfer of the function of the infralanguage to a representation. The *Incwala*, from beginning to end, is but a long elaboration of this representation, which is not the image of the king's body itself, but that of a new body, full of potencies, whose gestures copy and direct the movements of the cosmic world and the nation.

We notice two series of things aiming at this result. One concerns all the sequences that tend to make ceremonial gestures coincide with cosmic movements; the other includes those which contribute to the elaboration of the image of the king's body.

In the first, the symbolism of the stars has to be highlighted, especially, at the beginning of the ritual, when the sun couples with the moon—through this the natural world progressively inscribes itself on the king's body. But other episodes contribute: the bull, the taking of medicines that are immediately symbolic—transfer of potency from plants that do not die, power from animal organs to the king. We could say there is nothing special about this, since this also happens with the body of the possessed, exfoliating to the point of embracing a symbolically overdetermined space. No doubt. However, there is a difference between the possession and enthronement rituals: the king's body is not exfoliated in a becoming-animal sense, his metamorphosis does not go right through to completion. It is more a case of transformation of the infralanguage into a *body*. The magician king acquires a body that possesses magical powers, and differs from that of the sorcerer or the ordinary magician who manipulates codes through objects. With the king the primordial tool, and the privileged object for manipulations, is his own body. At the end of the *Incwala*, when they wash the paints from the king's body, the water that falls "helps the rain."

Now we have to understand how the inscription of the movements of the world in the body of the king works. If we compare it with possession, we note that in the enthronement ritual there is a *fixing* of the powers of the possessed; the king certainly takes supernatural potencies into his body, but instead of expelling them at the end of the session, as in the therapeutic ritual, he keeps them forever. Of course, the administration of medicines from diverse codes—vegetable, animal, mineral—contributes to making the king's body a translator of signs and forces. The specificity of the process lies in the fact that its translating activity is manifest in corporeal gestures that involve the whole body.

How does this fixing of supernatural potencies in the body of the king come about, changing him into a new body and a representation of the body? This question carries two problems: (1) to know how the *representation* of the king's body is built up, that is, how it becomes a totality where the whole world is inscribed; (2) how this representative totality has the property of fixing supernatural potencies in it (that is, why these don't abandon the king's body, as happens in the possession ritual).

The difficulties set up by these questions will only allow me a tentative approach to their solution.

Incwala is, at different points, punctuated by an alternation: between the naked and the dressed body of the king. The crowd reacts in opposite ways corresponding to these states. When the king appears nude, they are sorry for him, the women cry, the men sing hostile songs. When he emerges in a resplendent costume, the crowd and the princes are gripped with fear. I think that this alternation is the pivot for the formation of the representation of the king's body. Because of it, two processes enter into play and join forces: on one side the nude-clothed oscillation follows a progression—the king begins by being completely naked, then he appears wearing a penis sheath, and finally his nudity is hidden, even when he is undressed, underneath the paints. Now clothes and paints have connotations of potency, while nudity (as the songs indicate) signify vulnerability. Dressing therefore plays an essential role in the construction of the image of the new body, which is a body of potency.

On the other hand, this image is constituted in a permanent reference of the king's body in the body of his subjects. Sometimes he dominates, sometimes he is the subject of his subjects, this movement ending up in the absolute supremacy of the king.[28] This reverberation—which is shown by the play of actions (of the king) and the replies (from the people) on multiple levels: dance, costumes, gestures, taboos—is isomorphic with possession in therapeutic rituals. Here, in fact, there is no possession,[29] but because of the link that has been created in this way between the singular bodies and the king's body, the latter allows himself an (exfoliated) body space that includes the former. The alternation between clothing and dress is similar to the death/rebirth poles alternating in therapeutic rites. This alternation is not the isolated product of an individual body, but is in a relationship between the king and his subjects designed to create a collective body, the body of the Swazi nation, and a reflected body of the former, the power of the king. The to and fro movement between the subjects' bodies and their monarch creates the latter as an *image*, an image that is a global surface for the inscription of specific bodies. The reflection of this global image onto the totality of the subjects reorganizes them into a new grouping. In this way two complementary representations are formed. The subjects see their potency and their behavior in the potency and the gestures of their king. And the king sees his power concretized in the effects that his behavior has on the totality of his subjects. All this is really only possible because there is a *fixation* of supernatural potencies working on the body of the king. This fixation, indicating the absolute power of the monarch, *releases* the representation of the body of the king from that of the "collective body" of the nation. Now, the fixation of divine potencies signifies the immortality of power. It is because *Incwala* is a ritual destined to abolish death and produce an immortal body that the representation of this body can arise.

The moment in *Incwala* that marks the division between the representation of the body of the king and that of the singular subjects (inasmuch as they belong to the nation) is no doubt that of the dance of the *Silo* monster. Here the absolute transcendence of the power of the king is affirmed: the monster is nameless, the dance is incomprehensible, only the king knows it, he makes it up as he dances; and the freakish form of the costume shows that this body is different from all other bodies. This costume is a concentration of the immortality feature of the king (via the animal skins). This is how the division between the bodies is organized, and the representation of the deathless body of the king is located beyond all representation: it is what is represented by a visible and unnameable representation (the monster's body).

To get to this point, they have had to manipulate first of all the king's real (naked) body and to make an object and basis for representation. It has had to have been prepared to become a surface for the inscription of the world, translating others (and its own mortal body) into itself. So, folding back on itself, the infralanguage transforms itself into a metalinguistic operator for the translation of codes.

Now we are even in a position to answer the question set up at the beginning of this section: why, with the emergence of State power, was a center for the accumulation of forces and goods created?

F   I   V   E

The Surplus Value of the Power of the State

HAVING TAKEN on board the magical functions of supernatural beings, the king's body gives life to the earth and assures the prosperity of the community. As a deathless, deified, curing body, it is the model of social health. Its magical functions are also social. As we have already said, the principle of the profane over the sacred, the political over the magical or religious, is installed with the first state formations. State law codes magical-religious functions according to its own tasks and goals.

The State apparatus is initially a large body containing the potencies capable of acting on people and the world. The State does not act like a god (which does not have a body), but like a body that has the capacity to act (magically or rationally) on nature and society. The "king's body" is no doubt a model for conceiving the State, but at a more profound level (and this is the reason for its use as a model), it is the cured body of the possessed, but hypostasized.

Incidentally, if we consider the *act* that transforms the prestigious leader into a power leader, the act that constitutes prestige in power, we notice that he identifies himself with a kind of submission through which the community not only agrees to recognize prestige in one person only, but to obey him legally, that is, always. Now in this contract, the forces that the community has given to the leader are not given back in the same form. The leader has appropriated them and created a device that can stock them. This device is, in the first instance, the hypostatized body of the leader. As a body it constitutes the way of unifying the forces; thinking about possessing them, accumulating them as a reserve of human forces; transforming them into power: it is the agency of force. The act of subjection through which State power is installed copies that of the submission to the gods that the community performs in the curing ritual.

Except that with the State, the curing ritual is always happening. It has never stopped, ever since the first act that established the State as a cured social body. This is why the community always has to pay tribute in goods and forces, because the existence of the state is like the perpetual epiphany of social potency transfigured into political power. So it is through this tribute that society is permanently being "cured" in (and through) the State. The State accumulates forces as if it were society itself that was piling them up in its body.

But there is another reason why the power of the State is installed, thanks to the agency of the "king's body." In the circuit of exchanges of goods and forces shown on page 257, the equivalence among them all stops any accumulation in individual social units. At the basis of this equivalence is found a certain coincidence between the exchange and use value of the goods, a coincidence that comes from the fact that both have the same standard: the symbolic value of these same goods. Now, this value depends on the capacity of the goods to "produce" forces (the most valuable goods are the ones that have the most forces concealed in them). This symbolic value is therefore itself a function of the quantity of forces moving from people to gods and those in politics. In short, the ultimate basis for symbolic value of goods is the power that produces them and that they always carry. It is because goods contain (i.e., can be transformed into) forces, and in a direct fashion (without any equivalence relation, on the one hand, and on the other because the forces are symbolized, in such a way that the force necessary for the production of goods is among those forces received from the dead and ancestors), that tribal societies can modulate the excess of goods by liquidating them in offerings to the gods, to get forces in return that will once more be used to produce goods. It is because in fact supernatural potencies are basically of the same nature as human potencies that they both "consume" goods (symbolically *at first*) and produce goods that the exchange circuit is possible. All this equivalence is established via symbolic thought. Because exchanges are symbolic, the value of goods is based on their power to procure forces; and this power is both symbolic and efficient (real). So exchanges with the dead constitute, as well, an economic circuit, with a real effect on the community's productive capacity.

With the formation of the "king's body" we are witness to this body's absorption of the symbolic value of forces. This is an aspect of the monopolization of potency by political power. While in therapeutic rites the accumulation of forces is produced to dismantle an excess of forces (sickness equals blocked forces), to destroy whatever is stopping forces from circulating (this is very clear in the Ndembu case: the woman is sick because she forgot to pay homage to a matrilineal ancestor, and the cure obliges her to sacrifice goods and to reinvest her forces and her affectivity once again, especially on the matrilineal side, since she had gotten too close to her husband's side),[1] the accumulation of potency in the body of the hypostatized leader only happens so it can be redistributed again: part of these forces remains blocked in the body to be used to consecrate it, build it up, or even proliferate it. The forces are no longer there to destroy the threat that the body will corporalize itself (in sickness) but, on the contrary, *to corporalize a cured body* (which means the body is functioning, from the point of view of the infralanguage, in a quite freakishly perverse way, since it actually acts in such a way as to stop the body from taking itself for a sign or a representation). The corporalization is first of all translated into the (political) unification of potencies—the body gives itself an image, an image that is going to be a model for the infralanguage. The image of the king's body will be the true image of the body and the interpretive grid for its functions. This body's gestures will have magical or political functions. The corporalization of the cured king's body thus transforms the infralanguage into a "spiritual" metalanguage. The model body will henceforth be a language, and the supreme language, the real way to speak and act about and on forces and potencies, will be the acts and discourses—the language—of the State. But this means that the State, as a "spiritual body," will take on board some of the functions of singular bodies (infralanguage), especially the production of the potencies needed for the symbolic circulations of goods and forces. Here we find the second major consequence of the constitution of the king's body," that is, his corporalization. It implies its oversymbolization, the absorption of forces in the supreme body of the monarch. This body stops being a singular body, which allows the symbolization of the world to set itself up (in the shape of its image) as the symbol of the world and of bodies. It will be both the supreme commodity and the supreme power.

From now on the exchange circuit of goods and forces will always lack a device immanent to the bodies that will control the relative value of them both. We can pinpoint two basic reasons for this imbalance:

1. Singular forces, stripped of their symbolic value, are only exchanged with other forces by way of goods for which the value is henceforth fixed by

the relationship and exchange with the State. This assumes an "obedience contract" through which the State always takes off a portion of the forces social units give it, using it to its own advantage. The forces given to the State are in part given back in the form of services, while these are meant to allow the community production of forces in a practical rather than a symbolic manner. Even when the political functions of the State are still confused with magical-religious fictions, the services rendered to the community by the king's body (guaranteeing the harvest, fixing the ritual calendar, and so on) are always accompanied by a dual obligation: work for the State and a tribute to be payed (a tax) so the State will be held to deliver these services. In short, these services are necessarily followed by a *symbolic deficit* vis-à-vis the symbolic value of the potencies specific units give. This symbolic deficit then reduces the value of singular potencies. To make it up (this is the "infinite debt" Deleuze and Guattari speak of in *Anti-Oedipus*) one has to work harder from this point on. Also this work for the State takes on the appearance of a symbolic tribute, that is, an effort to produce the symbolic — in the vain expectation of an equal return in the form of public services. At the same time as a symbolic deficit is created on the side of society, a surplus of symbolic value builds up on the side of the State. The latter accumulates both social forces, becoming the largest reserve of potency and symbolic value. There is this value, but, paradoxically, the State can no longer fulfill its function of symbolic transformation, which the gods previously had. It is different from the gods in that it is public and visible, constantly intervening in exchanges; it is constituted as a political body and as a social body with an apparatus that is involved in exchanges and that must be fed, so that it can carry out its political and social tasks. It is thus condemned to *real* and not just symbolic consummation (that is, real *at first*) of goods and forces. As both a social partner and symbolic operator it cannot, as the gods would in a symbolic mode, receive everything for giving everything. In actually consuming forces and goods, it brings about their progressive desacralization, instigating a waste of social symbolism.

The excess accumulated by the State represents the surplus value of State power. Founded on the appropriation of potencies and symbolic value, it then entails, cyclically, the accumulation of a new surplus value in potency and wealth. As I have already said, part of this surplus value will be used for the conservation and the development of the State apparatus (from the administrators through to the indispensable symbolic pomp it dresses itself up in: ornaments, ceremony, and so on).

The break in the equivalence of exchanges therefore originates, primordially, from the unification of potencies that come to fill the empty form of the traditional political establishment. This is not a result of the political will of the chieftains, but obeys an internal logic. From the moment that this unification necessarily implies the oversymbolization of what brings it about (the king's body), the mechanism that deducts symbolic surplus values in specific social units comes into play. From this point on these are affected by a lack, and they have to try to fill it through work, work that is not just measured by the symbolic value of the goods produced, but more on their "exchange" value, which is an offshoot of the contract signed with the State.

2. The second reason for the nonequivalence of goods and forces introduced by the State's activities is related to the very nature of the new exchange circuit. When the magical-religious system was the sole symbolic agency, what men gave to gods was recompensed by what they got back: the symbolic value modulated the value of goods offered and produced, such that one gave what one had to in order to receive the equivalent. "Excesses" and "surpluses" were given, and one got back what one needed once more produce surpluses. The control brought about thanks to symbolic exchange with gods and the dead allowed an equivalence between an excess of goods (to offer) and a lack of forces (to receive). What was asked of the gods was not just the reproduction of the minimal conditions for biological survival of the community, but the conditions for its cultural life, beginning with the management of "abundance."

Now, with the emergence of the State, this system is reversed: what is given to the State ends up being insufficient for the State to give the same back again. The act of submission that inaugurates the State's activities monopolizing the singular potencies creates a lack (of goods and forces) in the heart of society. And the services that the State returns represent the minimal conditions for community life (in principle). It is no longer a matter of receiving what will allow the production of an excess of goods, since that—an excess of forces—is henceforth the property of the State; it is a matter of receiving what will allow the reproduction of the symbolic lack (i.e., a lack of potency) in specific social units. Because the State also consumes, because it really holds goods and forces, this part that is retained is no longer transformed into forces and goods (spread around the community). What the community gets is not enough to allow it to produce a surplus in relation to its normal situation, rather it is just enough to make up the lack in the symbolic. So, when a new cycle of exchanges starts up, what the specific social units give to the State does not just come from an excess produced by the society, but again produces a double lack (symbolic and real) that leaves these units once again under the sign of privation. And as the natural tendency of the State is to proliferate and increase its surplus value of power, social lack will not stop growing (this is the

general case: it is clear that with different concrete types of state political power organization, there are different regimes of surplus value extraction, taking multiple
and even contradictory forms).

These then are the conditions under which *determined work* produces goods of which some go to the State and the rest goes to the community; the
first is used to install state power, power to make people work, for example, because
it is affected by a symbolic lack, work becomes *naked* force, the force of work that
must produce goods to acquire a symbolic value (i.e., potency). Previously, in the
prestate situation, the value of goods was fixed as a function of their capacity to
produce forces. Forces and potencies were therefore the basis for value. Now it is
the value of forces that is fixed as a function of their capacity to produce goods
(which may or may not come to support forces). The State receives goods and is
supposed to transform them into forces that it returns to the collectivity; in reality,
by holding on to singular potencies, it becomes itself the basis for the value of goods,
upsetting the exchange system. Since the potency of specific social units has stopped
being the basis for the value of goods, the latter, produced by the former, will have
a value (symbolic, a power value) that will determine the value of forces. And as the
State only gives back, in the form of services — guaranteeing the protection of society against enemies, assuring justice, the survival of the community in times of need,
and so on — what will allow the reproduction of forces for which the value is measured against the value of goods, this measure tends to become quantified, shedding
its symbolic connotations. So the value of forces will be measured by their capacity
to produce more and more goods (which are socially necessary to the reproduction
of forces). The quality of the goods is of little importance, as it happens, since it
also depends on its capacity to feed a new circuit of exchanges, determined by the
power of the State and the needs of society. Under these conditions one always has
to work to excess to return to the State the tribute that its power demands.

Note that the goods continue to carry their potency, even though
it may be monopolized by the State, but in another form. Besides, this regime —
because of a certain quality of investment of forces in work — allows the State to
maintain the submission of social units (creating a dependence on social exchanges
vis-à-vis its power, and using its potency to make work).

Henceforth people's work obeys the necessity to pay a tribute to
the State to contribute to the feeding of this "huge leviathan" that is the "king's
body." Henceforth these bodies, stripped of their singular potencies, corporalized
by lack of symbolization, will increasingly only entertain political relations among
each other. These find their model in the functioning of the State, which acts as a

metalanguage. As such, it is an agency for all the equivalences between all social activities (even if this does not actually come about, even if at the actual stage of development of the modern State this has not come about, it is inscribed from the start, in its vocation and its destiny). All social activities, all individual and collective acts, now possess a "general equivalent to civic value," for which the principle is contained in State law, the apparatus that decodes this value in each particular instance.

Several consequences should be highlighted from the preceding. First we note that State organization always takes on the magical-religious mantle in its initial form. Magical States, theocratic States—these are the result of the overlay (or the partial fusion) of the magical-religious establishment on the political establishment. This overlay is accompanied by a monopolization of social powers. In this sense, the formation of political power is equivalent to the fixing of the "floating signifier," to its encasement in a "regime of signs" that functions, in its first modalities, under the aegis of a "supreme (or despotic) signifier." This regime of signs controls the circulation of forces in the interior of the social field.

Second, the emergence of the State form upsets the exchange of forces and goods, and the order of subordination of the political and the symbolic is reversed. From now on what is installed is the principle of the domination of the political over the symbolic, if not the actual domination. What characterizes State-less societies is the subordination through exchanges of the political under the (social) symbolic. The various forms of tribal justice are witness to this subordination, especially to the extent that sanctions applied—for example, supernatural, or by way of the pressure of public opinion—have the aim of restoring specific potencies that have been wronged. Even when the mechanism for the control of conflicts is related to a "weakened" symbolism—for example, when Eskimos have a joking match instead of a vendetta—that is, one that plays itself out in a public space without supernatural powers intervening, it is still symbolism that allows for the return to the situation preceding the conflict, where the balance of the rights of each party is based in a certain balance of potencies. If, in stateless societies, the political has not seized the social, it is because the political does not have enough power.

With the birth of the State, a permanent center for the accumulation of power is created. Now, as we have seen, the extraction of surplus value of power becomes the very condition for social functioning. Political power moves from the edges toward the center of the social domain. And as the development of the State apparatus entails the proliferation of a stratum of administrators (and, in the West, the "political professionals" whose emergence Max Weber has studied), all those who belong to this class will naturally benefit from the surplus value of the power of the State. They will benefit in a double way—as agents of the State and as members of civil society. This will create problems in certain cases. If it is true that membership of the social stratum of administrators (where we include the "clientele" that accompanies so many monarchical powers, especially in the West, at the end of the Middle Ages) implies privileges that are repeated at the level of civil society (because one benefits from power in order to enjoy its privileges, also, outside of power), then from another perspective this same layer of administrators or the class it emerges from can enter into conflict with State power. This is even, in a way, inevitable. Since the State apparatus constitutes a machine to draw surplus value from the whole society, even as it privileges a stratum or class, it nevertheless takes it unawares and picks it up in the net of the exchanges that it uses to accumulate power.

When I speak of "exchanges with the State," I do not mean direct exchanges. If specific social units must pay a "tribute" to the State, it is in the very heart of their normal social activity. Here lies the specificity of state action and its specific way of keeping society subjected. In reality one does not work *for* the State; one works, and in working socially, one pays taxes to the State. There is no exchange with the State (except when one becomes a "social partner," but in this case it is the State that puts itself at the same level as individual units, like any other "legal personage"); one exchanges, and in exchanging socially, one "pays" a tax to the State; one gets married, one is born, one dies—one "pays" to the State (in the form of a mark, an inscription on the official register, that is, an inscription on the body of the State) to get married, to have a name at birth, to die, to live, to inherit; taxes, duties, all sorts of services rendered to the State punctuate its intrusion everywhere in social life. It acts indirectly, short-circuiting social acts, imposing itself between people to take its dues. In this sense, nothing has changed, except that from now on each exchange will bring with it a deduction taken off by the State. It thus becomes the major mediator of collective human relations.

Notes

Introduction

1. *Primitif*, in French usage, is used nonpejoratively in relation to certain societies, while "primitive" in English has fallen out of anthropological and general usage. "Traditional" or "tribal" will be used to gloss *primitif*, as in "tribal societies" or "traditional peoples." On this page *primitif* is retained in connection with Deleuze and Guattari's technical usage. It is important to bear in mind that the author originally used *primitif* to designate societies deploying a particular form of power, so it could, in some cases, refer to "us." *Trans.*

2. Gilles Deleuze and Félix Guattari, *A Thousand Plateaus*, trans. Brian Massumi (Minneapolis: Minnesota University Press, 1987), chap. 10.

3. Edmund Leach, *Culture and Communication: The Logic by Which Symbols Are Connected: An Introduction to the Use of Structuralist Analysis in Social Anthropology* (Cambridge: Cambridge University Press, 1976), 44.

Part I, The Antinomies of Power

1. Claude Lévi-Strauss, *Introduction to the Work of Marcel Mauss*, trans. Felicity Baker (London: Routledge and Kegan Paul, 1987), 64.

I.1, First Antinomy (on the Means of Power)

1. The two French words for "power," *puissance* and *pouvoir*, correspond to two quite different concepts, which ultimately derive from Latin *potentia* and *potestas*. In the "Notes on the Translation" in Deleuze and Guattari's *A Thousand Plateaus*, Brian Massumi points out that Deleuze and Guattari use *puissance* to refer to a "range of potential" or "a capacity to affect or be affected" (xvii). To the extent that Gil seems to be following this meaning, I will render *puissance* as "potency," except occasionally where "efficacy" seems better. *Pouvoir*, on the other hand, is used to refer to a social or political force in Gil, corresponding to Michael Hardt's rendering of Negri/Spinoza's *potere/potestas* as "Power" (with the capital): "the centralized, mediating, transcendental force of command" (Antonio Negri, *The Savage Anomaly*, trans. Michael Hardt [Minneapolis: University of Minnesota Press, 1991], xiii). *Trans.*

2. The partial or total destruction of the "coppers" of the Kwakiutl is designed, in any case, to free the energy they contain. By breaking them, the chieftains assert their superiority, that is, the superiority of their force over signs.

3. Luc de Heusch, *Essais sur le symbolisme de l'inceste royal en Afrique* (Brussels: University of Brussels, 1958).

4. On the meaning of *charis*, see J.-P. Vernant, *Mythe et pensé chez les grecs*, vol. 1 (Paris: Maspéro, 1965), 131.

5. Countryside of Western France marked by intermingling patches of woodland and heath, small fields, tall hedgerows, and orchards (Catherine Cullen's note, p. 3 of Jeanne Favret-Saada, *Deadly Words: Witchcraft in the Bocage*, trans. Catherine Cullen [Cambridge, Cambridge University Press, 1980]; *Les Mots, la mort, les sorts* [Paris: Gallimard, 1977]).

6. Edmund Leach, *Rethinking Anthropology* (London: Athlone Press), 1971.

7. See Catherine Cullen's note for this translation of *désorcelleur*, in Favret-Saada, *Deadly Words*, 3. *Trans.*

8. On this topic, see the Third Antinomy, Part I, chap. 3.

9. E. E. Evans-Pritchard, *Witchcraft, Oracles, and Magic among the Azandie* (Oxford: Clarendon Press, 1976).

10. A classification that is adopted without changes by L. Mallart Guimera in *Ni dos ni ventre: Religion, magie et sorcellerie Evuzok* (Paris: Société d'ethnologie Université de Paris X, 1981).

11. Estienne de La Boétie, *Slaves by Choice* (Egham: Runnymede, 1988); Wilhelm Reich, *The Mass Psychology of Fascism*, trans. Vincent R. Carfagno (Harmondsworth, England: Penguin, 1975); Gilles Deleuze and Félix Guattari, *Anti-Oedipus: Capitalism and Schizophrenia*, trans. Robert Hurley, Mark Seem, and Helen R. Lane (Minneapolis: University of Minnesota Press, 1983).

12. See Part II, 5.1.

I.2, Second Antinomy (on the Forms of Power)

1. See Part III, 3.1.3.

2. I am adopting the Kelsenian conception of the norm. Cf. Hans Kelsen, *Théorie pure du droit* (Paris: Dalloz, 1962), translated as *Pure Theory of Law*, from the 2nd (rev. and enl.) German ed. by M. Knight (Berkeley: University of California Press, 1967).

3. On this point see José Gil, "Costituzione," *Enciclopedia Einandi* (Turin) 4 (1978).

4. Plato, *The Republic*, trans. Allan Bloom (New York: Basic Books, 1968), book VIII, 562c.; Aristotle, *Politics*, Book V, V, § 1–6.

5. Plato, *Republic*, book VIII, 562e–563d.

6. Cf. E. E. Evans-Pritchard, *The Nuer: A Description of the Modes of Livelihood and Political Institutions of a Nilotic People* (1940; reprint, Oxford: Clarendon Press, 1968), and *Nuer Religion* (Oxford: Oxford University Press, 1974).

7. Emile Benveniste, *Le Vocabulaire des institutions indo-européennes*, vol 2 (Paris: Minuit, 1969), 148–151.

8. I have taken these rituals as symbolic compensations. It is obvious, as has often been pointed out, that power always withholds real potentiality (*puissance*).

9. What Gilles Deleuze and Félix Guattari call, in the *Anti-Oedipus*, the "surplus value of the code" of prestige.

10. Claude Lévi-Strauss, *Triste tropiques*, trans. John and Doreen Weightman (London: Jonathan Cape, 1973), 316–17.

11. Cf. Lorna Marshall, "!Kung Bushman Bands," in R. Cohen and J. Middleton, eds., *Comparative Political Systems* (New York: Natural History Press, 1967).

12. Claude Lévi-Strauss, *Triste tropiques*, 316.

13. Luc de Heusch, "Pour une dialectique de la sacrality du pouvoir," in *Le Pouvoir et le sacré* (Brussels: Université Libre de Bruxelles, 1962).

14. See the third antinomy.

I.3, Third Antinomy (on the Ends of Power)

1. Jack Goody, *Death, Property and the Ancestors* (Stanford, Calif.: Stanford University Press, 1962), 73.

2. Ibid., 73.

3. Ibid.

4. This spelling, following Goody, is retained in the translation. In Gil it is spelled "LoDagaa." *Trans.*

5. Jack Goody, *Death, Property*, 74.

6. Ibid., 309.

7. Ibid., 408.

8. Ibid., 409–410.

9. Marshall Sahlins, "The Spirit of the Gift," in *Stone Age Economics* (Chicago: Aldine Atherton, 1972) [p. 160: "a third party is necessary to show a *turnover*." *Trans.*].

10. Marcel Mauss, *The Gift: Forms and Functions of Exchange in Archaic Societies*, trans. Ian Cunnison with an introduction by E. E. Evans-Pritchard (London: Cohen and West, 1966). See Part II, chapter 3 in this volume for the Maori text translated in full.

11. Sahlins, *Stone Age Economics*, 165–66.

12. Ibid., 168.

13. Ibid.

14. Ibid.

15. Lévi-Strauss, *Introduction to the Work of Marcel Mauss*.

16. Ibid., 64.

17. Elsdon Best, *The Maori*, vol. 1, Memoirs of the Polynesian Society vol. 1, no. 5 (1924), 299, quoted in Sahlins, *Stone Age Economics*, 166.

18. Sahlins, *Stone Age Economics*, 166–68.

19. It is not by chance that in a book called *Pouvoirs de vie, pouvoirs de mort* (Paris: Flammarion, 1977), Marc Augé makes particular reference to doubles. See also the same author's *Théories des pouvoirs et ideologie* (Paris: Hermann, 1975).

20. Goody, *Death, Property*, 394.

21. Commenting on the way that the Ndembu think about the different supernatural forces at play in a ritual, Victor Turner wrote: "It is impossible to draw the line here between animism and dynamism. All one can say is that Ndembu try to tap many sources of power (*ng'ovu*), treating their dominant symbols as power-accumulators" (*The Drums of Affliction: A Study of Religious Processes among the Ndembu of Zambia* [Oxford: Clarendon Press, 1968], 85).

22. See Part III, 2.3, for a discussion of this process.

23. I will present later a model for the origin of the state, where the political sphere falls back on the magical-religious one.

24. On this point, see Pierre Legendre, *Jouir du pouvoir* (Paris: Minuit, 1976).

25. Georges Duby, *Guerriers et paysans* (Paris: Gallimard, 1973), 67, and *The Early Growth of the European Economy: Warriors and Peasants from the Seventh to the Twelfth Century*, trans. Howard B. Clarke (London: Weidenfeld and Nicolson, 1974). On the question of bequests, see Philippe Jobert, *La Notion de donation, convergences: 630–750* (Paris: Publications de l'Université de Dijon, XLIX, Société des Belles Lettres, 1977).

26. For this history, see Louis-Vincent Thomas, *Anthropologie de la mort* (Paris: Payot, 1975).

27. See Part III, 2.3, for the development of this aspect of the exchange circuit between the dead and the living.

I.4, Fourth Antinomy (on the Limits of Power)

1. E. E. Evans-Pritchard and Meyer Fortes, *African Political Systems* (London: Oxford University Press, 1970).

2. On this topic, see the analyses of Deleuze and Guattari on the body full of the earth, in *Anti-Oedipus*, 144.

3. Victor Turner, *The Drums of Affliction: A Study of Religious Processes among the Ndembu of Zambia* (Oxford: Clarendon Press, 1968), 272.

4. Ibid., 52.

5. Ibid., 63–64.

6. Ibid., 64.

7. Arnold Van Gennep, *Rites of Passage*, trans. Monika B. Vizedom and Gabrielle L. Caffee (London: Routledge and Kegan Paul, 1960).

8. Under which category of which classification should the ritual be classed? This is a question that

anthropology has not settled. Rites, it is true, like myths, make up their own categories, on the side, under other headings like "beliefs," "practices," "representations"— all resembling Borges's famous fantastical taxonomy.

9. In *The Savage Mind* (London: Weidenfeld and Nicolson, 1966), Lévi-Strauss analyzes the way in which ritual makes mythical time closer to human time: "Thanks to ritual, the 'disjoined' past of myth is expressed, on the one hand, through biological and seasonal periodicity and, on the other, through the 'conjoined' past, which unites from generation to generation the living and the dead" (236). After having shown how ritual captures diachronic time, he concludes, "It can thus be seen that the function of the system of ritual is to overcome and integrate three oppositions: that of diachrony and synchrony; that of periodic or non-periodic features which either may exhibit; and finally, within diachrony, that of reversible and irreversible time" (237).

10. The fact that one of the functions of the dead is to halt the irreversibility of time—or to create "cyclical" time—is already shown by the belief of traditional peoples in the unchanging foundations of their social model. As Lévi-Strauss notes, "That endlessly repeated justification of every rule, technique and custom in the single argument: the ancestors taught it to us" (236).

11. Max Gluckman, *Analysis of a Social System in Modern Zululand*, Rhode-Livingston Paper, no. 28 (Manchester: Manchester University Press, 1958), 54.

12. Turner, *Drums*, 274.

13. Ibid., 275.

14. Ibid., 275–76.

15. The Latin word *ritus* is derived from the Indo-European "flow" (ibid., 269).

16. Ibid., 64.

17. Ibid., 62.

18. Ibid., 68.

19. Ibid., 65.

20. Ibid., 82.

21. In *The Forest of Symbols* (Ithaca, N.Y.: Cornell University Press, 1967), Turner writes on this matter. The woman who loses too much blood and is incapable of bearing children "is behaving like a male killer (i.e., a hunter or a murderer), not like a nursing woman."

22. Turner, *Drums*, 58.

23. Victor Turner, *The Ritual Process: Structure and Anti-Structure* (London: Routledge and Kegan Paul, 1969), 42–43.

24. Ibid., 25: "The second medicine collected . . . represents another theme of Ndembu ritual—that of representing the patient's inauspicious condition. This is the *mulendi* tree. It has a very slippery surface, from which climbers are prone to slip (*ku-selumuka*) and come to grief. In the same way the patient's children have tended to 'slip out' 'prematurely.' "

25. Ibid., 28.

26. Ibid., 31.

27. Which Turner clearly distinguishes from therapeutic rituals for illnesses.

28. Ibid., 33–37.

29. Ibid., 25.

30. Ibid., 39.

31. Ibid., 41–42.

32. Edmund Leach, *Culture and Communication* (Cambridge: Cambridge University Press, 1976), 44.

33. Turner, *Ritual Process* 11–12. "Thus the implicit aims of *Isoma* include: restoration of the right relation between matriliny and marriage; reconstruction of the conjugal relations between wife and husband; and making the woman, and hence the marriage and lineage, fruitful" (ibid., 18).

34. Turner, *Drums*, 52.

35. Ibid., 42.

36. This opposition is, of course, too rough, but it remains relevant in the context of the *Isoma* ritual.

37. Ibid., 42–43.

38. See in Part II, chap. 1, my commentary on Lévi-Strauss's conception of shamanistic cure.

39. These mediations include mythic discourse, know-how, coded social behavior, technical activity, things, and tools.

40. The worst thing one can do is to make gods human. Like Christ, they have become subject to illness, and humans have become incurable.

41. Which thus appears as a product of this disjunction between space and time.

II.1, The Floating Signifier

1. Claude Lévi-Strauss, *Introduction to the Work of Marcel Mauss*, trans. Felicity Baker (London: Routlege and Kegan Paul, 1987), 61.

2. Ibid., 62–63.

3. Ibid., 63.

4. When American slang says that a woman has got "oomph." *Trans.*

5. Marcel Mauss, *Sociologie et anthropologie* (Paris: Presses Universitaires de France, 1960), 104.

6. Lévi-Strauss, *Marcel Mauss*, 72 n 18.

7. Mauss, *Sociologie et Anthropologie*, 117–20.

8. Ibid., 120.

9. Ibid.

10. Roman Jakobson, *Essais de linguistique générale* (Paris: Minuit, 1963), 80.

11. Edmund Leach, *Culture and Communication: The Logic by Which Symbols Are Connected* (Cambridge: Cambridge University Press, 1976), 11.

12. Ibid., 41.

13. Lévi-Strauss, "The Sorcerer and His Magic" and "The Effectiveness of Symbols," in *Structural Anthropology* (Harmondsworth, England: Penguin, 1977).

14. In English in the original.

15. On this point see Mircéa Eliade, *Shamanism: Archaic Techniques of Ecstasy*, trans. Willard R. Trask (1951; reprint, Princeton, N.J.: Princeton University Press, 1964).

16. Claude Lévi-Strauss, *Structural Anthropology*, trans. Claire Jacobson and Brooke Grundfest Schoepf (New York: Anchor/Doubleday, 1967), 175–76.

17. Ibid., 193.

18. See Michel Leiris, *La Langue secrète des Dogon de Sanga (Soudan français)* (Paris: Institute d'Ethnologie, Musée de l'Homme, 1948), introduction.

19. See Georges Charachidze, *Le Système religieux de la Géorgie païenne* (Paris: Maspéro, 1968), 135.

20. Lévi-Strauss, *Structural Anthropology*, 181.

21. Nils M. Holmet and Henry Wassen, *Mu-Igala or the Way of Muu: A Medicine Song from the Cuñas of Panama* (Göteborg, 1947).

22. See Part I, 4.4.4.

23. Maurice Merleau-Ponty, *Phenomenology of Perception*, trans. Colin Smith (London: Routledge and Kegan Paul, 1962).

24. Claude Lévi-Strauss, *The Savage Mind* (London: Weidenfeld and Nicolson, 1966).

25. See Gilbert Rouget, *Music and Trance: A Theory of the Relations between Music and Possession*, revised by Brunhilde Biebuyck in collaboration with the author (Chicago: University of Chicago Press, 1985), chaps. 1 and 2.

26. See Alfred Métraux, *Voodoo in Haiti*, trans. Hugo Charteris (London: Deutsch, 1959).

27. Cf. Michel Leiris, "La Possession et ses aspects théatraux chez les Ethiopians de Gondar," *L'Homme* 2 (1958).

28. The *Ku-Tumbuka* rite in Turner, *Drums of Affliction,* 86–87.

29. All these points are elaborated in 2.7.

30. Mary Douglas, *Purity and Danger: An Analysis of Concepts of Pollution and Taboo* (London: Routledge and Kegan Paul, 1966), 81.

31. Douglas, *Purity and Danger,* 99.

32. Ernesto de Martino, *Italie du Sud et magie* (Paris: Gallimard, 1963), 24.

33. See Douglas, *Purity and Danger.*

34. Maurice Leenhardt, *Do Kamo: Person and Myth in the Melanesian World,* trans. Basia Miller Gulati with a preface by Vincent Crapanzano (1947; reprint, Chicago: University of Chicago Press, 1979), 18.

35. Leenhardt, *Do Kamo,* 18.

36. Ibid., 19.

37. Ibid., 21.

38. Geneviève Calame-Griaule, *Ethnologie et language: La parole chez les Dogons* (Paris: Gallimard, 1965), 35.

39. Ibid., 34, n. 6.

40. Traces of this idea can be found in Galen's *rete mirabilis* or Descartes's pineal gland.

41. In English in original. *Trans.*

42. Lévi-Strauss, *Marcel Mauss,* 64.

II.2, The Body, Transducer of Signs

1. Béla Balazs, *Theory of the Film: Character and Growth of a New Art* (New York: Arno Press, 1972; Paris: Payot, 1979), 71; emphasis added.

2. Balazs, *Theory of the Film,* 55.

3. Here there is something like a "prepredictive" understanding of spatial forms.

4. See Part II, chap. 4.

5. Cf. Deleuze and Guattari, *Anti-Oedipus,* chap. 1.

6. Bernard Koechlin, "A propos de trois systèmes de notation des positions et mouvements des membres du corps humain...," in *Langages et techniques, Nature et Société,* vol. 1 (Paris: Klincksieck, 1952), 168.

7. Paul Bouissac, *La Mesure des gestes, prolégomènes à la sémiotique gestuelle* (Paris: Mouton, 1973), 16.

8. Ibid., 172.

9. Ibid., 176.

10. Ibid.

11. Ibid., 108.

12. K. L. Pike, *Language in Relation to a Unified Theory of the Structure of Human Behavior* (Glendale, Calif.: Summer Institute of Linguistics, 1954), 31.

13. Leenhardt, *Do Kamo,* 17.

14. The seme being the minimal unit of meaning; for example, the lexeme "high" contains the semes "dimensionality," "verticality," and so forth. See Alain Trognon, Jean-Louis Beauvois, and Gérard Lopez, "Topologie et théorie de la métaphor," *L'Homme* 12 (July–Sept. 1972): 71–72.

15. Ludwig Binswanger, *Introduction à l'analyse existentielle* (Paris: Minuit, 1971), 201.

16. "*Comme tombé des nues.*" The original has the metaphor of falling (*tomber*) essential to the argument. *Trans.*

17. Ludwig Binswanger, *Introduction,* 199.

18. Ibid., 200.

19. Ibid., 201.

20. Ibid., 132.

21. Ibid., 136.

22. Ibid.

23. Ibid.

24. Ibid., 137.

25. Ibid., 132.

26. Ibid., 147.

27. Gisela Pankow, *L'Etre-là du schizophrène* (Paris: Aubier-Montaigne, 1981).

28. Ibid., 114.

29. Ibid., 115.

30. Ibid.

31. Ibid., 116.

32. Ibid., 111.

33. Ibid., 117.

34. Ibid., 116.

35. Ibid., 117; Pankow's emphasis.

36. Ibid.

37. Ibid., 127.

38. Ibid., 129.

39. Ibid., 130.

40. In, for example, Pankow, *L'Etre-là du schizophrène; L'Homme et sa psychose,* (Paris: Aubier-Montaigne, 1973); and "The Body Image in Hysterical Psychosis," *International Journal of Psycho-analysis* 55, no. 3 (1974).

41. Pankow, "L'Etre-là du schizophrène," 17.

42. Gisela Pankow, "La Dynamique de l'espace et le temps vécu," *Critique*, no. 297 (1972): 171.

43. Ibid., 178.

44. Ibid.

45. This is the single-body version of the same phenomenon analyzed earlier concerning the relation between the mime's gestures and the spectator's decoder-body.

46. Reference should be made here to the familiar critique of the conception of body image that centers around the self and conscious intentionality: the unconscious is neglected. I take this critique on board: the space of the body is not conscious, but neither is it unconscious, in the psychoanalytic sense.

47. See France Schott-Billman, *Corps et possession* (Paris: Gaulthier-Villars, 1977), 121.

48. This example was not chosen by chance. Research going on by ethnographers shows that "petrifications," as they appear in stories and legends, cover quite a vast array of codes; in theory anything can be petrified. This would signify that stone would be like an infralanguage projected into space and fixed there. There, codes can no longer be exchanged, but all find their translation, which precisely stops them from being translated among themselves ever again. In certain stories, characters are petrified by a magic spell because they did not know how to translate the codes: for example, they have not been able to go through an initiation procedure.

49. We will see later that such an absorption constitutes one of the operations that allows the emergence of despotic signifiers in a symbolic system, which precisely tend to take the place of the infralanguages by becoming the master decoders of all codes.

50. It seems to me that it is in this way that we have to understand the recent redevelopments of Pankow's method. She is more interested in the "structuration" of space than in the notion of body image, reduced more and more to an analogical referential, as I have already noted: "I take the body to be a model of spatial structure" (Pankow, "Image du corps et objet transitionel: Une contribution à la structuration de l'espace potentiel," *Revue Française de Psychanalyse* 40, no. 2 [1976]: 288). In this same article she gives the following characterization of symbiosis: "In symbiosis, object relations are spatialized: the other who could be loved becomes space, a protective envelope" (289). In the end she arrives at a conception of her modeling method that comes close to the interpretation à la creation I have given of the production of the spaces of the body: "In considering the modeled object in relation to its spatial environment, the dynamic of the relations between objects (objects or living things,

including humans) allows the structuring, in a sort of wakeful dream, of the object relations that are inscribed in temporality. *This modeling process is found in potential space; but the modeled object is not a transitional object*, because the patients do not discover it as a ready-made, they create it. Both the transitional object as well as the model should help patients to symbolize. But this process would not be able to take place without a symbiosis, that is, without this hinge in the dialectic of space. Only this gives access to the elaboration of a transference, and thus to an analytical cure of the psychosis" (299; Pankow's emphasis). I think that these notions of "potential space," "transitional space," and "transitional object," which psychoanalysis gets from Michael Balint and Donald Winnicott, can be comprised in the framework of "the space of the body." What is presented, in potential space, as the play of the transitional object is an apprenticeship in the infralanguage; transmission, via the mother, of "gestures," which, deploying the exfoliations of potential space, will allow the child to assimilate knowledge and the mechanics of corporeal space—in other words to learn to dissociate and reassemble, to put things (and his or her body) into spatial relationships, in short to decode information with the body, and also to metaphorize (symbolize) by making several exfoliations of the space of the body coincide in the transitional play.

51. Pierre Kaufmann's critique of Binswanger's conception of dream spaces in relation to emotional givens is quite justified (Pierre Kaufmann, *L'Expérience émotionelle de l'espace* [Paris: Vrin, 1967], 105 n. 52). Kaufmann says that "there can be no systematic conception of dream spaces at the moment," and this is so independently of the repression of emotional experience. Nevertheless, if one envisages space in dreams not as "the topographies for the ways our desire comes about"—which makes topographic description depend on unconscious contents for which the conscious representations might turn out to be the disguise—but, on the contrary, since the mechanism of the space of the body conditions the very emergence of desire, a mechanism that then brings into being another topography, which is neither that of the represented contents nor of their symbolic sense, it seems that certain obstacles can be lifted. Invariably, in psychoanalytic conceptions, as in "existential analysis," one moves from the meaning (of desire) in order to determine space and its relations; this perspective should be reversed, putting forward the idea that the mechanism of the spaces of the body allows the "linkages" of desire to be noted. For a discussion of the merging of metaphor with "condensation" in the Freudian sense, see Umberto Eco, "Metafora," *Enciclopedia Einaudi* (Turin) 9 (1980): 205. Similarly, for the merging of condensation to linguistic "metaphor," see S. Leclaire and J. Laplanche, "Langage et inconscient," in *L'Inconscient* (Paris: Desclée de Brower, 1966).

52. Although I have decided to limit myself to space, it is clear that I should make a reference to time. These forms are spatial-temporal: corporeal rhythms like the pulse of the blood, breathing, or the rhythm of the movement of things, sound, or astronomical cycles—all these things have form. Thus there are twisted spaces, spaces that expand or shrink, gulflike spaces, and voluminous expansions. J. P. Lovecraft was a wonderful creator of such spaces.

53. Cf. René Thom, *Structural Stability and Morphogenesis* (Reading, Mass. Benjamin, 1975), 124.

54. There is a convergence because physical forms are not "other" than corporeal forms, since the body is also a product of nature. Man's anatomical and physiological structure is part of a "natural plan," as Geoffroy Saint-Hilaire has shown.

55. Thom, in an article criticizing the psychogenetic conception of Piaget's "representative" space, stresses the importance of linking it with the body: "conscious individuals have an (inner) representation of the space which surrounds them, and of the positions of their bodies in that space. I cannot see how one could fail to see in this local map containing the organism anything other than 'representative' space. Because if representative space is other than this local map at the very least it contains it as an originary and essential part of it associated with the body and its activities." Further on when discussing the stages of children's drawing, Thom evokes man's "symbolic function" as it is associated with language: "The child responds to the instruction to draw object A as if he had been asked what is object A? He makes his drawing the graphic equivalent of the word [in a graphic space which is a real space]. In the same way that the word in the listener's mind is going to stimulate the signification of the concept, the drawing is going to stimulate the graphic deployment of the concept. Now, a concept can be broken down into sub-concepts, this analysis being done linguistically through the transformation into the genitive. Thus a "dog's tail" defines a sub-concept of the object dog, expressed topologically through the area of space occupied by the tail belonging to that occupied by the dog. The correct use of grammar thus presupposes a perfect mastery of the implicit topology pertaining to connections, contiguities and which object belongs with which other" (René Thom, "The Genesis of Representational Space according to Piaget," in *Language and Learning: The Debate between Jean Piaget and Noam Chomsky*, ed. Massimo Piattelli-Palmarini (Cambridge, Mass.: Harvard University Press, 1980), 361–368. I believe that this "implicit topology," which presupposes not so much an analysis of the concept as one of information according to forms and abstract forms, can be furnished by bodily space.

56. Henri Maldiney, *Regard parole espace* (Lausanne: Editions L'âge d'homme, 1973), 160.

57. Ibid., 166.

58. Is this not the meaning of this famous text by Hokusai? "From the age of six onward I had an obsessive desire to draw the shape of objects. Toward the age of fifty I had published an infinite number of drawings, but everything I produced before the age of sixty-five is scarcely worth counting. It was at the age of seventy-three that I more or less understood the structure of true nature, animals, plants, birds, fish, and insects. Consequently by the age of eighty I would make even more progress; at ninety I would penetrate the mystery of things; at a hundred I would definitely reach a degree of perfection, and when I am one hundred and ten, for me, every point, every line, will be all alive."

59. Unlike cadence, rhythm implies "critical instances" where the energy is condensed. This is because of the process of energetic concentration of what comes out of form in order to move onto some elements appearing because of rhythm.

60. See Edmund Husserl, *Formal and Transcendental Logic,* trans. Dorion Cairns (The Hague: Nijhoff, 1978). "However much ["The Kreutzer Sonata"] itself consists of sounds, it is an ideal unity; and its constituent sounds are no less ideal. They are obviously not the sounds dealt with in physics; nor are they the sounds pertaining to sensuous acoustic perception, the sounds that come from things pertaining to the senses, and are really extant only in an actual reproduction and the intuiting of it. Just as the one sonata is reproduced many times in the real reproductions, each single sound belonging to the sonata is reproduced many times in the corresponding sounds belonging to the reproduction" (ibid., 21).

61. This could be rephrased in the terms of Deleuze and Guattari. All concrete stances are on a "plane of consistency," which is equivalent to what I am calling "abstract stance" (Deleuze and Guattari, *Thousand Plateaus*, 70–73).

62. Ibid., 308.

63. The work of M. J. Herskovits, Alfred Métraux, Michel Leiris, J. Rouch, Roger Bastide, and L. Mars, among others, has become classic in the African and Afro-American domains.

64. Rouget, *Music and Trance*.

65. The following passage characterizes the role of music for the possessed. If music does not hold the "mysterious power of triggering possession," it aims to "create a certain emotional climate for the adepts…; it leads the adept towards that great mutation, occurring at the level of the imagination, that consists in becoming identified with the spirit which is possessing him," an operation for which other factors are needed. Music is of course indispensable. "Why? Because it is the only language which speaks simultaneously (if I may so put it) to the head and the legs, because it is through music that the group provides the entranced person with a mirror in which he can read the image of his borrowed identity; and because it is the music that enables him to reflect this identity back again to the group in the form of dance. There is no mystery to it at all. Or, if there is, then it lies in the trance state itself, as a special state of consciousness; and if we must seek an explanation for this, it may be found in the overriding power of a certain conjunction of emotion and imagination. This is the source from which trance springs. Music does nothing more than socialize it and enable it to attain full development" (ibid., 325–26).

66. A good example of this would be A. Adler and A. Zempléni, *Le Baton de l'aveugle* (Paris: Hermann, 1972).

67. On this topic see Willy Apollon, *Le Vaudou* (Paris: Editions Galilée, 1976), pt. 1.

68. As in the space of the Kabyle house. See Pierre Bourdieu, *Outline of a Theory of Practice*, chap. 2, "Structures and the Habitus," trans. Richard Nice (Cambridge: Cambridge University Press, 1977); also 218 n. 44.

69. This obviously sets up a problem of interpretation. At what level does meaning have to stop? I would simply like to make one point in relation to this. Whether one likes it or not, one is always, in a certain way, condemned to hermeneutics. But there are two ways of proceeding. Either one looks for signs to interpret with the help of other signs, such that one remains forever cloistered in a semiotic system, or the interpretation brings itself to bear on the breaks between signs and systems such that there are repercussions on the decoding system chosen. In the first case one falls easily into the trap of believing that the system itself contains the final meaning of the signs being decoded, and that nothing remains to be interpreted. Plenty of work (including the "archaeology of knowledge" of Michel Foucault) has shown that our signs have a history and that their meaning is different from what we believe. Here too there are breaks, beyond the factual level. For example, the interpretation of the "holes" in the *Isoma* ritual, if one sets out to find a definitive meaning. If the new hole, the "cold" hole (which is opposed to the anteater's "hot" hole) represents the mother's womb, what does the mother's womb signify? In traditional symbolic systems it relates to a whole series of symbolic levels, and in the end leaves an opening (these levels do not form a circle). In our system it relates to self-evident psychoanalytic and conceptual ideas, for example, but ideas that in reality open on to other meanings that are not necessarily inscribed in a history of facts, in the Husserlian sense. In other words, the foundation of psychoanalytic facts is but a false historical limit, simply a "marker." From the other point of view, choosing to attend to the breaks among semiotic systems, one is less likely to become enclosed within

globalizing and totalizing semiotic systems, so increasingly one has to allow these breaks to act on our own signs. This does not mean breaking (up) signs as such ("they are still signs," one could say), but to refer them to that which, in us, is also on the level of the break, the transemiotic (this is the drift of the methods of both Foucault and Deleuze and Guattari, although each in their own way). In this case, our facts do not become the clear reflection of the obscurities in the signs of others; the evidence that results from the clash of two breaks is no more than itself another diversifying break that does not seek to enclose in another evidentiality any future signs, but it is the evidence that, in the obscurity of the break, calls forth other transemiotic breaks (past and future).

70. See Part I, 4.4.4.

71. For related matters among the Songhay, see Paul A. Stoller, "The Epistemology of Sorkortarey: Language, Metaphor and Healing among the Songhay," *Ethos* 7 (Summer, 1980).

72. Here it is not just a language of the spirit (le *gurri*-screams—of the *zâr* among the Ethiopians [Michel Leiris, "La Possession," 15]), but quite uncodified movements and sounds. Among the Bochiman, the chants relating to bewitching are not made up of words but of sounds without meaning (Lorna Marshall, "The Medicine Dance of the !Kung Bushmen," *Africa* 39, no. 4 (London: Oxford University Press), 370.

73. Thanks to a whole series of techniques used, which are often the same as those that facilitate overcoding, like music and dance.

74. This is a rough sketch of one precise detail (the start of the trance) taken from therapeutic rituals, in particular bewitchment. It is possible, in this context, to understand certain particular stages of the ritual, like that of "exorcism" (*dépossession*), which prepares the body as a surface of inscription.

75. From the fact that the ritual space is the space of the exfoliated body emerges the impossibility of assigning a particular status to it—symbolic, imaginary, or real. Here are some statements made by Willy Apollon on the Haitian voodoo: "The organization of this space is centered around an axis: the *Poto-Mitan*. Here we should not imagine that this is a temple because of everything that is connoted by that idea. We are confronted by a particular organization of space, seemingly with a centre and four directions. The voodoo priest says that, via the Poto-Mitan, we are linked symbolically to another space, that of the *loas*. It is not quite an elsewhere, another physical space. There is no other physical space. All the places are moving through each other. One is always both here and over there. The outside traverses the inside and the surface does not cover up the depths. The Poto-Mitan is at the same time the center, the axis, the borders and the outside limit, and everything happens around it as well. Here is a concept of space which is not structured by writing, nor already oriented by the work of the text. Voodoo spaces are at the crossroads of multiple places. Thus the bottom of the sea, which represents IFE's country, is the place where contact is made with Guinea in Africa—symbolic Guinea and real Africa. And yet this deep water is brought into being just as easily with an earthenware crock filled with water as with the Atlantic Ocean or the Grande Rivière du Nord. Deep water is nothing but deep water. All these places come together. Here the writing has not endorsed the usual distinctions among distances. And the earthenware crock does not represent the bottom of the sea. It is the bottom of the sea. It is from here that the spirits called forth by the *houngan* will emerge, during the ceremony which must make them come out of the water where they have resided since the moment they died" (Apollon, *Le Vaudon*, 100).

76. This concept has the advantage of encompassing both possession and shamanism, the spirit's "entry" into the body of the possessed, and its "exit" from the body of the shaman.

77. The organization of the current work has obliged me to place an analysis that could have occurred here in Part II, chap. 4.

78. Here is a description of "possible, but scarcely codified, motor and verbal behaviour" in the *ndöp* rite among the Wolof of Senegal: "The behaviour in question is located in the confines of strictly ritual activities—classical dancing, miming behaviour, 'crisis work,' 'falling'—and it is sometimes difficult to distinguish the one from the other. The dance itself is occasion for personal manifestations of the following type: certain possessed subjects strike their heads or chests rhythmically, leap on the stage, do some rough dance steps, then suddenly, joining their hands behind their back, begin hopping, then shouting, fall and strike themselves again, begin dancing once more, and so on. Others grab the *laar* of a priestess, shake it, and threaten the crowd with it while dancing. Another group might begin by dancing, then begin to run around the stage, wild-eyed, stopping and gesticulating like boxers. They make inviting gestures to the first griot before making their bodies move in loose undulatory movements and their arms circulate out of time with the music" (Andras Zempléni, "La Dimension thérapeutique du culte des *rab, ndöp tuuru et samp:* Rites de possession chez les Lebou et les Wolof," *Psychopathologie africaine* 2, no. 3 [1966], 410).

79. For instance, in the *ndöp* rite of the Wolof, "measures" of the body and its articulations are important. This has a bearing on the one-multiple dimension of the spaces of the body (Zempléni, "La Dimension thérapeutique," 364).

80. It is clear that the ritual culminating in a trance is a "process," as Turner says. The patient, too, while previously prepared to undergo the overcoding implied by submission to the norms of the rite, does not lend herself to it in the same manner at the beginning compared with at the moment of the trance. It is the process of intensification of energy that leads her to the high point of overcoding. At the beginning she is more or less forced; in any case she is not "living" the coding as intensely as at the end. In this perspective one could take up other possession phenomena: "theatricalization," for instance, comes from the transformation of the body into an expressive corporeal language.

81. See Paul A. Stoller, "The Discourse of Magic: Force and the Power of Words" (unpublished manuscript). Stoller shows that among the Sanghay, where he underwent an apprenticeship in order to be initiated as a sorcerer, magic words, names of medicines that possess magical virtues, the names of powers, sorcerers, and the like, must never be uttered. The initiate learns to use an oblique sibylline language to name these prohibited things. The overt designation of the object is a blunder that earns the initiate a lecture and the reputation for being "dangerous." The prohibited words, which will be used in ritual and magical practice, are charged, in this way, with forces. Stoller affirms that it is the same process as in Favret-Saada's study (*Deadly Words*) of sorcery in the Norman bocage, which he compares with the Songhay, which leads to "deadly words."

82. In this instance similar to Stoller's analysis.

83. Material collected in Pierrette Bertrand-Rousseau, *Ile de Corse et magie blanche: Etude des comportements magico-thérapeutiques* (Paris: Publications de la Sorbonne, 1978).

84. This is an example—a formula for curing burns: "Le Christ est né / Oint avant d'être mouillé / La Madone fut certaine / Que chair cuite devendrait crue" (Pierrette Bertrand-Rousseau, *Ile de Corse*, 71; Gil's translation). English approximation: "Christ was born / Anointed before being wet / The Madonna was certain / That cooked meat would become raw."

85. But then we can understand the meaning of the linguistic changes: create a short text, a condensation of metaphors and synecdoches, which precisely appears *as if complete*, that is, as completing what the "original text" leaves ineluctably open because it is incomplete. What is this "original text"? It is the "final" text that would result from the set of decipherings, associations, and symbolic correspondences carried out on the *historiola*. This could bring up the whole history of the passion of Christ, as well as the magical-religious system of traditional Corsican society: it is clear that this is an inexhaustible corpus.

86. This is no doubt a similar phenomenon to that which in yoga consists in reducing a whole treatise to a few *bija-mantra* (see Mircéa Eliade, *Yoga: Immortality and Freedom*, trans. Willard R. Trask (1954; reprint, Princeton, N.J.: Princeton University Press, 1969), 217.

87. Deciphering symbolic-metaphoric syntagms of a myth with structural or other types of analysis only gives the *ordinary* way in which energy is circulated, and which is then worked on, filtered, transformed by behavior, techniques, and so on.

88. In one sense the case of the *historiola* is much more complex, because the sick people do not seem to put themselves in any particular psychic state or move in any particular way, and it is the same case in Italy as in Corsica. How then can we comprehend the direct action of the discourse? More careful observations discover, however, (1) that the patient's situation is nonetheless special; (2) that the regime for the circulation of the unconscious in rural Mediterranean societies is such that all that is needed is a slight "conditioning" to allow the magical action of discourse on the body. A study on this topic would, I believe, allow us to envisage the cure in the framework being set out here.

89. Here, it seems, we are in a sphere where the traditional aporias of knowledge of "being" are found to be resolved. There is no longer any break between the relative and the absolute, the conditioned and unconditioned, language and action, sign and thing, appearance and reality. It is a "noumenal" sphere where *points of view* disappear. In a sphere where other-becoming is capable of immediately translating all the codes, there ceases to be a privileged point of view, or privileged space and time, or a privileged system of signs. It is the nature of other-becoming to not work from a particular system of signs toward a translation, but to put them all on the same plane. Decontextualized in this way, they are all equivalent. The "real" is therefore everywhere, and is not opposed to the "imaginary" as "truth" would be to "illusion." So where would the "real" of metaphysics be? A privileged system of significations. What is the "reality" of common knowledge? A privileged system of significations. The problem is to know how they become privileged systems.

90. See, for instance, the case of the *natt*, "measures" of the body in the *ndöp* ritual: "Finally, it can be remarked in passing that we note that the 'measure' of different parts of the body via different species of roots suggests the idea of a system of correspondences, now no longer in operation, between 'families' of vegetables and organs of the body, such as have been described among other Sudanese peoples" (Zempléni, "La Dimension thérapeutique," 388).

91. Jacques Fédry, "L'Expérience du corps comme structure du langage: Essai sur la langue sàr (Tchad)," *L'Homme* 16 (January–March 1976): 72.

92. This would explain the transformations of space perceived in trance experiences. Material furnished by ethnography is, in this area, very thin; on the other hand, the works of Carlos Castañeda contain many extremely interesting descriptions.

93. So in alchemical and medical thought the body becomes the mirror of macrocosmic relationships, a field of *effects* of these relationships, and a field of *symptoms*. Subsequently it will be in the symptom that the relationships find their signs, their marks in the body— they will be translated there. And also in political-juridical thought on the "social body," the king is the head, the bankers are the belly, the people the limbs, and so on. The image of the macrocosm thus serves to hierarchize relationships. I should have shown how the one-multiple of infralanguage basically makes metonymy possible. Let me just state one thing: already in the very nature of the articulations of the body the possibility of a certain play between the whole body and a sequence or segment of a sequence exists. This is because a long segment (containing several shorter ones) can also be a gestural unity, and because the body as a whole can become an element in a gestural sequence—for example, in *diving*—and thus be integrated in another sequence. It can therefore be replaced in an intersection (let us say "semic") by a part of the body; in metonymy, the part is metaphor for the whole. But the reverse is also true. If there is a metaphor of *a* unity (let us say "lexemic"), it is because in the play of metamorphoses between the part and the whole of the metonymy, it is the *one*, the same of the metonymized body, which is thus constituting itself as "plan," or model of all individuation. In metaphor, semic intersection therefore makes elements come in to play a role in identity in the metonymic mode of the *one*. It is because metonymy speaks of the same *one* as difference that an equivalence between two diverse elements can be established. And if it speaks of the same *one*, that then relates to this specific phenomenon of the body: in each of its partial movements, as in each of its exfoliations, there is the presence of the *one*.

94. Franz Kafka, *Metamorphosis and Other Stories*, trans. W. and E. Muir (Harmondsworth, England: Penguin, 1961).

95. Ibid., 9.

96. Ibid.

97. "It struck both Mr and Mrs Samsa, almost at the same moment, as they became aware of their daughter's increasing vivacity, that in spite of all the sorrow of recent times, which had made her cheeks pale, she had bloomed into a pretty girl with a good figure. They grew quieter and half unconsciously exchanged glances of complete agreement, having come to the conclusion that it would soon be time to find a good husband for her. And it was like a confirmation of their new dreams and excellent intentions that at the end of their journey their daughter sprang to her feet first and stretched her young body" (62–63). This ending allows for the interpretation of "The Metamorphosis" under the perspective of an initiation of a pubescent girl, as in folkloric tales (the ordeal undergone by Gregory, and his death, allow his sister to reach maturity). This is a pertinent angle on the story, justified by the text, but I cannot go into it here.

98. This analogy is not artificial, however contrived it may seem: in the other perspective, which interprets "Metamorphosis" as being the story of a girl's initiation, the boarders occupy exactly the same place as the ogre (or its variants) in popular folklore.

99. Through to the cause of the illness, scarcely mentioned, which suggests a ritual to cure it—the cause recalling an attack of witchcraft: "You know very well that the traveller who is never seen in the office almost the whole year round, can easily fall victim to gossip and ill luck and unfounded complaints, which he mostly knows nothing about, except when he comes back exhausted from his rounds, and only then suffers in person from their evil consequences, which he can no longer trace back to their original causes" (ibid., 22). At another time Kafka speaks of "Sioux whistles," which his father makes while following Gregor.

100. Ibid., 12–13.

101. Ibid., 13.

102. He cannot become human again, because this would imply incest with his sister. The whole passage about the attraction Gregor feels when he hears his sister play the violin leaves no doubt on this subject. In any case, it is this episode that brings about the total rejection of Gregor by his sister, then his death, and finally Grete's release. The interpretation of "Metamorphosis" as a backward possession ritual links up with the interpretation of it as an initiatory story (we know that Propp thinks folktales have their roots in ancient Indo-European initiation rites). Gregor's illness was his incestuous desire, and his failed metamorphosis the trial that liberates his sister. This is the relevant passage: "Her face leaned sideways, intently and sadly her eyes followed the notes of music. Gregor crawled a little farther forward and lowered his head to the ground so that it might be possible for his eyes to meet hers. Was he an animal, when music had such an effect upon him? He felt as if the way were opening before him to the unknown nourishment he craved. He was determined to push forward till he reached his sister, to pull at her skirt and so let her know that she was to come into his room with her violin, for no one here appreciated her playing as he would appreciate it. He would never let her out of his room, at least, not as long as he lived.... His sister ... would burst into tears, and Gregor would then raise

himself to her shoulder and kiss her on the neck, which, now that she went to business she kept free of any ribbon or collar" (53–54).

II.3, The Body and the Traditional Community

1. Lévi-Strauss, *Marcel Mauss*, 63.

2. Here lies the "phenomenological" basis for the monster's aptitude for becoming a soothsayer.

3. There is no doubt a good reason for the fact that Arcimboldo, unique in his genre as a mannerist among his contemporaries, was never very well received by art historians (this fashion has recently changed). It is not just that he is considered an average painter, but that he is not considered a "painter" at all. Let me propose a (no doubt excessive) hypothesis: independently of the play—here purely compensatory—of color and form, in Arcimboldo there is no place for a true pictorial language. If he has created a following, his success has only been due to the idea that he "put forward" or discovered; his imitators and followers have been seduced by the technique of the representation of anomalous elements in composing the body, and by the gestaltist game of part/whole perception. Without a pictorial language there is no authentic communication between viewer and author, and in the end this would relate to his being in the position of not being able to represent nudity. There is no surface on which to inscribe signs—as in any other "nude"—and which would be like a blank sheet, or magic mirror (like the bodies in Bronzino's painting *Venus and Cupid between Time and Madness*, which are of a smooth nakedness, without shadows, quite similar to the ones in the *Portrait of Gabrielle d'Estrées and the Duchess of Villars in the Bath* by the Fontainbleau School), which sends back to the viewer, on the wings of their stimulated emotion, the floating signifiers that it puts into circulation. With Arcimboldo, there is no space for metaphorical combination. Without inside or outside, with no thickness, these bodies without space are only metaphors of the body by a stretch of the imagination.

4. Claude Lévi-Strauss, *Jean-Jacques Rousseau, fondateur des sciences de l'homme* (Neuchâtel: Ed. de la Baconnière, 1962).

5. See Tatiana Slama-Cazacu, "Sur la formation du systeme phonématique chez l'enfant," in *To Honor Roman Jakobson: Essays on the Occasion of His Seventieth Birthday*, vol. 3 (The Hague and Paris: Mouton, 1967), 1862.

6. Jean Lohisse, *La Communication tribale* (Paris: Editions Universitaires, 1974), 49.

7. Marcel Mauss, "Techniques du Corps," in *Anthropologie et sociologie*, 368.

8. Anatoly Martchenko, *My Testimony*, trans. Michael Scammell (London: Pall Mall Press, 1969).

9. Emmanuel Le Roy Ladurie, *Montaillou: Cathars and Catholics in a French Village, 1294–1324*, trans. Barbara Bray (London: Scolar, 1978).

10. Lohisse, *La Communication tribale*, 52.

11. In the traditional Corsican village, each quarter had its special place where everyone, men and women, fulfilled their needs. It played an important role in "social life."

12. Margaret Mead, *Coming of Age in Samoa: A Psychological Study of Primitive Youth for Western Civilization* (New York: Morrow, 1961).

13. This problematic is dealt with in relation to Corsican society in José Gil, *La Corse entre la liberté et la terreur* (Paris: Editions de la Différence, 1984), chaps. 2 and 4.

14. Leenhardt, *Da Kamo*, 164.

15. This was discussed in relation to Marshall Sahlin's analyses in Part I, 3.3.

16. Marcel Mauss, *The Gift: Forms and Functions of Exchange in Archaic Societies*, trans. Ian Cunnison with an introduction by E. E. Evans-Pritchard (London: Cohen and West, 1966), 8–9. Mauss notes that the word *utu* means satisfaction in blood vengeance. [And Gil adds: "compensations, repayments, responsibility, etc. It also designates a price. It is a complex notion of morality, law, religion and economy."]

17. This analysis of the Maori text only confirms the analysis that Sahlins has done. In his commentary, the first terms of the exchange are the powers of the forest. And in each exchange they are present, like the first terms whose place I should not usurp ("I" second term)—to acquire a profit. All exchange thus implies a screening (as if the object were coming from me) and the requirement to return (the object does not come from me). The aim being to bring about an equivalence in difference, an exchange of different goods while at the same time inhibiting the development of profit. This is precisely the function, on the economic level, of supernatural powers.

18. It is interesting to note that in the Maori text the word *utu*, which elicits a note from Mauss, designates also a "vendetta" type of compensation—this is the extreme pole of the erasure of the symbolic to the benefit of immediate corporeal relations. We can see the role played by the community body inasmuch as it is signified by ancestors or supernatural powers. In the space of the traditional Corsican village, for example, the "parade," the contest of insults, is made up of a series of elements—of which the family name is one—designed to halt escalation and the slide toward vendetta. One of these elements is attached to the cult of the dead and its relation to the spilling of blood. For a brief account of this problematic, see José Gil, "Vendetta et pouvoir dans la tradition orale corse," *Les Temps Modernes*, August–September 1978, and *La Corse entre la liberté et la terreur*.

19. Mauss, *The Gift*, 22.

20. Ibid.

21. Clifford Geertz, "Notes on the Balinese Cockfight," in *The Interpretation of Cultures* (New York: Basic Books, 1973), 423.

II.4, Dance and the Laughter of Bodies

1. In this regard, see R. Jaulin, *La mort sara* (Paris: Plon, 1967). The ethnologist, trapped between the levity shown by the Sara and the "ideological" seriousness with which he considered his own initiation, no longer knows what to believe and what not to believe.

2. See Part I, 4.4.4.

3. This distinction between two types of dance more or less repeats that of Gilbert Rouget's between "figurative dance" and "abstract dance": "In a certain number of cults it is possible to distinguish between two types of dance. There are what I shall term abstract dances, whose function is to trigger trance, and figurative dances (or simply mimes), whose function is to manifest the possession state.... If, in possession, dance oscillates between these two poles, figurative and non-figurative, the one being that of dance as identificatory behavior, the other that of dance as trance behavior, this is because it provides the adept with the means to assuming his new personality, and living intensely at the motor level" (Rouget, *Music and Trance*, 114, 117). I make this distinction move between two symbolic regimes, the two different roles that infralanguage plays in dance.

4. Rouget, *Music and Trance*, 118.

5. "It is non-figurative, it is pure physical expenditure. In this sense it is already liberation, catharsis" (ibid., 175).

6. Zempléni, "La Dimension thérapeutique," 401–2.

7. Rouget, *Music and Trance*, 410–11.

8. Ibid., 121.

9. Ibid., 120–21.

10. Ibid., 121.

11. It is true that at a certain end point, they would come together, because in both cases what is happening is a transformation of energy. So the difference lies with the regime of signs that makes this energy circulate (see Part II, section 6).

12. "It would no doubt be difficult—and possibly futile—to draw precise boundaries between abstract dance, figurative dance, and mimicry. A particular dance may seem to be non-figurative only because we do not know (or it is no longer known) what it represents or symbolizes. These three categories do nevertheless exist, and they furnish the elements of a system of combinations which vary from cult to cult, and which undoubtedly tell us a great deal about the underlying logic of these cults" (Rouget, *Music and Trance*, 115). It is this logic I am trying to define here.

13. Enaksi Bhavnani, *The Dance in India* (Bombay: Taraporevala's Treasure House of Books, 1970), 82.

14. Ibid., 83.

15. Ibid., 82.

16. Ibid., 38.

17. See above.

18. A. R. Radcliffe-Brown, *Structure and Function in Primitive Society*, chaps. 4 and 5 on "joking relationships," which Leenhardt called "free talk relationships" ("*parenté à libre parler*").

19. Mikhail Bakhtin, *Rabelais and His World*, trans. Hélène Iswolsky (Cambridge, MIT Press, 1968).

20. Among the growing number of works on carnival, I should cite the work of Gaignebet Claude, especially Gaignebet Claude and Marie-Claude Florentin, *Le Carnaval: Essais de mythologie populaire* (Paris: Payot, 1974).

21. Mikhail Bakhtin, *Rabelais and His World*, 318.

22. Ibid., 26.

23. See, in particular, Jurgis Baltrusaitis, *Le Moyen Age fantastique* (Paris: Colin, 1955); *Révieils et prodiges* (Paris: Colin, 1960); *Aberrations: An Essay on the Legend of Forms*, trans. Richard Miller (Cambridge: MIT Press, 1989).

II.5, Seriousness of Symbols and Incarnation

1. See Part III, chap. 1.

2. Jean Baudrillard, *Symbolic Exchange and Death*, trans. Iain Hamilton Grant, with an introduction by Mike Gane (London: Sage, 1993), especially the introduction.

3. See Franz Boas, *The Social Organization and the Secret Societies of the Kwakiutl Indians* (New York: Johnson Reprint Corporation, 1970), 341–58.

4. See Part III, chap. 2, for the discussion of Clastres's theses about society against the State, and the sketch of a model of mechanisms that would favor the emergence of the State.

5. For example, the *vaygu'a* acquire prestige in the course of their trips; "in the same way the North-West American coppers and Samoan mats increase in value at each *potlatch*" (Mauss, *The Gift*, 94 n).

6. This quantity "appears" in a number of ways, from the function of credit (ibid., 38) in *potlatch* through to simple "greed": see the *kwakuitl* text on the "small chiefs" who are "working secretly for property, ... traitors" (ibid., 102 n).

7. Mauss, *The Gift*, 43.

8. Ibid., 113 n.

9. See my analysis of the Corsican story, *Muschinu* (Gil, "Vendetta et pouvoir," 192–93), where I concluded (1) that the vendetta (as here with potlatch) is a device that prevents the accumulation of goods, because it is in deflecting the process of revenge that Muschinu succeeds in monopolizing the herds of cattle and the women of the village; and (2) that the transformation of the (false) symbolic value of the hero's fortune-telling machine into an exchange value (money) procures a monetary surplus value for the latter. In reverse, it is the same process as described above, relating identical mechanisms.

10. It is therefore sufficient that a symbolic value concentrated in a given power (in a despotic political signifier, for example) "latch onto" this surplus of things for it to be fixed, not removed from the circulation of goods (by sacrifice, *potlatch*, or some other means), and justified. This is one of the sense I will be giving here to the "incarnation of symbols." The regime of exchanges has changed, at the same time as the regime of signs. But it is first of all necessary for this symbolic surplus value to be produced for the economic surplus value to be engendered. For more on this, see Part III, chap. 5.

11. For example, under conditions that give rise to prophecy (commotion or disintegration of traditional cultural structures for a variety of reasons: wars, colonial invasions, epidemics, natural catastrophes).

12. A rich and complex example of the way in which violence exercised on the body has been used to frame the floating signifier, in the service of a supreme signifier as a seat for political power, is the sorcery trial at Loudun, in the seventeenth century. See especially Michel de Certeau, *La Possession de Loudun* (Paris: Julliard, 1970).

13. See Part I, 1.5.

14. See Louis Dumont, *Homo Hierarchicus: The Caste System and its Implications*, trans. Mark Sainsbury (London: Weidenfeld and Nicolson, 1970), 184–87 and especially 235–36.

15. See Part I, 1.5.

16. This is what happens as medicine replaces traditional therapies; with teaching and writing, which replace know-how and oral memory; with the juridical space of behavior induced by laws and state regulation, which replaces community space where singular laws are in immediate relationship with forces (see Part III).

17. See, on this subject, the analysis of transformations of this type in the modern Far East in Geertz, "Religion as Culture," in *The Interpretation of Culture* (New York: Basic Books, 1973).

18. Cited in Julius Evola, *Le Yoga tantrique* (Paris: Fayard, 1971), 105.

II.6, The Body and the Voice

1. See Jacques Derrida, *Speech and Phenomena, and Other Essays on Husserl's Theory of Signs*, translated with an introduction by David B. Allison (Evanston, Ill.: Northwestern University Press, 1973).

2. Mark 14: 24.

3. Derrida, *Speech and Phenomena*, 75–76.

4. One last question: Why discourse? Why the voice? Where does its effectiveness come from? Later on I will investigate the properties of breathing, but the problem of the voice remains. Articulate language is also a metalanguage, the only metalanguage. In the mechanism of the double translations of the two levels, indicative and expressive, the first (the voice) translates, therefore, a metalanguage, which is difficult to understand. What is it that is translated, then? Not the message itself, but its whole linguistic context, the set of tacit significations that surround the message. If the voice can take the place of articulated metalanguage, it is no doubt because it already contains metalinguistic potentiality. We could say by way of setting up a hypothesis that the human vocal apparatus is made up in such a way that it can express what is given in the infralanguage: gaps, differences, articulations on the kinesic as well as the affective levels. This "expression" is still not semantic, it is presemantic. One must see in the expressivity of the voice a sort of expressive extension of the infralanguage, and allow into the amorphous level of the voice the already inscribed metalinguistic potentiality of articulate language. Now this potentiality can only be understood as an infralinguistic relation, to the extent that infralanguage is a focal point from which all the meanings of all possible languages spread out. If a language can speak of colors, it is because infralanguage preordains the colors in their relations to objects in space, to movement, and so on. And this "preordaining" is "preexpressed" in the voice.

5. Derrida, *Speech and Phenomena*, 88–89.

6. This whole analysis concerns what happens at the threshold of the constitution of body images. Voice, if it is absorbed by the expressive layer, can make infralanguage move over to the side of body images.

7. In the French original this is *corps de l'armée*. While "Army corps" might be a literal translation, mine reverts to the French for "body." *Trans.*

II.7, The Body in Penal Settlements

1. Kafka, *Metamorphosis and Other Stories*, 169–99.

2. Ibid., 176.

3. Ibid., 179–80.

4. Ibid., 184.

5. Ibid.

6. Ibid.

7. Ibid., 196.

8. Ibid., 191.

9. Ibid., 196.

10. Ibid., 198.

11. Ibid., 185.

12. Ibid., 173.

13. Cf. José Gil, "Costituzione," *Enciclopedia Einaudi* (Turin) 4 (1978).

14. The role of the old commandant, to the extent that it is possible to characterize it, seems to be that of a founder, the founder of a despotic system, rather than a despot as such.

15. Kafka, *Metamorphosis*, 170.

16. Ibid., 185.

17. Ibid., 183.

18. Ibid., 176.

19. Ibid., 172.

20. French *écorché*, "flayed"—a figure in which the muscles are represented as stripped of the skin, for scientific or artistic study. *Trans.*

21. In relation to this an author evokes some poetry that a writer composed for a crucifixion: "Un homme massacré pedoit sure cette croix / Sa peau sanglante estoit cousue avec ses os / Et son ventre attaché aux vertèbre du dos / Sans entrailles sembloit ... Ce qui restait encore de sa chair détranché / Pendoit horriblement par lambeau écorché ... L'on voyoit au profond ses large ulcères / Ses veines, ses tendons, ses nerfs et ses artères" (Jacques Bousquet, *La Peinture maniériste* [Neuchatel: Ides et Calendis, 1964], 250).

22. Otto Benesch, *German Painting from Durer to Holbein*, translated from the German by H. S. Harrison (Geneva: Skira, 1966), 87.

23. Ibid.

24. Ibid.

25. Pietro Berretini de Cortone, *Tabulae Anatomicae* (Rome: Rubéis, 1741).

26. Juan Valverde, *Anato Mia del Corpo Humano* (Rome: A. Salamance and A. Lafreri, 1560). This plate is also called "The Masked Man."

27. Mondino de Luzzi, *Anatomica Corporis Humani*, 1319.

28. Thomas Bartholin, *Anatomia Reformata* (Leyden: F. Hackius, 1651).

29. It has certainly been noted that *écorchés* "make sure they show the inanity of death" (Roger Caillois, *Au cœur du fantastique* [Paris: Gallimard, 1965], 146).

30. Kafka, *Metamorphosis*, 197.

II.8, Note on the Frontispiece of *De Humani Corporis Fabrica* by Vesalius

1. See Michel Foucault, *The Order of Things: An Archaeology of the Human Sciences* (London: Tavistock, 1970).

2. See Alexandre Koyré's discussion of the problem of the infinitude of the world in Nicholas of Cusa, in *From the Closed World to the Infinite Universe* (Baltimore, Md.: Johns Hopkins University Press, 1957).

3. "Leonardo on the Figure," in *Leonardo on Painting: An Anthology of Writings*, by Leonardo da Vinci, with a selection of documents relating to his career as an artist, ed. Martin Kemp, selected and translated by Martin Kemp and Margaret Walker (New Haven, Conn.: Yale University Press, 1989), §351.

4. Ibid.

5. See Johan Huizinga, *The Waning of the Middle Ages* (New York: Garden City, 1954), Esp. chap. 11, "The Vision of Death."

6. Lynn Thorndike, *A History of Magic and Experimental Science* (New York: Macmillan, 1923), book 1, 126.

7. Andreas Vesalius, *De Humani Corporis Fabrica* (Basel: J. Oporinus, 1543).

8. See Georges Cangulhem, "L'Homme de Vésale dans le monde de Copernic: 1543," in *Etudes d'histoire et de philosophie des sciences* (Paris: Vrin, 1970).

9. Jacopo Berengario da Carpi, *Commmentaria cum Amplissimis super Anatomia Mundini* (Bononiae: H. de Bebedictic, 1521); Charles Estienne, *Dissectione Partium Corporis Humani Libri Tres* (Paris: Simon de Colines, 1545), contains plates dated 1530, 1531, and 1532.

10. Huizinga, *Waning of the Middle Ages*, 129.

11. As Jean Baudrillard seems to do in *Symbolic Exchange and Death*, although his thought is more subtle than this: "In medicine, one's corpus of data is in the corpse. In other words, the corpse is the ideal limit of the body in its relation to the medical system. It is the corpse which produces and reproduces medicine in its main task, under the sign of the preservation of life" (117).

12. Explanation of the characters marked in the table of figures belonging to women's instruments serving reproduction, in *L'Abrégé de l'Anatomie de Vésale*, by Jacques Grévin, de Clermont en Beauvoisis, Médecin à Paris, chez André Wechel (Paris: 1569), 91.

13. Vesalius, *Fabrica*, V, 15, p. 531: "[Theologran's students], who have a more populous discussion about the genitalia and the seed than do the doctors and whom we have in our audience in great numbers when we display the organs of generation in lectures" (trans. Frances Muecke).

14. Ibid., I, 28, p. 126.

Part III, The Body and the Origin of the State

1. On the subject of such a system see José Gil, "La Lutte des envies: Un modèle du fondement d'une society égalitaire," *Etudes Corses 2* (1984), special number dedicated to F. Ettori.

2. Ernst Kantorowicz, *The King's Two Bodies: A Study in Medieval Political Theory* (Princeton, N.J.: Princeton University Press, 1957).

3. Claude Seyssel, *The Monarchy of France*, trans. J. H. Hexter, edited, annotated, and introduced by Donald R. Kelley, additional translation by Michael Sherman (1515; New Haven, Conn.: Yale University Press, 1981); E-J Seyès, *Qu'est-ce que le Tiers Etat?*, critical edition by R. Zapperi (Geneva: Droz, 1970).

4. Jean-Yves Guyomar, *L'Idéologie nationale* (Paris: Champ Libre, 1974).

III.1, Anthropology and the Problem of the Origin of the State

1. Pierre Clastres, *Society against the State*, trans. Robert Hurley (Oxford: Basil Blackwell, Mole Editions, 1977).

2. Ibid., 12.

3. Ibid., 10.

4. Clastres refers here to the work of Jean-William Lapierre, *Essai sur le fondement du pouvoir politique* (Aix-en-Provence: Ophrys, 1968).

5. Clastres, *Society against the State*, 14–15.

6. Ibid., 167–68.

7. Ibid., 34–35.

8. Estienne de La Boétie, *Slaves by Choice*, translation and commentaries by Malcolm Smith (Egham: Runnymede, 1988).

9. Clastres, *Society against the State*, 32.

10. Ibid., 33.

11. Ibid., 35.

12. In English in the original. *Trans.*

13. Ibid., 176.

14. Ibid., 177.

15. Ibid., 16.

16. Ibid., 33.

17. Ibid., 34.

18. Ibid.

19. Ibid., 173–76.

20. Ibid., 176.

21. Ibid., 176–77. See also Clastres, "Le Malheur du guerrier sauvage," in *Recherches d'anthropologie politique* (Paris: Seuil, 1980), 209.

22. Clastres, *Society against the State*, 173.

III.2, Conditions under Which Societies without States Can Become State Societies

1. Clastres, *Society against the State*, 16.

2. Marc Swartz, Victor Turner, and Arthur Tuden, eds., *Political Anthropology* (Chicago: Aldine, 1966), 4–5.

3. Ibid., 6–7.

4. Ibid., 7.

5. The French word is retained here in reference to Jean-François Lyotard, *The Differend: Phrases in Dispute*, trans. Georges Van Den Abbeele, (Minneapolis: University of Minnesota Press, 1988). *Trans.*

6. See Paul Bohannan, *Social Anthropology* (New York: Holt, Rinehart and Winston, 1963), 283.

7. Isaac Schapera, *Government and Politics in Tribal Societies* (New York: Schocken Books, 1967), 8, 203, 217.

8. This assumes that in tribal chieftainships, the chief does not really accumulate wives. In fact, his women are not *wives*; these women do not enter into the circuit of exchanges with the collectivity (unlike the case with the king's women), and the chief has no kinship (which benefits political privileges). This means, on the one hand, that the society that gives women to the tribal chief finds itself in a situation of superiority (as giver of women) vis-à-vis the person who takes them (a situation that is going to reverse in a singular fashion with the state power of the king). On this level, socializing prestige is to precisely transform this prestige coming from the possession of women into "general" prestige. Polygyny, in this sense, carries out this mutation because (1) the chief's women work for the community, and (2) they are not wives, which denies accumulation and

inequality in the system of social exchanges of women. From this, the possession of women (and not wives) by one man gives him an ambiguous status: he enjoys the possession personally, and can only use it socially for collective ends — his prestige as (individual) holder of women is transformed into a general attribute, linked to his status.

9. Marcel Gauchet, "La Dette du sense et les racines de l'Etat," in *Libre*, 77–2 (Paris: Payot, 1977), 23.

10. Ibid., 22.

11. Ibid., 32.

12. Ibid., 33.

13. Ibid., 38.

14. Ibid., 42.

15. Ibid., 41.

16. Ibid., 21.

17. E. E. Evans-Pritchard, *Witchcraft, Oracles and Magic among the Azande* (London: Oxford University Press, 1937).

18. Robert Gessain, *Ammassalik ou la civilisation obligatoire* (Paris: Flammarion, 1969).

19. Bronislaw Malinowsky, *The Argonauts of the Western Pacific* (London: Routledge and Kegan Paul, 1953), and *Trois essais sur la vie sociale des primitifs* (Paris: Payot, 1968).

20. Favret-Saada, *Deadly Words*.

21. Sahlins, *Stone Age Economics*.

III.3, The Origin of the State

1. Max Weber, "Politics as a Vocation," in H. H. Gerth and C. Wright Mills, eds., *From Max Weber: Essays in Sociology* (London: Routledge and Kegan Paul, 1948), 78.

2. Despite Malinowski's disclaimer (that he was attempting any sort of "classification exercise" of tribal norms) we are able, thanks to him, to sketch out certain basic types of customary norms: (1) norms that regulate individual behavior in relation to the community, and for which the violation impinges initially on the individual in question; (2) norms that regulate individual behavior in relation to an initial, basic relation, of the individual to the community. The second group is controlled by the *do ut des* principle, the mutual obligation of presation, for which the violation entails a reaction on the part of the other. This is the domain of litigation and of "civil" law.

3. H. Kantorowicz, *The Definition of Law* (Cambridge: Cambridge University Press, 1958), 78.

4. Bronislaw Malinowski, *Crime and Custom in Savage Society* (London: Routledge and Kegan Paul, 1926), 58.

5. Ibid., 31.

6. Ibid., 30.

7. Ibid., 66.

8. Ibid., 68.

9. Ibid., 69.

10. Ibid., 67.

11. Ibid., 79.

12. Ibid., 80.

13. Ibid., 60.

14. Paul Bohannan, *Justice and Judgement among the Tiv* (London: Oxford University Press, 1957).

15. See José Gil, "Vendetta et pouvoir dans la tradition orale corse," *Les Temps Modernes*, August–September, 1978.

16. Malinowski, *Crime and Custom*, 29.

17. E. Adamson Hoebel, *The Law of Primitive Man: A Study in Comparative Legal Dynamics* (New York: Atheneum, 1970), 94–95.

18. Ibid., 93.

19. Ibid., 98–99.

20. Max Gluckman, *Politics, Law and Ritual in Tribal Society* (Oxford: Basil Blackwell, 1965), 304.

21. Ibid., 306.

22. See John Comaroff and Simon Roberts, "The Invocation of Norms in Dispute Settlement: The Tswana case," in *Social Anthropology and Law* (London: Academic Press, 1977), 104.

23. See François Chatelet, "La Grèce classique, la raison, l'Etat," in *L'Occident et ses autres* (Paris: Aubier-Montaigne, 1978).

24. Cf. Max Gluckman, *The Judicial Process among the Barotse of Northern Rhodesia* (Manchester: Manchester University Press, 1955).

25. Beyond the specific histories of one or another state that waned only to cede its place to a more powerful state formation, or for whom the decline and then the collapse allowed a new beginning for history, in another site, based on more original stages.

26. Bohannan, *Social Anthrolopogy*, 296.

27. See Lucia Desideri, "La Violence humiliée," *Les Temps Modernes*, August–September, 1978.

28. Plato, *Gorgias*, 482e.

29. *Republic* 1.1, 338c.

III.4, The Body of the State

1. This is why prestige exceeds the field of its original competence, especially political prestige. Setting itself up as the knowledge of all knowledges, it claims to have the key to all possible translations.

2. Leach, *Culture and Communication*, 44. See Part II, chap. 1.

3. James G. Frazer, *The Golden Bough* (London: Macmillan, 1957), 221–22.

4. Ibid., 222–23.

5. This point will be developed later.

6. In the same way as the "king's portrait" (Louis XIV) is part of his being, as Louis Marin showed in *Le Portrait du roi* (Paris: Minuit, 1981).

7. As Frazer's examples showed. See also, for an inventory of "divine" royalties, Laura Makarius, *Le Sacré et la violence des interdits* (Paris: Payot, 1974), chap. 4.

8. We can see how the power of magical royalties implies a loss of power among singular bodies. The latter are deprived of the possibility of exfoliating to the extent that the exfoliation of the body of the king has appropriated the exclusive power to act, in certain ways, on concrete space. Thus begins the history of power cutting up space into grids.

9. For the detailed description of this ritual, see Hilda Kuper, *An African Aristocracy: Rank among the Swazi* (London: Oxford University Press, 1947). The commentary has been extensive; I will simply cite Max Gluckman, "Rituals of Rebellion in South-East Africa," in *Order and Rebellion in Tribal Africa* (London: Cohen and West, 1963); T. O. Beidelman, "Swazi Royal Ritual," *Africa* 36 (October 1966), no. 4; Pierre Smith, "Aspects de l'organisation des rites," in M. Izard and P. Smith, *La Fonction symbolique* (Paris: Gallimard, 1979).

10. See Pierre Smith's interpretation, "Aspects de l'organisation des rites."

11. Kuper, *An African Aristocracy*, 202.

12. This is how the Swazi characterize the ritual, as a theatrical performance. Kuper, following the indigenous language, calls it the "drama of kingship" (ibid., 207).

13. Ibid., 209.

14. Ibid., 210.

15. Already in the Little *Incwala*, reference was made to the king as a bull. Before the king spits to the east and the west, a priest shouts to the crowd: "Eh eh. He stabs it with both horns. Our bull" (205).

16. Kuper, *An African Aristocracy*, 212.

17. Ibid., 214.

18. Ibid., 214.

19. Ibid.

20. Ibid., 215.

21. Ibid., 216.

22. Ibid., 217–18.

23. Ibid., 218.

24. Ibid., 219–20.

25. This logic is perfectly described on one point — the splitting of the king's body — by Alfred Adler in his study of Moundang rituals (see A. Adler, "Le Dédoublement rituel de la personne du roi," in M. Izard and Pierre Smith, *La Fonction symbolique*. Adler uses the notion of the "splitting of the person of the king," which in fact includes that of the splitting of the body. Only the study of the relations between the notions of "person" and "body" in tribal languages would be able to cast some light on a very complex process, which my exclusive use of "body" rather simplifies. (At the time of writing, Adler's book *La Mort et le masque du roi* (Paris: Payot,

1982) had not yet come out, which is why I have been referring only to the 1979 text.

26. See Adler, "Le Dédoublement rituel," 198. Here I am designating with the general and inappropriate term of "enthronement ritual" the ritual ensemble that accompanies an enthronement. So the *Incwala* is only a harvest ritual serving at the same time for enthronement.

27. I cannot undertake this analysis here; in any case a ritual should not be analyzed on the basis of a text. All the difficult-to-describe corporeal elements like dance, voice, variable intensities of rhythm, and so on, are decisive for its understanding.

28. If this is the case, the *Incwala* is therefore neither a rebellion ritual (Gluckman) nor a separation ritual (Beidelman).

29. We should recall that the Swazi themselves say that the *Incwala* is a representation, a theatrical performance.

III.5, The Surplus Value of the Power of the State

1. See Victor Turner, *The Drums of Affliction*.

Index

José Gil is professor of philosophy at the University of Lisbon. He has also taught at the Collège International de Philosophie in Paris. Gil is the author of a novel, *La Crucifiée*, and *Un'anthropologia delle forze*.

Stephen Muecke is professor of cultural studies and editor of the *UTS Review: Cultural Studies and New Writing* at the University of Technology, Sydney. He is the coauthor of *Reading the Country: Introduction to Nomadology* and author of *Textual Spaces: Aboriginality and Cultural Studies* and *No Road (Bitumen All the Way)*.